BALLET AND OPERA IN THE
AGE OF *GISELLE*

PRINCETON STUDIES IN OPERA
CAROLYN ABBATE AND ROGER PARKER,
SERIES EDITORS

Reading Opera, edited by Arthur Groos and Roger Parker

Puccini's Turandot: *The End of the Great Tradition*
by William Ashbrook and Harold Powers

Unsung Voices: Opera and Musical Narrative in the Nineteenth Century
by Carolyn Abbate

Wagner Androgyne: A Study in Interpretation by Jean-Jacques Nattiez,
translated by Stewart Spencer

Music in the Theater: Essays on Verdi and Other Composers
by Pierluigi Petrobelli, translated by Roger Parker

Leonora's Last Act: Essays in Verdian Discourse by Roger Parker

*Richard Wagner, Fritz Lang, and the Nibelungen: The Dramaturgy
of Disavowal* by David J. Levin

Monstrous Opera: Rameau and the Tragic Tradition by Charles Dill

*The Culture of Opera Buffa in Mozart's Vienna:
A Poetics of Entertainment* by Mary Hunter

Metaphysical Song: An Essay on Opera by Gary Tomlinson

Mad Loves: Women and Music in Offenbach's Les Contes d'Hoffmann
by Heather Hadlock

Siren Songs: Representations of Gender and Sexuality in Opera
by Mary Ann Smart (editor)

Ballet and Opera in the Age of Giselle
by Marian Smith

MARIAN SMITH

Ballet and Opera in the Age of *Giselle*

PRINCETON UNIVERSITY PRESS
PRINCETON AND OXFORD

Copyright © 2000 by Princeton University Press
Published by Princeton University Press, 41 William Street,
Princeton, New Jersey 08540
In the United Kingdom: Princeton University Press, 3, Market Place,
Woodstock, Oxfordshire OX20 1SY

All Rights Reserved

Library of Congress Cataloging-in-Publication Data
Smith, Marian Elizabeth.
Ballet and opera in the age of Giselle / Marian Smith.
p.   cm. — (Princeton studies in opera)
Includes bibliographical references (p.) and index.
ISBN 0-691-04994-7
1. Opera–Europe—19th century.   2. Ballet—Europe—History—19th century.
3. Adam, Adolphe, 1803–1856. Giselle.   I. Title.   II. Series.
ML1720.4 .S65   2000
782.1'09'034—dc21   00-060622

This book has been composed in Times Roman

The paper used in this publication meets the
minimum requirements of
ANSI/NISO Z39.48-1992 (R 1997)
(*Permanence of Paper*)

http://pup.princeton.edu

Printed in the United States of America

1 3 5 7 9 10 8 6 4 2

*This book is gratefully dedicated
to our many happy memories of*

Sophia Lauderdale
Carl Oscar Bergquist
Forrest Cullen Hallmark
Bryce Carlson Hallmark

CONTENTS

LIST OF TABLES AND ILLUSTRATIONS	ix
PREFACE	xi
ACKNOWLEDGMENTS	xix
NOTE TO THE READER	xxi
CHAPTER ONE Introduction: Music and the Story	3
CHAPTER TWO A Family Resemblance	19
CHAPTER THREE The Lighter Tone of Ballet-Pantomime	59
CHAPTER FOUR Ballet-Pantomime and Silent Language	97
CHAPTER FIVE Hybrid Works at the Opéra	124
CHAPTER SIX *Giselle*	167
APPENDIX ONE Ballet-Pantomimes and Operas Produced at the Paris Opéra, 1825–1850	201
APPENDIX TWO The *Giselle* Libretto	213
APPENDIX THREE Sources for Musical Examples	239
NOTES	241
INDEX	301

LIST OF TABLES AND ILLUSTRATIONS

TABLES

1.1	*Lady Henriette*, Act One, First Tableau.	7
1.2	Rationales for Dancing in Operas and Ballet-Pantomimes.	17
2.1	Settings of Operas and Ballet-Pantomimes at the Opéra.	22
2.2	Plot Situations in Operas and Ballet-Pantomimes at the Opéra.	26
2.3	*Giselle* and *Les Huguenots*, First Acts.	29
2.4	Placement of Divertissements in Ballet-Pantomimes and Operas.	35
2.5	Minor Characters in Ballet-Pantomimes and Operas at the Opéra.	47
2.6	Numbers of Costumes Used for Various Productions.	49
2.7	Shocking Penultimate-Act Events.	55
2.8	Abrupt Endings to Divertissements.	56
3.1	Numbers of Male and Female Characters Named in Miscellaneous Opera and Ballet-Pantomime Libretti.	61
3.2	Settings of Ballet-Pantomimes and Operas.	62
3.3	Operas Converted into Ballet-Pantomimes (*mis en pantomime*) at the Paris Opéra, 1778–1845.	73
3.4	*Paul et Virginie*, Opera and Ballet-Pantomime Versions.	83
3.5	The "Marriage of Figaro" Play, Opera Buffa, and Ballet-Pantomime.	86
4.1	Borrowed Music in Ballet-Pantomime Scores at the Paris Opéra, 1777–1845.	104
5.1.	*La Muette de Portici*, The Unfolding of the Action.	130
5.2.	*Le Dieu et la Bayadère*, The Unfolding of the Action.	146
5.3.	*La Tentation*, The Unfolding of the Action.	155
6.1	Time of Composition of the *Giselle* Score.	173
6.2	*Giselle*—Scenes Often Cut in Current Productions.	176
6.3	Argument between Loys and Wilfride.	179
6.4	Argument between Berthe and Giselle.	181

ILLUSTRATIONS

1.	The Paris Opéra, rue le Peletier.	xii
2.	The Paris Opéra, rue le Peletier.	xii
3.	The Paris Opéra, rue le Peletier.	xiii
4.	*Les Mohicans* (ballet-pantomime), design for tomahawk, peace pipe, and moccasin.	37
5.	*L'Ile des Pirates* (ballet-pantomime), Octavio disguised as an islander.	38
6.	*Manon Lescaut* (ballet-pantomime), "Nymphe, Nayade."	38
7.	*Manon Lescaut* (ballet-pantomime), shepherdesses.	39

8. *La Révolte au sérail* (ballet-pantomime), dignitary. 39
9. *La Révolte au sérail* (ballet-pantomime), women's costumes, including martial attire. 40
10. *La Belle au bois dormant* (ballet-pantomime), peasants. 40
11. *La Juive* (opera), Archbishop. 41
12. *La Juive* (opera), the cardinal's trumpeter. 41
13. *Robert le diable* (opera), nun. 42
14. *La Sylphide* (ballet-pantomime), Scotsmen. 42
15. *La Sylphide* (ballet-pantomime), Effie (James's fiancée). 43
16. *Guillaume Tell* (opera), peasants, chorus, and *corps de ballet*. 43
17. *Guillaume Tell* (opera), ladies, chorus, and *corps de ballet*. 44
18. *Guillaume Tell* (opera), Mathilde. 44
19. *Gustave III*, Act V, tableau 2, ballroom in the palace of Stockholm, sketch by Charles Cambon. 46
20. *Gustave III ou le Bal Masqué* (opera), Polichinelle costume for the masked ball. 46
21. Performance of *Les Huguenots* (opera). 51
22. Eugène Lami, *Foyer des acteurs à l'Opéra*. 69
23. The *loge infernale*. 69
24. Jean-Louis Forain (1852–1931), *Abonné et danseuse*. 70
25. *Le Page inconstant* full score, at curtain-up, Act One (quoting the Fifth Symphony of Beethoven). 91
26. *Le Page inconstant* full score, a few measures later. 91
27. *La Muette de Portici*, Act V, Viceroy's palace with Mt. Vesuvius in the background, engraving by Lemaître (based on the design of Ciceri). 125
28. *La Muette de Portici*, nondancing *figurantes*. 126
29. *La Muette de Portici*, *figurant*, chorus and *corps de ballet*. 126
30. *La Muette de Portici*, Neapolitan costume, *corps de ballet*. 127
31. *La Muette de Portici*, women of the people, chorus, and *corps de ballet*. 127
32. *La Muette de Portici*, costumes for the *bolero* and *guarache*. 128
33. *Le Dieu et la Bayadère*, bayadere costume. 139
34. *Le Dieu et la Bayadère*, chorus costume. 139
35. *La Tentation*, the hermit. 150
36. *La Tentation*, Miranda. 150
37. *La Tentation*, the sultan. 151
38. *La Tentation*, an angel. 151
39. *La Tentation*, amazon. 151
40. *La Tentation*, demon. 152
41. *La Tentation*, demon. 152
42. *La Tentation*, the angel Mizaël. 153
43. *Robert le diable*, Bertram and Alice. 169
44. *Giselle*, Albrecht and Giselle (Anton Dolin and Alicia Markova, photographed by Gordon Anthony). 169

PREFACE

THEATERGOERS today know ballet as an autonomous art form, reliant on neither opera nor words, but rather entirely self-sufficient. This was not always so. As scholars have told us, ballet was often performed as an integral part of opera in the seventeenth and eighteenth centuries. It took the efforts of strong-minded reformers in the eighteenth century to challenge the tradition of mingling singing with dancing in a single work, and ultimately to prove that ballet could thrive on its own as an independent, wordless theater art. As Jean-Georges Noverre argued in 1760:

> A well-planned ballet can dispense with the aid of words [which] chill the action and weaken the interest.... Words will become useless, everything will speak, each movement will become expressive, each attitude will depict a particular situation, each gesture will reveal a thought, each glance will convey a sentiment; everything will be captivating....[1]

Noverre and others promoted the merits of a new independent type of ballet, sometimes called the *ballet d'action,* which eschewed altogether the use of intoned words and told a complete story with dance and mime.[2] By the end of the eighteenth century, this new sort of ballet had gained acceptance on many European opera stages—in Milan, Paris, Stuttgart and Vienna, for instance—though stodgy spectators at the Paris Opéra still took offense at Noverre's "manner of making the principal subject of the spectacle what ought only to be the accessory."[3] By about 1830—the point at which this study begins— most of the fuss seems to have died down (though there was still a bit of grumbling, as I will explain later). The independent ballet had attracted an enthusiastic following and was thriving in many a European opera house, even though at many houses it was not yet performed on an evening alone, without opera.

This book is about the ballet-pantomimes created at one particular house in one particular period: the Paris Opéra during the 1830s and 1840s, an age celebrated among both opera and dance historians as one of the most successful in that institution's long and illustrious history.[4] (See Figures 1, 2, and 3.) These ballet-pantomimes are lauded as particularly forward-looking works that exerted a profound influence on theatrical dance for the rest of the nineteenth century in Europe and beyond and indeed laid the foundations for "classical" ballet as we know it today. It was at the Paris Opéra during these two decades that the ballet-pantomimes *La Sylphide* and *Giselle* were first performed; that the first *ballets blancs* (or "white ballets") were popularized; that the ballerina wrested control of the stage from the *danseur;* that Marie Taglioni stunned audiences and other dancers with a supple technique and ethereal style that set new standards for lyrical dancing.[5]

Figure 1. The Paris Opéra, rue le Peletier. By permission of the Bibliothèque nationale de France.

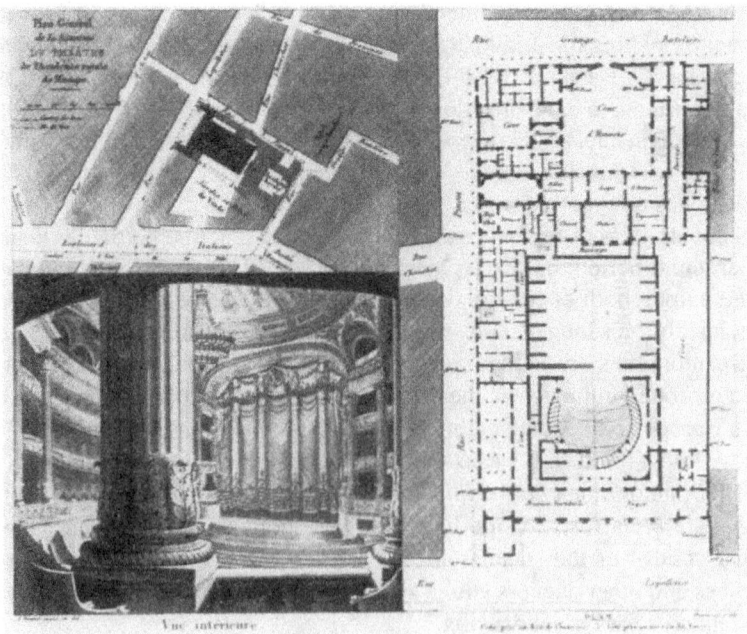

Figure 2. The Paris Opéra, rue le Peletier. By permission of the Bibliothèque nationale de France.

Figure 3. The Paris Opéra, rue le Peletier. By permission of the Bibliothèque nationale de France.

Yet, despite these innovations, ballet-pantomime's old connections with opera and its indebtedness to words had not vanished entirely. The argument I wish to make in this book is simple: that the longtime marriage between opera and ballet at the Opéra had not yet fully ended in the 1830s and 1840s. This may seem an odd proposition, since the affinities of these ballet-pantomimes with opera are no longer obvious to today's theatergoer. Indeed, few spectators of these Parisian ballet-pantomimes as they are currently performed would guess that they had originated in a milieu in which ballet-pantomime shared its stage, and its audience, with opera. Yet, though we cannot fully reconstruct that world, we can at least map the correspondences that existed between the ballet-pantomimes and the lyric works created alongside them; correspondences that, as I contend in the pages that follow, were many and various.

A side-by-side comparison of the two types of works discloses, first of all, a strong family resemblance between them—in scene types, character types, settings, overall shape, staging, and even, to a certain extent, music (Chapter Two). It also reveals, however, that ballet was lighter in tone, a circumstance that may be explained in part by new ideas about verisimilitude in ballet as well as the old custom at the Opéra (flourishing in the years leading up to the

July Monarchy) of turning well-known comic operas into ballet-pantomimes (Chapter Three).

Given this tradition of interchange between the genres, it is not surprising that ballet-pantomime's plots were nearly as complicated as opera's. This reveals another crucial point of intersection between ballet and opera (Chapter Four), for imparting complicated ballet plots to the audience called for strategies—including the distribution of detailed libretti and the coordination of speechlike music with lines of dialogue printed therein—that were closely akin to those used in lyric works. Thus language lurked just beneath the surface of the ballet-pantomime, even though the performers never actually intoned words.

Three hybrid pieces produced at the Opéra during this period (Chapter Five) reveal still more common ground: in them, silent ballet characters and singing opera characters mingled freely, proving that they could not only occupy the same stage on the same evening in separate works but could also meet face to face and "talk" to one another.

The disappearance from the repertory of so many of these ballet-pantomimes and the operas performed alongside them has made it difficult to remember the many points of intersection between them. *Giselle,* by far the best-known today of all the ballet-pantomimes created at the Opéra during the July Monarchy, serves as a fitting case study in this regard (Chapter Six). A comparison of its earliest incarnation to the versions currently performed shows plainly that many of its more opera-like verbal characteristics—most strikingly, its coordination of gesture to music—have been discarded in the process of streamlining that the ballet has undergone in the century and a half since its first production. While the alterations to *Giselle* have, of course, kept it abreast of the times as ballet has become more abstract, they have also effectively hidden from our view some of the narrative features that made this piece so alluring to its first audience, and in the process erased clues that would allow us to gain a fuller sense of that audience's crossover fluency in the languages of both ballet and opera.

HISTORIOGRAPHICAL habits have made these ballet-pantomimes' old connections with opera hard to uncover. First, there is a certain mutual exclusivity in the way latter-day scholars approach the Paris Opéra of this age—a mutual exclusivity that mirrors the virtual segregation of opera and ballet late-twentieth-century performance practice and incidentally renders comparisons of the two arts unlikely.[6] Most musicologists tend to depict the Paris Opéra of the July Monarchy as the house of "French grand opera"—of *Guillaume Tell, Les Huguenots,* Meyerbeer, Scribe, Damoreau, Nourrit—and if they sometimes acknowledge that operas entailed ballet segments, they rarely mention the Opéra's famous ballet-pantomimes. Many dance historians, on the other hand, overlook the operas (except for the ballet divertissements therein) and portray the Opéra mainly as the place where the Romantic ballet-pantomime flourished—the house of *La Sylphide, Giselle,* Taglioni, Elssler. These two kinds of accounts run in loose parallel, largely ignoring one another, so sharply specialized that the unknowing reader blundering across only one set of them or the other could wrongly gather that the Opéra was a place where *only* ballet-pantomime or *only* opera truly mattered—or worse, that it was a house where only one of them was performed at all.

It must also be admitted that a streak of distaste for dance runs through traditional musicology and has made the prospect of studying ballet and the fortunes of its relationship with opera less than appealing to many music specialists. Much of this ill feeling probably stems from Wagner's unequivocally stated contempt for the French ballet of his time, some of which may have been inspired by the Opéra's deliberate policy of showing off its danseuses' sexual appeal during the years of Wagner's tenure in Paris in the 1840s and 1860s (a policy that surely helped fuel the composer's disdain for the house and its audience, and which to this day has helped make ballet look like a trivial sideshow to musicologists by lending to the art itself a lingering aura of promiscuity).[7] Echoes of his scorn reverberate in many standard accounts of nineteenth-century French opera, some of which treat the French liking for ballet as nothing more than a peculiar fetish and could even suggest to the uninformed reader that ballets at the Opéra were generally imposed only after the opera's completion and against the composer's will, bearing no plausible connection to the drama. The same echoes may be heard in the occasional attacks on ballet disparaging not just the French operatic ballet segments Wagner so disdained, but all ballet. Recently, for example, a critic dismissed as "a mistake" the publication of articles about ballet in a new music-theater encyclopedia, writing that "truly musico-dramatic pieces otherwise qualified for inclusion had to be sacrificed on the altar of Terpsichore" because so many pages were "dedicated to the kings of fancy footwork."[8] According to this point of view—not an uncommon one— ballets are not "truly musico-dramatic pieces" and ballet is ipso facto no more deserving of a place in musicology than it was of a place in *Tannhäuser.*

Indeed, the *Tannhäuser* disaster of 1861 probably contributed significantly to the formation of this attitude about ballet's relative triviality.[9] For the Jockey Club's insistence upon ogling the Opéra's ballerinas serves as a nagging reminder of something we might rather forget: that ballet's expressive instrument was the human body. Ballet's very physicality has surely helped prevent it from receiving its due notice among musicologists, who like most scholars tend to overlook the corporeal in favor of the cognitive.

Yet another scholarly tradition impedes musicologists when it comes to studying ballet: the long-standing belief that music attached to words and drama is less worthy of serious attention than "absolute" music. Though this belief is now breaking down, it has put nineteenth-century ballet music, much of which was composed to follow stage action very closely, at a particular disadvantage. Consider, for example, this gingerly wrought defense (published in 1973) of the *Giselle* score. Adolphe Adam, says the author, is severely attacked in the first edition of Grove's Dictionary of Music.... We do not feel so harshly about poor Adam these days, but there is no doubt that the continued success of *Giselle* depends far more on its dancing than on its music. Nevertheless Adam's score for *Giselle* is, at least, extremely competent, and often very apt for the dramatic action. Indeed the music is very closely related to the dance, and there is no elaborate symphonic development.... Such music is of course ineffective in the concert hall—but that is not its place. It is intended to be listened to as an adjunct to the dance, and it supports the dancing by adding its rhythmical, emotional, atmospheric, or dramatic qualities. I am not saying that all ballet music should be like *Giselle*—Heaven forbid—but I do feel that the simplicity of the music here does disguise a greater dramatic power than many people realize.[10]

Roland John Wiley's more recent—and utterly unapologetic—writings about ballet music indicate that ballet, if still disparaged in some quarters, is now being taken quite seriously in others. In his introduction to *Tchaikovsky's Ballets,* for instance, he matter-of-factly offers one reason among many why the dancing and the stories of nineteenth-century Russian ballet cannot reasonably be left out of a scholar's reckonings:

Complementing the [ballet composer's] sensitivity to the visual was his awareness that the aural attractions of concert music could be defects in ballet. He attempted to adjust the level of inherent musical interest at any given moment to enhance the choreography, and realized that any competition of eye and ear for the audience's attention risked the weakening or loss of a desired effect. This procedure tends to produce in a ballet an inverse relationship between interest in music and interest in dance, whereby music makes its strongest impact when solo dance is the least commanding, and vice versa. The climactic moments of pure music and pure dance almost never coincide, a fact which should give pause to the analyst who seeks to judge ballet music only for its sounds.[11]

As Wiley has found it helpful to explain the value of looking beyond the score, opera scholars in recent years have been compelled to do much the same. They have argued that calling an opera "symphonic" degrades its poetry and its drama; that the "critic who proceeds with the goal of demonstrating coherent musical structure may demonstrate only that"; that examining the music without the libretto impoverishes opera study.[12] The academic preference for purely instrumental music exerted for quite a long time just as dampening an effect on opera scholarship as it did on ballet scholarship.[13] And just as opera achieved academic respectability only after old canonical norms had been challenged, so has this been the case for ballet. Moreover, ballet, like opera, has been subjected to analyses that seek coherent musical structures but pay little attention to the libretto or the drama. And ballet, like opera, has similarly been affected by the concomitant bias against works created in the nineteenth century: the operas of Berg and Monteverdi and the ballets of Stravinsky and Lully, for example, were sooner considered worthy of scholarly scrutiny than, say, the operas of Donizetti and the ballets of Tchaikovsky. Thus the recent musicological historiographies of ballet and opera (like the genres themselves) have much in common. But they are taking shape quite separately.

THE PRESENT study by no means constitutes an exhaustive account of the long-lived relationship between ballet and opera as it was played out in all the opera houses of Europe. But it does demonstrate that, at one of the most influential houses of all, close ties between the two types of works persisted well into the nineteenth century, long after opera and ballet had been solidly established as separate genres. Thus while it is true, as dance historians have long averred, that the ballet reformers of the eighteenth century created "the first ballets in the modern sense of the term"[14] and dealt what proved to be the deathblow to ballet's traditional coziness with opera, it is also true that ballet and opera in Paris in the 1830s and 1840s had not yet come to be driven by such widely separate aesthetic impulses as they are today; that the breaking apart of the two arts was a process that took longer than is generally believed, and was far from over by the time of the July Monarchy (1830–1848).

Historians of the arts have long since recognized that fracturing any theater piece into its component parts and studying one without the others can yield only a limited interpretation. And, clearly, isolating one type as though it bore no kinship to any other types can do the same. No composer, choreographer, or librettist in the nineteenth century learned about opera while remaining ignorant of ballet, nor learned ballet while remaining ignorant of opera. Such a thing would have been impossible. For us, as distant observers trying to imagine what these works were like and how they were perceived, such compartmentalization can make our readings unnecessarily narrow. By viewing opera and ballet together, in the same frame, we stand to discover a rich array of connections that can increase our understanding of both of them and, at the same time, allow us to experience some of the same pleasures of recognition and familiarity that helped attract their first audiences to the opera house.

A NOTE ON SOURCES

Imagining how Parisian ballet-pantomimes of the 1830s and 1840s were performed is difficult because of the relative paucity of sources when it comes to rock-solid information about choreography and staging. By an unhappy twist of fate, choreographers of this period (falling as they did in the gap between Feuillet notation and Sténochorégraphie) used no systematic method for notating their ballet-pantomimes. Nor, it seems, were they particularly inclined to preserve them for posterity even through informal ad hoc kinds of notations. And nobody wrote staging manuals for ballets, as they sometimes did for operas. (The prolific opera-manual publisher Louis Palianti, apparently, was even approached about doing so but never did.[15]) Therefore, though tantalizing notations and partial descriptions of choreographies for a few of these Parisian ballet-pantomimes do exist (for instance, in the Aumer and Taglioni collections), dance historians attempting to describe the steps and gestures of these ballets have relied for the most part on reviews and other anecdotal testimony from ballet-goers, oral tradition, iconographical evidence, and ballet libretti.[16]

One largely untapped resource, however, is the musical score. Though very few have been published, a good many have been carefully preserved in archives: full scores, orchestral parts, autograph composing scores, and *répétiteurs* (rehearsal scores), some even annotated with prose descriptions of stage action and occasional diagrams. (As I write, David A. Day, Knud Arne Jürgensen and others are uncovering such annotated scores in various European archives; I am confident that these scores will have a major impact on dance historiography.) Even those lacking annotations offer a gold mine of valuable information because they were composed to follow the actions and moods of the ballet characters very closely. Indeed, the composers' close adherence to the choreography makes their music in some ways the best and most faithful witness to the first productions of these works. It also allows us to enter into the sonic world of these ballets, opening up new possibilities for reexperiencing a genre that was, after all, not strictly visual.

Nearly all the archival materials I consulted in the writing of this book are housed in Paris, at the Bibliothèque nationale, the Bibliothèque de l'Opéra, the Bibliothèque de l'Arsenal, and the Archives nationales. They include scores for ballets and operas (unpublished manuscript full scores, orchestral parts, and *répétiteurs*, published full scores of operas, piano reductions of ballets, and sheet music), libretti for ballets and operas, staging manuals for operas, newspapers, memoirs, letters, lithographs, design sketches for costumes and sets, costume and materials lists, contracts, police reports, and various office memoranda. I also examined (on microfilm) an annotated Parisian *répétiteur* for *Giselle* that is kept at the Theater Museum in St. Petersburg. In the Dance Collection of the New York Public Library, I studied a *répétiteur* for *La Somnambule* as well as microfilm copies of various Parisian ballet scores. All annotations in my musical examples, except those in brackets, are found in the scores, and I have tried to reproduce as precisely as possible the placement of these words as I found them in the music. All translations into English are my own unless otherwise indicated.

Library Sigla

New York Public Library	US-NYp
Bibliothèque nationale, Paris	F-Pn
Bibliothèque de l'Opéra, Paris	F-Po
Archives nationales, Paris	F-Pan
Bibliothèque de l'Arsenal, Paris	F-Pa
Theatre Museum, St. Petersburg	RU-SPtob

ACKNOWLEDGMENTS

I HAVE incurred many debts in the writing of this book, and I am happy to mention them here. First, Ivor Guest—without whose magisterial work this volume could never have been imagined and without whose encouragement it would surely never have gotten off the ground—patiently answered my every question about the workings of the Opéra in the nineteenth century and the disposition of its archive today. Roger Parker and Stephanie Jordan gave me opportunities to try out my ideas publicly; Giannandrea Poesio and Lisa Arkin shared with me their expertise and artistry. David Charlton asked incisive questions about some of my related research, and Roland John Wiley offered crucial insight into two rare *Giselle* répétiteurs. M. Elizabeth C. Bartlet, Maribeth Clark, David A. Day, Sarah Hibberd, Steven Huebner, Margaret Miner, Cormac Newark, John Speagle, Reinhard Strohm, and Rebecca Wilberg all allowed me to read pieces of their research at the prepublication stage. At Princeton University Press, Elizabeth Powers, Malcolm Litchfield, Fred Appel, Elizabeth Swayze, Marta Steele, Robert Brown, and Jan Lilly each contributed significantly to the realization of this volume, from its first stages to its final production. The Bibliothèque nationale de France and the Picture Library of the Victoria and Albert Museum granted permission for the illustrations. The National Endowment for the Humanities, the University of Oregon and the Oregon Humanities Center supported my research with grants that allowed me to travel to Paris and take sabbatical time from my teaching. Thomas Christensen, Carol Marsh, and Rebecca Harris-Warrick offered thoughtful and blunt criticism of early versions of my manuscript (though any mistakes or infelicities that remain are, of course, my own).

In Paris, the Lebas, Weill, and Curie families, whose graciousness I shall never forget, selflessly opened their homes to me, tolerating my American habits and wardrobe and including me in many a merry evening around the dinner table. (And Germaine Curie taught me the specialized terminology of the *bal masqué* and of the *chasse!*) Janet Johnson and Elizabeth Bartlet sacrificed precious research time to help me better mine various archives, and along with Nancy Keeler, John Smith, and John Ferguson made my sojourns in Paris even more fun. Jean-Louis Tamvaco surprised me with the gift of his invaluable annotated transcription of *Les Cancans de l'Opéra*. At the Bibliothèque de l'Opéra, Nicole Wild, Marie-José Kerhoas, Martine Kahane and Pierre Vidal extended a most hospitable welcome and patiently responded to my sometimes-peculiar requests. In Brussels David A. Day took me on a thrilling tour of the annotated scores he is cataloguing at the Archives de la Ville. In St. Petersburg, Natalia Metelitsa of the Theater and Music Museum generously arranged for me to receive the microfilm of two rare *Giselle répétiteur* scores; my mother,

Linnea Smith, served as courier. And in New York, Genevieve Oswald kindly helped me gain access to the amazing new ballet-music microfilm collection she has amassed at the Dance Collection at the New York Public Library; Madeleine Nichols, Dorothy Lourdou, and Lacy McDearmon further facilitated my work there.

Here in Eugene, Marc Vanscheeuwijck, Nathalie Ricci-Whaley, and Carolyn Bergquist helped me negotiate the shoals of their native languages, and Lorri Froggét adeptly prepared the musical examples. Anne Dhu McLucas translated Russian manuscript scribblings and offered deanly encouragement. Peter and Dorothy Bergquist supported me in various ways, including stepping in with editorial triage every time I asked for it.

Finally, I wish to record my gratitude to my families in Texas—Smiths, Bergquists, and Harrises—for teaching me, early on, the pleasures of music and of the visual, and the power of good storytelling. Nor can I overstate my debts, for inspiration and sustenance of many kinds, to Rita Pisk, LaVerne Morrison, Nora Shattuck, Nelita True, Carrie Lemuel, Maurice Price, Sophia Lauderdale, Stanley Hall, Phil Niles, Bob Bonner, George Soule, Steve Kelly, Hazel McCanne, Marion Strahan, Grace Smith, Judith Ballan, Holly Slocum, Dave Penticuff, Kathryn Oberdeck, Margot Fassler, Brenda Dalen, Carrin Patman, Reinhard Strohm, Jeanne Swack, my aunt Kate Bergquist (who first conveyed the magic of ballet to me), and my brother and soul mate Thomas Smith (who supported my research in so many ways). And I am most grateful to my remarkable husband, Carl Woideck, who frequently accompanied me on my journeys through the "labyrinthe enchanté de verdure, de gaze, de sourires, de gambades, de fleurs, d'épaules nues, d'aurore naissant, de crépuscule flamboyant, de poésie, de rêverie, de passions, de musique et d'amour" and helped me find my way back to our hearth every time I got lost.

NOTE TO THE READER:
A FEW TERMS

THE Paris Opéra, or the Opéra, is the institution officially known during the July Monarchy (the reign of Louis-Philippe, enduring from 1830 to 1848) as the Académie royale de musique.[1] The term *ballet-pantomime,* used frequently at that time to denote the self-standing dramatic ballet, which told a story through dance and mime—for instance, *La Sylphide, Le Diable boiteux, Paquita*—was considered by some observers a synonym for the older terms *ballet en action* and *ballet d'action,* dating from the late eighteenth century. The term "ballet," on the other hand, was applied in its strict sense only to a danced segment within an opera or ballet-pantomime.[2] (Such segments could also be referred to as "divertissements.") Though I do wish to preserve the perceived distinction between the terms "ballet" and "ballet-pantomime," I occasionally refer to a "ballet-pantomime" by the shorthand term "ballet" (for instance, calling *Giselle* a ballet instead of a ballet-pantomime), as critics, choreographers, and theatergoers sometimes did in the late eighteenth and nineteenth centuries. I also use interchangeably the terms "choreographer" and "ballet master" to denote the person who devised the steps and gestures of a ballet, though the latter term was more widely used in the nineteenth century.

BALLET AND OPERA IN THE
AGE OF *GISELLE*

CHAPTER ONE

Introduction: Music and the Story

> If music doesn't express the feelings of players, what else
> is there to express them? Big arm movements are a poor
> language.
>
> *Le Siècle,* 23 Sept. 1836

SEVERAL of the arguments in this book depend on my reading of ballet-pantomime music composed at the Opéra during the July Monarchy. Before setting out, then, I would like to offer a brief general description of this music, since it is for the most part unknown today.

Most important of all is the fact that for each new ballet-pantomime created at the Paris Opéra during the July Monarchy, a new score was produced. The reason for this is simple: these ballet-pantomimes told stories—elaborate ones—and music was considered an indispensable tool in getting them across to the audience. Therefore, music had to be newly created to fit each story.

Music tailor-made for each new ballet-pantomime, however, was only one weapon in the Opéra's explanatory arsenal. Another was the ballet-pantomime libretto, a printed booklet of fifteen to forty pages in length, which was sold in the Opéra's lobby (like the opera libretto), and which laid out the plot in painstaking detail, scene by scene. Critics also took it upon themselves to recount the plots (of both ballet-pantomimes and operas) in their reviews of premières. So did the publishers of souvenir albums, which also featured pictures of famous performers and of scenes from favorite ballet-pantomimes and operas.

Why were these stories made available to the public in so many ways? The mere fact that elaborate ballet-pantomimes were created at breakneck pace at the Opéra (about two new ones per year) is one reason: audiences had to learn a lot of stories if they were to understand what they were seeing (unlike today's ballet-goers, who are usually offered a rich variety of plotless ballets, and a handful of familiar old "story ballets" like *Romeo and Juliet* and *Sleeping Beauty,* but very few *new* highly detailed "story ballets"). The more often they could read the stories, the more likely they would understand them in the theater.

Why the French were so partial to such stories is another matter. Théophile

Gautier protested that, as far as he himself was concerned, a ballet story need "have no ending, no beginning, no middle, for all we care," so long as the dancer's foot "is tiny and well arched . . . if her leg is dazzlingly pure in shape and moves voluptuously in its mist of muslin . . . if her smile bursts forth like a rose filled with pearls . . . " But he did venture a guess about his countrymen's affection for stories:

> In England and Italy [the plot] does not matter very much, but in France the choice of subject is very important. The French are not artistic enough in the true sense of the term to be satisfied with the plastic content of poetry, painting, music and the dance. They also require a clear-cut meaning, a theme, a logical dramatic development, a moral, a clearly defined ending . . . This is both a shortcoming and a merit. This attitude, which has produced one of the most rational dramatic literatures in the world, makes us at times very critical, particularly towards ballets and operas, which three times out of four fail or succeed because of the scenario or libretto and not because the music is good or bad . . . If one dared, one would be invoking Aristotle in connection with a *cabriole* that is well or badly executed.[1]

In any case, composers were expected to play their part in communicating ballet-pantomime's elaborate plots to the Opéra's audiences, and to do so by creating a new score for each new work. They did sometimes weave borrowed music into these scores (though as the years went by critics came to look askance at this practice) (see Table 4.1). But in every instance—whether the score was fully original or not—the composer was expected to hew to the action, tailoring the music to fit the choreography.[2] For this reason the composer customarily worked closely with the ballet master, and sometimes with the dancers as well. As one observer wrote, "[d]ance airs are no longer based on a known model; the composer consults with the choreographer about the forms, character and length . . . ;" another described rehearsals at the Opéra in which the ballet master and the composer together indicated the movements for the dance and pantomime to the dancers.[3] Collaborating so closely with a choreographer—whose artistic ideas took precedence—could be vexing for the composer, and it is hardly surprising that the latter's task was often considered a servile one.[4] The plight of the composer Jean-Madeleine Schneitzhoeffer, for example, stirs the sympathy of one critic in a review of *La Tempête* (1834):

> There is no task more painful and thankless than that imposed on the composer of ballet music. When he has finished, they make him start all over again. He is pleased with one passage, which he has carefully cultivated and nurtured; then the ballet master arrives and says he must cut it, elongate it, cut out a phrase or even the whole passage. Then at the rehearsals the dancers ask for another instrumentation—trombones, or bass drum in place of, perhaps, flutes with a pizzicato accompaniment. The poor composer! . . . when the musician is a distinguished artist like M. Schneitzoeffer [sic], one must truly feel sorry that he has found himself placed in such a frightful position.[5]

A later account, by Alphonse Duvernoy (who wrote music for ballets at the end of the nineteenth century), concurs:

> In olden days, the scenarist began by finding a choreographer . . . Between the poet and the dancer a close collaboration was formed. Once the plan of the piece and the dances were arranged, the musician was called in. The ballet-master indicated the rhythms he had lain down, the steps he had arranged, the number of bars which each variation must contain—in short, the music was arranged to fit the dances. And the musician docilely improvised, so to speak, and often in the ballet-master's room, everything that was asked of him. You can guess how alert his pen had to be, and how quick his imagination. No sooner was a scene written or a *pas* arranged than they were rehearsed with a violin, a single violin, as the only accompaniment. I forgot to say that even after having servilely done everything the ballet-master had demanded, the composer had to pay attention to the advice of his principal interpreters. So he had to have much talent, or at least great facility, to satisfy so many exigences, and, I would add, a certain amount of philosophy.[6]

Creating a new score to suit the needs of each new ballet is, of course, no longer the norm (though the style of moment-to-moment musical shadowing is known to us from the music for cartoons and some early films). As Michel Fokine wrote in 1914, "The new ballet . . . in contradistinction to the older ballet . . . does not demand 'ballet music' of the composer as an accompaniment to dancing; it accepts music of every kind, provided only that it is good and expressive."[7] Stringent requirements were imposed on ballet-pantomime music in the 1830s and 1840s, however. It simply cannot be overstated that, unlike most ballet music today, it was expected to help the audience follow the action; to provide something that the silent performers could not. As Carlo Blasis put it: "Ballet music and in general music . . . in dances must, so to speak, supplement [and] clarify for the audience all the mental movements which the dancer or mime artist cannot convey in gestures and the play of the physiognomy."[8] Thus, according to critical consensus in Paris at least until the mid-nineteenth century, much of the burden for making ballet-pantomime performances understandable to the spectator lay on the shoulders of the composer. Some critics even saw the ballet composer's role as akin to that of a storyteller and stated outright their conviction that "the music has a *mission* to explain or translate [the scenes]."[9] These remarks divulge high expectations:

> By their character, their expression and their style, the melodies [in ballet music] can and must complete the meaning of the gestures and the play of the physionomie.[10]

> Ballet music has a particular character; it is more accented, more *parlante* [i.e., communicative, lively], more expressive than opera music, because it is not destined only to accompany and enhance the words of the librettist, but to be itself the entire libretto.[11]

> Generally, one does not ask for music from a ballet-pantomime composer, but for an orchestra that is the translation, the commentary of the text which one would not otherwise be able to understand.[12]
>
> If music doesn't express the feelings of players, what else is there to express them? Big arm movements are a poor language.[13]
>
> The composer is virtually charged with telling the action....[14]

Only by understanding these strict exigencies can we fully understand why composers were hired to study the libretto, work with the choreographer, and follow the action so closely in their music.

TWO TYPES OF BALLET MUSIC

Anyone who glances through ballet-pantomime scores of this era may easily see that they are constituted of two distinct types of music (as the very term *ballet-pantomime* indicates they should be). One type—dramatic or "pantomime" music—changes frequently in meter, key, and tempo, reflecting the action and following the vagaries of the characters' emotions. The other, intended specifically for dancing, tends to fall evenly into 8-bar phrases, and to remain within a single key, meter, and tempo for longer segments than pantomime music (see Table 1.1). Contemporary observers acknowledge the clear distinction between these two types:

> [E]ach situation, each passion which comes momentarily to predominate, requires a new rhythm, new motifs, changes of tone and of phrasing. The skillful composer, despite the difficulties of these requirements, knows how to make a pleasing ensemble out of this mixture. This music must be imitative, capable of depicting images and exciting all sentiments which fit to diverse circumstances of the action. This imitation can be, it is true, objective: that is, this music can depict the physical phenomena of nature, for example a storm. But it must especially be subjective, in order to arouse in the spectator's soul the sentiments which he would feel if he found himself in circumstances similar to those created in the performance.... As for the dance airs, one conceives that they must be characteristic and analagous to the place where the action takes place, thus the dance airs of the Indians, the Scots, the Hungarians must have the character of the music of their countries....[15]
>
> In a ballet-pantomime, the *symphonie,* meant to depict the action and the sentiments of the characters, differs very much from the airs meant for the *pas* executed by the dancers. These airs are like the cavatinas, the duos, the trios of the singers, placed between recitatives....[16]

It is true that dance music was sometimes introduced for a few moments into dramatic scenes when the situation required it. Yet these two separate types of

TABLE 1.1 *Lady Henriette*, ACT ONE, FIRST TABLEAU

Tempo	Key	Meter	Action	Number of Measures
			Dramatic Action and Mime	
Andante	A♭	6/8	Lady Henriette is dressing.	17
			She dismisses her friends.	21
un peu plus animé	E♭	6/8	She is sad.	8
			Nancy presents her with a book.	3
Andante maestoso	C	2/4	A valet announces Tristan Crakfort, who begins to make a declaration.	15
Allegretto	G	2/4	Lady Henriette demands her fan.	5
			Tristan looks for the fan.	15
Andante maestoso	A	2/4	He recommences his declaration.	7
	C	2/4	She asks him to open the window.	8
			He responds.	8
			She asks him to close it again.	13
			She asks him to leave.	6
			She calls him back.	4
			She sends him away.	16
			Tristan falls exhausted into an armchair.	9
Allegro non troppo	E♭	6/8	Nancy runs to the window.	21
			She returns to her mistress.	8
			The servants are going to the festival.	19
			She tells Nancy to summon the young women.	23
même mouvement	G	2/4	The women tell Lady Henriette of the festivities.	43
			Dance	
Danse un peu moins vite	C	2/4	They perform character dances, which Nancy and Lady Henriette try to imitate.	109
un peu plus animé	F	2/4		82

NOTE: It is typical for the danced segments of a ballet-pantomime to be marked as such in the score (usually with the terms "danse," "pas," "divertissement," or "ballet"), and for the dramatic music immediately following the danced segment to be marked "après la danse" [after the dance].

This table is based on a *répétiteur* for *Lady Henriette*, F-Po Mat 19 [346 (22)].

music still remained recognizable as such and were consistently distinguished from one another quite clearly in contemporary commentary. Let us consider the two types in turn.

Dramatic or Pantomime Music

Composers went to great lengths to satisfy the requirements of depicting "the action and the sentiments of the characters" by providing a continuous current of music, through-composed and shaped by the constantly shifting needs of "each situation, each passion which comes momentarily to predominate."[17] In so doing, they deployed a wide variety of techniques, writing all manner of descriptive music imitating the characters' moods, actions and personalities, providing diegetic music and noises as appropriate (sounds heard by stage characters as such, like village-band music and knockings on doors), weaving in snippets of obviously "ethnic" music when the action required it, and using recurring motifs associated with particular characters or concepts and—sometimes—connotative borrowed music as well. They also brought a verbal aspect to bear (as will be discussed further in Chapter Four) by imitating the human voice in various ways and using so-called *airs parlants* (short snippets of melodies from folksongs or opera arias, which could introduce actual explanatory words into the viewers' minds). This music, then, offered up a mélange of different types of music, and could deftly switch from type to type—one moment following gestures or action, the next providing diegetic sounds (including imitations of the human voice), the next expressing a character's feelings.

In the famous opening scene of *La Sylphide,* for example, Schneitzhoeffer first imitates, with thirty-second-note neighbor figures, the flutter of the sylphide's wings as she hovers near the unsuspecting James (Example 1.1). Then, after the sylphide disappears up the chimney, James's mood is depicted with a dreamy adagio as he tries to convince himself that the Sylphide was merely a

EXAMPLE 1.1. The sylphide's fluttering wings.

[Note: Annotations in the score refer to "Tom" and "Garne," with various spellings for the latter; in the libretto these characters are called James and Gurn.]

EXAMPLE 1.2. James summons Gurn.

figment of his imagination. He summons Gurn (who is reclining nearby in the hay, and whose lack of refinement is pointed out by Schneitzhoeffer with a few bars of "country music" with a heavy drone) to inquire if he, too, had seen her (Example 1.2). The composer mirrors the dialogue between the two men by assigning them, alternately, the antecedent and consequent phrases of the melody (Example 1.3). Ferdinand Hérold is similarly attentive to the action and characters in the closing scenes of Act Two of *La Somnambule,* wherein the sleep-

EXAMPLE 1.3. Conversation of James and Gurn.

EXAMPLE 1.4. Thérèse walks in her sleep.

[Noise outside / She comes down from the window / She advances in measured steps / Surprise of M. Rambert]

walking Thérèse climbs through a window into Saint-Rambert's chamber. The scene opens with a fortissimo *tremolo,* which imitates the startling noise that Saint-Rambert and Gertrude hear outside the window. Hérold then accompanies Thérèse's descent through the window into the room with suitably delicate, anticipatory thirty-second notes, all preparing the new E-major tonic of the pizzicato walking melody ("Che sarà" from Rossini's *La Cenerentola,* a piece sometimes translated as "What a fix!") which accompanies her initial sleepwalk. After this moment of commenting on the action, the music then switches to Saint-Rambert's surprise (Example 1.4).

A few moments later, a group of merrymakers from a village festival (including Thérèse's fiancé Edmond), come up to Rambert's room. For this scene, Hérold supplies first the actual music of the festival and then depicts, in rapid succession, the sentiments of various characters: the shock and anger of the vil-

EXAMPLE 1.5. Edmond becomes furious.

[The villagers, coming from the festival / O heaven! Thérèse in the room . . . / Furor of Edmond]

lagers; the befuddlement of the awakening sleepwalker, the furor of her fiancé, Edmond (Example 1.5). Another rude awakening is depicted in Act Two scene i of Adolphe Adam's *Le Diable à Quatre,* which finds an imperious countess asleep in a basket-maker's humble hut. (She has been forced by magic to trade places with the basket-maker Mazourki's wife.) Her placid little pastoral "slumber" melody—ironically far too "country" for a countess, like the setting itself—alternates with short bursts of sixteenth notes as Mazourki vigorously attempts to awaken her. The Countess's startled arising is reflected by a fortissimo ascending scale; the busy little agitato melody in g minor that follows expresses her ensuing displeasure (Example 1.6).

The overture and opening moments of *Le Diable boiteux* provide an apt illustration of locale-setting. The rhythmic pattern, ♪♫ ♫♪, a reliable cliché indicating Spanishness, pervades the overture as an accompaniment (Example 1.7). It then returns as the curtain rises on the ball scene, set in the resplendent foyer of the Royal Theater in Madrid; this time it is used in one of two alternating melodies (one played on the stage and the other in the orchestra pit), which, emanating from separate places, help re-create the chaotic sonic effects of the masked ball (Example 1.8).[18] The music of a later scene, set in the *salle* of the same theater (with both performers and audience in view), provides many

EXAMPLE 1.6. The Countess is awakened.

EXAMPLE 1.7. *Le Diable boiteux* overture

EXAMPLE 1.8. *Le Diable boiteux* masked ball, two alternating melodies.

of the sounds of the theater: the call-bell signaling the impending curtain-up, the tuning up of the orchestra, the music of a *pas de deux* (performed by dancers with their backs to the real audience), and the curtain speech made by the stage manager.[19]

Recurring melodies figured prominently in this repertory as a dramatic device (more copiously, in fact, than in the operas usually listed as predecessors in this regard to Wagner's operas—works of Méhul, Cherubini, Weber, and Meyerbeer, for example). Reminiscence motifs (or "recalling" motifs), for example, were used fairly often, whether the character doing the recalling was crazy, sleepwalking, or in a state of regular consciousness.[20] One may also find plenty of examples of the recurring identifying themes (of the type later disparaged by Debussy in his attack on Wagner as "calling cards").

Composers who favored the use of recurring melodies, however, did not limit themselves to transparent identifying and recalling motifs alone. Consider, for example, Adam's transformation of a motif that is first heard when the starry-eyed Giselle dances with her dissembling lover in the Harvest Festival (Example 1.9). After returning as a recalling motif during the mad scene as her heart breaks, this motif comes back again, mournfully, at the beginning of Act 2 as Hilarion points out Giselle's grave to a group of hunters (Example 1.10). A transformed version—a shorter fragment stripped of its countrified drone bass and given a less stable harmony—is sounded when the Wili Giselle is first summoned from her grave by Myrthe (Example 1.11). The first three pitches of the melody ($\hat{3}, \hat{4}, \hat{2}$) are answered ethereally, by solo flute, with a configuration of pitches similar in contour; this solo returns when the grief-stricken Albrecht first catches a glimpse of the Wili Giselle, who to his shock emerges from behind her own gravestone (Example 1.12).

EXAMPLE 1.9. *Giselle,* Harvest Festival *pas de deux.*

EXAMPLE 1.10. Pointing out Giselle's grave.

The significance of the "Harvest Festival" motif was not lost on the composer in Russia who later used it—quite fittingly—as the basis for a new variation for Giselle he added to the second-act *pas de deux,* wherein the two lovers express their undying love for each other.[21] Nor, perhaps, was it lost on Wagner, who attended a performance of *Giselle* in Paris the week of its première in 1841.[22] In any case such recurring motifs, along with the many other devices at the ballet composer's disposal, proved valuable within a textless dramatic music to which the audience regularly turned for help in following the story.[23]

EXAMPLE 1.11. Giselle's first appearance as a Wili.

EXAMPLE 1.12. The Wili Giselle surprises Albrecht.

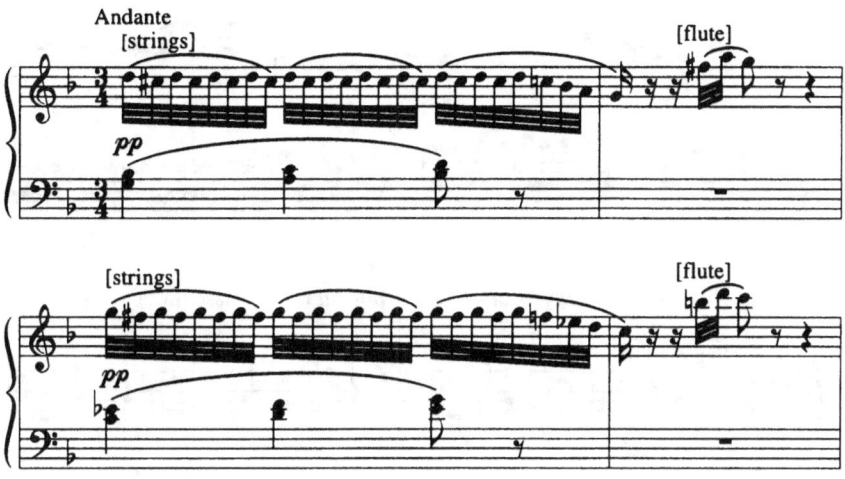

Dance Music

The style of the music written specifically for *dancing* in these ballet-pantomimes was legion in Europe for much of the nineteenth century and remains familiar even now because it has been carried over in works that are still in the repertory—for example, danced divertissements from French grand operas (*Les Martyrs, La Favorite, Les vêpres siciliennes*), and such enduring post-1850 ballets as *Don Quixote, Coppélia,* and *Le Corsaire*.[24] Standard stylistic features include a regularity of phrasing and simplicity of melody, harmony, and texture (two-voice textures are common; and often, for solo dances, composers wrote simply a solo for an obbligato melodic instrument and a pizzicato accompaniment[25]), repetition by the full orchestra of a melody first stated by solo instrument, punctuation of sparsely textured passages with occasional tutti chords, extended tutti cadences increasing in volume and sometimes quickening in tempo toward the end, and a heavy reliance upon repetition, both of melodies and of catchy rhythmic patterns. Dances for solo dancers, or small ensembles, are often preceded by a short, very anticipatory-sounding introduction lasting eight or sixteen measures and dwelling on the dominant.

One may also identify certain distinctive melody types favored in this repertory. One is characterized by a nearly uninterrupted flow of sixteenth-notes—often making much use of repeating notes—well exemplified by this flute solo from a divertissement in *La Volière* (Example 1.13).[26] This melody-type was used for what Wiley has called the "coquettish" dance.[27] Its later masculine counterpart, the "bravura" dance, was not as common in this earlier repertory, though it was not unknown. Labarre, for example, composed this bravura-style music for the arrival of Myssouf in *La Révolte au sérail* (Example 1.14).

EXAMPLE 1.13. Flute solo from *La Volière* (feminine).

EXAMPLE 1.14. Myssouf, in *La Révolte au sérail* (masculine).

THE DIVERTISSEMENT.   Dance music found its most concentrated use in the danced divertissements (referred to sometimes as the "ballets") that were featured in both opera and ballet-pantomime. These divertissements, indeed, constituted one of the most obvious points of similarity between opera and ballet-pantomime. In all cases the dancing within these divertissements was diegetic (that is, perceived by the other characters as dancing). Dramatic rationales included, for example, village festivals, wedding celebrations, masked balls, and entertainments performed for royalty (see Table 1.2). The same dancers were likely to turn up in both opera and ballet-pantomime divertissements, including Marie Taglioni and Fanny Elssler, for the custom of saving the best dancers only for the ballet-pantomime had not yet fully taken hold.

Formal construction of the divertissement adhered to certain rules: it usually featured dances both for the *corps de ballet* and for smaller small ensembles and soloists. (This sometimes included a *pas de trois* or *pas de deux,* dances that sometimes took a shape that by the time of the Tchaikovsky ballets had congealed into the formula of entrance / adagio / variations / coda.[28]) The composer also customarily ensured a contrast in tempo, key, or meter from dance to dance, which could make for a pleasing variety of mood (a sweet and sentimental adagio, for example, was likely to be followed by a brisk and vigorous allegro). In addition, divertissements commonly ended rousingly (often with multisectioned music entitled *final*).

TABLE 1.2 RATIONALES FOR DANCING IN OPERAS AND BALLET-PANTOMIMES

Guillaume Tell (Act One) Opera, 1829	Celebration of a village wedding.
Guillaume Tell (Act Three)	Tyrol peasants are forced to dance during festivities celebrating Austria's dominion over Switzerland.
La Sylphide (Act One) Ballet, 1832	Celebration of a peasant wedding.
Nathalie (Act One) Ballet, 1832	Village girls demonstrate their joy at gifts from a lord and lady.
Nathalie (Act Two)	Celebration of a village wedding
La Révolte au sérail Ballet, 1833	Zulma and her friends sport in the water.
Don Giovanni (Act Two) Opera, 1834	Masked ball at the don's palace
La Juive (Act One) Opera, 1835	Spontaneous dancing as the emperor and victorious soldiers march into the city.
La Juive (Act Three)	Festivities in honor of Léopold's victory over the Hussites.
Les Huguenots (Act Three) Opera, 1836	Spontaneous dancing by gypsies on the banks of the Seine.
Les Huguenots (Act Five)	Celebration of a noble wedding.
Le Diable boiteux (Act Three) Ballet, 1836	Festival on the banks of the Manzanares.
La Fille du Danube (Act One) Ballet, 1836	Ball at which the Baron's squire is expected to choose a bride.
Le Diable Boiteux (Act One) Ballet, 1836	Masked ball in Madrid.
La Chatte (Act One) Ballet, 1837	Imperial festival at which the princess is expected to choose a bridegroom.
Les Mohicans (Act Two) Ballet, 1837	Dancing of the Mohicans, who can't resist the sound of the pocket violin.
Les Martyrs (Act Two) Opera, 1840	Dances of celebration in honor of the new proconsul.
Giselle (Act One) Ballet, 1841	Celebration of the grape harvest.
La Gipsy (Act Two) Ballet, 1839	Dancing by gypsies at the great fair of Edinburgh.
Le Prophète (Act Two) Opera, 1849	Dancing of villagers at Jean's inn.
Le Prophète (Act Three)	Spontaneous dancing by peasants near the Anabaptists' army camp.

Any given divertissement, however, was likely to be altered to suit the talents of new dancers and the latest tastes of the ballroom. So receptive was the Paris Opéra to social-dance fashion, in fact, that dances new to the city's ballrooms in the 1830s and 1840s—for instance, the polka and galop—were virtually guaranteed to appear on the Opéra's stage.[29] Among these popular ballroom dances were so-called "national" dances (or "character dances," as they are more commonly called in the twentieth century), such as the cracovienne and the Jaleo de Xeres. (By the same token, the Opéra's dancers sometimes ignited social-dance crazes with their spectacular, crowd-pleasing performances of national dances.) Though these national dances tend to be overlooked in many latter-day accounts of nineteenth-century ballet, they were so popular in the 1830s and 1840s, both in the ballroom and on the stage, that choreographers of divertissements often created not only a national dance appropriate to the setting of the work—like a jig in Scotland—but "foreign" dances as well. On at least one occasion, for example, a Hungarian dance was performed in the ball scene of *Don Giovanni,* the rationale being that the Hungarians were providing entertainment for the maskers, even though the ball was taking place in Spain.[30]

The demands placed on ballet-music composers, then, were many: they were expected to provide dance music for divertissements and to "tell the action" and help "express the feelings of players" in dramatic sections, to mingle these two distinct types of music together as the situation required, and to include music appropriate for the setting and ethnicity of the characters.[31] Because it is only the style of the dance music, and not the dramatic music, that is familiar to our ears today, we tend to think of these ballet-pantomimes as largely centered around dancing. Yet, as I hope to show in the pages that follow, dancing was only one element of the ballet-pantomime, a genre whose relationship to opera cannot be revealed unless one takes into account the non-dancing segments of these works and the music composed for them.

CHAPTER TWO

A Family Resemblance

> [The Paris Opéra] has song and dance as its lord and master.
>
> Théophile Gautier, *La Presse,* 23 January 1841

IN THE 1830s and 1840s, the Paris Opéra—situated in the rue le Peletier, not far from where the old Bibliothèque nationale still stands today—was celebrated as one of the continent's most vibrant public theaters. The most famous singers and dancers in Europe performed on its stage, and the goings-on within its walls commanded the attention of a steady throng of spectators, many of whom took pen in hand to record their experiences or to weave fictional tales using the Opéra as a setting. Delacroix, Berlioz, Musset, George Sand, Mendelssohn, Balzac, and Dumas (among other luminaries) attended performances there, and even outside of Paris theatergoers eagerly awaited its premieres, for many of the operas and ballet-pantomimes created there were quickly taken up in the French provinces and by foreign houses across the continent and sometimes as far away as St. Petersburg, Helsinki, New Orleans, and Buenos Aires.[1]

Happily, the many manuscripts and printed documents left behind by the Opéra's patrons, critics, and employees have supplied plenty of fodder to the historian. And there is an underlying theme that seems to be taken for granted in nearly all of them: that the Paris Opéra was a house where both opera and ballet fully belonged and flourished. The director's contract, for instance, stipulates that he produce works in both of "the two genres allocated to this theater up to the present time, that is, grand opera . . . and ballet-pantomime."[2] The posted playbills list both singers' and dancers' names. Commercial picture albums offer portraits of both the Opéra's singers and dancers and plot summaries of both operas and ballet-pantomimes.[3] Contemporary chronicles of the Opéra include both kinds of works in their published narratives and repertory lists.[4] Newspaper reviews for both operas and ballet-pantomimes appear under the heading "Théâtre de l'Opéra" and often follow the same rough format.[5] News columns mix information about opera and ballet together[6]:

> News: . . . Tomorrow, on Monday at the Opéra: *Stradella* [an opera], followed by *Le Diable amoreux* [a ballet-pantomime]; in the second act M. Coralli and Mlle

Maria will dance the Polka. All week *Le Lazzarone* [an opera] has been rehearsed; the first performance is set for next Wednesday. Today the final rehearsal is taking place.... Two famous dancers of diverse styles, Mmes Cerrito and Lola Montez, found themselves together in Paris. The former has already departed for Brussels....[7]

Nowhere, perhaps, is this sense of the Opéra's shared purpose better expressed than in its schedule: every performance included both opera and ballet. That is, if a four- or five-act opera were performed in its entirety, it comprised at least one lengthy ballet divertissement; if a ballet-pantomime were performed, a short opera—or truncated version of a longer one—was given either before or afterward.[8] Thus, no ballet-pantomime was ever given without an opera, and no opera was ever given without some sort of ballet. Simply put, spectators were presented with both singing and dancing every night the Opéra was open.

Behind the scenes, too, the mingling of opera and ballet seems to have been a common practice. Every Monday morning, the Director began his week by convening the key members of his staff—including specialists in both opera and ballet—to discuss "important questions regarding *mimo-dramatico-lyrique* performance...."[9] And many of the Opéra's creative artists habitually plied their skills both to operas and ballet-pantomimes. The sets, costumes, machines and choreography of all new works, in fact, were designed by precisely the same people. Many of the libretti and scores, too, were created by artists experienced in both genres, most notably the composers Adolphe Adam and Ferdinand Hérold (known as particularly adept with ballet and opéra comique) and the librettists Eugène Scribe and Vernoi de Saint-Georges (who between the two of them supplied libretti for more than twenty operas and ballets at the Opéra during the July Monarchy). (See Appendix One.) Moreover, the Opéra's dancers regularly performed in both opera and ballet-pantomime. The singers, though they did not perform in ballet-pantomime, were given ample opportunities for exposure to it—so taken with ballet was the renowned tenor Adolphe Nourrit, in fact, that he even wrote the libretti for the ballet-pantomimes *La Sylphide*, *La Tempête*, and *L'Ile des pirates*.

This sort of artistic ecumenicism contributed to the state of affairs that is the subject of this chapter: that operas and ballet-pantomimes created at the Opéra during this period actually *resembled* each other. That is, they were not only created under the same roof and performed for the same audiences; they bore many features in common. This close family resemblence is an apt starting point for any study of the relationship that existed between them.

Before I launch into my list of their common features, however, a bit of background is in order. First, it must be recalled that the Opéra's practice of creating ballet-pantomimes and operas in such close conjunction with one another in the 1830s and 1840s—a practice now virtually dead—was a holdover from the seventeenth and eighteenth centuries, when dancing and singing were regularly mixed in various proportions in single dramatic works at that house (in tragédies lyriques and opera-ballets, for example). And though ballet-pantomime had certainly become well established as an independent genre by the period under scrutiny here, and was to become ever more removed from opera as time passed, the practice of performing it alongside opera had still not been called into question by the Opéra's administrators. They were simply carrying on the long-standing tradition of presenting singing and dancing, together, to the Opéra's audience, as that institution had always done.

Remember, too, that at the time of *La Sylphide*'s première in 1832 (the inaugural event of ballet's Romantic age, in the opinion of many historians) only fifty-six years had passed since the advent at the Opéra of the *ballet d'action* itself in 1776; since "the lost art of pantomime had been found by Noverre," as one observer put it.[10] The independent ballet, in which singers played no role, was still regarded as a relative novelty in the first three decades of the nineteenth century, as these words attest:

[B]allets, since about a half-century ago, have taken their place alongside operas, [sharing] . . . with them the empire of Polyhymnia and Terpsichore. . . . (1827)[11]

The execution of the music [of ballet] is *entrusted entirely* to the orchestra. . . . (1839)[12]

[Instrumental music] *no longer* has a rival in ballet. . . . Everything is the province of the orchestra, and it is the orchestra that must express all. (1828)[13]

If in retrospect we can call the Opéra's repertory of Romantic ballet-pantomimes an important stepping-stone toward the full-evening works by Petipa and Tchaikovsky, we must also remember that patrons of the Opéra in the July Monarchy, naturally, could regard it as nothing of the kind. They viewed the independent ballet as something rather new and were still inclined to look back to the days before ballet had broken apart from opera. The mere fact that it had become established as an independent, self-standing genre in no way meant that audiences expected it to be performed without opera. Nor did they think the two genres should suddenly to take on strikingly different appearances, nor "behave" in entirely separate ways.

THE similarities between the two independent genres of opera and ballet-pantomime would surely not have been at all difficult for spectators of the 1830s and 1840s, if asked, to enumerate. First of all, both types of work had a plot, and an elaborate one at that, usually featuring several principal characters and a large *corps de ballet* or chorus. Though this may seem too obvious a point to make, it is perhaps the most important of all, for it shows that all of these works started from the same basic premise: that they could, and should, tell a story. (This premise, of course, has long since been abandoned in the case of ballet, and plotless self-standing ballets comprise a significant segment of the current repertory.) Indeed (as noted in Chapter One), public exposition of the stories was an important feature of the external ritual attending a work's première, in that both opera and ballet-pantomime plots were customarily related at length in newspaper reviews and souvenir albums. These stories were also laid out for the audience in the libretti made available for sale in the Opéra's lobby, opera libretti supplying the words sung by the performers, and ballet libretti describing the action scene by scene. (Written in prose, ballet libretti often included bits of dialogue that its characters "spoke," even though, of course, these words were never actually intoned.)

The two basic plot ingredients of the Opéra's ballet-pantomimes and operas of this period were also the same: first, political or social contrasts, and second, affairs of the heart (though they were given different weight in the two different types of works—a matter to which I return in Chapter Three). Their action, too, tended to transpire in the same places: Western Europe and its colonies (France, Spain, and Italy being especially favored; see Table 2.1).[14] They existed within the same broad historical time span: the medieval and early

TABLE 2.1   SETTINGS OF OPERAS AND BALLET-PANTOMIMES AT THE OPÉRA

This is a list compiled around 1853 at the Opéra, with the heading "Indication of the Countries where these works take place."[1] It lists a few works twice (for instance, *Le Prophète*, *Le Freyschutz* and *Les Cinq Sens*), includes two different categories for Portugal, and in some cases fails to account for all the settings of a single work; for instance, it gives no indication that the last act of *Manon Lescaut* is set in the United States (the last scene being in the "vast desert of New Orleans," according to the libretto). But it gives a good overall picture of what settings were used, and shows that ballet-pantomime and opera favored the same settings, and in the same general proportions. I have included some of the original annotations, in italics. For information about the authorship of works not listed in Appendix One, see the endnotes to this table.

Country	Opera	Ballet-Pantomime
France	Le Comte Ory *1410*	La Somnambule
	Le Philtre *1740*	La Fille Mal gardée
	Le Serment *1800*	La Servante justifiée[2]
	Robert le diable *1032*	Manon Lescaut
	Les Huguenots *1572*	Ozaï *1768*
	Esmeralda	Le Violin du diable[3] *1718*
	Le Drapier	Paquerette[4] *1740*
	Charles VI *anglais et français*	Vert-Vert *Louis XV*
	La Bouquetière[5] *1774*	
	Jerusalem *1095 à 1099*	
	Le Fanal[6] *1845*	
	La Fronde[7] *1643 minorité de Louis 14*	

(*continued*)

TABLE 2.1   Continued

Country	Opera	Ballet-Pantomime
Italy	La Muette de Portici *1647* Stradella *1660* Guido et Ginevre *1460* Cellini Le Comte de Carmagnola Reine de Chypre *1473 1ᵉ acte* Le Lazzarone Othello *1530*	Le Carnaval de Venise[8] La Tempête L'Ile des Pirates La Tarentule *Calabre* Le Diable amoureux *Calabre* La Jolie Fille de Gand *2ᵉ acte* Stella *fin du 18ᵉ siècle*
Spain [and Portugal]	Don Juan [Don Giovanni] La Xacarilla La Favorite *1340* Fernand Cortez *1521* Dom Sébastien *1578 Portuguesa* Etoile du Séville *15ᵉ siècle* L'Apparition *Espagnol et français* Jeanne la Folle *1506*	L'Orgie Le Diable boiteux *1660* Paquita *1810 L'Empire* Alma [La Fille de Marbre] *1500*
Germany and Switzerland	Guillaume Tell *suisse* La Juive *1420* Le Lac des Fées *1517* Le Freyschutz *1650* Le Prophete *allemand et hollandais* Louise Miller[9] *Bavière Louis 15*	La Fille du Danube Giselle Nathalie *suisse*
Scotland and England	Le Vaisseau-fantôme *1655 ecossais* Charles VI *1422* Richard en Palestine *1191* Marie Stuart *1561 à 1587 écossais* Lucie de Lammermoor *Louis 13 1610 à 1643* Robert Bruce *1307 à 1330 anglais et eccosais*	La Sylphide *écossais* La Gipsy *écossais* Lady Henriette *anglais*
Corsica	La Vendetta	
Flanders	Juif errant *1420 1ᵉ acte*	La Jolie Fille de Gand *1620*
Sweden	Gustave *1792*	
Persia	Ali-Baba	Le Diable amoureux *3ᵉ acte*

[(*continued*)]

TABLE 2.1 Continued

Country	Opera	Ballet-Pantomime
The Americas]		Brézilia
"Créole"		La Volière
Mythological		Les Filets de vulcain
		Flore et Zéphire[10]
Fantastic	La Tentation	La Péri
		Les Nayades
		La Filleule des fées *1660*
India	La Bayadère	La Révolte au sérail
Ancient Rome	La Vestale[11]	Aelia et Mysis[12]
	Les Martyrs	
Ancient Greece	Iphigénie en Aulide[13]	Eucharis
	Iphigénie en Tauride[14]	
	Orphée[15]	
	Oedipe[16]	
	Sapho[17]	
China		La Chatte metamorphosée
Egypt	Moïse *16 siècle*	
	L'Enfant prodigue	
	avant Christ	
Greek - low empire	Le Siège de Corinthe	
	Le Juif errant	
Poland		Le Diable à Quatre
The Tyrol	L'Ame en peine	
Holland	Le Prophète	
Portugal	Dom Sébastien *1578*	Les Amazones *1520*
	Le Guerillero	
Bohèmia and Hungary	Le Freyschutz	Les Cinq Sens [Griseldis] *1500*
		La Vivandière
Moldavia and Vluachia		Les Cinq Sens [Griseldis] *1500*
Palestine	Roi David	
	Jérusalem *1095 à 1099*	
Iceland		Orfa[18]
Before Christ	L'Enfant prodigue	

(*continued*)

TABLE 2.1 Continued

[1] "Indication du Pays ou se passant les ouvrages désignés ci-dessous." F-Pan AJ13 215.
[2] Ballet-pantomime in two acts by P. Gardel, music by Schneitzhoeffer, first performed at the Opéra 18 February 1818.
[3] Ballet fantastique in two acts by Arthur Saint-Léon, music by Cesare Pugni, first performed at the Opéra 19 January 1849.
[4] Ballet-pantomime in three acts by Théophile Gautier, music by François Benoist, choreography by Arthur Saint-Leon, first performed at the Opéra 15 January 1851.
[5] Opera in one act by Hippolyte Lucas, music by Adolphe Adam, first performed at the Opéra 31 May 1847.
[6] Opera in two acts by Vernoi de Saint-Georges, music by Adolphe Adam, first performed at the Opéra 24 December 1849.
[7] Opera in five acts by Jules Lacroix and August Maquet, music by Louis Niedermeyer, choreography by Lucien Petipa, first performed at the Opéra 2 May 1853.
[8] Ballet-pantomime in two acts by Louis Milon, music by Louis-Luc Loiseau de Persuis and Rodolphe Kreutzer, first performed at the Opéra 22 February 1816.
[9] *Luisa Miller*, opera in four acts by S. Cammarano, music by Giuseppe Verdi, created in Naples, first performed at the Opéra 2 February 1853.
[10] Ballet anacréontique in two acts by Charles-Louis Didelot, music by Frédéric-Marc-Antoine Vénua, created in London, first performed at the Opéra 12 December 1815.
[11] Opera in three acts by Etienne de Jouy, music by Luigi Spontini, choreography by P. Gardel and Louis Milon, first performed at the Opéra 15 December 1807.
[12] Ballet-pantomime in two acts by Joseph Mazilier, music by Henri Potier, first performed at the Opéra 21 September 1853.
[13] Opera in three acts by Marie François Roullet after Racine, music by Christoph Gluck, first performed at the Opéra 19 April 1774, with ballets by M. Gardel (Act One) and G. Vestris (Acts Two, Three), revived in 1822.
[14] It is unclear whether the compiler of this document was referring to the opera in four acts by Nicolas François Guillard, music by Gluck, first performed at the Opéra 18 May 1779, and revived in 1821, or the opera in four acts by A. de C. Dubreuil, music by Niccolò Piccinni, choreography by M. Gardel, first performed at the Opéra 23 January 1781. The former seems more likely.
[15] Opera in three acts by Ranieri de' Calzabigi, tr. by Moline, music by Gluck, first performed at the Opéra 2 August 1774 with ballets by G. Vestris (Elysian Fields, Cupid), and M. Gardel (Funeral, Underworld), revived in 1783.
[16] Opera in three acts by Guillard, music by Sacchini, first performed at the Opéra 1 February 1787, choreography by M. Gardel, revived in 1793.
[17] It is unclear whether the compiler of this document was referring to the opera in four acts by Emile Augier, music by Charles Gounod, first performed at the Opéra 16 April 1851, or the tragédie lyrique in three acts by Adolphe-Joseph Simonis, music by Anton Reicha, choreography by P. Gardel, first performed at the Opéra 16 December 1822.
[18] Ballet-pantomime in two acts by Henri Trianon, music by Adolphe Adam, choreography by Joseph Mazilier, first performed at the Opéra 29 December 1852.

modern periods, having outgrown together the taste for the ancient and the mythological that had prevailed in the eighteenth century.[15] Both types of works also made use of the "well-made" libretto, deploying a set of a formulas popularized by Eugène Scribe including startling reversals, suspense, and the cause-to-effect arrangement of incidents.[16] Thus, they relied on many of the same stock devices and situations—nobles appearing in disguise; a man loving a woman above his station, and so on (see Table 2.2). They also relied on many of the same scene types, including magnificent processions, bathing scenes,

TABLE 2.2 PLOT SITUATIONS IN OPERAS AND BALLET-PANTOMIMES AT THE OPÉRA

This is based on Karin Pendle's table listing plot situations in Scribe's operas (see *Eugène Scribe and French Opera*, 390–93); I have simply added titles of ballet-pantomimes. Brackets around a title indicate that the work contains a variant of the situation listed.

1. A woman loves (and may marry) a man who seems (but may not be) above her station.

OPERAS	BALLET-PANTOMIMES
La Muette de Portici (1828)	*L'Orgie* (1831)
Le Dieu et la Bayadère (1830)	*Nathalie* (1832)
[*La Juive* (1835)]	*Betty* (1846)

2. A man loves (or may marry) a woman who seems (but may not be) above his station.

OPERAS	BALLET-PANTOMIMES
Guido et Ginevra (1838)	[*L'Ile des Pirates* (1835)]
Le Drapier (1840)	*La chatte metamorphosée* (1837)
La Favorite (1840)	*La Gipsy* (1839)
Zerline (1851)	*La Tarentule* (1839)
Le Juif errant (1852)
Les Vêpres siciliennes (1855)

3. A man searches for and finds a woman with whom he has fallen in love. (In most cases he does not know her name until he finds her.)

OPERAS	BALLET-PANTOMIMES
Les Huguenots (1836)	*La Sylphide* (1832)
Guido et Ginevra (1838)	*La Fille du Danube* (1836)
La Favorite (1840)

4. A woman falls in love with a man whose name or identity she does not know.

OPERAS	BALLET-PANTOMIMES
La Muette de Portici (1828)	*Giselle* (1841)
La Juive (1835)	[(*La Volière* (1838)]
Les Huguenots (1836)	*Betty* (1846)
Carmagnola (1841)
Jeanne la folle (1848)

5. An impending marriage is broken up in favor of a rival for the hand of one of the partners.

OPERAS	BALLET-PANTOMIMES
Le Philtre (1831)	*La Fille Mal Gardée* (1828)
Le Serment (1832)	*La Sylphide* (1832)

(*continued*)

TABLE 2.2 Continued

OPERAS	BALLET-PANTOMIMES
Ali-Baba (1833)	La Fille du Danube (1836)
Le Lac des fées (1839)	La Tarentule (1839)
La Xacarilla (1839)	La Jolie Fille de Gand (1842)
Le Drapier (1840)	Ozaï (1847)
Le Juif Errant (1852)	

6. Nobles appear unidentified or disguised.

OPERAS	BALLET-PANTOMIMES
La Muette de Portici (1828)	La Gipsy (1839)
Le Comte Ory (1828)	Giselle (1841)
Le Dieu et la Bayadère (1830)	Lady Henriette (1844)
La Juive (1835)	Le Diable à Quatre (1845)
Carmagnola (1841)	Betty (1846)
Jeanne la folle (1848)	

7. A character discovers he or she is of noble birth.

OPERAS	BALLET-PANTOMIMES
Le Juif errant (1852)	La Gipsy (1839)
Les Vêpres siciliennes (1855)	Paquita (1846)

8. A character sings a ballad about a legend or in a mime scene explains a past event or story that has some bearing on the plot.

OPERAS	BALLET-PANTOMIMES
Le Philtre (1831)	L'Orgie (1831)
Robert le Diable (1831)	La Gipsy (1839)
Le Serment (1832)	Giselle (1841)
Le Juif errant (1852)	Paquita (1846)
La Nonne sanglante (1854)	
L'Africaine (1865)	

9. The devil, or his agent, attempts to secure the soul of one of the characters.

OPERAS	BALLET-PANTOMIMES
Robert le diable (1831)	Le diable amoureux (1840)

"OPERA-BALLET"
La Tentation (1832)

10. A woman agrees to marry a man to save the life and/or honor of the man she really loves.

OPERAS	BALLET-PANTOMIMES
Le Dieu et la Bayadère (1830)	La Révolte au sérail (1833)
Le Lac des fées (1839)	La Tarentule (1839)
Dom Sébastien (1843)	

prayer scenes, celebrations of betrothals, masked balls, letter-reading scenes, and infernal bacchanales. Both types of works made frequent use of musicians *sul palco* or in the wings, and featured the *corps* or chorus quite prominently, populating the Opéra's stage with the same types of minor characters—for instance, peasants, children, pilgrims, soldiers, black people, courtiers, ladies-in-waiting, penitents, musicians, monks, masquers, and huntsmen. Both tended to switch frequently between styles and moods—from noisy festive celebrations to poignant soliloquies; from sedate gatherings to rancorous confrontations—laid out in such a way as to afford the audience plenty of variety in mood, pacing, and musical style (see Table 2.3).

TABLE 2.3 *Giselle* AND *Les Huguenots*, FIRST ACTS

This table should give some notion of the range of scene types of ballet-pantomime and opera. In the first act of *Giselle*, the audience is presented with a country dance by peasants, a grand procession of lords and ladies in a hunting party (who pointedly do *not* dance), both a long and a short *pas de deux* between the leading couple, six conversations (ranging in tone from tender to enraged), a grand waltz danced by the *corps*, three monologues by the frustrated Hilarion, two solo dances by Giselle, a mad scene, and a death scene. The first act of *Les Huguenots* includes three rousing male choruses, one solo rendition of a Protestant chorale, seven conversations, and three short arias—a charming one by the soprano Urbain, a poignant one in the high tenor range by Raoul, and Marcel's "Piff paff," in a comic folk style.

Giselle ACT ONE

This is based on an annotated *répétiteur*, RU-SPtob 7114/8 and Adam's autograph manuscript, F-Pn MS 2639. The titles for the numbers (in bold) are taken from the published piano score arranged by V. Cornette and published by Le Boulch & Régnier (n.d.).
Please note: Loys and Albrecht are the same character. Albrecht is a nobleman who disguises himself as a peasant and calls himself Loys.

No.	Key/Meter	Tempo	Who's Onstage	Action	Number of Measures
Introduction					
Overture	G C	All° con fuoco	—	—	28
	E♭ 9/8	Andante			
1. Les Vendanges					
	G ¢	Allegro	2 groups: seigneurs and dames; peasants	Each group crosses the stage and exits.	34
	G ¢	Allegro	Hilarion	In a monologue, Hilarion expresses his love for Giselle and distaste for Loys	43

(*continued*)

TABLE 2.3 Continued

No.	Key/ Meter	Tempo	Who's Onstage	Action	Number of Measures
2. Entree du Prince					
	C C	Allegro non troppo	Hilarion (who is hidden), Wilfrid, Loys	The 2 men argue; Wilfrid disapproves of Loy's scheme	45
3. Entree de Giselle					
	~2/4	Allegro non troppo	Hilarion (who is hidden), Loys	Loy knocks on Giselle's door	25
	G 6/8	Allegro moto di danza	same + Giselle	Giselle emerges from her cottage and dances	41
	G C	Andante	same	Loys convinces the skittish Giselle that he loves her	40
	G 6/8	Allegro non troppo	same	They flirt and dance	24
	e 2/4	All° mosso	same (Hilarion no longer hidden)	Hilarion bursts from his hiding place to chastise the lovers; Loy chases him away	64
4. Retour de la Vendange					
	G ¢	All° loure	Giselle, Loys, peasants	The peasants bid Giselle join them in the vineyard	53
Valse	D 3	Moderato	same	Giselle leads them in a gay waltz instead	126
	D 6/8	Allegro	same + Berthe	Giselle's mother Berthe upbraids the waltzing peasants	25
	B♭ 3	All° mod^{to}	same	Giselle argues with her mother	8
	~ ¢	All° mod^{to}	same	Berthe says Giselle is risking her life	10
	~ C	And^{te} mod^{to}	same	Berthe tells the story of the Wilis to the peasant girls	36

(continued)

TABLE 2.3 Continued

No.	Key/ Meter	Tempo	Who's Onstage	Action	Number of Measures
5. La Chasse					
	D 6/8	Allegro	same; then empty stage	Loys and peasants depart	32
	G ¢	Allegro	Hilarion	Hilarion is sad; wants revenge	30
	D 6/8	Allegro	Hillarion; then hunting party arrives	Hilarion breaks into Loys's cottage; the Prince and hunting party arrive	104
	B♭ 2/4	Andantino allegretto	same + Giselle and Berthe	Berthe and Giselle serve refreshments to the hunting party; a lady takes an interest in Giselle	89
	B♭ 3	Mvt de valse	same	Giselle tells the lady of her love for dancing	8
	~B♭ 2/4	Allegro	same	Berthe says dancing is dangerous; Giselle continues chatting with the lady	72
	D 6/8	Allegro	same	The prince leads his suite back to the hunt	104
6. Scène d'Hilarion					
	G ¢	[Allegro]	Hilarion	Hilarion emerges from Loys's cottage carrying a sword; he anticipates revenge	35
7. Marche des Vignerons; pas de deux; galop general [Divertissement]					
Marche	D C	All° marcato	peasants	Peasants arrive	6
	D 6/8	All° con moto	same	They begin the celebration	120
Pas de deux	E♭ 3	Andante	same + Loys and Giselle	The 2 lovers dance	38
	E♭ ¢	Moderato	[Loys' solo]		41
	G 3	All° mod^to	[Giselle's solo]		37
	A♭ 2/4	Allegro		[closing duo]	119
Galop	A 2/4	Allegro	same	Everyone dances	80
	D 2/4	Allegro			40
	A 2/4	Allegro			38

(*continued*)

TABLE 2.3 Continued

No.	Key/ Meter	Tempo	Who's Onstage	Action	Number of Measures
8. Final					
	e C	Allegro	same + Hilarion	Hilarion confronts Loys	28
	e ¢	All° mosso	same	Hilarion presents the sword; Giselle is alarmed	39
	G 6/8	Allegro	same + hunting party	Hilarion summons hunting party	36
	e ¢	Allegro	same	The prince asks why Albrecht is wearing a peasant disguise; Giselle is distraught	69
Scène de folie	~ C	Andante	same	Giselle goes mad	38
	A♭ C	Allegro	same	—continuing—	3
	A♭ C	Andantino	same	—closing—	48
	e C	Allo mosso	same	Reason returns; Giselle dies; onlookers are horrified	97

There is no dancing at all in the finale except for the few weak steps Giselle takes in the mad scene. Nor is there dancing in nos. 1, 2, 5, or 6 (except when Giselle waltzes for 8 measures as she tells the visiting lady of her love for the dance).

Les Huguenots, ACT ONE

This is based on a reprint (New York and London: Garland, 1980) of a published score (Paris: Schlesinger, n.d. [1836]) of *Les Huguenots.*

No.	Key/ Meter	Tempo	Who's Onstage	Action	Number of Measures
1. Overture et Introduction					
A) Overt.	E♭ C	Poco and^{te}	(overture)	—	94
	E♭ 2	All° con spirito	(overture)	—	19
	E♭ 12/8				5
B) Choeur	A C		7 seigneurs, Nevers, chorus of seigneurs	Seigneurs enjoy a banquet	66
C) Morceau d'Ensemble	F C	All^{to} mod^{to}	same	They discuss Raoul	72
et Entree de Raoul	A♭ 3/4	And^{no} quasi All^{to}	same + Raoul	Raoul enters	43

(continued)

TABLE 2.3 Continued

No.	Key/ Meter	Tempo	Who's Onstage	Action	Number of Measures
D) Orgie	C 2/4	All° con moto	same	They sing gaily of Bacchus	185
	3/8	All° con spirito	same	—continuing—	22
	3/8	Presto	same	—continuing—	32
	6/8	(tutta forza)	same	—continuing—	6
	9/8		same	—end—	4
2. Scène et Romance					
Récitatif	~ C	[various]	same	Nevers asks Raoul to tell of amorous adventure	43
Scène	~ C	All° mod^{to} /récit	same	Raoul introduces his story	21
	D C	Andante /récit	same		18
Romance	B♭ C	Andante cantabile	same	Raoul describes a beautiful woman he rescued	63
3. Scène et Choral					
Scène	a C	Molto mod^{to} /récit	same + Marcel	Marcel arrives; is appalled to see Raoul socializing with Catholics	46
Choral	C 2	molto mod^{to}	same	Marcel sings the chorale; onlookers interject comments	50
4. Scène et Chanson Huguenote					
Scène	C C	Récitatif	same	Amused seigneurs ask Marcel for another song	32
Chanson Huguenote	c 3/8	All^{to}	same	He obliges them; sings "Piff paff"; onlookers interject comments	149
5. Morceau d'Ensemble					
Morceau	B♭ C	All° mod^{to}	Seigneurs, Marcel, Raoul	Nevers's men watch as he meets a lady in the garden	24

(*continued*)

TABLE 2.3 Continued

No.	Key/ Meter	Tempo	Who's Onstage	Action	Number of Measures
	B♭ C	un poco meno mosso	same	Marcel confers with Raoul as the men sing of the lady outside	
	G 3/8	All° con mo^{to}	same	They sing of their curiosity	59
	G C	Récitatif	same	They ask Raoul why he's not curious	6
	~ 3/8	Tempo primo	same	Raoul, shocked, recognizes her as the woman he rescued	18
	B♭ C		same	He declares his disinterest while the men continue watching through the window	34
Récitatif	G 3/4	Andantino	Nevers	Nevers, reflectively,	7
	~E C	Récitatif		says in a monologue	11
	a 2/4	Allegro		that his betrothed has broken their engagement by order of the Queen	7
6. Final					
A) Choeur	D C	Allegro con spirito	Seigneurs, Nevers, Raoul Marcel	The Seigneurs tease Nevers about the mysterious lady	48
B) Cavatine du Page	B♭ C	Andantino	Same + Urbain	Raoul welcomes Urbain	5
	B♭ C	Maestoso			5
	B♭ 9/8	Andantino	same	Urbain greets the Seigneurs	31
C) Suite	E♭ C	Tempo primo/ Récitatif	same	Urbain reveals that he bears a note for Raoul; the seigneurs are shocked	47
	~ C	Poco andante	same	The seigneurs see that the note is from the Queen	12
	3/4				5
	e C	All^{to} ben moderato	same	They congratulate Raoul exaggeratedly	23
D) Stretta	D 3/8	Molto vivace	same	They continue their congratulations; Raoul is confused	151
	D 2/4	M^{vt} de l'orgie	same		72

Indeed, variety was the order of the day for both types of works, and audiences could usually count on seeing a mixture of large choral or *corps* numbers (ranging in mood from the rancorous to the joyful), set pieces for solo or small ensemble (similarly varied in mood), and action scenes for the principal characters often witnessed by the chorus or *corps,* which participated to varying degrees. Librettists in both cases also made the most of the dramatic possibilities supplied by the contrast between forward propulsion and stasis, calling upon composers to write set pieces which took place when the forward motion of the plot came to a halt (aria and *pas de deux,* for example), as well as scenes in which the story was advanced through action, mime, recitative or conversational singing (or some combination thereof).[17] These two types—one static, one kinetic—existed at opposite ends of a continuum, but in between there were found all manner of gradations: the *pas de trois* interrupted by a few actions and gestures (*La Somnambule,* Act One scene 4); the vocal duo interspersed with bits of recitative ("Ta fille en ce moment est devant le concile," *La Juive* Act Four); the action scene interwoven with half-minute bursts of full-out dancing or singing (*Giselle,* Act One scene iv); the vocal ensemble that restlessly propelled the plot forward without resorting to recitative but without ever falling into a songlike melody or regular phrases either ("Des beaux jours de la jeunesse," *Les Huguenots,* Act One).

In neither opera nor ballet-pantomime did the vast cornucopias of arias, divertissements, pantomimes, action scenes, and so forth spill out in any predictable order. But librettists did follow certain general structural rules in both genres. For instance, they liked to open a work with a choral or *corps* number, following it with a more soloistic piece in which the basic conflict was set up. Librettists also provided some sort of contrast between one segment and the next in both genres—a rousing number for large ensemble might follow a tender love duet, for example. They also frequently worked the action into some sort of obvious conflict (or even crisis) at the end of at least one act and often placed a crowd onstage at the end of the final act. And, without fail, they included at least one danced divertissement in every ballet-pantomime, and in every opera of four acts or more (see Table 2.4). In rough outline, in fact, the form of grand opera and ballet-pantomime was precisely the same: action punctuated by danced divertissements.

In order to help tell the stories of opera and ballet-pantomime, composers, like librettists, relied on stock devices of their trade. The arrival and departure of large groups, for example, was usually expressed (respectively) by a building up and winnowing down of musical forces. Crises were often marked by rapid minor-key scales and arpeggios, or bold, tutti, unison statements. For tense recitative and mime scenes, great dynamic contrasts in the orchestra were favored. Changes of subject or mood in conversation scenes were often signaled by the introduction of new rhythms and melodies. Certain formulas of instrumentation turned up in both genres as well—bass drums and cymbals marking every beat in cadential passages for crowd scenes, string or wind pedal drones

TABLE 2.4   PLACEMENT OF DIVERTISSEMENTS IN BALLET-PANTOMIMES AND OPERAS

Ballet-Pantomimes	Operas
La Belle au bois dormant (1829)	Guillaume Tell (1829)
I —X—	I —X—
II ———	II ———
III ———X	III —X—
	IV ———
La Révolte au Sérail (1833)	Robert le diable (1831)
I —X—	I ———
II ———	II —X—
III ———X	III ———X
	IV ———
	V ———
La Tempête (1834)	Don Juan (1834)
Intro ———	I ———
II —X—X—	II —X—
III ———X	III ———
	IV ———
	V —X—
La Gipsy (1839)	La Juive (1835)
I —X—	I —X—
II ——X—	II ———
III ———X—	III —X—
	IV ———
	V ———
Le Diable à quatre (1845)	Le Prophète (1849)
I —X—	I ———
II ———X—	II X———
	III —X—
	IV ———
	V ———

There was no hard and fast rule about the placement of the divertissement, though ballet-pantomimes tended to have more of them, and librettists generally avoided putting them at the very beginning of the first act.

The divertissements shown here were in most cases designated as such in the scores, were of varying lengths, and were altered frequently. Please note that in operas, dancers' time onstage was by no means limited to the divertissement (this is borne out by rehearsal scores). Also, in ballet-pantomimes shorter danced segments (sometimes mixed with mime in dramatic scenes) occurred frequently but are not shown in this table.

for peasants, harps for scenes featuring tender declarations of love or dominated by females, brass for nobility.

Composers were called upon to write pantomime music in both opera and ballet-pantomime (though voiceless action scenes in opera were short and relatively infrequent). They were also expected to write music appropriate for "talking" in both genres—in opera, this meant recitative and *arioso* singing; for ballet it meant various types of so-called *parlante* music (literally, "talking" music), some of which was borrowed from opera, most notably, the recitative. (I will return to the topic of *parlante* music in Chapter Four.) In addition, composers of ballet-pantomime music sometimes used the strophic forms that were the stuff of many opera arias (in both comic and grand opera)—for instance, the flute *romance*, complete with cadenza, that accompanied a *pas* in Act Two of *La Révolte au sérail*. They also preserved the poignant quality of the vocal adagio solo aria in certain mimed and danced scenes, giving the "vocal" part to an oboe, viola, or other suitable *récitant*—for instance Albrecht's sorrowful visit to his lover's grave early in Act Two of *Giselle,* a touching oboe aria in modified ABA form.[18] (The tradition of the poignant instrumental "voice" in ballet is preserved in the famous cantabile cello and violin solos of *Swan Lake.*)

This is not to say, of course, that audiences would not have noticed the musical differences between opera and ballet-pantomime. Aside from the most obvious one of all—that opera incorporated vocal music and ballet did not—the latter type entailed much more pantomime music since it was far more frequently called upon to accompany mime scenes and to stick closely to particular actions taking place on stage (in keeping with the "mission to explain or translate"[19]). Composers of ballet music were also expected to include borrowed music (until the 1840s at least), while opera music was expected to be entirely new and original.[20] Ballet composers were also called upon to write relatively shorter set pieces, since set pieces in ballet were more physically demanding of the onstage performers than those in opera. Furthermore, as Escudier put it, "music occupies only second rank in a choreographic composition, though it dominates in opera, because the dancer is the object of interest and one pays less attention to the music."[21] Given this circumstance, ballet music, to be frank, was of lower quality than opera music, for composers were reluctant to squander their best ideas on ballet music. As Castil-Blaze pointed out, "The composer finds a naive and simple idea, a solemn and pompous motive, a phrase of graceful melancholy, a martial passage, proud and accented; all of these different motifs are notable for their elegance and their originality. Do you believe that the composer, caring little about his own glory, will sacrifice these fruits of his genius and allow these pearls and diamonds to be lost in a choreographic shuffle?"[22]

Yet, despite the salient differences in the composers' tasks and the generally lower quality of ballet music, the two types of scores nonetheless shared the goal of helping tell a story by projecting such necessary qualities as (to quote Castil-Blaze again) the "naive and simple," the "solemn and pompous," the "martial," and the "proud," and, most important, relied upon many of the same techniques and formulas for doing so.

FURTHER similarities between the two types of works may be found in their visual presentation, for both were staged opulently and with an eye to "realistic" detail. (See Figures 4–18.) (As Gautier said of this age, "[W]e are no longer living in a time when the inscription 'magnificent palace' nailed to a post suffices for the illusion of the spectators."[23]) It is true that the scenic effects of operas were on the whole more dazzling and violent than those of ballet, in keeping with its libretti's demands. The eruption of Mt. Vesuvius in the opera *La Muette de Portici,* for instance, was clearly more spectacular—and more unsettling—than the highly praised mobile riverbank panorama of the ballet *La Belle au bois dormant* created in the subsequent season.[24] Yet audiences of this period expected—and usually got—marvelous scenic display in both operas and ballet-pantomimes.[25] Among the most admired accomplishments of the

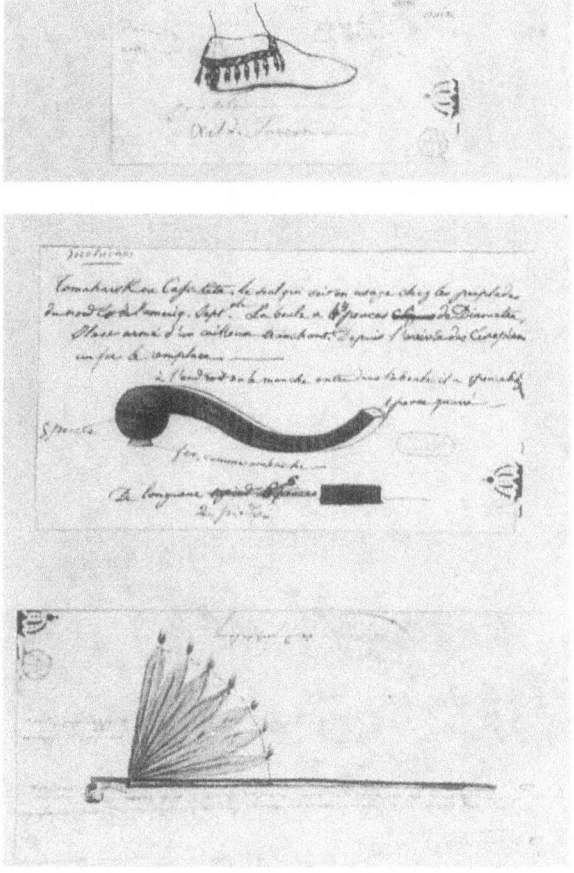

Figure 4. *Les Mohicans* (ballet-pantomime), design for tomahawk, peace pipe, and moccasin. By permission of the Bibliothèque nationale de France.

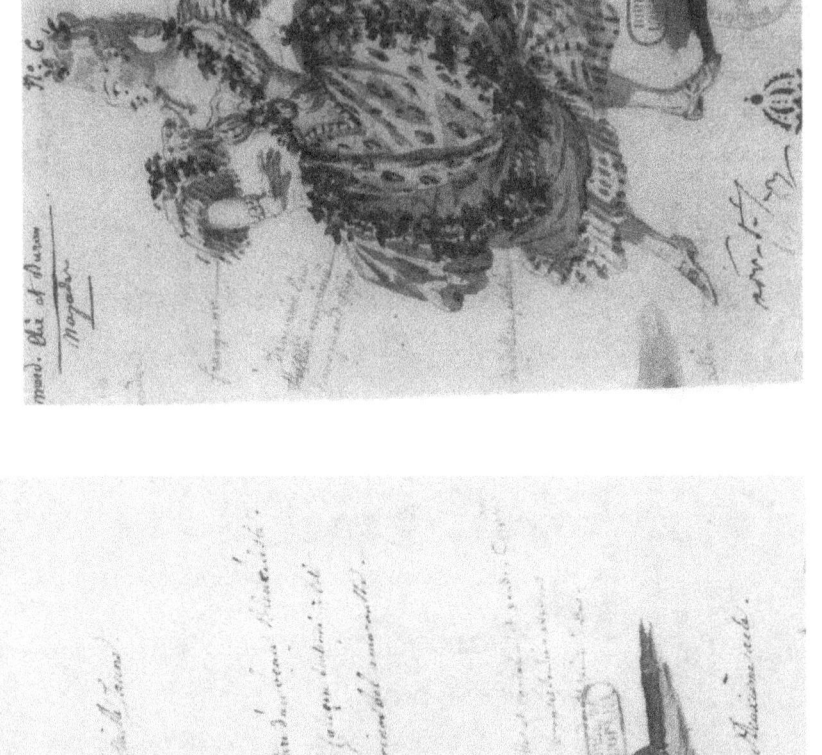

Figure 5. *L'Ile des Pirates* (ballet-pantomime), Octavio disguised as an islander. By permission of the Bibliothèque nationale de France.

Figure 6. *Manon Lescaut* (ballet-pantomime), "Nymphe, Nayade." By permission of the Bibliothèque nationale de France.

A FAMILY RESEMBLANCE 39

Figure 7. *Manon Lescaut* (ballet-pantomime), shepherdesses. By permission of the Bibliothèque nationale de France.

Figure 8. *La Révolte au sérail* (ballet-pantomime), dignitary. By permission of the Bibliothèque nationale de France.

Figure 9. *La Révolte au sérail* (ballet-pantomime), women's costumes, including martial attire. By permission of the Bibliothèque nationale de France.

Figure 10. *La Belle au bois dormant* (ballet-pantomime), peasants. By permission of the Bibliothèque nationale de France.

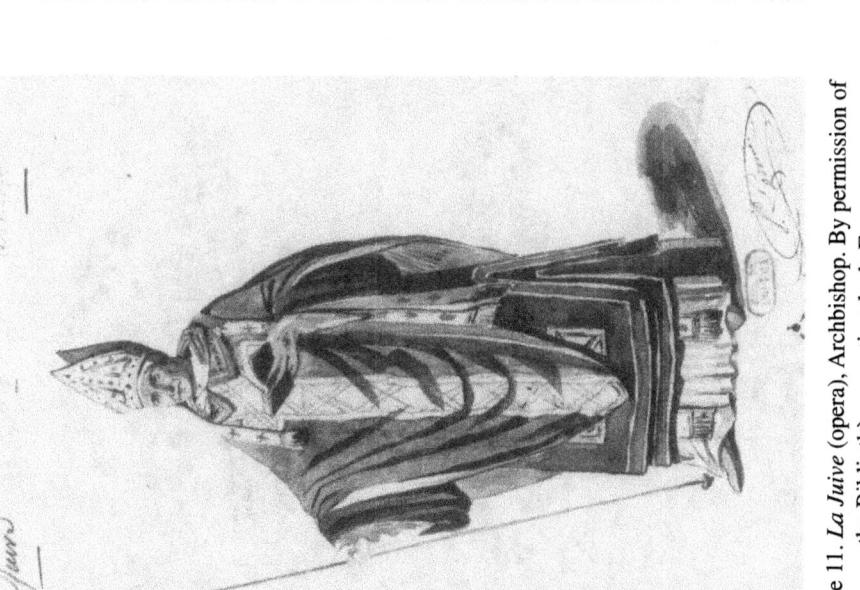

Figure 11. *La Juive* (opera), Archbishop. By permission of the Bibliothèque nationale de France.

Figure 12. *La Juive* (opera), the cardinal's trumpeter. By permission of the Bibliothèque nationale de France.

Figure 13. *Robert le diable* (opera), nun. By permission of the Bibliothèque nationale de France.

Figure 14. *La Sylphide* (ballet-pantomime), Scotsmen. By permission of the Bibliothèque nationale de France.

Figure 15. *La Sylphide* (ballet-pantomime), Effie (James's fiancée). By permission of the Bibliothèque nationale de France.

Figure 16. *Guillaume Tell* (opera), peasants, chorus, and *corps de ballet*. By permission of the Bibliothèque nationale de France.

Opéra's designers and machinists were the finale of *Le Prophète* with its burning Palace of Münster, the flying sylphides of *La Sylphide* (in which several dancers were conveyed through the air on wires[26]), the reconstruction of the eighteenth-century Opéra itself in *Manon Lescaut*,[27] the instantaneous transformation of flowers into flame-breathing reptiles in *La Belle au bois dormant,* the underwater landscape of *La Fille du Danube,* the burning lake of hell and the riotous orgy scene in *Le Diable amoureux,* and the masked ball in *Gustave III* (which one critic called "an unbelievable profusion of women, gauze, velvet, the grotesque and the elegant, good taste and bad, trifles, affectations, wit, folly, verve . . ."[28] It is no wonder that Edmond Duponchel, the Opéra's stage director from 1829 to 1841, was called "the Alexander of the *mise en scène . . .* the Ceasar of the costume"[29]). (See Figures 19 and 20.) Fireworks were regularly used in works of both kinds; horses in operas were "elevated to the office of indispensable actors . . . and equally invade the ballet."[30]

Figure 17. *Guillaume Tell* (opera), ladies, chorus, and *corps de ballet*. By permission of the Bibliothèque nationale de France.

Figure 18. *Guillaume Tell* (opera), Mathilde. By permission of the Bibliothèque nationale de France.

Costumes were even occasionally lent back and forth between opera and ballet-pantomime—an easy way to economize in a house in which large numbers of costumes were called for, and in which operas and ballets shared so many character types (see Tables 2.5 and 2.6).[31] Dominoes from the masked ball of *Gustave III* were worn by revelers in *Le diable boiteux,* for example; costumes for demons and skeletons used in *La Tentation* were also worn in the last act of *Don Giovanni;* habits villageois used in *Guillaume Tell* were borrowed for *La Fille du Danube;* pilgrims' clothing from *L'Orgie* was used in *Robert le diable.*[32]

Visual similarities between these two types of works may also be found in the ways actors moved on the stage.[33] For despite their disparate specialties, and despite the fact that performers of ballet-pantomime surely deployed a vocabulary of specific mime gestures far more extensively than those of opera did, it is likely that the actors in both genres were instructed to carry out some of the same kinds of blocking and gestures.[34] They used some of the same specific bits of stage business in both types of works, for instance—the waving of hats in the air in public celebrations; the inclining of banners to honor the presence of dignitaries.[35] The evidence also suggests that they executed dramatic scenes on different parts of the stage but went downstage to the center to perform their set pieces (duos, arias, *pas de deux,* for example), playing directly to the audience. (See Figure 21.) And, in both opera and ballet, principal characters are known to have sometimes formed a *chartron* (semicircle) at center stage.

For both types of performance, too, the actors' movements would probably seem stylized and stilted by today's tastes. Both the *corps de ballet* in the ballet-pantomime and the chorus in French grand opera were often configured symmetrically and sometimes formed a straight line across the back or side of the stage. They also tended to file on and off the stage in tidy rows, sometimes singly and sometimes two or three abreast.[36] ("Disorderly" entrances and exits of crowds were often saved for moments when chaos was called for by the libretto, though this restriction was somewhat loosened by the 1840s.[37]) And at least occasionally, they carried out dramatic gestures in unison, a practice that subsequent trends toward naturalism have rendered obsolete. (In the ballet-pantomime *La Gipsy,* for example, thirty-odd Bohemians mime the words "But who are you?" by "throwing their forearms" according to one unsympathetic critic; in *Le Prophète* a group of menacing Anabaptists simultaneously step forward and raise their swords to threaten Fidès.[38]) The same may be said of the actors' custom of following the music "à mesure." Jonas strikes the match in time to the beat in *Le Prophète,* for example, moving to a pulse in a manner that was perhaps derived from "pantomime mesurée" of the eighteenth century—something that might strike an audience today as dangerously close to Mickey-mousing.[39]

Actors in both types of works were also called upon occasionally to freeze in place for a few seconds, sometimes at moments of high drama in the middle

Figure 19. *Gustave III,* Act V, tableau 2, ballroom in the palace of Stockholm. By permission of the Bibliothèque nationale de France.

Figure 20. *Gustave III ou le Bal Masqué* (opera), Polichinelle costume for the masked ball. By permission of the Bibliothèque nationale de France.

TABLE 2.5 MINOR CHARACTERS IN BALLET-PANTOMIMES AND OPERAS
AT THE OPÉRA

Note: The terms *chant* and *danse* were usually used in libretti of this period as headings of lists of minor characters portrayed by the chorus and *corps de ballet*.

Work	Minor Characters
Guillaume Tell Opera, 1829	*Chant*: Swiss peasants, a hunter, women on horseback, squires, whippers-in, old men, pages of the hunt, men from Unterwald, Schwitz, Uri, soldiers *Danse*: Fiancés, Tyroleans, Swiss pastors, peasants, men from Unterwald, Schwitz, Uri, soldiers, pages of the court, fighters
Manon Lescaut Ballet, 1830	*Danse*: Young lords, old marquis, financiers, little knights of Malta, little countesses, pages, blacks, young duchesses, old duchesses, merchant of jewels, bourgeois men and women, men and women of the people, noble and bourgeois children, children of the people, characters of the Intermède (cupids, bacchants, shepherds), young lords, creoles, Native Americans, sailors, soldiers
Robert le diable Opera, 1831	*Chant*: Demons, knights, hermits, lords, ladies of the court, heralds, people, squires *Danse*: Demons, knights, hermits, ladies in waiting, pages, pilgrims, nuns, peasants
L'Orgie Ballet, 1831	*Danse*: Monks, pilgrims, mendicants, drinkers, dancers, a bride and her suite, villagers in festive costumes, Alguazils, guitarists, peasants
Nathalie Ballet, 1832	*Danse*: Hunters, goatherds, small goatherds, peasants, whippers-in, villagers, musicians, children, hunters
La Révolte au sérail Ballet, 1833	*Danse*: The king's women, suite of the king, pages, suite of Ismael, men, women, and children of the people, bathers, slaves, soldiers, suite of the Spirit of Womankind
Gustave III Opera, 1833	*Chant*: The king's officers, ambassadors, gentlemen and deputies, men and women of the people, officers and ambassadors disguised as sailors, conspirators *Danse*: Ballet dancers in Gustave Vasa's ballet (including Dalécarliens, children, and peasants), ballgoers in various costumes, including a Russian lady, Indians, Pierrot and Pierrette, Arlequine, a clown
Don Giovanni Opera, 1834	(*Chant* and *danse* not listed separately by character type) Spanish ladies and knights, Moorish knights, slave-women, blacks, pages, people, villagers, monks, alguazils, servants, young girls and children at the palace of Don Giovanni
La Juive Opera, 1835	*Chant*: Bourgeois and artisans, Jews, princes of the empire, cardinals, gentlemen, ladies of the emporer's court, the princess's ladies in waiting, penitents *Danse*: Gypsies, clerks, grisettes, pages of the emperor, of the cardinal and of the different seigneural

(*continued*)

TABLE 2.5 Continued

Work	Minor Characters
	manors, artisans, artisans' wives, characters of the Intermède (knights errant, enchanted princesses, a Sarazin magician, a dwarf), dukes and princes in the service of the emporer, cardinals and archbishops in the suite of the Council president
L'Ile des Pirates Ballet, 1835	*Danse*: Peasants from near Rome, peasants from the Villa Montalbano, "women of different countries, distinguishable by their costumes," small peasants, disguised pirates, a black, a Créole, slaves of the pirates, sailors of the Barbary coast, Asian sailors, Albanian sailors, sailors, cabin-boys, English sailors, Dutch sailors and cabin-boys, French sailors and cabin-boys, Turkish and Greek cabin-boys, Spanish sailors and cabin-boys, a Russian sailor, a Russian woman, a Spanish woman, an English woman, a peasant of Fondi
Les Huguenots Opera, 1836	*Chant*: Catholic and Protestant lords, Protestant soldiers, students, officers, gypsies, women of the people, peasants, bourgeois, magistrates, monks, counting masters, Protestant women, Catholic men of the people *Danse*: Ballplayers, footmen and pages of the Duke of Nevers, masked footmen of the queen of Navarre, ladies in waiting, bathers, pages of Queen Marguerite, children of the people, gypsies, Catholic soldiers, pages of Charles IX, the queen's squires, Swiss guard, Protestant lords and ladies, pages of the Medicis, grisettes, clerks
La Fille du Danube Ballet, 1836	*Danse*: Undines, nymphs, ladies of the court, chevaliers, pages, heralds, soldiers, peasants, children, young women from the valley of the flowers, lords, noblemen and noble women, child nymphs
Stradella Opera, 1837	*Chant*: Desperados, students, henchmen, maskers, merchants of fashions and wigs, monks, bourgeois, men and women of the people, Dalmatians, saltambiques *Danse*: Desperados, maskers, nobles, people, children, the nine Muses, the squires of the Doge, ambassador from the Orient, blacks, inhabitants of Albania, Tivoli, Frascati, and the Roman countryside
La Reine de Chypre Opera, 1841	*Chant*: Gondoliers, Venetian lords, sailors, French lords, noble Venetian women, children, courtesans, Cypriots, bourgeois and merchants, priests *Danse*: Lords, courtesans, pages, Cypriots, Venetian senators, children, maidens, pages, Knights of Malta, pages of the king
La Jolie Fille de Gand Ballet, 1842	*Danse*: Merchants and shop assistants, titled men and bourgeois, farmers, boys from the inn, peasants, children, a page, crossbowmen, fiancées, musicians, lords, a valet, ballgoers in various costumes, the four parts of the world (Europe, Asia, Africa,

(continued)

TABLE 2.5 Continued

Work	Minor Characters
	America), Suite of Diane, Flore and Galatée, blacks, nymphs, bacchants, gypsies
Charles VI Opera, 1843	*Chant*: Peasants, children, English soldiers, lords and ladies of the court, students, women of the people, English lords, bourgeois, ghosts of Jean, Clisson, and Charles, French knights, French soldiers *Danse*: Hunters, ladies, English soldiers, pages of Henri VI and Charles VI, flower merchants, women of the court, people, false Charles VI, Dauphin, assassins, French knights, English knights, pages

TABLE 2.6 NUMBERS OF COSTUMES USED FOR VARIOUS PRODUCTIONS

This table, a list compiled by the Opéra's costume shop, should give at a glance some notion of the large numbers of costumes needed for operas and ballet-pantomimes during this period as well as the pervasiveness of the practice of borrowing and restoring costumes originally used in other productions.
B = ballet-pantomime; O = opera.

Title	New	Borrowed and/or Restored	Total
La Tempête (B, 1834)	199	139	338
La Juive (O, 1835)	524	76	600
Brézilia (B, 1835)	36	26	72
L'Ile des Pirates (B, 1835)	248	136	384
Les Huguenots (O, 1836)	272	232	504
Le Diable boiteux (B, 1836)	154	180	334
La Fille du Danube (B, 1836)	150	25	175
Esmeralda (O, 1836)	111	361	472
Stradella (O, 1837)	293	322	615
Les Mohicans (B, 1837)	82	93	175
La Chatte (B, 1837)	234	54	288
Guido et Ginevra (O, 1838)	124	395	519
La Volière (B, 1838)	8	33	41
Benvenuto Cellini (O, 1838)	37	334	371
La Gipsy (B, 1839)	145	179	324
Le Lac des Fées (O, 1839)	211	315	526
La Tarentule (B, 1839)	80	74	154
La Vendetta (O 1839)	97	68	165
La Xacarilla (O, 1839)	16	39	55
Le Drapier (O, 1840)	112	49	161

(*continued*)

TABLE 2.6 Continued

Title	New	Borrowed and/or Restored	Total
Les Martyrs (O, 1840)	369	46	415
Le Diable amoreux (B, 1840)	208	214	422
La Favorite (O, 1840)	208	114	322
Carmagnola (O, 1841)	13	147	160
Le Freyschutz (O, 1841)	55	159	214
Giselle (B, 1841)	82	78	160
La Reine de Chypre (O, 1841)	301	341	642
Guerillero (O, 1842)	4	123	127
La J. Fille de Gand (B, 1842)	100	462	562
Le Vaisseau Fantôme (O, 1842)	23	119	142
Charles VI (O, 1843)	383	397	780
La Péri (B, 1843)	93	101	194
Dom Sébastien (O, 1843)	239	443	682
Lady Henriette (B, 1844)	168	233	401
Le Lazzarone (O, 1844)	5	187	192
Eucharis (B, 1844)	117	52	169
Otello (O, 1844)	28?	255	283
Richard en Palestine (O, 1844)	39	78	117
Marie Stuart (O, 1844)	162	127	289
Le Diable à Quatre (B, 1845)	195?	88	283
L'Etoile de Séville (B, 1845)	154	247	401
Lucie de Lammermoor (O, 1846)	6	180	186
Paquita (B, 1846)	170	194	364
David (O, 1846)	36	166	202
L'Ame en Peine (B, 1846)	37	120	157
Betty (B, 1846)	70	214	284
Robert Bruce (O, 1846)	426	146	572
Ozaï (B, 1847)	171	134	305
La Bouquetière (O, 1847)	37	106	143
La Fille de Marbre (B, 1847)	104	308	412
Jérusalem (O, 1847)	290	312	602
Griseldis (B, 1848)	196	190	386

This table is based on a list in F-Pa AJ13 183. In AJ13 184 the inventory-taker explained in a few cases how many costumes in this category were borrowed (as opposed to restored). For example, 300 costumes for *Benvenuto Cellini* were borrowed, 162 for *La Gipsy*, 14 for *La Lac des Fées,* 38 for *La Tarentule,* 49 for *Le Drapier,* 328 for *La Jolie Fille de Gand.* See also AJ13 215.

Figure 21. Performance of *Les Huguenots* (opera). By permission of the Bibliothèque nationale de France

of a scene, and sometimes to close out the action at the fall of the curtain. *Giselle* Act One, for example, ends with the "*triste tableau*" of Berthe cradling in her arms the lifeless body of her daughter Giselle, an encircling frame provided by the peasants and the noble hunting party who look on, aghast. *Robert le diable* ends with a *tableau tout religieux,* the entire cast on its knees in the cathedral of Palermo, the newly converted Robert joining them at the high altar. (Frozen stage *tableaux* were, of course, not restricted to the Opéra alone; they were used in French spoken drama, mélodrame and Italian opera as well. Parisian audiences could also satisfy their taste for live pictures by going to see *tableaux vivants* and attending the Diorama theatre.[40])

Creating striking pictures was also an important choreographic goal of the danced segments of ballet-pantomime, wherein a favorite device was the series of "poses succeeding one another":

> [Gemma] devises a plan to restore the artist to his senses [in *Gemma* Act Two, "pas du tableau"]. She takes the picture out of the frame and, standing behind it, assumes the same attitude. Massimo enters and sees the woman in painting smile at him, hold out her arms, step from the frame, and go towards him. After a series of captivating poses, Gemma makes Massimo realize that she is not a phantom but a woman of flesh and blood. Slowly Massimo recovers his reason.[41]

When performed by the *corps de ballet,* a succession of poses could create a kaleidoscopic pictorial effect.

> Zulma and her friends sport in the water [in *La Révolte au sérail* Act Two]. Slaves burn perfumes, others prepare to dress the king's wives. Zulma emerges first and is enveloped in a light veil behind which she makes her toilet. Soon her companions follow her example and dress in the same manner. Then the women dance and admire themselves in mirrors, forming a succession of the most captivating pictures [*tableaux*], which center upon the beautiful Zulma.[42]

> The bayadères seize the lovely materials [in *Le Dieu et la Bayadère* Act One] and, draping them about their bodies, form innumerable pictures [*tableaux*]. The dance grows more and more animated until suddenly interrupted by a trumpet-blast.[43]

One critic even referred to an entire ballet as a set of pictures: "[i]t must not be forgotten that these hastily arranged pictures [*Betty*] are only an excuse to present the very youthful person who comes to us from Milan [Sofia Fuoco]."[44] It may have been precisely these sorts of poses and pictures that later frustrated Bronislava Nijinska and other innovative choreographers of the early twentieth century who espoused the aesthetic of the new Ecole de Mouvement. "The choreographer must make movement visible to the artist/interpreter," she wrote; "[the choreographer] must teach the artist to reveal the movement, and make it visible to the spectator.... Up to now the dancer simply moved from position to position. He sought to *reproduce accurately the pose he had learned,* but between one pose and the next he left a dead and unconscious space. He did not join the positions to one another with living movement."[45] She declared simply that "[m]ovement is the principal element of dancing," an idea we are likely to regard as self-evident in this more kinetic age. In any case, in Romantic ballet, the pose existed as an important choreographic category, warranting mention as such in ballet libretti and newspaper reviews (the Wilis' poses were "voluptuous"; Urielle's were "ravishing"; Miranda's were sometimes decent, sometimes voluptuous).[46] Indeed, it is clear from the comments of contemporary observers that a strong pictorial sense often lay behind both the design and the appreciation of the ballet-pantomime. Critics refer frequently (favorably and otherwise) to the appearance of the groupings; they liken sets to paintings, and dancers to statues.[47] Gautier even goes so far as to declare that a "ballet should be a picture before being a drama"; that "the best combination for the production of a fine theme for a ballet [would be] a poet explaining his ideas to an artist who expresses them in sketches."[48]

BUT far more important than the miscellaneous mannerisms, stylized gestures, and taste for the *tableau* (frozen and otherwise) that made opera and ballet-pantomime look similar on the surface, is the fact that both opera and ballet-pantomime subscribed to the dramaturgical principle of "pantomimic intelligibility"—the idea that, as Louis Véron said, the dramatic action of an opera should be "as readily grasped by the eye as the action of a ballet."[49] Carl Dahlhaus has even argued that the stories of French grand opera were communicated more through visible action than exchanges of words: "It is not dialogue [in French grand opera], which is virtually swallowed up by the music, but the striking, "speechlike" arrangement of the agents—among whom Véron also includes the chorus—that constitutes the primary expressive means of a dramatic technique as legitimate in the opera as it is inconceivable in spoken theater, except perhaps in melodrama, by which Scribe was doubtless influenced."[50] In so saying, he owes much to the analysis of William Crosten, who wrote in 1948 that

> Scribe's libretti, then, as well as his dramas, are plays of movement, not of character or reflection. Moreover, like the stage works of Alexandre Dumas and the melodrama to which they are so closely related, grand opera is not merely a drama of action, but of spectacular action full of violent turns and stormy irruptions. . . . In this scheme of drama nothing is left to the imagination. There is neither intimacy nor ambiguity. Everything is open and expressed, but *expressed through action not through language*. Realizing that music is a constant threat to the intelligibility of the words, Scribe was never verbose and never allowed an action to be told instead of seen. He believed with Gautier that "any well-made drama must have a skeleton of pantomime" and he arranged his material in a plastic form that would be both clear to the eye and as self-acting as possible.[51]

But what specific techniques did the librettists and *metteurs en scène* of opera and ballet-pantomime rely upon to make the action so "visible and palpable"?[52] An examination of the extant evidence allows us to discern several of their habitual practices. First, they made plentiful use of the *éclat* (shock), a technique effective for visual storytelling because of the immediate and obvious reactions (of joy or horror, for example) it provoked in the onstage characters—reactions that plainly demonstrated the weight and the tone of the shocking event itself.[53] And they sometimes encased these reactions in *tableaux* of "*stupéfaction*" when an event was so shocking as to render its witnesses inert for a moment (thus deploying the *tableau* as a dramatic device). For instance, Oswald's unexpected request of Milord Rewena for the hand of his daughter in *Nathalie* was met with the astonishment of "tout le village"; everything stopped cold for a moment in *La Juive* at Albert's wholly unexpected command to the murderous mob to retreat.[54] In ballet-pantomime, the frozen moment lasted only a few seconds; in opera, it could last a few seconds or be sustained for several minutes while the characters (usually principals and chorus) continued singing. The shorter kind often came in sets of two or three, in both opera and ballet—one shock followed by another, and then perhaps another. Indeed, scenes of particularly high tension sometimes called for two or more such *éclat/stupéfaction* pairings within the span of a few minutes.[55] To name only two examples: in the ball scene of Act Two of *La Jolie Fille de Gand,* Césarius first shocks his daughter into a state of frozen fright by unmasking to reveal his identity; he then puts a curse on her, causing the crowd of onlooking revellers to become "terror-struck."[56] In the final scene of *La Juive* Act Two, Rachel is "stupefied" at her father's sudden unexpected arrival; within minutes, Léopold shocks first Eléazar with his revelation, "I am a Christian!" and then Rachel, by shouting "Never!" and refusing to take her hand.[57] Moreover, it was common to find a major crisis-inducing *éclat* at precisely the same place in both French grand opera and ballet-pantomime: the closing minutes of the penultimate act (though it was by no means restricted to this place alone) (See Table 2.7). Milder *éclats* were also handy for ending *divertissements,* taking the form perhaps of a thunderstorm (which broke up a divertissement in *La Jolie Fille de Gand*) or the sudden entrance of an angry character who disapproves of the festivities (like the Countess in *Le Diable à Quatre* or Abayaldos in *Dom Sébastien*). Such *éclats,* which sometimes gave the appearance of terminating a divertissement prematurely, could also serve to propel events into a state of instant chaos or consternation (see Table 2.8). Thereby, the librettist could both end the dancing and summon the instant momentum required to push the post-divertissment action forward after several minutes of static respite from the narrative.

Further bolstering the visual impact of events in these plays were characters who engaged quite obviously in the act of witnessing (temporarily joining the audience in the passive role of spectator) and showing plainly their responses to what they saw. Raoul in *Les Huguenots,* for example, standing at a window, watches Nevers's meeting with a mysterious woman and evinces horror on seeing that she is the same person with whom he himself was falling in love. Hilarion in *Giselle* spies on Wilfride and Albrecht and shows his astonishment as the former salutes the latter—a sure sign of Albrecht's noble status. Cleophas in *Le Diable boiteux* (one of the most celebrated gazers in the Opéra's repertory) looks on disapprovingly from a rooftop in full view of the audience as Florinde dances the suggestive cachucha before a group of admirers in her salon.[58]

Both kinds of works also featured pantomime scenes, though opera's were generally shorter. Described under the rubric "pantomime" in the staging manuals for opera, they range from brief, trivial interchanges between characters to scenes of silent acting crucial to the progress of the plot (like the pivotal scene in Act Four of *Le Prophète,* in which Fidès first displays her internal struggle

TABLE 2.7 SHOCKING PENULTIMATE-ACT EVENTS

Work	Shocking Penultimate-Act Event	Reaction
La Sylphide Ballet, 1832	James abandons Effie at their wedding	General surprise
Les Huguenots Opera, 1836	The tolling of the bells indicates indicates that the massacre has begun	Valentine faints
La Fille du Danube Ballet, 1836	Fleur-des-champs jumps into the Danube	Despair of the baron; cruel delight of the ladies
Le Diable amoureux Ballet, 1840	Lightning strikes a bride; she is revealed as an imposter	Onlookers are terrified
La Jolie Fille de Gand Ballet, 1842	Beatrix's father curses her	The crowd is terror-struck
Dom Sébastien Opera, 1843	Abayaldos throws off his disguise and accuses Zayda of adultery.	Everyone is astonished

and then her determination to save her son's life by pretending not to know him). In some cases, whether the actors were actually miming or not, they could capture "in a single drastic image" (as Dahlhaus has put it) the underlying mood or theme of a work—for instance, the image of the disrobing nuns in *Robert le diable* that demonstrates the ambivalence of saintliness and depravity that is the theme of the opera;[59] the image of Sarah Campbell discarding her Scottish plaids in favor of gypsy garb and a tambourine in *La Gipsy* that demonstrates the transformation of her identity;[60] the image of Jean denying his mother before a hostile crowd in *Le Prophète* that demonstrates the depths to which he has sunk in the face of vanity and uncontrollable social forces.[61]

It was not just the climactic scenes, of course, that called for such obvious displays. In the extant sources, one may find case after case of stage placements and gestures that simply help make things clearer. Characters draw swords and yield them; they bare their breasts to each others' daggers; they pass signifying objects back and forth to one another (flowers, miniature portraits, weapons, letters); they point meaningfully at one another's dwelling places.[62] One can imagine, reading the staging manuals and annotations, that even with the sound turned down, so to speak, the spectator would be able to follow the basic outline of the story, because of the constant barrage of visual information. In Effie's first scene in *La Sylphide,* for instance, she imparts the fact that she is betrothed

56 A FAMILY RESEMBLANCE

TABLE 2.8 ABRUPT ENDINGS TO DIVERTISSEMENTS

Work	Reason for Dancing	Reason for Abrupt Ending
Manon Lescaut (Act I) Ballet, 1830	Ballet performance at the eighteenth-century Paris Opéra.	Des Grieux rushes onto the stage.
Gustave III (Act I) Opera, 1833	Ballet rehearsal overseen by Gustave.	The Minister of Justice, carrying orders for the king to sign, interrupts.
La Juive (Act I) Opera, 1835	Spontaneous dancing as the emperor and victorious soldiers march into the city.	A mob harrassing Eléazar and Rachel pushes people aside.
Le diable boiteux (Act I) Ballet, 1836	Ballet performance at the Madrid Opera.	Florinde pretends to break her ankle; falls to the floor.
La Favorite (Act II) Opera, 1840	Festivities to celebrate victory over the Moors.	Don Gasper runs in excitedly with an intercepted love letter.
La Jolie Fille de Gand (Act II) Ballet, 1842	Masked ball in Venice	A mysterious domino hurls a garland to the ground and unmasks.
Dom Sébastien (Act II) Opera, 1843	Celebration in honor of Zayda's homecoming.	Abayaldos, enraged by the festivities, rouses his warriors to battle.
Lady Henriette (Act II) Ballet, 1844	Court entertainment in the theater at Windsor palace.	Lovestruck, Lyonnel interrupts the performance to seize Henriette.

to James by taking his hand and kneeling with him before her mother; Fernand in *La Favorite* makes obvious his contempt for King Alphonse by tearing off the chain Alphonse had earlier bestowed upon him, breaking his sword and throwing it at the king's feet.[63] Even the famous opening narrative of *Robert le diable* is turned into a visual event by the presence of Robert, the disgruntled subject of Raimbaut's story whose irritation in the first couplet turns quite clearly to anger in the second.[64]

It was for the benefit of a public accustomed to being presented with precisely such obvious visual cues that the following preposterous compliment was paid to the soprano Rosine Stoltz:

> One night a deaf man was seated beside me on the parterre at the Opéra: they were presenting [Halévy's] Charles VI. Because of his affliction, [my neighbor] could apprehend the plot of the opera only through facial expressions and gestures. He

tried to translate these by writing on his program the ideas he had grasped from this or that gesture made by Stoltz. When the curtain fell, he presented me with his manuscript, and I read there, word for word, the text sung by Madame Stoltz.[65]

Though these words convey far more about the hagiographic tendencies of puff journalism than about Madame Stoltz's acting technique, it is not surprising that an encomium should be manufactured along these lines at a house where so many of the actors never intoned words, and at a time when visual palpability was the order of the day. In opera as well as ballet-pantomime, the drama was designed to be "readily grasped by the eye"—or even (as Crosten went so far as to suggest) "expressed through action not through language."[66]

THUS did the Opéra's spectators of the 1830s and 1840s encounter ballet-pantomimes and operas that resembled one another in a multitude of ways. Most of them were set in the world of medieval and early modern Europe and its colonies. They were staged opulently, their designers laboring to create sets, costumes, and props that seemed "accurate" down to the smallest detail. Their special effects were frequently spectacular. They featured many of the same kinds of scenes and leavened their plots with the same kinds of danced divertissements. Their action was designed to be visibly palpable and at crucial moments was subject to the momentary freeze. Their characters, many of whom were of the same types, wore the same kinds of clothing, engaged in many of the same types of gestures, and formed some of the same patterns on the stage. Their scores were subject to some of the same principles of construction and, when necessary, could accommodate the need for the characters to "talk," whether they actually used their voices or not. Their plots were complicated—their characters facing many of the same kinds of pitfalls—and were clarified for the audience in libretti available for sale in the lobby.

This is not to deny the obvious differences between opera and ballet, nor to suggest that audiences could ever have confused one for the other. Nor is there any doubt that the trend toward the ballet-pantomime's greater independence—the trend that led eventually to today's habit of performing ballets and operas on separate evenings, or separate seasons, or in separate houses—was already well underway in the 1830s and 1840s. The advent of the *ballet d'action* at the Opéra in 1776 may be interpreted as the first blow to the marriage of the two arts at the Opéra, and the radical changes in technique in the Romantic ballet that eventually helped catapult ballet out of the realm of the narrative is perhaps another.[67] One may identify many post-1850 trends in the relationship's deterioration as well—the decline of the cross-generic double bill; the establishing of more separate constituencies and rules of etiquette; ballet's continuing liberation from the strictures of the narrative plot and the rise of the abstract ballet; the virtual disappearance of the Opéra's prima ballerinas from the operatic ballet.

But it cannot be overemphasized that the polarization of the two types was still in its early stages in the 1830s and 1840s, despite the incontestable self-sufficiency of ballet-pantomime and opera of that era, and despite the illusion of utter segregation unintentionally created by the divergence of their latter-day chroniclers. The Opéra's audiences came to the house to see two kinds of works that were not yet fundamentally different from one another, two kinds of works that still looked and operated enough alike that grasping their meaning did not require two separate sets of competencies, two kinds of works that were not yet driven by separate aesthetic impulses nor attended by separate audience rituals.[68] Dance was still held to belong comfortably with sung drama—in part because, quite simply, there had not yet arisen between opera and ballet-pantomime any dissimilarities great enough to cause anyone to put the two asunder. Thus it had always been at the Paris Opéra, and thus it would remain for many more decades. The kind of segregation between opera and ballet that we know today lay far in the future, still an unthinkable thought.

CHAPTER THREE

The Lighter Tone of Ballet-Pantomime

> To make the heroes of modern history jump around is utterly contrary to illusion.
>
> A. Baron, *Lettres et Entretiens sur la danse,* 282

GÉRARD DE NERVAL, the poet, in 1845 suggested that "it would be asking too much to seek philosophy within the superficial canvas of a ballet."[1] Louis Véron, the entrepreneur, had arrived at a similar conclusion upon assuming the directorship of the Paris Opéra in 1831. As he recalled later in his memoirs:

> I studied the receipts earned by all the old works, and I ascertained that those ballets that had succeeded most were *Les Filets de Vulcain* and *Flore et Zéphyre.* The ballets *Clary, Alfred le Grand, Manon Lescaut,* and *La Somnambule* never succeeded financially. On the other hand, *La Sylphide,* with its numerous flights and the prodigious talent of Mlle Taglioni, and *Le Diable boiteux,* a fairy-tale ballet imbued with the charming talent of Mlle Fanny Elssler, obtained a durable popular success. Dramas and morality plays do not belong in the domain of choreography. In a ballet the public demands above all varied and striking music, new and unusual costumes, great variety, contrasting sets, surprises, changes of scene, and action which is simple and easy to follow, in which the dance develops naturally out of the situation. One must also add the seductions of a young and pretty dancer who dances better and in a different manner than those who have come before her. When one appeals neither to the mind nor the heart, one must speak to the senses and especially to the eyes.[2]

Indeed, Véron and his successors did work hard to ensure that many ballet-pantomimes at the Opéra adhered to a strategy relying on variety, contrast, and the "young and pretty dancer." This helps account for the principal difference between opera and ballet-pantomime plots of this period at the Opéra: the latter type was generally much lighter in tone, and more likely to end happily.[3] For though ballet-pantomime did depict the same world that opera did, it was deemed the less appropriate medium for the presentation of heavy, sober, and overtly political plots.

In other words, although the plots of both kinds of works did usually consist of the same two elements—public political contrasts and private affairs of the heart—opera often emphasized the former, and ballet-pantomime the latter. Therefore, although nearly all of these plots included a love story, the operatic ones usually functioned mainly as private, ancillary subplots to weighty stories revolving around public political conflict, and often ended unhappily. The cruel treatment of Fénella by Alphonse in *La Muette de Portici,* for example, dramatizes the oppression of the Neapolitan peasants by their Spanish overlords, and the story ends with a bloody battle and the suicide of the title character. In ballet-pantomime, on the other hand, the love story served as the centerpiece, and any contrasts between social classes or ethnic groups—while very carefully presented to the audience—remained discreetly in the background of the plot.[4] When the peasant Hilarion and the nobleman Albrecht in *Giselle,* for instance, come to sword's point, it is strictly a matter of rivalry over Giselle's affections, and nobody ever accuses Albrecht of exploiting, as a class, the poor grape-harvesters who live on his land.

When depicting European encounters with colonized peoples, too, opera and ballet-pantomime took decidedly different slants. In the ballet-pantomime *Ozaï,* a charming south sea island female lovingly welcomes the French explorer Surville; in the opera *L'Africaine,* by contrast, hostile natives of Madagascar climb up the sides of a Portuguese explorer's shipwrecked vessel with the intention of massacring the Europeans aboard, and the perfume from a poisonous native plant nearly kills Vasco da Gama's fiancée Inès.[5] Opera and ballet-pantomime also used historical settings in different ways, for while the former was seen as an appropriate vehicle for the recounting of actual historical events, the latter was not. So, though designers took no less care in presenting particular locales in identifiable historical periods in ballet-pantomimes (for instance, Stuart London in *Betty* and mid-eighteenth-century France in *Manon Lescaut,*) librettists very rarely used such settings as anything more than a picturesque backdrop for the characters' private love affairs. Many an opera plot, on the other hand, was centered around a particular (and infelicitous) historical trend or event—for example, anti-Semitism during the time of the Council of Constance (*La Juive*); the slaughter of the Huguenots in 1572 (*Les Huguenots*); the insurrection of the Neapolitans against their Spanish rulers in 1647 (*La Muette de Portici*); the Anabaptist revolt in sixteenth-century Holland (*Le Prophète*).[6] Such themes lent themselves handily to a kind of opera which thrived on sensational—even gruesome—public scenes, such as Rachel's being thrown into a pot of boiling oil, the fatal leap of Fénella into the stream of hot lava, and the immolation of Jean and Fidès in the Palace of Münster. Scenes of this sort were not at all characteristic of the ballets, wherein deaths were depicted only rarely, were always brought about by the souring of love affairs and did not affect the fate of an ethnic group or social class.[7]

Given this disparity, it is not surprising to discover that operas featured *per capita* a higher proportion of males than ballet—characters who in opera (like males in real life) were far more prone to assume the roles of power brokers in

TABLE 3.1   NUMBERS OF MALE AND FEMALE CHARACTERS NAMED
IN MISCELLANEOUS OPERA AND BALLET-PANTOMIME LIBRETTI

Operas	Male	Female	Ballet-pantomimes	Male	Female
Gustave III	6	3	Manon Lescaut	4	5
Ali-Baba	8	2	La Sylphide	2	8
La Juive	12	2	L'Ile des Pirates	9	7
Les Huguenots	7	3	Le Diable boiteux	11	4
B. Cellini	8	2	La Tempête	3	3
Les Martyrs	6	1	La Fille du Danube	4	4
La Favorite	5	2	Les Mohicans	8	1
Dom Sébastien	7	1	Giselle	5	6
Marie Stuart	15	5	Le Diable à Quatre	6	4

These characters are mentioned by name in the section of the libretto listing (in most cases) *personnages* and *acteurs,* as opposed to the section listing minor characters (under the titles *danse* and *chant*) portrayed by the *corps de ballet* and the chorus.

matters of politics, war and religion (see Table 3.1).[8] Too, the action of French grand operas was more inclined to transpire in a city, or indoors, than in the peaceful valleys and enchanted woods of ballet-pantomime, even though operas and ballet-pantomimes favored the same countries as settings (see Table 3.2). And the role of the crowd—prominent in both types of works—varied widely. Ballet-pantomime's crowds lacked the sort of agency that opera's crowds were often accorded, their plot function usually being limited to that of collective witness to the vagaries of the principal characters' love affairs.[9] Opera's crowds, of course, served this function well, too, but could also take an active role as a willful, capricious mob, dangerously susceptible to demagoguery and capable even of murder.[10] Indeed, Dahlhaus drew a direct connection between these crowds and those Parisians were likely to encounter in real life: "The crowd scenes in these [opera] plots," he wrote, "betray the temperament of an age which still believed that major political decisions are made in the street."[11] One could even argue, as Anselm Gerhard does in his 1992 study *The Urbanization of Opera,* that French grand opera reflects in many ways the realities of urban life in the fast-growing Paris of the nineteenth century—not only its street politics, but its striking juxtapositions between the grotesque and the pleasing, its confusing influx of foreigners and provincials, its harried pace.[12] At the same time, I would suggest, the ballet-pantomimes created in the same house allowed the audience to retreat into a far more soothing and pastoral realm.

WHY, aside from the need for sheer escapism, did ballet-pantomimes at the Opéra—following public tastes as Véron read them—privilege private love

TABLE 3.2 SETTINGS OF BALLET-PANTOMIMES AND OPERAS

This is by no means an exhaustive list of the setting for every scene of all the works produced at the Opéra during the period under scrutiny in this book, but it does offer a few examples of such settings, showing that ballet-pantomime tended more toward outdoors and the countryside while opera tended more toward indoors and the city.

Ballet-Pantomimes

Nathalie (1832)
Switzerland, on Lord Rewena's estate
   I. A farm; a farmer's residence and a Lord's elegant summer residence are visible; in the background, a picturesque Swiss landscape.
   II. An elegant room in Lord Rewena's castle; a window to the right; in the background, a large drapery concealing an alcove.

La Révolte au sérail (1833)
The Kingdom of Grenada, during the period of Moorish domination
   I. A vast room at the Alhambra; circular tiers of seats to the left; a gallery leading to a mosque above; a door covered with rich draperies to the right.
   II. A splendid bathing room; in the center beneath a kiosk surrounded by thin columns is a circular bath of white marble; in the background is a secret door masked by a gold curtain.
   III. A savage landscape in the Alpuxaras; steep mountains in the background. / The gardens of Generalife.

Brézilia (1835)
America
   I. A forest; through the trees, high mountains are visible in the distance. To the right, a chain of high rocks forming a natural rampart, defending this forest from all exterior communication. Hammocks are suspended from a tree.

L'Ile des Pirates (1835)
The Roman states
   I. The gardens of a villa; to the right, the principal facade of Casin, of which one of the terraces, shaded by curtains, shelters an orchestra. To the left, large trees, through which the sea is visible, lapping up onto the walls of the garden.
   II. Close alongside a ship at anchor, near the Barbery coast.
   III. The garden of women, on the Isle of the Pirates.
   IV. The tent of the Pirate chief.

La Fille de Danube (1836)
The Valley of Donaueschingen
   I. A beautiful valley, with white, red, and blue flowers on the banks of the Danube, and mountains in the background. / A room in the baron's castle; through a window the Danube is visible.
   II. The same beautiful valley. / Beneath the Danube.

(continued)

TABLE 3.2 Continued

Les Mohicans (1837)
North America
   I. A picturesque site with an encampment of English soldiers; mountains in the background.
   II. An Indian camp; a temple to Fétiche to the left, large idols in front of it; a stake; wooded hills in the background.

La Volière (1838)
The Spanish part of the island of Santo Domingo
   I. Elegant garden.

La Tarentule (1839)
Calabria
   I. A village; an inn to the left, a church to the right; a mountain in the distance.
   II. Lauretta's room in the post-house. / A mountain landscape; a convent in the foreground.

Giselle (1841)
Thuringia
   I. A cheerful valley; two thatched cottages in the foreground; vine-covered hills and a castle in the background.
   II. A humid forest on the banks of a pool.

La Jolie Fille de Gand (1842)
Ghent and environs, and Venice
   I. A goldsmith shop in Ghent; through stained-glass windows, the main street of the city is visible. / The principal plaza of the city of Ghent./ Beatrix's room; a bed, a window, a prie-Dieu, a crucifix, a clock.
   II. An opulent boudoir in the palace of San Lucar in Venice. / A magnificent ballroom.
   III. The park of San Lucar's villa; flowers and greenery are everywhere. / The ballroom again, but in moonlight. / The town square of a village near Ghent. /Beatrix's room.

Paquita (1846)
Saragossa
   I. The valley of the bulls; a gypsy camp; immense rocks to the right in the distance.
   II. Interior of a gypsy dwelling. / Magnificent ballroom in the Moorish style with French embellishments.

Operas

Gustave III (1833)
Stockholm and environs
   I. A large and opulent waiting room in the royal palace in Stockholm.
   II. The fortune-teller's house; there is a fire in the fireplace; through the window the harbor of Stockholm is visible.

(continued)

TABLE 3.2 Continued

III. A scary, wild place near Stockholm; lugubrious rocky landscape; gallows.
IV. Ankastrom's study.
V. A gallery adjacent to the ballroom of the Opéra. / The ballroom of the Opéra, brightly lit.

La Juive (1835)
The city of Constance and the Canton of Thurgovie
   I. A city street; one may see a church with open doors, a jeweler's shop, a plaza.
   II. The interior of Eléazar's house.
   III. Magnificent gardens; in the distance, the lovely countryside of the canton of Thurgovie.
   IV. A gothic apartment adjacent to the Council Chamber.
   V. A huge tent, supported by gilded gothic columns; it dominates the city of Constance; the principal edifices of the city are visible.

Les Huguenots (1836)
Touraine and Paris
   I. A room in the castle of Nevers; a lawn and gardens may be seen through a window.
   II. The gardens of Chenonceaux; a river runs among the trees; a large staircase at the right ascends from the garden to the chateau.
   III. The pré au clercs on the banks of the Seine; the principal edifices of Paris are visible in the background.
   IV. An apartment in the castle of Nevers, with family portraits on the walls.
   V. The magnificently lit apartments in the hôtel de Sens. / Old Paris, with a cloister and a Protestant church.

Les Martyrs (1840)
Mélitène, the capital of Armenia
   I. Catacombs; stairway cut out of rock.
   II. Felix's study. / The grand plaza of Mélitène, with statues, obelisks, and an arc de triomphe.
   III. Pauline's bedroom. / A large staircase leading to the temple of Jupiter; a sacred wood around the temple
   IV. The apartment of the governor of Armenia./ A grilled cavern adjacent to the cirque. / A part of the cirque; the stadium seats; the grilled cavern where the lions are kept.

La Favorite (1840)
The kingdom of Castile
   I. The courtyard of Saint-Jacques de Compostelle; on the right, trees and tombs; on the left, the entrance to the chapel. / A beautiful site on the shore of the Isle of Léon.
   II. The gardens of the palace of Alcazar.
   III. A rich salon in the palace of Alcazar.
   IV. The cemetery of the cloister of Saint-Jacques de Compostelle.

(continued)

TABLE 3.2   Continued

Charles VI (1843)
Paris and environs
   I. The interior of a farmhouse.
   II. A brightly lit salon at the hôtel Saint-Paul.
   III. A tent in front of the home of Raymond. / Old Paris, in brilliant autumn sunlight. The Bastille may be seen in the distance.
   IV. The royal bedroom.
   V. Nighttime on the banks of the Seine. / The interior of the church of Saint-Denis.

Marie Stuart (1844)
France; Scotland
   I. Calais. A tavern on one side; an inn on the other; the port in the background.
   II. A salon in Darnley's palace in Edinburgh./ The bedroom of Marie Stuart.
   III. A salon in Marie Stuart's palace at Holyrood./ A ballroom in Marie Stuart's palace at Holyrood.
   IV. A room in the castle of Loch-Leven. / A picturesque site; the castle of Loch-Leven may be seen in the background.
   V. A room in the castle of Fotheringay. / The gardens of Fotheringay; at left, the castle-keep. / The room of execution in Fotheringay castle.

---

affairs over public strife, females over males, and light-hearted plots over more serious and violent ones? In this chapter I seek an answer to this question by exploring two customs: first, that of treating dancing in the Opéra's ballet-pantomimes in quite a literal fashion (which put a special focus on the dancers' bodies, as I discuss below); and second, that of turning comic operas into ballets (a custom that had flourished particularly in the years leading up to 1830). Both of these customs contributed significantly to the disparity in tone between opera and ballet-pantomime at the Opéra of the July Monarchy. The first did so by helping sort out what kinds of characters were appropriate, respectively, for ballet and for opera. The second established, long before the July Monarchy began, an important precedent for creating light and comical ballet-pantomimes at the Opéra.

THE DEMANDS OF VERISIMILITUDE

Ballet-pantomimes at the Opéra in the 1830s and 1840s were required—just like operas—not only to tell complicated stories to the audience but to do so while treating the activity of dancing with a fairly strict literalism. The critic Alfred Baron explains the ramifications of these strictures for ballet in no uncertain terms:

> Rarely are historical characters dancing characters.... The dance is so essential to a ballet that all actors who didn't dance at all would seem out of place, espe-

cially when the action depends on dance for its interest. It is the same on stage as at our society balls; the attention there is concentrated on the dancers. One doesn't ever pay attention to the grandmothers and the old men, because they aren't dancing at all. And if they did dance, they would be ridiculous. To make the heroes of modern history jump around is utterly contrary to illusion. Serious medieval topics lend themselves even less to *pirouettes* and *entrechats*.[13]

He declares himself at odds with Noverre's conviction that "history [is] . . . an inexhaustible source for ballet." Gustave Chouquet, too, finds fault with Noverre's notions of what constituted proper subject matter for a ballet plot:

> Was this choreographer [Noverre] right to believe that his art lent itself to the presentation of the most serious fables and most tragic actions translated into gestures, noble steps, and attitudes? We think that it is asking too much of the mimic [art], and that it is imprudent, to change the ballet into a somber tragedy that would be incomprehensible without the aid of a libretto. . . . It is important to avoid carefully all that demands long expositions, all that resembles deep reasoning, and all that even the best mime can't render clearly. The simplest, shortest, most picturesque and animated dramatic subjects appear to us . . . to be those that are most appropriate for choreography.[14]

Complicated ideas and "deep reasoning" remained off limits for ballet-pantomime, according to this set of rules, because they were the province of the mind. But, presumably, private emotion constituted a perfectly appropriate subject, since the body, ballet's primary instrument of expression, was so closely linked to it.

This acute sense of what was proper and improper subject-matter for the ballet-pantomime—as a body-centered genre in which the characters' onstage movements were taken somewhat literally—dictated quite simply that ballet-pantomime characters unlikely to dance in real life (Giselle's mother, for instance) should refrain from dancing on the Opéra's stage. It also encouraged librettists to supply rationales for characters who did dance.[15] (Why does the gamekeeper Hilarion dance in the second act of *Giselle?* Because he is forced to do so by the Wilis.) This, of course, excluded the sorts of characters that appeared so often in French grand opera: care-ridden men and women caught up in painful public events, and the "heroes of modern history"—people who were disinclined (at least according to these rules of verisimilitude) to dance.

It also meant that dancing itself became the focus of many ballet-pantomime scenes—danced entertainments, balls, social-dance lessons, ballet classes, for instance.[16] (Staged dancing lessons were so common that Castil-Blaze referred to them, with some annoyance, as "these eternal lessons which seem to make a dancing master out of a coryphée."[17]) And, naturally, it dictated that a good many ballet characters be dancers, whether professional or amateur. Zulma in *La Révolte au sérail,* for example, is a dancing slave; Florinde in *Le Diable boiteux* is a professional ballerina at the Madrid opera house; Beatrix in *La Jolie Fille de Gand* takes lessons from a dancing master and attends balls; Diana, in the same ballet, is the *première danseuse* at La Fenice in Venice; Giselle, a village girl, calls dancing "my only pleasure" and, as her mother put it, "she is mad about it."[18]

This stricture also meant that supernatural characters fared particularly well in ballet-pantomime, in part because certain physical movements were implied to be natural to their species. Wilis "fluttered here and there," the Péri "glide[d] over the ground without touching it"; the daughter of the Danube in one moment was beside her lover, in the next was "a shade, intangible"; the Sylphide "flutter[ed] around [her mortal lover James] and over his head, cooling the air he breath[ed] by agitating her wings."[19] Such movements could be realized by dancing (and, in some cases, with the aid of wires, seesaws, and trapdoors). Unlike mere mortal characters, for whom rationales for dancing had to be invented, supernatural ones, simply by being themselves, could dance without violating the audience's sense of illusion.

Expressing emotions through dance steps, too, made sense when it was done by supernatural characters, as Gautier explained, even though it struck him as odd when regular mortal characters did so. Supernatural people are not real, he says, and therefore are not constrained to express themselves as real people would:

> Fairyland is the place where the action of a ballet can most easily be developed. Sylphides, salamanders, undines, bayaderes and nymphs of every mythology are the obligatory characters. For a ballet to be at all convincing, it must be entirely unrealistic. The more fabulous the action, the more chimeric the characters, the less will be the shock to authenticity, for it is easy enough to believe that a sylphide can express her sorrow in a pirouette and make a declaration of love with a *rond de jambe*. But all that is not very convincing, despite optical illusions and theatrical conventions, when it comes from a person in a powder-blue silk dress whose father is a rather portly colonel in white leather breeches and riding boots.[20]

Of course, supernatural characters were not "obligatory" as Gautier asserts. Indeed, the Opéra during this period produced more nonmagical ballets than magical ones—a fact easily forgotten in the light of the modern-day popularity of *Giselle* and *La Sylphide*. And it goes without saying that many a mortal ballet character did express emotions with dance steps and gestures. But the urge to reduce ballet's "shock to authenticity"[21] did center around the notion that bodily motion onstage was to be taken somewhat literally, and, moreover, that the sorts of creatures most prone to express themselves with ballet steps were unlikely to partake in weighty historical events on the order of those depicted in, say, *La Juive*. In this post-Enlightenment world, the heavy thinkers were not very inclined to dance, and dancing itself was coming more and more to be seen as a feminine, frivolous activity.

This acute sense of the body's presence in ballet also allowed it to be objectified, which in turn made ballet characters seem all the more reasonably suited to be lovers first and foremost. For there is no doubt that many members of the audience found themselves quite distracted by ballet's chief expressive instrument, particularly when the instrument in question happened to be young, supple, and female.[22] Consider, for example, Gautier's description of Carlotta Grisi's portrayal of Leila, a dancing slave-girl in *La Péri* who dances the "bee dance" before the approving eyes of the slave-master Achmet:

> If you only knew with what modest embarrassment Carlotta takes off her long white veil; how she poses, while kneeling beneath its transparent folds, like Venus of old smiling in her pearly shell; with what child-like fright she is seized as the angry bee comes out of the calix of the flower; how well she expresses the hopes, the anxieties all the phases of the struggle, as the bodice and scarf, and the skirt which the bee attempts to pass through, fly quickly to right and left and disappear in the whirl of the dance.[23]

And recall Charles de Boigne's oft-quoted description of Fanny Elssler's rendition of the cachucha in *Le Diable boiteux:*

> Those swayings of the hips ... those provocative gestures, those arms which seemed to reach out for and embrace an absent being, that mouth which asked to be kissed, the body that thrilled, shuddered, and twisted, that seductive music, those castañets, that unfamiliar costume, that short skirt, that half-opening bodice, all this, and, above all, Elssler's sensuous grace, lascivious abandon, and plastic beauty were greatly appreciated by the opera-glasses of the stalls and boxes....[24]

The tendency of many male patrons to focus on the medium instead of the message, and the willingness of the Opéra to cater to their "erotic daydreaming" (as Louise Robin-Challan has recently put it) have been well chronicled.[25] Louis Véron is especially remembered for the fact that he raised the hemlines of the *danseuses* in the *corps* (even as he lowered their salaries) and encouraged the patronage of the Jockey Club, whose reputation for regarding ballet performances as voyeuristic free-for-alls inspired Albéric Second, in his fictionalized account of the Opéra, to spin a tale about ordering from the engineer Chevalier special binoculars that enlarged objects thirty-two times.[26] ("With these awful binoculars," he wrote, "underwear becomes a joke. They reveal as much of even the best-harnessed legs as if the dancer had slipped out of her dress."[27])

Véron and his successors granted certain lucky male patrons even closer proximity to the ballerinas by admitting them to the *foyer de la danse,* a favor that came automatically with a subscription to the *loge infernale* and was also bestowed upon " ... deputies, on peers, on upper ministerial employees, on journalists, on distinguished artists; in a word on all the people whose relationships could be useful or at least agreeable" to the Opéra director.[28] Here, as the lightly clad ballerinas stretched out their muscles in preparation for perfor-

Figure 22. Eugène Lami, *Foyer des acteurs à l'Opéra*. By permission of the Bibliothèque nationale de France.

Figure 23. The *loge infernale*. By permission of the Bibliothèque nationale de France.

Figure 24. Jean-Louis Forain (1852–1931), *Abonné et danseuse*. By permission of the Bibliothèque nationale de France.

mance on stage, their male admirers, in elegant suits and top hats, hovered around them, and the president of the Jockey Club held forth like a "Sultan in a seraglio."[29] (See Figures 22–24.) Flirtations in this setting, moreover, sometimes played themselves out in more private venues under a system of "prostitution légère" which dancers found tempting because, without outside income, many of them were too destitute to pay for food, fuel, and lodging.[30] (So inadequate were the *corps* dancers' salaries, in fact, that many of them suffered from malnutrition.) Thus were some of the Opéra's dancers subjected not only to the male gaze, but to the male touch.

As dance historians have noted, the Opéra's ballet-pantomime plots tended to mirror this backstage relationship by promoting in no uncertain terms a particular set of values that upheld the notions of masculine power and feminine submissiveness.[31] Indeed, the ballet-pantomime's subtextual admonishments to maintain a male-dominated order in the private realm might even be perceived as the counterpart to what Jane Fulcher has identified as the Opéra's attempts, through the plots and stagings of certain French grand operas, to maintain a state-dominated order in the public realm.[32] Among the object lessons taught by ballet-pantomime plots were these: that marriageable women should not behave in an overtly sexual or excessively adventurous manner; that men could not find domestic happiness with women who did so, or with women of a distant class or race; that if the need arose good women sacrificed their own happiness in favor of their husbands' or lovers'. Whether by negative or positive example, these values were reinforced time and again: a good-hearted South Sea Islander, Ozaï, sacrifices her own happiness so that her French lover may marry his proper white fiancée. The fiery Florinde dances the sexually explosive *cachucha* before a throng of male admirers and is consequently abandoned by her lover, who chooses a virginal illiterate country girl instead.[33] Beatrix, the daughter of a goldsmith of Ghent, rashly considers eloping with a dashing marquis but is then so terrified by a violent dream revealing the ghastly consequences of such an action that she gladly marries her dull cousin at the end. And so on.

Such plots instructed women as to proper comportment and recommended to men that they marry only women who had learned these lessons well. Yet they further taught that exoneration could be readily found for the man who occasionally departed his monogamous existence to avail himself of the pleasures offered by such an inappropriate woman.[34] Even the guilty dissonance between the enticements offered to the Opéra's male patrons in the *foyer de la danse* and the licit (if unglamorous) affection of their wives is reflected—and nicely resolved—in the plot of *Giselle,* as Susan Manning has recently suggested, wherein Albrecht is forgiven by his noble fiancée for his dalliance with the pretty dance-loving peasant Giselle. Plenty of the Opéra's ballet-pantomime plots of this age, in fact, feature male characters who enjoy—serially or simultaneously—love relationships with two women (the safe one of their own station, and the dangerous one of a distant class, or darker skin, or otherworldly pedigree) and, in the end, forswear the "other" woman and find forgiveness. (Sometimes the dangerous woman even sanctions her lover's union with the safe woman at the end of the ballet.[35]) Thus, one could argue, the Opéra under a single roof afforded men both a temptation and a species of ballet plot that provided absolution for yielding to it.[36]

Of course the ballerina's onstage sexual allure could work just as powerfully in an operatic divertissement as in a ballet-pantomime. (Lola Montez's scandalous renditions of *L'Ollia* and *Las Boleras de Cadiz* during the ball scene in *Don Giovanni* provide one of the more interesting cases in point.) But the perceived connection of ballet with sex in the public mind—a perception encouraged by Véron and publicized even further by gossipy stories about the *foyer de la danse* in the popular press—must be counted among the reasons for ballet-pantomime's perceived suitability as a genre focused on the private realm, and its strong inclination toward plots lighter in tone than opera's and strongly seductive in presentation. Because it was body-centered and its actors were silent, ballet-pantomime could more readily be construed as overtly sexual (and therefore less proper a medium for recounting tales of public struggle) than French grand opera. Thus, though ballet-pantomimes and operas depicted the same world—early modern Europe and its colonies—ballet tended to depict the more pastoral, sexual, private, and pleasing side of this world, and French grand opera, the more urban, intellectual, public, and violent. The two genres complemented each other well at the Paris Opéra, remaining grounded in the same basic fictional reality but splitting this reality into two segments, allocating each to what was deemed the appropriate medium.

BALLET PARODIES OF COMIC OPERA

A glance back through the sixty-odd years before 1830 reveals another phenomenon that can help explain the light tone of the ballet-pantomimes that held sway at the Opéra during the July Monarchy: the custom of turning comic operas into ballets, or as one critic put it, "translat[ing] familiar situations into the language of the choreographer's art."[37] This entailed borrowing the plots, characters and, usually, the titles of the original works, copying much of the action scene by scene and often taking over goodly portions of the original score as well. The comic opera was by no means the choreographer's only inspiration for ballet plots during the pre-Romantic era at the Opéra. Nor, of course, was the intercourse between the two genres in general restricted to opera-to-ballet parodies alone; at other houses operas were taken over from ballet plots.[38] But ballet parodies of comic opera did constitute an important part of the Opéra's repertory from the 1780s until the practice fell into decline during the July Monarchy; these parodies invite our attention here not only because they set an important precedent for the light-hearted ballet plot of the Romantic era, but because they expose another link between opera and ballet-pantomime: a veritable pipeline from the Opéra Comique to the Opéra.[39] In the pages that follow, I offer a summary sketch of the practice, speculating about the reason for its rise and fall and offering, for the sake of illustration, details about three such parody ballets.

THE first parody ballet to appear at the Paris Opéra was Maximilien Gardel's *La Chercheuse d'Esprit* in 1778, a ballet version of Charles-Simon Favart's popular one-act "opéra comique" of the same name. The success of Gardel's version of this comedy, perhaps, led to the stagings of two more such ballet parodies within six months (see Table 3.3), and indeed, the fairly steady production of parody ballets until about 1830 (excepting the Revolutionary years).

Critical reception of the parody ballet was generally favorable until the 1820s, when it became somewhat ambivalent (though shareholders at the Opéra Comique, understandably, objected strenuously for decades to the Opéra's co-opting of their works[40]). "Everyone knows the pretty opera by Grétry which gives its name [*L'Epreuve Villageoise*] to the new ballet," wrote one critic in 1815, in a typically positive review. "M. Milon has followed the action rather faithfully. . . . The author of the music has very appropriately used most of Grétry's music. . . . It seems that this ballet, very gay and well executed, will

TABLE 3.3 OPERAS CONVERTED INTO BALLET-PANTOMIMES (MIS EN PANTOMIME) AT THE PARIS OPÉRA, 1778–1845

Title and no. of acts	1st Paris perf.	Genre[1]	Librettist or Choreographer	Composer[2]
La Chercheuse d'Esprit (1)	20 Feb. 1741	opéra comique	Favart	——
La Chercheuse d'Esprit (1)	1 March 1778	ballet-pantomime	M. Gardel	——
Annette et Lubin[3] (1)	15 Feb. 1762	comédie en un acte, mêlée d'ariettes et de vaudevilles	Mme Favart	——
Annette et Lubin (1)	9 July 1778	ballet-pantomime	Noverre	Grenier or Gossec[4]
Ninette à la Cour[5] (2)	12 Feb. 1755	comédie en deux actes, mêlée d'ariettes	Favart	Duni
Ninette à la Cour (1)	18 Aug. 1778	ballet en action	M. Gardel	——
Le Déserteur (3)	6 March 1769	drame en trois actes, en prose, mêlée de musique	Sedaine	Monsigny
Le Déserteur[6] (3)	21 Oct. 1786	ballet d'action	M. Gardel	Miller
Le Coq du Village (1)	31 March 1743	opéra comique	Favart	——
Le Coq du Village (1)	18 Feb. 1787[7]	ballet comique	M. Gardel	——
Le Barbier de Seville (4)	14 Sept. 1784	opéra comique	Petrosellini	Paisiello
Figaro ou la Précaution inutile (3)	30 May 1806	ballet-pantomime	Blache, Duport	Lefebvre
Paul et Virginie (3)	15 Jan. 1791	comédie en trois actes, en prose mêlée d'ariettes	de Favrières	Kreutzer

(continued)

TABLE 3.3 Continued

Title and no. of acts	1st Paris perf.	Genre[1]	Librettist or Choreographer	Composer[2]
Paul et Virginie (3)	12 June 1806	ballet-pantomime	P. Gardel	Kreutzer
L'Epreuve Villageois (2)	24 June 1784	opéra-buffon en deux actes en vers	Desforges	Grétry
L'Epreuve Villageois (2)	4 April 1815	ballet comique	Milon	Persuis
La Servante Justifiée (1)	19 March 1740	opéra comique	Favart, Fagan	——
La Servante Justifiée (1)	30 Sept. 1818	ballet villageois	P. Gardel	Kreutzer
Les Promesses du Mariage (2)	4 July 1787	opéra-bouffon en deux actes et en verse	Desforges	Berton
Clari (3)	19 June 1820	ballet-pantomime	Milon	Kreutzer
Les Pages du Duc de Vendôme (1)	17 June 1807	comédie en un acte, mêlée de vaudevilles	Dieu-le-Foi, Gersin	——
Les Pages du Duc de Vendôme (1)	18 Oct. 1820	ballet	Aumer	Gyrowetz
Cendrillon[8] (3)	22 Feb. 1810	opéra-féerie en trois actes et en prose	Etienne	Isouard
Cendrillon[9] (3)	3 March 1823	ballet-féerie	Albert	Sor
Nina ou la Folle par Amour[10] (1)	15 May 1786	comédie en un acte, en prose, mêlée d'ariettes	Marsollier	Dalayrac
Nina ou la Folle par Amour (2)	23 Nov. 1823	ballet-pantomime	Milon	Persuis

(*continued*)

TABLE 3.3 Continued

Title and no. of acts	lst Paris perf.	Genre[1]	Librettist or Choreographer	Composer[2]
Le Mariage de Figaro (4)	20 March 1793[11]	opéra buffon	DaPonte	Mozart
Le Page Inconstant (3)	18 Dec. 1823	ballet-pantomime	Aumer	Habeneck
Aline, Reine de Golconde[12]	3 Sept. 1803	opéra	de Favrières	Berton
Aline, Reine de Golconde[13]	1 Oct. 1823	ballet-pantomime	Aumer	Dugazon
Zémire et Azore (4)	9 Nov. 1771	comédie-ballet en vers et en quatre actes	Marmontel	Grétry
Zémire et Azore (3)	20 Oct. 1824	ballet-féerie	Deshayes	Schneitzhoeffer
Joconde (3)	28 Feb. 1814	opéra-comique	Etienne	Isouard
Astolphe et Joconde (2)	29 Jan. 1827	ballet-pantomime	Aumer	Hérold
La Belle au Bois dormant (3)	2 March 1825	opéra-féerie	Planard	Carafa
La Belle au Bois dormant (4)	27 April 1829	ballet-pantomime-féerie	Aumer	Hérold
Léocadie (3)	4 Nov. 1824	drame lyrique	Scribe, Mélesville	Auber
L'Orgie (3)	18 July 1831	ballet-pantomime	Coralli	Carafa
La Chatte Metamorphosée en Femme	9? March 1827	vaudeville	Scribe, Mélesville, Bouchard	—
La Chatte Metamorphosée en Femme (3)	16 Oct. 1837	ballet-pantomime	Coralli	Montfort

(continued)

TABLE 3.3 Continued

Title and no. of acts	1st Paris perf.	Genre[1]	Librettist or Choreographer	Composer[2]
Victorine, ou La Nuit Porte Conseil (5)	21 April 1831	drame en cinq actes, mêlée de couplets	Dumersan, Gabriel, Dupeuty	——
La Jolie Fille de Gand (3)	22 June 1842	ballet-pantomime	Albert	Adam
Lady Henriette (3)	21 Feb. 1844	ballet-pantomime	St.-Georges, Mazilier	Flotow, Burgmüller, Deldevez
Le Diable à Quatre[14] (3)	30 Nov. 1809	opéra comique	Sédaine	Solié
Le Diable à Quatre (2)	11 Aug. 1845	ballet-pantomime	Mazilier	Adam

[1] The names by which the genres of these works were called sometimes varied; I have listed the earliest genre names known to me in each case.

[2] The scores of many of these works were attributed to a single composer, though in many cases they included extensive borrowings.

[3] Other versions of this work include that with text by Marmontel and music of de la Borde (first performed in Paris 30 March 1762), and that with text by Mme Favart and Voisenon, with music of J.P.E. Martini, first performed at Versailles, 16 February 1789, and in Paris, 18 April 1800. Another version of this text, with music by Touchemolin, was performed in Regensburg in 1778.

[4] Scores of this ballet at F-Po (A.255, 1778; A 366, 1799; and Rés. A.255) are attributed to Gossec. Considerable portions of this score are borrowed from other sources.

[5] Other versions of this work include a ballet choreographed by Angiolini (Vienna, 1765), and a comic opera with a revised version of Favart's text by Creuzé de Lesser and music by Henri Berton (Paris, 21 December 1811).

[6] An earlier ballet version of *Le Déserteur*, by Jean Dauberval, was performed in England before Gardel's version was performed in France. See Mme Dauberval's letter of protest to *Le Mercure*, 27 August 1785, 186–87.

[7] According to an annotation in the orchestral parts (F-Po Mat 18[71]), this ballet was first performed on 17 February 1787; according to the *Journal de l'Opéra* (F-Po usuels), it was first performed on 18 February 1787.

[8] For this score, Isouard made musical borrowings from Anseaume's *Cendrillon* (text by Larrette), first performed 20 February 1759.

[9] This work was first performed in London at the King's Theatre on 26 March 1822.

[10] Later versions of this work include one by Paisiello (*Nina, o sia La pazza per amore*) first performed in Naples, 21 November 1789.

[11] See Sherwood Dudley, "Les Premières Versions Françaises du *Mariage de Figaro* de Mozart," *La revue de Musicologie* 69 (1983): 55-83.

[12] The de Favrières/Berton version of this work was based on a ballet héroïque of the same title, first performed on 10 April 1766, by Sedaine and Monsigny. Later versions of the opera include those by Boieldieu (text of de Favrières and Vial), first performed in St. Petersburg, 5 March 1804, and by Donizetti (text of Romani), first performed in Genoa, 12 May 1828.

[13] The ballet version of this work, *Aline, Königin von Golkonda*, was first performed in Vienna, 18 May 1818. Aumer revived it as *Aline, Reine de Golconde* in London, 16 May 1823.

[14] Sedaine's *Le Diable à Quatre* was first performed in Paris, 19 August 1756, with known airs; the music was rearranged in a later version by François-André Danican Philidor; it was performed at Laxenburg on 28 May 1759 with additional airs by Gluck. Adolphe Adam rescored the music of Solié's setting for a revival of this work, which was first performed on 15 October 1853 at the Théâtre Lyrique.

attract large audiences to the *Académie impériale de musique*."⁴¹ It was also common for critics to equate the two versions of the same piece:

> It would be perfectly futile to give a summary of a ballet [*Astolphe et Joconde*, 1827] known by heart to all of those who have seen the opera *Joconde*—and who hasn't seen the opera *Joconde?* Wit translated into pirouettes; the grace of cadenced steps substituting for graces of style, situations that are the same except for the language: the exchange of the medallion and the scarf, the apparition of the two women as gypsies, their maliciously concerted strategy for appearing unfaithful, and to confound the incessant infidelity of their lovers; the nocturnal scene of the double kiss, the crowning of the rose-queen, the jealous pedantry of the bailiff, all of this is found equally in the two works. Such a thorough resemblance fully justifies the word of a witty man who said while leaving the performance: "I just *heard* a ballet with charming words."⁴²

Some critics even preferred the ballet parodies to their lyric models. One of them wrote, for example, in a review of *Le Coq du Village* (1787), that "we should be grateful to the elder Gardel, author of this ballet, for thus calling to life these little plays . . . under this new form, they have something more lively and more piquant about them."⁴³ The next year, the success of *Le Déserteur* was attributed in part to the fact that "pantomime, obliged to exaggerate expression because it lacks words, has more powerful means to electrify us."⁴⁴ Of *Nina* (1813), a critic wrote, "the piece at the Feydeau [Opéra Comique], despite the suavity of its melody, and the extreme talent of the two actresses who, in turn, have distinguished themselves in it, never made half the impression on me of that seen at the Opéra."⁴⁵ A. Delaforest wrote that the "choreographic translation" of *Aline, Reine de Golconde* (1823), "shining with freshness and opulence, will make the Opéra Comique, which includes *fêtes* and dances that are of necessity inferior to those of the Académie royale, seem cold and pale."⁴⁶

The popularity and success of the Opéra's parody ballets were owed in part to the fact that audiences took pleasure in going to the theater to be regaled with familiar stories—and this was of course nothing new. Popular stories knew no generic boundaries and frequently cropped up in a variety of incarnations—operas, spoken dramas, street improvisations, melodramas, vaudevilles—and it is significant that ballet, a wordless genre, was fully included in the mix.

Yet at the same time, there is another element in the success of the Parisian parody ballet that is not to be underestimated: the confusion of the Opéra's audience upon being confronted with wordless drama. Although many Parisians had surely grown accustomed to pantomime by the late eighteenth century by seeing it at the Fair theaters, the Ambigu-Comique, and other places, there was still a strong sense of bewilderment expressed in reviews when the new *ballets d'action* began to be performed at the Opéra.⁴⁷ "There is no need to offer a plot synopsis of this ballet here", wrote a critic in 1778, in a review of *La Chercheuse d'Esprit*. "It is a great advantage for pantomime to represent only subjects already well known to the spectators, and to leave to them the pleasure of interpreting themselves the airs, the gestures and the dances."[48] And in the above-cited review of *Le Coq du Village* (1787), the critic contended that by showing "action known in advance, one thus forestalls obscurity, the biggest inconvenience of this art."[49] Even as late as 1831, Castil-Blaze could still write that "These plagiarisms must be forgiven. The author reproduces a story that is already known; scenes which the public knows; they easily divine the details of a piece of this type."[50]

Three Parodies

I have referred generally to the lyric works upon which the Opéra's parody ballets were based by the broad term "comic operas," although in fact they are too varied to fit under a single rubric and were known by a variety of designations. The term *opéra bouffon,* for example, referred to broadly comic operas, especially those influenced by *opera buffa* models. The term *comédie mêlée d'ariettes,* referred to light works (most of them pre-Revolutionary) featuring spoken dialogue and newly composed music. Many works employed both old tunes and newly composed *airs* and were often designated as *comédies mêlées d'ariettes de vaudevilles* (the word *vaudevilles* referring to the traditional tunes, or *timbres,* to which new words had been set, often to hilarious effect).[51] Before the Revolution, the term *opéra comique* also commonly referred to a work with spoken dialogue that used pre-existing tunes, though under the Empire and Restoration the same term came to designate operas with spoken dialogue and newly composed music—arias, choruses, recitatives, and so on.[52] No mere list of labels, however, can fairly convey the richness and variety of French comic operas, which formed a vital part of Parisian culture in the late eighteenth and early nineteenth centuries. For they reflected the heritage of a multitude of lively theatrical traditions, not the least of which were the earthy humor and biting social satire of the *vaudevilles* of the Fair Theaters, the slapstick of the commedia dell'arte, the witty repartee and word play of Molière's comédie-ballets, and the sweetness of "larmoyant" sentimental comedies.

Just as there was no single type of "comic opera," there was no single strategy for converting these pre-existing lyric works into ballets.[53] But in most instances the plot was simplified to make it more accessible to the eye and adjusted to take advantage of the opportunities provided by performers who could dance and mime, while at the same time the music from the original version was usually reused to some extent.[54] A closer look at three parody ballets—*La Chercheuse d'esprit* (1778), *Paul et Virginie* (1806), and *Le Page inconstant* (1823)—will provide a few clues about how choreographers and composers (or arrangers) went about creating such works. The first is based on an *opéra comique,* the second on a *comédie* "mêlée d'ariettes," and the third on a pair of related stage works: a Beaumarchais comedy (mixed with singing) and the *opera buffa* that it inspired.

La Chercheuse d'Esprit

As noted above, Maximilien Gardel's ballet-pantomime *La Chercheuse d'Esprit* (1778) was based on Charles-Simon Favart's *opéra comique* of the same name (1741), a one-act comic piece in twenty-one scenes with spoken dialogue and new words sung to approximately seventy known airs.[55] The ballet unfolds over eleven scenes, and its unattributed score consists of twenty-eight discrete numbers, many of them in binary form and some of them based on the melodies used in the *opéra comique* version.[56] Both the opera and ballet versions end with a danced divertissement, celebrating the happy uniting of three couples after a series of misadventures:

A notary, Subtil, declares his love for Nicette, a simple innocent girl, whose mother (a rich farmer) agrees to the match on the condition that Subtil allow her, Mme Madré, to marry his vapid son Alain. Mme Madré idly tells her daughter to go and get some wits into her head, whereupon the girl, taking the words literally, sets out to do so. She first asks the bookworm Narquois if he can sell her any. She then asks her sister's fiancé L'Eveillé the same question. He is eager to help but the sister (Finette) intervenes. Finally, Nicette and Alain (who is as simple as she) decide to seek wits in Paris, but before their journey is undertaken, Mme Madré (hoping to ensnare a husband for herself) begins to instruct Alain in the art of courtship. Soon thereafter, Alain and Nicette fall for each other, and Mme Madré, at first seeming furious, is becalmed when Subtil, admitting his foolishness in proposing to Nicette, invites Mme Madré to marry him instead. The three happy couples are paired, and all ends with a celebration.[57]

A comparison of the layout of the opening scenes of these two pieces, during which the characters are introduced and the comic conflict is set up, will suffice to show Gardel's approach to distilling Favart's piece into visually palpable scenes. Consider, first, the Favart piece, the first two scenes of which are presented to the audience with a combination of speaking and singing, featuring twelve discrete sung numbers (incorporating sixteen known airs), and relying upon the usual ironic interplay between the old and new song texts. (Subtil, for example, sings of Nicette's virtue to the song "Ces filles sont si sottes" [These girls are so silly][58]).

SUMMARY of Favart's opéra comique *La Chercheuse d'Esprit*, scenes 1 and 2 (based on a libretto published in Paris by Duchesne in 1768[59])

SCENE I
Spoken dialogue: Monsieur Subtil tells Mme Madré that he would like to remarry; Mme Madré reveals that she, too, would like to remarry. Then Subtil expresses his desire

to marry Mme Madré's daughter Nicette. Amused and astonished, Mme Madré reminds him that Nicette is simplicity itself.

Singing interspersed with spoken dialogue: The pair sing to the melodies of three known airs,[60] of Subtil's matrimonial wish, of Mme Madré's incredulity, and of Nicette's extreme youth. Subtil elaborates, in the next song, on Nicette's beauty;[61] Mme Madré, in turn, sings of her daughter's dull-wittedness.[62] Finally, Subtil offers to Mme Madré his son Alain in exchange for the fair Nicette; she eagerly accepts.[63] After a short spoken dialogue, Mme Madré herself then sings of the advantages of taking a young spouse.[64]

Spoken dialogue: In the scene's closing dialogue the older couple agree to the exchange and congratulate themselves upon their cleverness. In an aside, Mme Madré reveals to the audience her hope that Subtil will change his mind.

Scene 2

Singing interspersed with spoken dialogue: The second scene begins with Nicette's arrival. She listens uncomprehendingly, repeating stupidly the final word of each of his couplets, as Subtil sings to her of her sweetness.[65] "You might as well be speaking Hebrew," Mme Madré tells him as he finishes his song. Undaunted, he sings his proposal of marriage to Nicette.[66] Despite her mother's instructions to accept his invitation, she refuses.

Subtil then sings of Nicette's virtue[67] and imagines the pleasures of applying his tutelage to her innocence as Mme Madré rejoins in another song that her daughter will be just as stupid after the wedding.[68] The tireless Subtil tells Nicette again that he wants her hand;[69] "What for?" she asks. After a short discussion, the two express their respective ardor and simplicity in the subsequent duet.[70]

Mme Madré vents her impatience once again and in the final song of the scene, instructs her daughter, "Go find some wits."[71] As the older couple exit, Nicette protests that she doesn't know where to look for wits, Mme Madré shrugs, and Subtil laughs.

The same dramatic territory is covered, in the ballet version of *La Chercheuse,* in seven discrete binary-form musical numbers, some apparently original, and at least one drawing on a melody sung in the opera. (This score is typical of ballet-pantomime scores of the time in that it consists of a succession of short pieces.) Annotations in the score suggest, further, that the choreography of each such number is dedicated mainly to a single action, concept, or interchange.[72] It appears, for instance, that Gardel employed three separate musical numbers to demonstrate—respectively—Nicette's simplicity, Subtil's ardor, and Mme Madré's reluctance to sanction the proposed match, concepts all raised briefly in the opera in a single dialogue at the beginning and then revisited several times.[73] Gardel also made slight alterations to the action in order to ensure, in mimed dialogues, the presence of whatever third party the two interlocutors are referring to, thus making it easier for the audience to comprehend visually what the dialogue was about.

SUMMARY of M. Gardel's ballet-pantomime *La Chercheuse d'Esprit*, first seven musical numbers (based on the *répétiteur*, F-Po Mat 18 [65])

1. Nicette "appears, dancing steps which characterize her simplicity."[74] (*Mme Madré, who shared the opening scene of the opera with Subtil, does not appear until later.*)
2. Subtil falls to his knees, declaring his affection for Nicette (*an idea imparted, in the opera, in a conversation with Mme Madré, with Nicette nowhere in sight*).
3. Mme Madré arrives and laughs at the sight of Subtil kneeling before Nicette (*thus demonstrating her lack of sympathy for his proposed match, another idea imparted in the opera in a simple conversation between the two older characters in Nicette's absence*).
4. Subtil asks the older woman for her daughter's hand; Mme Madré is discouraging.
5. Subtil's son Alain appears and shares a laugh with Nicette. Mme Madré, upon noticing the young couple's interplay, asks Subtil if she herself may marry his son. (*The Alain of the opera was absent when this match was suggested.*)
6. Subtil eagerly assents, and Mme Madré breaks the news of the engagement to Alain, who retreats quickly.
7. The older couple gaily sets out for the notary's office to draw up the marriage contracts, Subtil bidding his beloved an affectionate farewell and Mme Madré scornfully suggesting to the girl that she should go "chercher de l'esprit."

The compiler of the score for Gardel's parody (probably Gardel himself) used relatively few of the tunes sung in Favart's version. In the opening sequence of this ballet, in fact, only one of the seven musical numbers—the seventh—is borrowed from the corresponding segment of the opera. It is the tune "L'éclat de mon bonheur," to which Subtil sang his only direct, formal proposal of marriage to Nicette in the opera. Perhaps the score's compiler, in keeping with the one-subject-at-a-time approach, wished to avoid using melodies that had, in the opera, been amalgamated into medleys. He may also have meant to place special emphasis on the ballet's proposal scene by accompanying it with a tune that would automatically remind some spectators of the comparable scene in the opera. In any case, one may see that this work adheres to the general principles of keeping the scenes clearly focused, reusing the original music effectively, and preserving the original story but adjusting it in ways that made it palpable through wordless mime and action.

Paul et Virginie

The comic opera *Paul et Virginie* (1791) was one of many stage works derived from the popular novel of the same name published in 1788 by Jacques-Bernardin Henri de Saint-Pierre (a novel inspired by a real event, the wreck of the *Saint-Géran* off the coast of Mauritius in 1744[75]). The novel had ended with the sorrowful death of the title characters, but the librettist of the opera, de Favrières, wrought a far lighter story, which, in turn, was taken up in the ballet parody version:

Paul and Virginie, dear friends since early childhood and now planning to marry, live with their mothers on an exotic island also inhabited by blacks and Creoles. The two lovers befriend Zabi, an old black man who is running from the hunters who sold him into slavery. They help him find his children and save him from the villain slave-hunter, Dorval. This adventure has taken them far from home; they realize that they are lost in the jungle. Happily, their servant, Domingo,[76] and his dog, Fidèle, rescue them. Meanwhile, the governor of the island has arrived unexpectedly at the home of Virginie's mother, demanding to take Virginie back to France to live with her cruel aunt. The young lovers return from the jungle only to find that Virginie, much to their horror, will soon be forced to board the governor's ship. As Paul watches in despair from a cliff, the ship sets sail. But it is sunk in a violent storm shortly thereafter, and Paul and Zabi swim to Virginie's rescue.[77] All the principal characters gather on the beach at the end, the governor good-naturedly declaring his willingness to allow Virginie to remain with Paul.

Maximilien Gardel's younger brother Pierre, who choreographed the Opéra's ballet version of *Paul et Virginie* (1806), streamlined the plot and made minor changes in the action, in keeping with custom, to ensure that the story could be imparted visually. In the ballet, for instance, the governor seizes Virginie and drags her away to the waiting ship, her hands outstretched toward Paul and her mother swooning in the servants' arms; in the opera she had merely pressed a handkerchief to her eyes and walked away, surrounded by soldiers. In the ballet, would-be wedding guests dance and wait for the nuptial couple, carrying flowers and a garlanded sign reading (rather unsubtly), "Mariage de Paul et de Virginie"; in the opera, wedding plans had merely been discussed.[78]

Gardel's version of this narrative, however, does not fall into the same sort of singly focused scenes that one finds in his brother's *La Chercheuse* ballet. Instead, he keeps the action pushing busily ahead by providing a steady stream of events. A comparison of the lyric and danced versions of *Paul et Virginie*, in fact, discloses that more events transpire in the first and third acts of the ballet than in the corresponding acts in the opera, even though the plot of the ballet is actually somewhat simpler (see Table 3.4). Gardel also introduces no fewer than nine characters during the ballet's first act, as opposed to the five introduced in the first act of the opera. He also fragments some events into several short episodes, splitting the Zabi affair, for example, into three segments—he introduces Zabi in Act 1, shows the slave hunter Dorval searching for Zabi in Act 2 (a scene not found in either the novel or the opera), and resolves the situation in a later scene in the same act, when Virginie confronts Dorval and frees Zabi from slavery.[79]

TABLE 3.4 PAUL ET VIRGINIE, OPERA AND BALLET-PANTOMIME VERSIONS

Opera	Ballet-Pantomime
Act One	**Act One**
P&V discuss the letter from France.	P&V playfully kiss and eat fruit.
Chansonette: "Ma zoé."	Dom. & Marie watch; P&V surprise them.
P&V meet Zabi.	Div.: Bamboula; general dance.
Trio: "Apprenez nous votre peine."	The mothers decide P&V should marry.
Duo: "Fatigué de si longue route."	The Pasteur arrives.
P&V rescue Zabi from Dorval.	Div.: Distribution of fruits
P&V playfully kiss and eat fruit.	P&V meet Zabi.
Couplets: "De ta main ceuilles ses fruits."	The mothers discuss wedding plans.
P&V are lost; Domingo finds them.	The governor arrives to claim V; dismay.
Rescue celebration.	Domingo and dog go to find P&V.
Choeur: "Petits blancs bien doux."	Domingo shows the dog Paul's clothing.
Act Two	**Act Two**
Duo: "Helas . . ." (worry over lost P&V).	Dorval hunts for Zabi.
Mothers discuss the past.	P&V and Zabi, fleeing, are exhausted.
P&V return to their mothers.	Dorval finds them; V wins the day.
Quatuor: "O bonnes mères."	P&V are lost; Domingo finds them.
V distributes gifts.	Div.: Rescue celebration.
The governor arrives to claim V.	
Pasteur reads aloud the aunt's letter.	
Virginie: "Elle propose à Virginie."	
Dismay; V talks to little boy; V departs.	
Finale: "Mère cruelle barbare."	
Act Three	**Act Three**
Duo: "Elle est partie, ma Virginie."	The mothers worry about the lost P&V.
P and Pasteur watch ship.	P&V return to their mothers.
Trio: "Regardons bien."	Div.: celebration of reunion; gifts.
P talks to boy.	The governor arrives to claim V.
A storm breaks out.	Dismay; V departs.
Choeur: "Courage, courage . . ."	Misinformed wedding revelers arrive.
The ship is wrecked; P saves V.	A storm breaks out.
	The ship is wrecked; P saves V.

Gardel's other modifications to the plot accommodate the need for at least one danced divertissement per act.[80] For the first-act divertissement, for example, Gardel invents a scene in which Domingo and his wife Marie spy on the amorous Paul and Virginie; the young couple catches the older couple in their act of voyeurism and gaily compels them to atone by dancing the bamboula, which they gladly do.[81] Paul and Virginie then reciprocate by dancing while

Domingo and Marie play tam tam and triangle (all-purpose instruments of exoticism); eventually a group of blacks joins in the merriment.[82]

Rodolphe Kreutzer's music of this ballet is like that for the *La Chercheuse* ballet in that it consists of discrete numbers. Each number, however (in keeping with other early-nineteenth-century ballet scores at the Opéra), is typically longer than those of the earliest ballets and is not in binary form. Its music falls into the two categories so well known by the 1830s and 1840s: dramatic and dance music.[83] Much of this ballet music was composed anew by Kreutzer, and when necessary it conforms nicely to the action (even supplying the sound of a dog barking). Yet Kreutzer also carries over a good deal of the music he composed for the opera—for instance, the storm music, and the melody for "Mère cruelle barbare" sung in the opera by Paul to express his anger upon Virginie's enforced departure, and played again in the corresponding scene of the ballet.

Le Page Inconstant

Because of its extensive musical quotations from Mozart's *Le Nozze di Figaro,* one parody ballet that could draw even upon the present-day theatergoer's fund of experience is *Le Page inconstant,* a danced version of Beaumarchais's famous story, choreographed by Jean Aumer for the Opéra in 1823 (and one of the few of the Opéra's parodies *not* co-opted from the Opéra-Comique). Aumer had based this ballet parody on an older one created nearly four decades earlier in Bordeaux by the choreographer Dauberval. As Aumer explained in his 1823 libretto:

> The origins of this work go back to the epoch when [Beaumarchais'] *Le Mariage de Figaro* found so much success. Dauberval was in Bordeaux. This comedy was performed and then banned. The people of Bordeaux could not hide their disappointment, and Dauberval believed that, to compensate, he could convert it to a ballet. Truly, the gaiety and comedy of the original work is reproduced in the situations so artfully drawn that the ballet became as successful as the play.[84]

Most of the alterations in the plot seem designed, in keeping with custom, to help make the action abundantly clear. Two newly created scenes added to Act One, for instance, serve this purpose nicely: a dinner party at the very beginning, and a visit by the Count to Fanchette's cottage shortly thereafter. The dinner party not only manages to introduce nearly all the characters at once, but makes plain their disparate social stations, and demonstrates the title character's appreciation for women:

> The count, the countess, and several noble guests are seated at the table. The page serves the countess, gazing at her very attentively. Antonio and Fanchette bring flowers to their masters. Suzanne walks around the table; Bazile plays a bacchanalian melody on his guitar; the musicians are on a raised platform; everything ex-

udes a sense of pleasure. . . . The page admires the beauty of the countess, the charms of Suzanne and the graces of Fanchette; Bazile does not miss a single one of Chérubin's admiring looks.[85]

The Count's visit to Fanchette's cottage, too, and his discovery there of the page—an episode not enacted in either the play or the opera, but described in both cases by the Count after the fact—also serves an important function. The humor of his finding Chérubin hiding under a dress in Suzanne's armchair later in the play and opera, is of course owed largely to the Count's declaration, even as he draws the garment away, that he had found Chérubin behind a curtain in Fanchette's cabin earlier in the day. The choreographer conveys the redundancy of the situation by allowing the ballet audience actually to witness the scene in Fanchette's cottage, thus showing them, explicitly, both unveilings.[86]

The libretto for this ballet-pantomime collapses the five acts of the play into three and changes the sequence of scenes, ensuring that its action, like that of the ballet-pantomime version of *Paul et Virginie,* is unrelenting, allowing little breathing room between events (see Table 3.5).[87] In one case, the choreographer alters the order so he can meet the need for divertissements: he pushes the Count's renunciation of his *droit de seigneur* from the end of the first act back to an earlier scene, probably so that the resulting celebration (an occasion for a danced divertissement) can be separated, by a few scenes, from the second divertissement, which occurs at the end of the act as everyone bids farewell to Chérubin. In the play the renunciation of the *droit* occurs nearly at the end of the act, immediately before the farewell to Chérubin, and the two occasions for merrymaking are merged.

The remaining three divertissements in the ballet-pantomime are carried over from actual musical numbers in the play. The first, Chérubin's singing of his ballad to the Countess, becomes in the ballet-pantomime a *pas de deux* between the two of them, danced as Suzanne mimes the plucking of a guitar.[88] The second is the joint wedding celebration, which in both play and ballet-pantomime serves as a backdrop to Suzanne's intrigue. (Choral and solo singing, as well as dancing, mark the occasion in the play; the celebrants in the ballet-pantomime, of course, dance.) The last divertissement is derived directly from the last round of singing and dancing in the play, which occurs at the very end and celebrates the favorable outcome of the *folle journée.*

Although the plot of Aumer's ballet was based more closely on Beaumarchais' script than Da Ponte's libretto, its score borrowed heavily from *Le Nozze di Figaro,* thanks to an 1819 Viennese version of the ballet-pantomime, for which Adalbert Gyrowetz had arranged a score that quoted Mozart's music extensively.[89] When Aumer restaged the ballet-pantomime in 1823 at the Opéra, he found it "necessary to rejuvenate the music" (presumably, that arranged by Gyrowetz) and assigned the task to Jean-François Habeneck, who kept much of Mozart's music and added, among other things, bits of Beethoven.[90] (See

TABLE 3.5 THE "MARRIAGE OF FIGARO" PLAY, OPERA BUFFA, AND BALLET-PANTOMIME

Le Mariage de Figaro (Beaumarchais)	Le Nozze di Figaro (DaPonte/Mozart)	Le Page Inconstant (Aumer after Dauberval/ arr. Habeneck)
Act One *A partly-furnished room*	**Act One** *A partly-furnished room*	**Act One** *A hall decorated with flowers with a banquet table in the middle*
Figaro measures the floor; Suzanne warns him of the Count's designs.	Figaro measures the floor; Susanna warns him of the Count's designs.	The Count and Countess dine, attended by their servants; Chérubin eyes the women.
Marcelline tells Bartholo of her desire to marry Figaro.	Marcellina tells Bartolo of her desire to marry Figaro.	The Count signs the renunciation of his rights; Divertissement.
Suzanne and Marcelline have a spiteful interchange.	Susanna and Marcellina have a spiteful interchange.	Marcelline and Bartholo interrupt the celebration; she claims rights to Figaro.
Chérubin takes the Countess's ribbon; tells Suzanne of his ardor for women; says he has written a ballad.	Cherubino takes the Countess's ribbon; tells Susanna of his ardor for women; says he has written a love song.	*Cottage of Antonio and Fanchette* Antonio arranges flowers; Fanchette thinks fondly of Chérubin.
Chérubin hides behind a chair as the Count woos Suzanne; the Count hides when Bazile arrives; the Count reveals himself and then discovers Chérubin.	Cherubino hides behind a chair as the Count woos Susanna; the Count hides when Basilio arrives; the Count reveals himself and then discovers Cherubino.	Chérubin enters; Fanchette dances with him; he hides as the Count woos Fanchette; the count discovers him and angrily sends him away.
The Countess, Figaro, Fanchette, and peasants enter; Figaro asks the Count for the renunciation of the privilege; he grants it; general joy.	The Count banishes Cherubino; Figaro and peasants enter; Figaro asks the Count for the renunciation of the privilege; he grants it; general joy.	*Suzanne's Chamber* Figaro measures the floor; he worries about Suzanne's coquettishness; Marcelline appears and reproaches Figaro when Suzanne is out of the room.
The count banishes Chérubin; Figaro hatches a scheme to help the page defy the Count's orders.	Everyone bids Cherubino farewell.	Suzanne and Marcelline have a spiteful interchange. Chérubin takes the Countess's ribbon; Suzanne discovers a *romance* he has composed for the Countess. Chérubin hides behind a chair as the Count woos Suzanne;

(continued)

A LIGHTER TONE

TABLE 3.5 Continued

Le Mariage de Figaro (Beaumarchais)	Le Nozze di Figaro (DaPonte/Mozart)	Le Page Inconstant (Aumer after Dauberval/ arr. Habeneck)
Act One	**Act One**	**Act One**
		the Count hides when Bazile arrives; the Count reveals himself and then discovers Chérubin.
		The Countess, Figaro, Fanchette, and peasants enter; everyone bids Chérubin farewell. Divertissement.
Act Two	**Act Two**	**Act Two**
A bedroom furnished splendidly	*The Countess's chamber*	*A bedroom*
Susanne and Countess discuss Count's desire for Suzanne, and Chérubin's desire for the Countess.	Alone, the Countess is sad; Susanna and Countess discuss Count's desire for Sus., and Cherubino's desire for the Countess.	Suzanne and Countess discuss Count's desire for Suzanne.
Figaro arrives, tells them of his scheme.	Figaro arrives, tells them of his scheme.	Figaro arrives; tells them of his scheme.
Chérubin arrives, sings his ballad.	Cherubino arrives, sings his love song.	Chérubin, alone with Countess, kisses the ribbon. Divertissement: Chérubin and the Countess dance to his *romance*.
The two women dress Chérubin as a girl.	The two women dress Cherubino as a girl.	
The Count demands entry; Chérubin hides.	The Count demands entry; Cherubino hides.	The Count demands entry; Chérubin hides.
The Count enters, is suspicious; Chérubin jumps out the window.	The Count enters, is suspicious; Cherubino jumps out the window.	The Count enters, is suspicious; Chérubin jumps out the window.
The Count is astonished to discover Suzanne instead of Chérubin; is ashamed.	The Count is astonished to discover Susanna instead of Cherubino; is ashamed.	The Count is astonished to discover Suzanne instead of Chérubin; is ashamed.
Antonio enters with flowerpot; furious Count wants revenge.	Antonio enters with flowerpot; furious Count wants revenge.	The Count secretly invites Suzanne to meet him in the garden; the Countess overhears. The Countess dictates a letter for Suzanne to send to the Count.
Countess and Suzanne agree to carry out their scheme without Figaro's knowledge.	Marcellina *et al.* are triumphant; Susanna, Figaro and the Countess are confounded.	

(continued)

A LIGHTER TONE

TABLE 3.5 Continued

Le Mariage de Figaro (Beaumarchais)	*Le Nozze di Figaro* (DaPonte/Mozart)	*Le Page Inconstant* (Aumer after Dauberval/ arr. Habeneck)
Act Two	**Act Two**	**Act Two** *A fine gallery* Chérubin, disguised as a girl, celebrates with the villagers, is discovered by Antonio. Brid-Oison tells the Count of Figaro's parentage. Divertissement. Wedding celebration. During dancing, Suzanne's letter is passed to the Count. Fanchette guilelessly reveals to Figaro Suzanne's plans to meet the Count.
Act Three *The throne room at the castle* The Count sends Pedrillo to Seville to find Chérubin. The Count is angry, realizing Figaro has tricked him. Suzanne agrees to meet the Count in the garden in the evening. In Court, Marcelline's case is argued; Figaro's parentage is revealed; Joy, reconciliation.	**Act Three** *A hall in the castle* The Count is confused, insulted. He sends Basilio to Seville to find Cherubino. The Countess persuades Susanna to carry out a scheme. Susanna agrees to meet the Count in the garden in the evening. Count becomes angry upon overhearing Susanna tell Figaro "you've won your case!" Don Curzio rules Figaro must marry Marcellina, but then Figaro's parentage is revealed. Joy; reconciliation. Barbarina plans to dress Cherubino as a girl. The Countess, alone, mourns	**Act Three** *A chestnut grove; pavilions on either side; an illuminated castle in the background; a garden seat downstage* Fanchette, with a lantern, seeks Chérubin; Bazile, Antonio, Brid-Oison, Bartholo and several valets wait to confound Suzanne and Count; Figaro is miserable. Marcellina, Susanna and the Countess arrive; Suzanne awaits the Count; the other women hide. Chérubin seeks Fanchette, instead finds the Countess, who is disguised as Suzanne. The Count arrives; receives a kiss from Cherubin, who meant to kiss the Countess, who is disguised as Suzanne;
Act Four *A gallery with candelabras, decorated with garlands and flowers for a fête* Suzanne promises Figaro she will not meet the Count. The Countess persuades her		

(continued)

A LIGHTER TONE

TABLE 3.5 Continued

Le Mariage de Figaro (Beaumarchais)	*Le Nozze di Figaro* (DaPonte/Mozart)	*Le Page Inconstant* (Aumer after Dauberval/ arr. Habeneck)
Act Four	**Act Three**	**Act Three**
to do so after all; she dictates a letter for Suzanne to send to the Count. Chérubin, dressed as a girl, celebrates with the villagers; is discovered by Antonio. Wedding celebration; Suzanne's letter is passed to the Count. Fanchette guilelessly reveals to Figaro Suzanne's plans to meet the Count.	the loss of the Count's affections; vows to regain his love. The Countess dictates a letter for Susanna to send to the Count; Cherubino, dressed as a girl, celebrates with the villagers; is discovered by Antonio. Wedding celebration; Susanna's letter is passed to the Count.	the page flees after touching the Count's clothes to confirm his hunch that he has kissed a man; the Count woos his wife, thinking she is Susanne. Figaro realizes his wife is in disguise; he pretends to woo the Countess; Suzanne is angry. The Count is furious with Figaro, demands punishment. General bewilderment and stupefaction. Everyone is reconciled; the Count is forgiven. Divertissement: Joy and celebration.
Act Five *A chestnut grove; pavilions on either side; a garden seat downstage* Fanchette, with a lantern, hides from Figaro; Figaro, Bazile, Bartholo, Brid'oison, Gripe-Soleil, valets, and workmen, all invited by Figaro, wait to confound Suzanne; Figaro is miserable. Marcellina, Susanna and the Countess arrive; Susanna waits for the Count while the other women hide. Chérubin seeks Fanchette, instead finds the Countess,	**Act Four** *The gardens of the castle at twilight* Barbarina guilelessly reveals to Figaro Susanna's plans to meet the Count. Figaro, furious, tells Marcellina and plans revenge; Marcellina, alone, bemoans the fate of women. Barbarina hides from Figaro; Figaro, Basilio and Bartolo wait to confound Sus.; Figaro, with a lantern, is miserable. Marcellina, Susanna and the Countess arrive; Susanna	

(continued)

TABLE 3.5 Continued

Le Mariage de Figaro (Beaumarchais)	Le Nozze di Figaro (DaPonte/Mozart)	Le Page Inconstant (Aumer after Dauberval/ arr. Habeneck)
Act Five who is disguised as Suzanne. The Count arrives; receives a kiss from Chérubin, who meant to kiss the Countess, who is disguised as Suzanne; the Count sends Chérubin away, woos his wife, thinking she is Suzanne. Figaro realizes his wife is in disguise; he pretends to woo the Countess; Suzanne is angry. Pedrillo returns from Seville The Count is furious with Figaro, demands punishment. General bewilderment and stupefaction. Everyone is reconciled; the Count is forgiven. Joy and celebration.	**Act Four** warmly summons the Count while the other women hide. Cherubino seeks Barbarina, instead finds the Countess, who is disguised as Susanna. The Count arrives; receives a kiss from Cherubino, who meant to kiss the Countess, who is disguised as Susanna; the Count sends Cherubino away, woos his wife, thinking she is Susanna. Figaro realizes his wife is in disguise; he pretends to woo the Countess; Susanna is angry. General bewilderment and stupefaction. Everyone is reconciled; the Count is forgiven. Joy and celebration.	

Figures 25 and 26. The first 125 measure of the finale of Beethoven's Fifth Symphony accompany the opening of Act One of *Le Page inconstant;* note that harp arpeggios were added sometime after this score had first been copied.)

Mozart's music from *Le Nozze di Figaro* is employed in only one of the five divertissements in *Le Page inconstant:* the music that Suzanne appears to be playing in the *pas de deux* between Chérubin and the Countess is a set of variations on "Voi che sapete." But melodies from *Le Nozze* do crop up fairly often in the dramatic scenes, usually corresponding directly to the action of the opera, thus making the action of the ballet easier to grasp for spectators familiar with Mozart's opera.[91] The arranger uses, for example, quotations from "Cinque, diece" as Figaro measures the bridal chamber; "Se a caso madama" as Suzanne warns Figaro of the Count's designs; "Giovanni liete, fiori spargete" as the peasants celebrate the Count's renunciation of his *droit de seigneur;* "Non più andrai" as Figaro bids farewell to the just-drafted Chérubin; "Dove sono"[92] as the Countess expresses her sadness; "Sull'aria che soave zeffiretto" as the

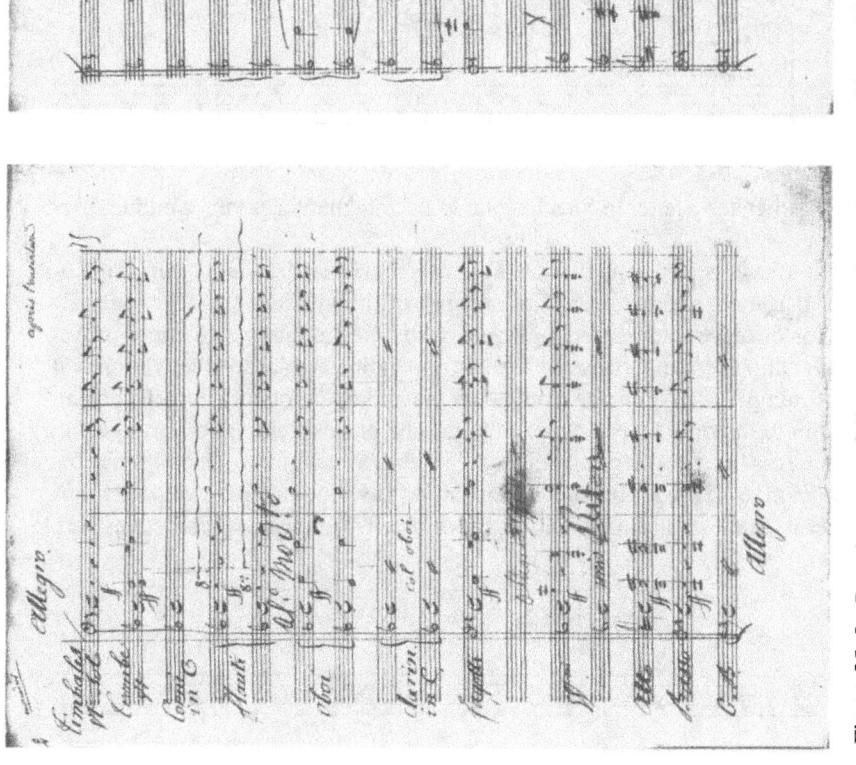

Figure 25. *Le Page inconstant* full score, at curtain-up, Act One (quoting the Fifth Symphony of Beethoven). By permission of the Bibliothèque nationale de France.

Figure 26. *Le Page inconstant* full score, a few measures later. By permission of the Bibliothèque nationale de France.

EXAMPLE 3.1. Figaro visits the Countess's chamber.

Countess dictates a letter to Suzanne; and "Ecco la marcia" as the wedding parties process.

In some cases short snippets from Mozart's music are used as identifying motifs for particular characters.[93] The opening of the overture and "Se voul ballare," for instance, are quoted as Figaro visits the Countess's chamber in Act Two, signaling perhaps (respectively) his impending arrival and then the arrival itself (Example 3.1). A phrase from "Non più andrai," probably quoted to bring Chérubin to mind, is played again as Figaro begins explaining to Suzanne and the Countess his scheme of disguising Chérubin as a woman. He continues his explanation as "Se vuol ballare" is repeated (this time in a new key), perhaps in order to draw attention back to Figaro himself. "Se vuol ballare" gives way

EXAMPLE 3.2. Figaro becomes angry.

to "Non so più" when the page enters. In the last act, the "Se vuol ballare" motif is subjected to a midstream change of mode as the angry Figaro prepares to witness Suzanne's assignation with the Count (Example 3.2). In this manner the arrangers of this score blended the common ballet-pantomime techniques of deploying both borrowed music and recurring melodies to help convey the story.

THE DECLINE OF THE PARODY BALLET

In the 1820s an increasing number of critics expressed reservations about the merits of the parody ballet. Delaforest suggested that, though the deficiencies of mime made parodying necessary, the public demanded some spark of originality, even in works with borrowed plots. *Zémire et Azore* (1824) had failed, he said, because it was nothing more than a "veritable facsimile of Marmontel's opera":

> Choreographers are quite right to choose the subjects for their ballets from popular stories. It is in order to spare spectators the intense application of mind necessary to understand and follow a thread of action that cannot be explained in gestures, because pantomime, one could say, is a dramatic enigma.... The intelligence of all spectators is not such that they can, without effort, rapidly and perfectly understand the desires, the passions, the interests of characters whose names they do not even know.... These inconveniences are avoided by staging well-known plots from mythology and fairy tales ...; they translate plays shown at other theaters into gestures. The public has welcomed these mimic translations.... [T]he *Barbier de Séville, Nina, Les Pages du duc de Vendôme* ... were only imitations of more or less notable works.... But the public accepts these translations only under certain conditions. There must be pretty tableaux, incidents, and a new character to throw some diversion and freshness into the old, washed-out effects and colors of the action, and to enliven a plot that otherwise would no longer have anything exciting about it.[94]

A critic of *Astolphe et Joconde* (1827), similarly, found the ballet to his liking but added that

> [t]ranslating well-known, trite operas into pantomime is not a means of exciting the curiosity of the public.... Can't we find subjects to copy at the Opéra other than those of *Zémire et Azore, Cendrillon, Joconde, Nina,* and the *Pages du duc de Vendôme?* Do we always have to stay in the same rut? and will the public, which is right to ask for something new, never be satisfied? ... Only with original works can public favor be earned.[95]

Castil-Blaze chided the Opéra for its lack of invention in his review of *Cendrillon* (1823): "After having tailored our most beautiful tragedies into opera libretti, the Académie royale turned to the operettas of the Théâtre Feydeau, to form a ballet repertory. You have already seen parading across its stage a great number of comic operas translated into *entrechats*. . . . *Cendrillon* . . . will not be the last borrowing of this type."[96] He wrote happily of Eugène Scribe's contribution of a libretto for the ballet-pantomime *La Somnambule* in 1827, implying that choreographers were sorely in need of a literary philanthropist:

> Choreographers had tried the patience of the public by showing old comedies and have made a repertory of old comic operas and even vaudevilles, adorned with *entrechats* and *pirouettes*. The makers of ballets, who have been bankrupt of ideas and wit for a long time, laid bare their complete indigence. A rich capitalist, an opulent financier of liberal views, takes pity on their wretchedness, opens his safe, and in two shakes of a lamb's tail, that silent copy of the best-known (and often most trivial) plays becomes a witty drama, palpitating with interest; with rare and lively originality.[97]

Plagiarism, too, became a concern of the critics of ballet parodies. "Was it entirely necessary, asked Delaforest, "one could even add, is it entirely fair, to take the work of a living author that is applauded every week? to follow this piece literally in its principal effects, in its most piquant situations, and probably—by the success obtained in this manner—to harm the best interests of the copied work?"[98] After attending a performance of *Astolphe et Joconde,* he exclaimed: "Never has the republic of letters better merited the name Republic of Wolves given to it by Beaumarchais! Here we have, in eight days, two pieces by M. Étienne which, thinly disguised under other titles, serve to make a reputation and a profit for those who doubtless seek one even more than the other."[99] The critic for *La Pandore* wrote sarcastically in his review of *Pages du duc de Vendôme* that choreographers were "too occupied with taking pains to pillage the Opéra Comique to compose what they have bizarrely named 'ballet d'action.'"[100]

Too, there may have been a growing sense that ballet differed in significant ways from texted stage drama. Gautier, at least, implied as much in 1846: "We have already expressed our distaste for this habit . . . of dressing up comic operas, melodramas, or comedies as ballets. Ballet is a special genre, which requires subjects of a very particular nature. . . . A play translated into mimic signs and accompanied by a divertissement is not a ballet."[101] Ballet's special and separate status goes without saying today, but such comments were far from common in Paris in the first half of the nineteenth century. Not everybody at the Opéra became accustomed to wordless ballet overnight, nor did they accept as a truism the idea that ballet could "require subjects of a very particular nature" and unlike those of opera.

To the contrary, as the angry shareholders of the Opéra Comique would have hastened to point out in the 1820s, the Parisian public had been taught that ballet and comic opera could be virtually interchangeable. After all, the Opéra's directors had managed with impunity to reach beyond the two genres it was legally allowed in order to parade "a great number of comic operas translated into *entrechats*" across its stage.[102]

Eventually, of course, public taste came around to Gautier's point of view and the Opéra began to forsake these ballet "facsimiles." Newly invented stories (like *La Somnambule* and *L'Ile des Pirates*) came to be more highly prized. And while choreographers never ceased entirely to draw inspiration from literary models, ballet came to be appreciated as an art form unto itself. By 1845, when the ballet parody version of *Le Diable à Quatre* was created, critics looked upon it as a charming retrospective work; indeed it was one of the last of the old breed of the comic opera parody. But for several decades both before and after the turn of the century, this practice of parodying had flourished, proving that the generic boundary between comic opera and ballet-pantomime could be very porous indeed.[103] Moreover, the long-lived success of the parody ballet had established in the public's mind, ipso facto, two important notions: first, that ballet-pantomime was enough like opera that a given plot could be imparted to an audience with comparable effectiveness in both mediums; and second, that comic opera lent itself well to pantomimic retelling. Thus had the precedent of the light, pleasant, or sentimental (and in some cases downright silly) ballet-pantomime been set at the Opéra nearly from the first days of the *ballet d'action* there in the 1770s.[104]

When Louis Véron, then, made his assessment in 1831 of what it took for ballet-pantomime to succeed, declaring that "dramas and morality plays do not belong in the domain of choreography," he was not breaking altogether with the past. Rather, he was casting his lot with a lighter strain of ballets of which the comic-opera parody had been a part, leaving to other houses the further development of "the most serious fables and most tragic actions" of the type Noverre and Angiolini had created and foreseen for the future.[105] If he rejected the notion of direct parody, he was happy to cultivate the light *tone* of the parodies that had flourished at the Opéra in an earlier age.

Of course, Véron's opinions did not dictate entirely the course of the ballet-pantomime at the Opéra during the July Monarchy.[106] Many of his contemporaries would dispute, for instance, his rather cynical comments about ballet speaking "neither to the mind nor to the heart" by noting the capacity of the Opéra's ballet-pantomimes to move audience's emotions profoundly. But in sizing up his audience and making his best effort to turn a profit, Véron did succeed at discerning important prejudices about ballet of his age in France when he referred clearly to the new notions of verisimilitude with his remark that the public expects "the dance [to develop] naturally out of the dramatic situations" and noted that the "seductions of a young and pretty dancer" were believed to hold a legitimate place in ballet. Clearly these beliefs, held by many in the Opéra's audience, helped make ballet seem a reasonable vehicle for the presentation of the funny, the light, the pastoral, the feminine, and even the erotic.

THE existence and popularity of the parody ballet also brings up an equation well worth considering: if French grand opera was designed to be palpable to the eyes, the parody ballet had, on the other hand, been designed to be dependent upon words (even if at second hand) to make its performances work. This meant that audiences at the Opéra had come to know the independent ballet-pantomime as a type of work that might refer to plots already imparted elsewhere through the use of language (and perhaps quite witty language at that). Therefore, while it is true that these parody ballets were intended to be as visually accessible as possible, they nonetheless swam in the intertextual sea as comic operas—indeed, as all dramas with words. Many critics even held that much of their merit lay in the palpability conferred upon them by such prior connections to a texted model. This raises the matter of ballet's dependence on words, to which I turn in Chapter Four.

CHAPTER FOUR

Ballet-Pantomime and Silent Language

> Today [ballet-pantomime] music is composed entirely according to the fantasy of the composers, and has as much need of explanation as the program. What we have gained is that both are unintelligible.
>
> *La Revue Musicale*, 16 August 1835

BALLET-PANTOMIME at the Opéra in the 1830s and 1840s depended far more upon words than we have imagined. This may seem a strange notion, given the prominent place allotted the Romantic ballet in the critical literature on the ineffability of dance—and the fame of such declarations as Gautier's, that "the real, unique and eternal theme for a ballet is the dance itself," and Mallarmé's, that "the dancer who expresses herself by dance steps understands no other eloquence, even that of gesture."[1] Yet, upon closer inspection of the performance materials of these ballet-pantomimes (particularly the scores and libretti), one may see that words—though never spoken or sung aloud—did play a role.

A few decades back, as we saw in the case of the parody ballet, words had figured quite prominently indeed in the Opéra's ballet-pantomimes, in which choreographers had assumed that some of the spectators had gotten the gist of the plot beforehand at a texted performance, and composers had quoted texted, memory-jogging melodies. But the parody ballet was by no means the only type of ballet in the late eighteenth and early nineteenth centuries to introduce language indirectly into the performance of ballet. One could even venture so far as to say that, in the half-century or so before *La Sylphide*'s première in 1832, composers, choreographers, and designers at the Opéra introduced words into ballet performances in every way but actually having the performers intone them. Thus they helped realize Noverre's glowing prediction of 1760 that "words will become useless, everything will speak . . . "—but did so by providing unspoken verbal cues for the audience.[2]

In this chapter I describe how words played a part in ballet at the Opéra, showing first how they continued to exist in ballet even after the advent of the *ballet d'action* in 1776 with its silent performers, and then demonstrating that certain difficulties arose in the 1830s and 1840s when these silent words, too, began to sink beneath the surface.

98   SILENT LANGUAGE

EXAMPLE 4.1. Instrumental recitative in *Psiché*.

[Psiché to expiate her crime on this rock will become the victim of a monster]
The text given in the score is written under the violin line.

LET us begin with the celebrated ballet-pantomime *Psiché* (1790), by Pierre Gardel and Ernest Miller, one of the most enduring works ever produced at the Opéra, its long life in the repertory stretching from 1790 until 1829. This ballet includes one particularly blatant example of the verbal cue. At a key moment in the action—as a set representing the Temple of Venus collapses onstage to reveal an inscription that is read with chagrin by the ballet characters—the orchestra plays an instrumental recitative in unison and "depicts the inscription in measured time," as the libretto says.[3] That is, the orchestra follows, fairly faithfully, the syllables of the inscription, so that the text could be fit to the music if it were intoned (Example 4.1). Thus the audience read the words onstage and heard, at the same time, a musical "depiction" of them. Further, they could read the sense of the text in the libretti that they held in their hands.[4]

This sort of simultaneous three-way co-ordination—of onstage sign, libretto, and instrumental recitative—was rare in ballets created after 1800. All three of these devices, however, continued to be deployed separately in ballet-pantomime productions at the Opéra well into the nineteenth century.

THE ONSTAGE SIGN

First, it was common through the 1830s for words to be displayed on stage props: on a flag carried by a band of Amazons in *Achille à Scyros* (1804) ("Courage knows no gender"); on a large parchment unfurled by the king's officers in *La Révolte au serail* (1833) ("At the demand of the valiant Ismaél, the king grants freedom to all his women. . . . Zulma alone will remain captive"); on signs affixed to the houses of two important characters in *La Somnambule* (1827) ("The Widow Gertrude, Matchmaker"; "Mother Michaud, Miller"); on a notice (complete with polite contingency clause) posted on the door to the princess's chamber in *La Belle au Bois dormant* (1829) ("She will sleep one hundred years. . . . He who awakens her will marry her, if he is not already married").[5] (Letters and other sorts of documents not legible to the audience were also read "aloud" occasionally by characters, and their text given in the libretto. For example, the title character in *Brézilia*, 1835, reads the words "eternal hatred to men" on a scrap of papyrus.[6])

THE LIBRETTO

Second, as noted in previous chapters, it was common far past mid-century for detailed ballet libretti to be sold to patrons of the Opéra for reading during the performance. (One hyperbolic critic even claimed in 1845 that "the beautiful *salle* of the Opéra [often] resembles a reading room where the readers look up at the performers from time to time."[7]) These libretti, fifteen to forty pages in length, told the story of the ballet-pantomime in great detail, scene by scene, in some cases even recounting the words the characters "spoke." (In fact, they may well have been enjoyed as storybooks by patrons at home as well as in the opera house.[8]) Consider these examples:

La Jolie Fille de Gand (1842) Act One, Tableau One, scene vi

Julia paraît. Elle court dans les bras de Béatrix. Après les premiers épanchements d'amitié, Julia raconte qu'elle s'est faite danseuse.
 «*C'est mon élève*»! s'écrie Zéphiros. Il la présente au Marquis, en la lui recommandant.
 Julia est accompagnée d'un jeune et beau seigneur, qu'elle paraît aimer beaucoup.
 «*Comment!* lui dit Béatrix, en lui rappelant la scène de la flèche dans la perruque de Zéphiros, *ce n'est donc plus don Bustamente, l'ami du Marquis?—Du tout*, répond Julia, avec embarras, en montrant le jeune homme qui l'accompagne; *je n'aime que le comte Léonardo, mon noble protecteur, mon amant.*» Béatrix paraît éprouver un sentiment pénible en entendant cet aveu, et s'éloigne de son ancienne amie avec une sorte de dédaine. Celle-ci se met à rire, et semble lui dire: «*Un jour, tu feras un jour comme moi.*»

Julia appears. She rushes to embrace Béatrix. After a friendly greeting, Julia tells her friend that she has become a dancer. "That's my student!" cries Zéphiros. He presents her to the Marquis.
 Julia is accompanied by a young and handsome nobleman, of whom she appears quite fond.
 "Well!" says Beatrix to him, reminding him of the time an arrow was shot into Zéphiros's wig [by Bustamente], "it is no longer Don Bustamente, the friend of the Marquis?" "Not at all," says Julia, with embarrassment, indicating the young man who is accompanying her. "I love only Count Léonardo, my noble protector, my love." Béatrix seems pained by this avowal, and distances herself from her old friend with a sort of disdain. This makes Julia laugh, and she seems to say, "Someday, someday, you will do the same as I."

La Somnambule (1827) Act Two scene ii

La Mère Michaud, Thérèse, *sortant du moulin*
Thérèse paraît dans le plus grand désordre, et se soutenant à peine. Elle regarde autour d'elle les apprêts de la fête, qui rendent encore son malheur plus cruel. Elle pleure, elle se désespère, elle atteste à la mère Michaud qu'elle est innocente, qu'elle n'a rien à se reprocher.—C'est difficile à croire; mais puisque tu me le dis, mon enfant, me voilà persuadée.—Quoi! vous me pardonnez! vous me rendez votre estime! Ah! je ne suis plus qu'à moitié malheureuse.—Et elle se précipite dans les bras de sa mère, qui essuie ses larmes.—Ma chère enfant, ce n'est pas moi qu'il faut convaincre; tiens, c'est celui-là (en montrant Edmond qui paraît), et tu auras de la peine.[9]

Mother Michaud, Thérèse, *leaving the windmill*
Thérèse appears, greatly distraught, and can scarcely sustain herself. She looks around her at the preparations for the celebration, which render her sorrow all the more painful. She cries, she is in despair, she swears to her mother that she is innocent; that she has done nothing wrong. "That's difficult to believe, but since you tell me so, my child, I am persuaded." "What! You pardon me! You restore my reputation! Ah! I am now only halfway miserable." She throws herself into the arms of her mother, who wipes her tears. "My dear child, it is not I that you must convince; it is he, over there (she points at Edmond, who appears), and you will find it difficult."

Yet for all their detail, these libretti are far shorter, scene for scene, than the explicit *notes de ballet,* that is, manuscript descriptions of action and gestures, apparently used by choreographers when blocking out the dance and mime in rehearsals. These *notes* not only lay out the action and dialogues in detail but also list the tempo marking (and sometimes the meter) of each musical segment. Few such *notes* survive, unfortunately, but those that do offer considerable insight into how precisely mime and action scenes were carried out. Here, for example, are the *notes* for the scene from *La Somnambule* described above:

La Somnambule (1827), Act Three, scene ii excerpt, from the *Notes de ballet.*

No. 2. [Allegro moderato]
1. Thérèse supplie. 2. La mère Michaud. Non, je ne veux rien entendre. 3. mais je t'ai vu sur le lit du seigneur. (Elle pleure)

No. 3 Agitato
1. Thérèse s'approche de sa mère, lui ôte la main de ses yeux et la prie de l'écouter. 2. ma bouche mon coeur vous ont-ils jamais mentis? La mère Michaud: non. 3. Eh bien pouvez-vous croire que je sois allée chez le seigneur pour m'y déshonorer? 4. Non non vous ne le croyez pas (et on se jetant à sa pied). Voyez, mes pleurs vous attestent que je ne suis pas

coupable. La mère Michaud avec attendrissement 5. Elle prend Thérèse par la main 6. mon enfant je te crois, mais c'est bien difficile. Thérèse: ah croyez moi! 7. la Mère Michaud: Je te rends mon amitiés. Elle la presse contre son coeur et lui essuie du larmes. 8. On entend du bruit. 9. La mère Michaud: apperçoit Edmond qui sort de chez Gertrude. 10. Celui-ci sera plus difficile à convaincre; il ne te croira pas.[10]

No. 2 [Allegro moderato]
1. Thérèse beseeches her mother. 2. Mother Michaud. No, I don't want to hear anything about it. 3. But I saw you on the seigneur's bed. (She cries)

No. 3 Agitato
1. Therese approaches her mother, takes her hands away from her eyes and begs her to listen. 2. My mouth, my heart; have they ever lied to you? Mother Michaud: no. 3. Well, can you believe that I went to the Seigneur's house to dishonor myself? 4. No, no you don't believe that (and she throws herself at her feet). See, my tears attest that I am not guilty. Mother Michaud with compassion 5. She takes Thérèse by the hand 6. My child I believe you, but it is very difficult. Thérèse: oh believe me! 7. Mother Michaud: I am so fond of you. She presses her to her heart and dries her tears. 8. A noise is heard. 9. Mother Michaud sees Edmond, who is leaving Gertrude's house. 10. He will be more difficult to convince; he will not believe you.

Thus the spectators saw an impassioned, carefully choreographed conversation taking place, and those with libretto in hand could even read the dialogue the gestures were meant to convey.

THE INSTRUMENTAL RECITATIVE

Third, the instrumental recitative, a device sometimes used in 18th-century *ballet d'action* scores, continued to accompany ballet characters' conversations in the first three or four decades of the nineteenth century.[11] (And, as David Charlton has pointed out, the recitative found its way into other sorts of instrumental music as well in the late eighteenth and early nineteenth centuries, including concert music, in which its expressive powers could be potent.[12]) Some were designed to match particular words; an oboe, for example, expresses the hermit's words as he responds to a knock at the door in *La Tentation* (1832) (Example 4.2).[13] Other such recitatives did not match the words written in the score or libretto. In many cases, in fact, no words were given at all, as in these trombone recitatives (Examples 4.3 and 4.4).

THE AIR PARLANT

Another device, and perhaps the most powerful verbal weapon in the composers' arsenal, was the *air parlant*. This was an excerpt of texted music (sometimes only a phrase or less) borrowed from opera or popular song. When prop-

EXAMPLE 4.2. The hermit responds to a knock.

[there is a knock / who could be knocking / there is a knock / he goes to open up]
Perhaps the composer bore the words "il va ouvrir" in mind as he wrote the music immediately following the second door-knock, or perhaps these notes restate the hermit's question, "Qui peut frapper?" until it melts into the anxious music of the final three measures.

erly deployed, the *air parlant*—which came into use in Parisian ballet scores shortly after the advent of the *ballet d'action* at the Opéra in the eighteenth century and remained a favorite tool of ballet composers there until the 1840s—could make *particular* words pop into the spectator's mind.[15] Like the commercial jingle that so readily recalls brand names and slogans to the listener's mind today, the *air parlant* took advantage of people's natural tendency to recall words linked with melodies.

EXAMPLE 4.3. The nurse offers an explanation in *La Gipsy* (1839).

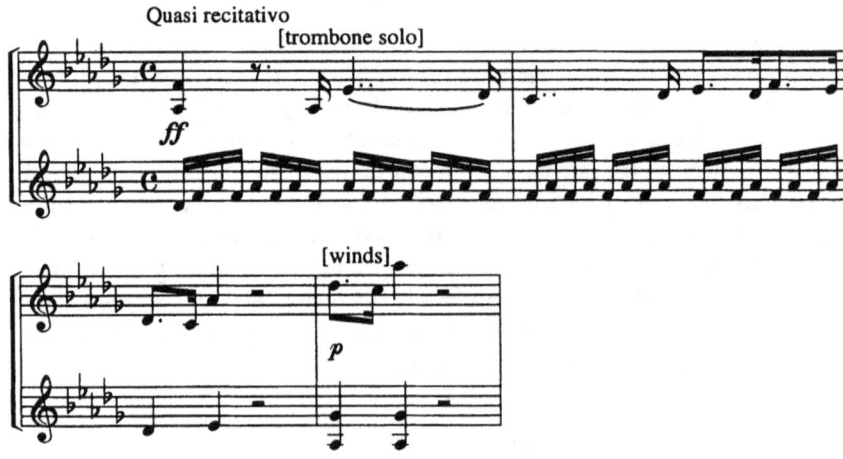

Lord Campbell has just asked the nurse Meg to tell him what has happened; here, according to the libretto, she falls to her knees and explains to him how Stenio saved his daughter. (Please note: this is a transcription for violin rehearsal score.)

EXAMPLE 4.4. The stage manager addresses the public in *Le Diable boiteux* (1836).

In this particularly lengthy trombone recitative, the stage manager of the Madrid Opéra is addressing an angry public after a ballet performance is interrupted by Florinde's feigned ankle injury. His deep voice, solemn mood, and self-important nature are communicated well.[14] (Please note: this is a transcription for a violin rehearsal score.)

The *air parlant,* one could say, was a subset of the borrowed music that (as noted above) composers since the late eighteenth century had relied upon (see Table 4.1). And even after the pastiche ballet score had fallen from favor in the early nineteenth century, composers continued to weave fairly lengthy borrowed snippets into original ballet scores. Ferdinand Hérold, for example, took over the opening chorus from Rossini's *Il Barbiere di Siviglia* ("Piano, pianissimo") for the heroine's tiptoe entrance in *La Fille mal gardée* (1828); Alexandre Montfort borrowed Rossini's music for the plague of darkness and prayer from *Moïse* Act Two for the prayers of the people in the eclipse scene in *La Chatte métamorphosé en femme* (1837); Jean-Madeleine Schneitzhoeffer quoted from Paganini's variations *Le Streghe* (The Witches) for the witches' scene in *La Sylphide* (1832); Gallenberg borrowed the opening of the "Tuba mirum" ("The trumpet, scattering a wondrous sound through the tombs of every land . . . ") from Mozart's Requiem (!) for a sunrise scene in *Brézilia* (1835) in which the protagonist discovers a group of slumbering young beauties in a forest, each in her own hammock. Not every snippet of borrowed music in these scores, of course, held a connotative value—the exposition of J. S. Bach's Fugue in F Major from Book II of the *Wohltemperirte Klavier,* for instance (the fugal subject entries of which Schneitzhoeffer co-ordinated with the appearances of three groups of witches in *La Sylphide*), carries with it no extramusical suggestion.[16] But many of them did. One critic explained the practice in 1836: "One can have recourse to tender and passionate melodies, grand and solemn movements, and, without copying in all its great length the trio of *La Gazza Ladra* or half an act from *Sémiramide,* one can explain the sense of the scene and the gestures of the characters by using known fragments that awaken the memory of an analogous situation or feeling."[17]

The *air parlant,* however (also known as the *proverbe musicale,* and less commonly the *carillon*), is special because—as noted above—it referred directly to particular words. It was defined by Léon Escudier as a "popular air, or

TABLE 4.1 BORROWED MUSIC IN BALLET-PANTOMIME SCORES AT THE PARIS OPÉRA, 1777-1845

Date of First perf.	Work	Composer/Choreographer
26 Jan. 1777	Medée et Jason	Garnier/Vestris, Noverre, Gardel

Final chorus from *Ismène et Ismias* by de la Borde. [F-Po A.236a-b]

| 17 Feb. 1787 | Le Coq du Village* | P. Gardel/M.Gardel |

Excerpts from the original opéra-comique and the "duo de Tic Tac" from *La Servante Justifiée*. [F-Po A.318, *Le Journal de Paris*, 19 Feb. 1787]

| 1 March 1778 | La Chercheuse d'Esprit* | ——/ M. Gardel |

Excerpts from the opéra-comique. [F-Po A.248]

| 9 July 1778 | Annette et Lubin* | Grenier or Gossec/Noverre |

A contredanse from *La Vénitienne* by Dauvergne, an allegretto by Porta, an andante by Della Maria, a romance by de la Borde, a gigue and menuet by Grétry, a menuet by Dezède, a menuet by Floquet, a trio by Fréderic, a tambourin by Grétry, and a contredanse by Dezède. [F-Po A.255 and A.366]

| 18 Aug. 1778 | Ninette à la Cour* | ——/ M. Gardel |

Music by Ciampi (*Bertholdo alla Corte*), Latilla, Cocchi, Sellitti, Jommelli, Vinci, Méhul and Cimarosa, and "Vive Henri Quatre." [F-Po A.257b; Chouquet, 360]

| 18 Nov. 1779 | Mirsa | Gossec/ M. Gardel |

One version of this score includes an air from Dezède's *Peronne sauvée*, Lefèbvre's *Imitations d'une parole*, and excerpts from a symphonie concertante of Widerkehr. [F-Po A.273a-b]

| 15 Feb. 1781 | La Fête de Mirza | Gossec/ M. Gardel |

A symphonie-overture for Act Four by Gossec, and excerpts from Gluck and Grétry. [F-Po A.284a-b]

| 26 July 1783 | Le Premier Navigateur | Grétry and others/ M. Gardel |

Excerpts of Méhul, Grétry, and of *Les Sauvages* by Rameau. [F-Po A.309]

| 14 Dec. 1790 | Psiché | Miller/ P. Gardel |

(Act One) Excerpts from Kreutzer, Haydn, an air from *Armide*, a "Romance pastoralle" by Bertelmont, "Villanelle Ranita" by Nomann, *Le Poisson d'Or* by Vogel, *Atine et Zamorin* by Rigel, *L'Embarras des richesses* by Grétry, a romance of Cambini, and *Peronne sauvée* by Dezède; (Act Two) Cherubini, Paisiello, the overture of *Panurge* by Grétry, a menuet by Fisher, *Richard Coeur de Lion* by Grétry, *Annette et Lubin* by Gossec, *L'Oracle* by Granier or Miller, an air from *Le Poisson d'Or;* (Act Three) *Theonis* by Trial, Haydn, *Iphigénie en Tauride* by Gluck, *Didon* by Piccini, *Orphée* by Piccini. [F-Po A.337]

| 7 March 1793 | Le Jugement de Paris | Méhul/ P. Gardel |

Excerpts from (Act One) a menuet of Pleyel, a rondeau from the clarinet concerto of Michell; (Act Two) Haydn, Nicolo, a violin concerto by Kreutzer, *Psiché*; (Act Three) "Que de grâce" from *Iphigénie en Aulide*, symphonic variation on Papageno's air from *Die Zauberflöte*. [F-Po A.317]

(continued)

TABLE 4.1 Continued

Date of First perf.	Work	Composer/Choreographer
31 Dec. 1799	*Héro et Leandre*	Lefèbvre/ Milon

The initials of composers from whom music was borrowed (L, H, D, M, P, and G) are noted in the score. [F-Po A.370]

| 14 Jan. 1803 | *Daphnis et Pendrose* | Méhul/ P. Gardel |

(Act One) An overture by Himmer, music of Haydn, horn solos and harp music by Duvernoy and Dalvimare, an air concertant by Devienne; (Act Two) an overture by Winter and Kreutzer, and excerpts from *Aspasie* by Miller, and *Echo et Narcisse* by Gluck. [F-Po A.384]

| 18 Dec. 1804 | *Achille à Scyros* | Cherubini/ Gardel |

Excerpts from (Act One) Haydn, Viotti; (Act Two) Weigel, Catel, Righini, Méhul, Haydn, horn solo and harp music of Cousineau; (Act Three) Righini. [F-Po A.397]

| 10 May 1805 | *Acis et Galathée* | Darondeau and Gianella/ Duport |

The air of *Atys* by Schneilroesser [Schneitzhoeffer?], an air of Dreuilhe, "Vive Henri IV," excerpts from *Le Jugement de Paris* and *Caravane* by Grétry, the finale of *Lys*, and a "pass russe." [F-Po A.399 I-II, LaJarte, 38]

| 12 June 1806 | *Paul et Virginie** | Kreutzer/ P. Gardel |

A "Polacca à Rondo" for the dancer Albert. [F-Po A.405]

| 20 Dec. 1808 | *Alexandre chez Apelles* | Catel/ P. Gardel |

Excerpts from Mozart, an allegretto of Haydn, an andante in A Major by Paër. [F-Po A.416]

| 4 Jan. 1810 | *Vertumne et Pomone* | Lefèbvre, arr./ P. Gardel |

Excerpts from *Les Sauvages* by Rameau and a rondo by Dussek. [F-Po A.421]

| 8 June 1810 | *Persée et Andromède* | Méhul, arr. and comp./ P. Gardel |

Excerpts from Haydn's *Creation*, *Ariodant*, and works of Paër. [F-Po A.423, Chouquet, 384]

| 11 April 1811 | *Vénus et Adonis* | Lefèbvre/ P. Gardel |

An air from *La Folle Soirée* and an air of Rossini. [F-Po A.415a]

| 27 June 1811 | *L'Enlèvement des Sabines* | Berton/ Milon |

An air from *Françoise de Foix* and excerpts from the finale of *Montano et Stéphanie*. [F-Po A.427, Chouquet, 385]

| 28 April 1812 | *L'Enfant Prodigue* | Berton/ P. Gardel |

(Act One) Excerpts from the prayer in *Joseph* by Méhul, the romance from Haydn's *Reine de France*, Viotti, and a symphony in C of Haydn. [F-Po A.429]

| 25 July 1815 | *L'Heureux Retour* | Persuis, Berton, Kreutzer, arr./ Milon, P. Gardel |

A set of variations on "Charmante Gabrielle" by Schneitzhoeffer, and the tune "Vive Henri Quatre." [F-Po A.442, LaJarte, 86]

(*continued*)

TABLE 4.1 Continued

Date of First perf.	Work	Composer/Choreographer
12 Dec. 1815	*Flore et Zéphire*	Venua/ Didelot

Airs of Hus-Desforges and Lefèbvre and the song "Réveillez-vous, belle endormie." [Chouquet, 387, Castil-Blaze, 320-323]

26 Nov. 1816	*Les Sauvages*	Lefèbvre/ Milon

Airs from Lefèbvre's *Vertumne et Pomone*. [F-Po A.448]

19 June 1820	*Clari*	Kreutzer/ Milon

"Ju suis braver les coups de sort" from Grétry's *Le Sylvain*, "Descends du Ciel, doux Hymenéee" from Salieri's *Les Danaïdes,* and "Ne doutez jamais de ma flamme" from Gluck's *Iphigénie en Aulide*. [*Le Journal des Débats*, 22 June 1820; *Clari* libretto, 1820]

18 Dec. 1823	*Le Page Inconstant**	Habeneck, arr./ Aumer

Excerpt from Beethoven's Fifth Symphony, from *Le Nozze di Figaro* by Mozart, and from an earlier version of the ballet by Gyrowetz. [Guest, 52]

29 May 1826	*Mars et Vénus ou les Filets de Vulcain*	Schneitzhoeffer/ Blache

Excerpts from Mozart, Haydn, and Grétry. [*Journal des Débats*, 1 June 1826]

29 Jan. 1827	*Astolphe et Joconde*	Hérold/ Aumer

Opera airs, *Joconde*, excerpts from a rondo by Hummel. [Guest, 70.]

19 Sept. 1827	*La Somnambule*	Hérold/ Aumer

"Dormez, mes chères amours," "Malbrouck s'en va-t-en guerre," a duo from Maçon, a fragment of a duo from Armida and from the sextet of *La Cenerentola* by Rossini, excerpts from *Elisa e Claudio*. [B.N. Vm6250, *La Revue Musicale*, 1827, pp. 215–16]

2 July 1828	*Lydie*	Hérold/ Aumer

An excerpt from the overture of Weber's *Der Freischütz*. [Guest, 88]

17 Nov. 1828	*La Fille mal gardée*	Hérold/ Aumer

The overture from Martini's *Le Droit du Seigneur*, the opening chorus from Rossini's *Il Barbiere di Siviglia*, the storm music from Rossini's *La Cenerentola*, the song "La jeune et gentille Lisette" (also used by Haydn in his 85th Symphony), and many excerpts from the score composed for the Bordeaux version of this ballet in 1789. [Guest and Lanchbery, "The Scores of 'La Fille Mal Gardée' "]

27 April 1829	*La Belle au Bois dormant*	Hérold/ Aumer

Excerpts from the overture from Weber's *Oberon* and a cavatina from Rossini's *La Pietra del Paragone*. [F-Pn MS Vm6253]

3 May 1830	*Manon Lescaut*	Halévy/ Aumer

Duo from Garcia's *Il Califfo di Bagdad,* excerpts from *L'Amour vainqueur;* the songs "La Camargo," "Dans les Gardes françaises," "Avant la bataille," and "Vive la vin de Ramponneau." [*La Revue Musicale*, 1830, 11-15; *Le Corsaire*, 5 May 1830; *Le Moniteur universel*, 5 May 1830]

(*continued*)

TABLE 4.1 Continued

Date of First perf.	Work	Composer/Choreographer
12 March 1832	La Sylphide	Schneitzhoeffer/ F. Taglioni

Excerpts from the trio of Boïeldieu's *Le Calife de Bagdad*, from the Fugue in F Major of J. S. Bach's *Wohltemperirte Klavier*, Book II, and from Gluck's *Orphée et Euridice*; an air by Pauline Duchambge, and Paganini's variations, "Le Streghe." [F-Po A.501; Castil-Blaze, cited in Guest, 117]

| 15 Sept. 1834 | La Tempête | Schneitzhoeffer/ Coralli |

"Dormez, mes chères amours," and excerpts of arias from *Alceste, Richard Coeur de Lion, Le Prisonnier, Le Pré-aux clercs, Le Nozze di Figaro, les Danaïdes*. [Castil-Blaze, cited in Guest, 135; *La Gazette Musicale de Paris*, 21 Sept. 1834]

| 12 Aug. 1835 | L'Ile des Pirates | Carlini, Gide/ Henry |

Excerpts from *Sémiramide* of Rossini and a Beethoven sonata. [Chouquet, 399]

| 1 June 1836 | Le Diable boîteux | Gide/Coralli |

Excerpts from works of Rossini, Auber, Hérold, and Grétry. [*Le Ménestrel*, 5 June 1836]

| 16 Oct. 1837 | La Chatte Metamorphosée en femme | Montfort/ Coralli |

Introduction to *Moïse*. [Guest, 166]

| 28 Jan. 1839 | La Gipsy | Benoist, Thomas, Marliani/ Mazilier |

"God Save the Queen," excerpts from Weber's *Preciosa* and from works of Mozart, Beethoven, Hummel, and Schubert [*La France Musicale*, 3 Feb. 1839; Chouquet, 401]

| 24 June 1839 | La Tarentule | Gide/ Coralli |

Excerpts from works of Grétry, Meyerbeer, Halévy, Auber, and Boïeldieu; the tune "La Danza." [The Times, qu. by Beaumont, 129; *La Revue et Gazette Musicale*, 27 June 1839]

| 12 Sept. 1840 | Le Diable amoureux | Benoist, Reber/ Mazilier |

Excerpts from Spohr's *Faust*, Kreutzer's *Lodoïska*, and works of Reber, including the "Pirate Song." [*Journal des Débats*, 26 Sept. 1840, *La Revue et Gazette Musicale*, 11 Oct. 1840]

| 7 August 1845 | Le Diable à Quatre* | Adam/ Mazilier |

An excerpt from Méhul's *L'irato*, a chorus of Cagliostro, a motif of Glinka, and the songs "Amusez-vous, oui, je vous le conseille," "Mon mari n'est pas là," "Moi, je pense comme Grégoire," [Guest, 249; *La France Musicale*, 17 Aug. 1845]

*Denotes a parody ballet (derived from another work).
  This table does not list every ballet that used borrowed music, nor does it offer in every case a complete list of borrowed music for those ballets included. The source of information about the borrowings is given in brackets and in many cases is the score itself (most often annotations therein).
  In this table I refer to the following books by author only: Beaumont's *Complete Book of Ballets*, Castil-Blaze's *La Danse et les ballets depuis Bacchus jusqu'à Mlle Taglioni*, Chouquet's *Histoire de la musique dramatique*, Guest's *The Romantic Ballet in Paris*, and LaJarte's *Bibliothèque musicale du Théâtre de l'Opéra, Catalogue*.

fragment thereof, which recalls to mind the words joined to the melody."[18] As another critic explained, "The spectator, through the motifs, recognizes the words that aren't heard."[19] There is a great advantage, wrote Gustave Chouquet, in using " . . . the words of a well-known motif to explain changes in the plot";[20] Castil-Blaze offers a lengthy definition in his dictionary of 1821:

> Music united with poetry makes such a strong impression on the mind that the melodies, even when they are divested of the charm of the words, still keep their meaning. They are only recollections, but this memorative expression acts in a very powerful manner. By analogy, the term "musical proverbs" is used for tunes, or fragments of tunes, which recall to the imagination a flash of slyness, a witty thought, a maxim, a compliment, a declaration of love, an oath, an invocation, an expression of admiration, of desire, of joy, of sadness, etc., which were included in the words joined to the melody. . . . These tunes which have been repeated for so long . . . are engraved in everyone's memories. . . .[21]

So familiar was the public with "these tunes," in fact, that Castil-Blaze—most unfortunately, from the standpoint of the historian—considered it unnecessary to name the sources, or to provide notation, of the thirty-odd *airs parlants* he lists in his dictionary entry on the subject. He lists texts only, for example:

> Que d'attraits, que de majesté!
> Où peut-on être mieux qu'au sein de sa famille!
> C'est ici le séjour des Grâces
> Quand le bien-aimé reviendra
> Jurons de nous aimer toujours
> Adieu, conservez dans votre âme
> Vive Henri Quatre[22]

(It should be noted that the tune "Vive Henri Quatre," which Tchaikovsky wove into the final scene of *Sleeping Beauty* to help conclude that ballet "with great pomp and ostentation," recalls the Parisian tradition of using it to suggest just those qualities.[23]) Castil-Blaze goes on to say that *airs parlants* provide

> ingenious allusions, and there never lacks applause for the musician who executes them appropriately in a serenade, a divertissement, a public festival. A clarinet sounds the motif and the words fly from mouth to mouth. The use of these *airs parlants,* these musical proverbs, is of great help for the understanding of the pantomime in ballets. They also add to the pungency of certain couplets of vaudeville. There is no subject in life, no passion which is not best expressed in music. *One would have to be a complete stranger to our lyric stage not to understand the meaning of most of the melodies.*[24]

Indeed, the popularity of operatic sources for *airs parlants* does suggest a very opera-literate audience, or at least an audience familiar with some of opera's more popular tunes. In one scene from *Le Jugement de Paris* (1793), for example, a shepherd, faced with three beauties from whom to choose, turns first to Juno as the orchestra plays the melody "Que d'attraits!" [Such allurement!] from Gluck's *Iphigénie en Aulide*. Next, as a critic described it, "he turns to Minerva, as the orchestra continues the same air, saying *such majesty!* Finally, he fixes on Venus, continuing to follow the same air in the orchestra, pronouncing *such grace! Such beauty!*"[25] (Note that the critic uses the verbs "say" and "pronounce." Another common phrase was *semble dire* [seems to say], which is used not only in ballet-pantomime libretti but in opera staging manuals, in descriptions of pantomime scenes.)

Further examples of operatic *airs parlants* in the Opéra's ballet-pantomime repertory in the first decades of the nineteenth century are plentiful. Often, the words of the *air parlant* were introduced by the composer as a way of commenting, like a narrator, on the action. In *La Somnambule* (1827), for example (see Chapter One, Example 4), the orchestra plays the opening phrases of "Che sarà" (a piece sometimes translated as "What a fix!") from Rossini's *La Cenerentola* when Thérèse sleepwalks into the Seigneur's chamber. In some cases the words seem to be enunciated by a particular character. In *Clari* (1820), the orchestra plays "Descends du ciel, doux Hyménée" [Descend from the sky, sweet Hymen] from Salieri's *Les Danaïdes,* as the heroine looks lovingly at the Duke, hoping that he will honor his pledge to marry her. Later, as described in the libretto, "she expresses that she *can face cruel fate but not the reproaches of a father . . .* " [from Grétry's *Le Sylvain*]. Her tears suffocate her."[26] In *La Sylphide* (1832), as James watches his beloved Sylphide die in his arms, the orchestra plays "J'ai perdu mon Euridice" [I have lost my Euridice] from Gluck's *Orphée et Eurydice* (Example 4.5). In *La Tempête* (1834), when Lea begins to fall in love, the orchestra plays "Je sens mon coeur qui bat, qui bat" [I feel my heart beating] from Grétry's *Richard Coeur de Lion;* when Oberon asks her what is troubling her, she mimes her reply as the orchestra plays "Voi che sapete" [You who know the nature of love] from *Le Nozze di Figaro.*[27]

Folksongs, too, were often quoted as *airs parlants:* "Dormez chères Amours" [Sleep, dear loved ones] is played as Thérèse settles down to sleep in *La Somnambule* (1827); "Réveillez-vous, belle endormie," [Wake up, lovely sleepers] is played in *Flore et Zéphire* (1808) as Zéphire awakens, one by one, a group of slumbering nymphs[28]; "Mon mari n'est pas là" [My husband isn't here] is played in *Le Diable à Quatre* (1845) as Mazurka explains that she enjoys dancing when her cruel husband is absent. (Later, as the devil arranges for the Countess and Mazurka to exchange places, the orchestra plays a Beethoven melody that had been given the words "Change, change-moi, Brama" [Change, change me, Brama] for a popular vaudeville at the Gymnase theater a few years earlier.[29]) For *Manon Lescaut* (1830), Halévy wanted the orchestra to play "Où allez-vouz, Monsieur l'abbé?" [Where are you going, Mr. Abbot?] as the abbot

EXAMPLE 4.5. Air parlant, "J'ai perdu mon Euridice" in *La Sylphide*.

[Despair of James / I have lost my Euridice.]
It was somewhat unusual for the text of an air parlant to be written into the score, as it is here.

attempted to steal into Manon's room, but the administration rejected the idea, perhaps for fear that it would be interpreted as anticlerical.[30] That an instrumental melody could be so censored gives some sense of how powerful the link between music and unsaid text was perceived to be.

To sum up: until the third and fourth decades or so of the nineteenth century, the Opéra's spectators were regularly offered reminders of ballet-pantomime's linguistic nature and at the same time were availed of several semiotic tools that helped them follow the action of ballet-pantomimes. They could read signs on the stage and libretti in their laps. They could also hear music that sometimes contributed to the illusion that the character was talking (the recitative), as well as music that offered them pertinent snippets of text (the *air parlant*).

The 1830s and 1840s, however, brought several changes. The first of these was a decline in the use of the texted sign. Another was the gradual falling away of the instrumental recitative, which lost favor to—and in some cases was subsumed within—other types of music still imitative of human speech but much more subtly so. For, while ballet libretti continued to recount characters' conversations, the music composed to accompany such talking scenes was becoming more abstract. That is, composers of ballet music, without forsaking their habit of offering a musical envoicing of onstage conversations, began to shift to a style of speechlike (or *parlante*) music that imitated the human voice in a far less obvious fashion.

One such imitative technique was to provide short bursts of instrumental laughter; for instance, this passage, in which snobbish ballerinas at the Madrid Opera laugh at the overly rustic dancing of Paquita in *Le Diable boiteux* (Example 4.6).

EXAMPLE 4.6. Laughing in *Le Diable boiteux* (1836).

Composers also wrote another sort of music that avoided specific "quotation" of words but did imitate the inflections of the human voice by employing the wide tessitura of spoken French, sometimes breaking the flow with rests (Example 4.7). Another common technique was to use syncopation (Example 4.8). Yet another kind of *parlante* music sounded as though it were following the speech-rhythms of particular words, like the recitative, but it avoided the repeating-note melodic formulas of many earlier recitatives (Example 4.9). Occasionally, the composer seized upon the speech rhythms of one of the opening words or phrases in a conversation and used them as the basis of several measures of music, though unless one is familiar with the practice it is difficult to

EXAMPLE 4.7. Parlante music in *La Fille du Danube* (1836).

EXAMPLE 4.8. Parlante music in *L'Orgie* (1831).

EXAMPLE 4.9. Parlante music in *La Gipsy* (1839).

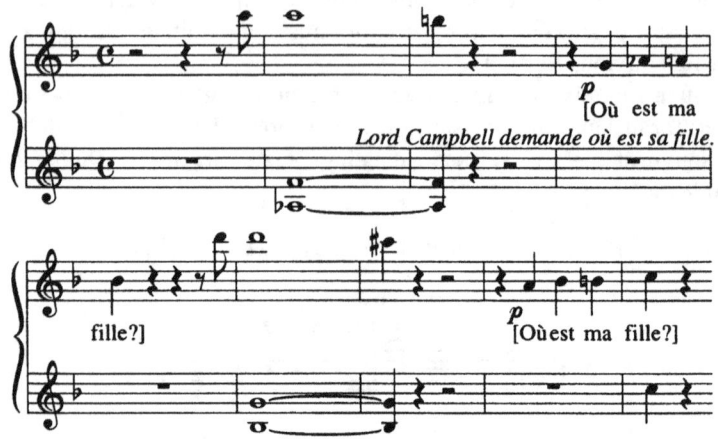

detect these passages as such without the aid of the libretto or an annotated score in which the echoed words happen to be written (Example 4.10).[31] One may also find melodies, only dimly reminiscent of recitative style, which are set in "questioning" and then "confirmatory" harmonies (to borrow David Charlton's terms)—for instance, in this passage from *Giselle* (Example 4.11).[32] The various kinds of speechlike music used in ballet-pantomime, both before and after the erosion of the recitative, were of course meant to echo vocal sounds of the sort that one would hear in everyday life. Ballet characters, after all, lived in a world that could be alive with sound, just as opera characters did—and in this world one could hear not only the "sound of a march," a "big noise"; a thunderstorm, or a village band, but the sounds of human speech: a "noisy and animated crowd," a quarrel, a laugh, a conversation.[33] Yet there is no doubt that, by the 1830s and 1840s, composers were finding more abstract ways to imitate the human voice in ballet-pantomime music.

At the same time, composers were beginning to eschew the *air parlant,* and indeed, all forms of borrowed music, which like ballet parodies, were falling

EXAMPLE 4.10. Parlante music in *La Somnambule* (1827).

EXAMPLE 4.11. Conversational phrases in *Giselle* (1841).

[Bathilde offers her a necklace / Giselle wants to refuse / she insists / Giselle accepts / she is so happy]
One can detect the skeleton of a recitative here, but it is nicely hidden in the melody.

victim to the new taste for originality. What had once been a desirable practice was now ceasing to be so, and a perusal of ballet reviews in the first half of the century demonstrates quite clearly this shift away from pre-existing melodies.

Up until approximately 1830, a good many critics praised composers who could use borrowed music in a skillful manner. These comments are typical: "The music [of *La Somnambule,* 1827] was arranged with infinite grace"; "... with exquisite taste by Hérold"; "The music [of *Nina,* 1813] is by M. Persuis, who has tastefully made selections from known airs which fit the situations the best"; "The music [for *Les amours d'Antoine et de Cléopâtre* (1808)]—a selection from Kreutzer and other eminent composers—is chosen with taste."[34]

COMPLAINTS ABOUT BORROWED MUSIC

In the fourth decade of the century, as the term "composer and arranger . . . " on the affiches and libretti gave way to "composer," the omnipresent praise in the press for skillful arranging gave way to stock compliments for those who could compose great numbers of motives and melodies. "Melodies came easily out of his pen like water from a spring," said a critic of Gyrowetz in a review of *Nathalie* (1832).[35] Pugni's *La Fille de Marbre* (1847), composed in two weeks' time, was said to have had " . . . more motives than other composers could have composed in six months."[36] "The music [for *Ozaï*, 1847] abounds in elegant motives that will be quarried to provide waltzes, fantasies, and contredanses . . . in the second act especially; the melodies are fresh and original."[37] And "the music of *La Péri* [1843] distinguishes itself by a succession of motifs that are, if not fresh and striking, at least elegant and distinguished."[38] And so on.

More important, critics also began to grumble in the 1830s that borrowing music was a less than laudable way to produce a ballet score. A critic of *La Gipsy*, for example, deemed it "unfortunate" that the three composers of the score had "all taken famous composers as their collaborators."[39] And, on the occasion of the debut of *Giselle*, the score of which was praised for being so original, Escudier drew a contrast between *Giselle* and other scores, saying disapprovingly that hardly any of the others had "cost the composer any imagination."[40] The same distaste for lack of originality is reflected in these comments about *Le Diable amoureux:* "[Though] I heard some people reproach [the composer] for not having used enough known airs . . . I believe, for my part, that what Messieurs Benoist and Réber lack in plagiarisms . . . they have amply won in dramatic expression."[41] These remarks, in a review of *La Gipsy*, make the point with a bit more vitriol:

> Ballets are antiliterary and antimusical works. I do not understand why people of good sense come to sit on the *banquettes* at the Opéra and remain planted there for four hours watching *entrechats*. This music, why is it important? If the *entrechats*, the *ailes de pigeon*, the hooped petticoats, the naive grimaces and the coy little hand-under-the-chin cuteness bore you, then too bad. "But one goes to the ballet to hear the music." I could have predicted you'd say that! And it would be just fine if there *were* music in the newer ballets. But, I ask, where is this ballet music? Who is familiar with this ballet music? Who has heard it? I beseech all honest people who have some knowledge of this alleged music to present themselves immediately at the office of *La France Musicale*—I will give them an honest reward, or an I.O.U. from Maurice Schlesinger, whatever their choice may be.

Really, I have never heard such a good joke: ballet music! That is, when you put on a new ballet, you apply to a known composer, and invite him to put in the accompaniments. The known composer applies to even better known composers; to ALL known composers. He opens all known scores, he chooses scads of known airs, he makes an inlay of Mozart, Haydn, Beethoven, Doche, Adolphe Adam, Monpou, Gluck, Rossini, Auber, and adds a head and a tail (several tails!) and—how thrilling—*voilà,* a new ballet.[42]

Escudier, in his review of *La Tarentule* in 1839, offers another indictment of the practice of borrowing:

Since it is agreed that [ballet] music must be only an arrangement, the composer finds that he is much better served by memory than by inspiration. Ballet music is a veritable mosaic into which one inserts pell mell the airs of Rossini, Boïeldieu, Auber, Meyerbeer, etc. etc. . . . These airs are most often denatured, because the rhythm has to be changed and the nuances altered. Thus the most respectable and most sacred things are confounded in a *mélange* of excerpts without cohesion and without a sense of continuity; the greatest masters have paid their tribute to this bastard genre. . . . Mozart and Beethoven have been denuded to cover the nakedness of [this] . . . music. . . .[43]

Further indication of the changing status of borrowed music is the fact that Opéra officials, in 1835 in the libretto of *L'Ile des Pirates,* for the first time listed the names of composers whose music had been borrowed (Rossini and Beethoven) along with the names of the composers and arrangers of this score (Carlini and Gide). One critic objected to this departure from the long-standing practice of leaving unmentioned the names of composers from whom excerpts had been borrowed:

These sorts of contributions (which one could call "forced") have always been permitted and are entirely authorized by custom. The public, which is not used to seeing composers cited by these musical pillagers, can mistakenly think that Beethoven was brought back to life to set these *pas* to music . . . or that Rossini, who seems not to want to write operas anymore, has resumed his career in order to compose a galop or a mazurka [for the ballet]. Will they be able to discern the difference?—the same public that cannot tell the difference between Carlini and Rossini, Gide and Beethoven. A vexing error for Gide and Carlini perhaps, but one even more deplorable from the standpoint of Beethoven and Rossini.[44]

Perhaps this unaccustomed billing was made in a deliberate attempt to lend prestige to this production, or even to imply (wrongly of course) that Rossini himself had taken part in the production of this piece. Or perhaps someone decided, in a break with longstanding policy, that any composer whose music was included in the score deserved credit in the playbill. In either case—though

Opéra officials never did it again—it may be read as a sign of the times, reflecting a shift in the way borrowed music was regarded.

MORE COMPLAINTS

In the 1830s and 1840s, borrowed music, *airs parlants,* and texted signs were falling from favor and speechlike music was becoming more abstract. These phenomena, taken together, served to erode much of the external assistance that ballet audiences had grown accustomed to. And not surprisingly, there arose during the same time two waves of complaints that point to a certain amount of confusion. The first of these concerned the "obscurities" of pantomime and foretold the post-1850 trend of shortening mime scenes and lengthening dance scenes at the Opéra. Some of these complaints bear quoting at some length because they offer a picture quite at variance with the rosier impression left by words of praise more often quoted in accounts of nineteenth-century ballet. Indeed, they make quite plain the nature of the audience's sometime confusion (and, incidentally, offer some of the best extant clues about what pantomime of the period looked like).[45]

This critic for *La Gazette Musicale de Paris,* for example, opines that a texted sign was needed to compensate for mime's insufficiencies:

> I have an aversion to ballets; I think that this spectacle, in which wordless gestures are the sole means of expressing the thought (when thought there be) is excessively absurd, a hundred times more so than a spoken drama [without gestures would be].... If such a thing were attempted by poets, it would certainly be unsuccessful.... Every day we see ... actors dislocating their arms, exposing themselves to the possibility of injuries to the spinal column, and disfiguring themselves by rolling their eyes and contorting themselves ridiculously in order to make us understand some dramatic commonplace.... Are their laborious efforts met with success? So little that every time they try to convey an idea on which the general sense of the piece depends, they are forced to write it out and display the words for all to see, as in *Sleeping Beauty:* "She will sleep a hundred years."
>
> ... A young Arab, newly arrived in Paris, said to me one day, "I went to see the mutes perform last night."
>
> "The mutes—what do you mean?"
>
> "Yes, I went to the Académie Royale de Musique. They were performing a piece which bored me a bit because, not having studied sign language, I understood nearly nothing. I was surprised by the beauty of your mute women; it is rare that these afflicted creatures don't have other, more obvious infirmities as well."
>
> "But I swear to you there are no mutes at the Opéra. If you'd sat closer to the stage, the immoderate babble of these ladies would have reassured you of this, perhaps much more than you would have desired."
>
> "Then why didn't the actors speak in this play that I saw?"

"Because, in that kind of show, the word is prohibited."

"You are kidding me! How could I ever believe that a people so advanced in civilization, so ingenious as the French people, would adopt as a special kind of entertainment such an enormously stupid thing. I would sooner believe that you would prohibit your writers from using more than a certain number of words in their writings, to the exclusion of the rest of the language; that in certain theaters in Paris, you have dancers who may not dance except on one foot, singers who can only use six notes, and a public that will applaud this foolish mutilation of their abilities."

One could see that my interlocutor, though well educated in the French language, still hadn't had enough time to adjust to European customs. . . . However, we share his viewpoint in regard to ballet-pantomimes. . . .[46]

Frédéric Soulié complains, similarly, about the obscurity of the mime passages in *La Fille de Danube,* finding fault with the choreographer (Filippo Taglioni) in particular:

An old woman pesters the young lover. On the stage and in a ballet, any old woman who pesters a young man is the mother of the young man's girlfriend. Wrong! In the libretto this woman is a benefactress who has found Fleur-des-champs on the banks of the Danube, and to whom the poor girl never said anything, because she's a mute. In truth, the libretto is very interesting!

Scarcely is the lover dispatched by the mother of Fleur-de-Champs than a squire arrives with trumpeters. The squire says,—"Monsieur, what does he say?" "I don't know—do you have a libretto?" "No. I don't understand." "Neither do I." "Here's a libretto." "Thank you." Ah! It's one of the baron's officers, who announces that his master is summoning all of the young ladies to his castle so he can choose a bride—one who won't die like the wives of his elder brother have. "By Jove, I like this libretto very much!" . . . Look; there she is in person, with a veil.—Read the libretto, you blockhead! It isn't she, it's her shadow. Since the libretto tells me so, I am sure of it. . . .[47]

Berlioz expresses a general distaste for pantomime in his florid review of *La Chatte metamorphosée en femme,* making the point that complicated details could not be conveyed through conventional gesture alone:

Writing a program for a ballet is not a difficult thing in itself; it is much harder to write a critique of the plot, especially when one has the bad luck of having understood nothing of the pantomime and of not wanting to consult the libretto. I find myself in precisely that situation here. . . . Innumerable experiences have shown me that the mimic art was a closed book for me, and that I could see the index finger of the right hand pointing toward the forehead hundreds of times without divining that they meant to say this: "You see this cap? Well, this cap is a magic cap; when you keep it on your head, the way that I'm wearing it now, there are no spirits about; but when you turn it around, you have all the spirits at your command.

You have power over them; they obey you instantly without a murmur, and should you have the fantasy of changing an animal into a woman, a dog, a cat; this wish would be granted as soon as it was made."

Yes, I confess, I would not yet know, even now, that this simple movement of the finger meant all that, without the obliging help of my colleagues . . . who have charmingly recounted the whole plot of the new piece [in the libretto]. . . .

. . . I have never been able to persuade myself, even now, that my mimic sense was so obtuse that I couldn't discover the . . . fundamental idea, the basic idea, the IDEA, at the first performance of a work of this nature. . . . This is why I was obstinate in passing up the libretto. Vanity! Vanity—all is but vanity! . . . [48]

The same complaint is expressed by A. Lorenz in the satirical publication *La Musée Philipon* in its lampoon of *Giselle:*

Pantomime, this sublime polyglot language, which says so many things in so few words, tells us that the action transpires in Thuringia; that it is early morning, and that the man who has just arrived, all dressed in green, is named Monsieur Hi, hi, là, rions [Hilarion]. . . . Notice the immense advantage of pantomime over spoken language! Some *ronds de jambe,* some *ronds de bras* and some slight wriggling around. . . . [tell] us the name of all the characters, their ages, their professions, their places of birth, and a host of other things.[49]

The failure of gesture to convey specific concepts particular to the situation at hand is similarly addressed in this review of *La Gipsy:*

While all the actors dislocate themselves in a disagreeable fashion to a melody you have known since early childhood, they have the audacity to distribute in the theater booklets in octavo, entitled, for example, "La Gipsy, ballet-pantomime in three acts and I don't know how many tableaux"; and in this booklet you read "Stenio says to the Bohemians: "I have strong arms; I am young, courageous; would you like me to join you?" Someone asks, "But who are you? Who are you?" "An unfortunate fugitive, without money without refuge, without hope." "Thus he may enter among us."

You may have noticed the expressions . . . "Stenio SAYS," etc. Well, Stenio, instead of SAYING, rotates his two arms like a windmill in a frightening manner, and then he socks the first Bohemian in the eye. Literal translation: "I have strong arms."

Then he caresses the backs of his legs in a friendly manner, as if he feels an itch; he . . . pinches his waist, he rubs his chin, he lightly curls his forelock. . . . Translation: "I am young."

Then he draws his sword, if he has one, and frightens two or three small children posted near the wings. . . . Translation: "I am courageous."

Then he strikes a haughty pose in the manner of Caesar. . . . Translation: "Would you like me to join you?"

The thirty or forty Bohemians first stamp their left feet, holding their right feet in the air; ... then they stamp the right feet, holding their left feet in the air ... they roll their eyes in a scary manner, ah these strapping blades! They gesticulate with an extraordinary vehemence, and they throw their forearms as though they wanted to unhitch the painted canvas that furnishes them a cloudless sky. Translation: "But who are you? Who are you?"

... For four hours they carry on dialogues like this. Do you know how long four hours is; that it's two hundred forty minutes, and that minutes in ballet are longer than others, and that two hundred forty minutes makes forty thousand four hundred seconds ... ?[50]

The same critic invokes the past, sarcastically ruing the day that text had been removed from ballet:

The ballet nowadays is only a parody of the old ballet, of true ballet, the only ballet that merits the name. In earlier days a ballet was nothing other than a grand opera in which they sang a good deal and danced a little. Today, a ballet is something where they dance a lot and never sing. Sung works occupy a place of prestige in the beaux-arts. Therefore one could compose a sung ballet. But since ballet has been reduced to pantomime, to this inconceivable mystification—during which a group of people run around after each other as though they wanted to pin small pieces of paper to each others' backs—we must admit that ballet is nothing more than a dream, an illusion, a nothingness that is of a lower order than something that truly exists.[51]

The jesting implication that the gift of speech should be restored to the Opéra's dancers is of course a conceit, but one that could work well since the readers of this critique were accustomed to reading ballet characters' dialogues in libretti, were aware that ballet-pantomime had severed itself from opera only a few decades before to become an independent theater art, and, moreover, readily embraced the notion that both genres were supposed to tell the audience a complex story involving linguistic characters. In retrospect, we can see that the "problem" of mime in the ballet-pantomime was ultimately resolved by limiting the length and significance of mime scenes and reducing the importance of the word. But during the July Monarchy—though mime was still seen quite favorably in some quarters—certain sardonic journalists and conservative curmudgeons could still recommend as a solution to the indecipherability of mime a return to the "old ballet," the "true ballet" that entailed singing. And though their comments must be taken with a grain of salt, the underlying frustration warrants our attention. These critics repeatedly point out pantomime's inadequacy for conveying vital information to the audience; information that was a *sine qua non* for the understanding of the complicated plots.

LET us now turn our attention to a second set of complaints, made in roughly the same period, about the inadequacies of original music to explain the action of ballet-pantomime. For by the 1830s and 1840s, though the majority of critics who partook in the argument about the relative merits of borrowed and original ballet music stated a preference for the latter, a handful of others lamented the failure of original music to help the spectator understand the action, and wistfully mourned the passing of the air parlant. Schneitzhoeffer's score for *La Sylphide* (1832), for instance, though generally well received, was deemed too original to be helpful by at least one critic:

> I will always vow that I do not approve of the system adopted by Mr. Schneitzhoeffer in the music of his ballets. The language of pantomime is quite imperfect; it leaves many things vague and uncertain, and music alone can supply what is lacking in clarity. But music is itself a vague art that needs the aid of the word in rendering positive ideas. Deprived of this help [i.e., the word] in ballets, it can at least recall situations or sentiments analogous to those which it must express by themes known to everyone. It is, in effect, by this procedure that several ballet music composers have known how to render mimic action intelligible; however, this is not at all how Mr. Schneitzhoeffer composes his own. Considering music as an art of expression, he seems to attribute to his means more power than [he should], disdaining, in general, known airs, and methodically *composing . . . all the music in his works*. From this, a fault of clarity has hurt him, perhaps more than he thinks, in his success.[52]

Castil-Blaze, ten years earlier in his review of *Alfred le Grand* (1822), had registered a similar complaint (and lamented the decline of *non*-connotative borrowed music as well):

> A ballet with original airs, that is, airs composed especially for the piece, is usually musically unremarkable. Trivial contredances, noisy marches, without design and without taste, a sort of orchestral tum-ti-tum that accompanies the mime gestures. . . . Such are the elements of which ballets are composed. . . .
> . . . Our old ballets, such as *Le Jugement de Paris, Psiché, Persée et Andromède,* were composed with known airs. The musician, who could choose from the rich repertory of symphonists and of dramatic composers, chose only what was excellent. Where will you find more elegant contredanses than the andantes and finales of Haydn, the rondos of Seibelt and of Viotti? Where could you find excerpts more dramatic, more strongly conceived than the overture of *Démophoon,* the magnificent *agitato* in F minor, taken from a violin duo of Viotti, the air of *Ariodan* [sic], placed by Méhul himself in *Persée et Andromède,* and a thousand others that I could cite? [If] the spectators were fatigued by the insipid monotony of the dance, the orchestra consoled them and restored their patience by providing them with well-played, beautiful music. A ballet was an interesting concert, where all the genres of music came together to please the audience with seductive variety. The lovers of the new style applauded Mozart and Beethoven. Those who continued to venerate our old airs found them sometimes [in ballet music], but embellished and presented with a rich, more tasteful harmony.

I will leave it to the reader to consider the effect that certain pieces of Rossini would produce, if they were introduced artfully in the ballets. Moreover the same opera airs, even after having lost their words, preserved a memorative expression very precious for explaining the enigmas of the mimic language, while a new music without originality wouldn't strike the imagination nearly enough for its expression to be felt, and its wit, if it had any, would escape the inattentive listener. *I would not [underestimate] the power of known melodies, and of the clarity they bring to the silent dialogues of pantomime.*[53]

The critic of *La Revue Musicale* again expressed general objections to the "new system" in this review of *L'Ile des Pirates* (1835):

In the old days, they didn't compose ballet music; they arranged it, compiled it. The arranger took motifs from operas or melodies—any well known melody whatsoever—and adapted them to situations of the libretto; the music explained the situations in the libretto through the meaning of the words which normally were associated with these motifs and melodies. That way, music gave meaning to the pantomime, which by the way is quite useful. Today music is composed entirely according to the fantasy of the composers, and has as much need of explanation as the program. *What we have gained is that both are unintelligible.*[54]

This critic's assertion that the scores of his day were entirely original is much exaggerated; they were not. (The very ballet that occasioned this complaint, as a matter of fact, included excerpts from Rossini's *Semiramide* and a Beethoven sonata.) But his overstatement is a good measure of the fact that some spectators felt bereft without familiar borrowed music, especially *airs parlants,* to help them understand the action.

CLEARLY, the transition to original ballet scores was not altogether smooth, for the composer was still expected to fill the tall order of "telling the action" and "translating" the text, but to do so without the help of the connotative borrowings that had served the purpose for so long.[55] Even though composers had not entirely abandoned the practice of echoing the sounds of human speech, it is no wonder that some critics called for a return to the more overtly helpful *air parlant*. Nor is it surprising that they should grouse about the inefficacy of mime as a means of disclosing information at precisely the same time that music was ceasing to do so.

This is not to say, of course, that the burst of complaints about mime can be neatly attributed solely to shifting musical practices. There were many other forces playing into critics' increasing impatience with the language of pantomime, not the least of which was the new taste for realism that was giving rise to a looser and naturalistic form of verse in spoken drama a few blocks away at the Comédie-française (the most controversial new play, perhaps, being Victor Hugo's *Hernani*).[56] The progressive aesthetic sensibilities that led Gautier to cringe when the lady in the powder-blue silk dress expressed her emotions with a *rond de jambe*[57] (and also compelled him to lead the charge at the Comédie-française against the old-fashioned, stilted verse forms), were also impinging on the ability of others to tolerate the codified poses and gestures of pantomime—the "haughty poses in the manner of Ceasar"; the rotating of the arms "like a windmill"[58]—and for precisely the same reason: it violated verisimilitude as they saw it. Real people would not "talk" that way.

But whatever the exact reasons for the wave of disenchantment with pantomime, and for the increasing abstraction of ballet music that imitated the sounds of human speech, and for the growing distaste for connotative borrowed music, one may view these concurrent trends as disparate elements in a single crucial paradigm shift that was leading ballet-pantomime away from words—away from the assumption at the Opéra that ballet-pantomime, like opera, should be a storytelling genre deeply entrenched in language. This step, of course, also constituted an inching forward toward today's view, which holds that ballet is an art form well suited to the abstract.

Indeed, in the above-quoted derogatory comments about pantomime we may find a foreshadowing of current-day standards. For when nineteenth-century ballets are performed nowadays—for example, *Giselle, La Sylphide, Sleeping Beauty*—most of the original mime scenes are usually either shortened or omitted. Nowadays, in fact, mime scenes can seem so ludicrously unrealistic as to be comical. Les Ballets Trockadero de Monte Carlo even plays the mime scenes for laughs in its satirical production of *Swan Lake*.

Likewise, the original stories of the nineteenth-century ballets are routinely cut and simplified. And only drastically condensed versions of the original libretti are offered to the audience. (For the New York City Ballet's annual production of *Nutcracker,* even the summary is sometimes omitted.[59]) Storytelling itself is even sometimes looked at askance. As George Balanchine has said, a "story or dramatic interest" can actually "detract from the steps and structure of the choreography" and can be used by a choreographer to "hide behind."[60]

To be sure, ballets with stories, or "story ballets", as they are now called in order to distinguish them from the self-standing plotless pieces that comprise a significant segment of the repertory, are still created and performed. (That there has been little need for the comparable term "story opera" suggests that the ballet repertory has changed more radically since the July Monarchy, at least from the narrative standpoint, than the opera repertory.) But few newly created story ballets (for example Balanchine's *Prodigal Son,* Agnes De Mille's *Fall River Legend,* Sir Frederick Ashton's *A Month in the Country*) focus nearly as much on words—either on stage or in the programs distributed to the audience—as did their nineteenth-century predecessors.[61]

Current-day performance practice has made it easy to forget ballet's one-time conversational quality, and to forget that ballet, like opera, featured characters who could talk. It has also obscured the fact that ballet, like opera, was meant to tell the kinds of stories that lent themselves to (indeed *required*) detailed recounting in words. Moreover, our adherence to a historiographical tradition that tends to favor the progressive has made it easy to overlook the continuing presence of language in post-Noverre ballet, because it is a strikingly conservative trait—one that smacks more of the Lullian *tragédie lyrique* and other old-fashioned mixed-medium genres than of the long line of successful, innovative and wordless Romantic and twentieth-century ballets (by Perrot, Petipa, Ivanov, Nijinska, Nijinsky, Ashton, Balanchine, and others) that the *ballet d'action* is credited with spawning.

Yet there can be no doubt that words played a part in the performance of ballet-pantomimes at the Opéra well into the nineteenth century, and well past the time when they had ceased to be intoned. And even as words began to recede by the 1830s and 1840s with the fading away of the texted sign, the instrumental recitative, and the *air parlant* they continued to make their presence felt—albeit in increasingly subtle ways. Thus, this era of ballet history at the Opéra, justly celebrated for its brilliant innovations, also deserves recognition as a period when language was still manifest in the ballet-pantomime (just as it was in the opera), and was still playing a vital part in the Opéra audience's appreciation of these mimed and danced dramas.

CHAPTER FIVE

Hybrid Works at the Opéra

> [The] prima donna executes a continuous tacet.
> Castil-Blaze, *L'Académie impériale*

THE LINGERING presence of language in the ballet-pantomime, and the existence of ballet characters who were as capable of using language as opera characters were, enabled the two types of characters to communicate effectively when they actually encountered each other. "Dialogues" between them, it is true, occurred relatively rarely, because in nearly all of the operas of this period, ballet and opera characters mingled together only in crowd scenes and divertissements, affording no opportunities for substantive interaction. But face-to-face conversations did take place in three works: the opera *La Muette de Portici* (1828), in which a dancer played the title role, the opera *Le Dieu et la Bayadère* (1830), in which a singer played the god and a dancer the bayadere, and the "ballet-opéra" *La Tentation* (1832), in which both singers and dancers played major roles.[1] These works—which have long since vanished from the repertory and might seem strange at first blush to the average theatergoer of today—reveal the close consanguinity of opera and ballet characters of this age, showing that they not only occupied the same world but could still convincingly interact within a single dramatic work. They might also be profitably seen as proof that the Opéra was becoming more sensitive to the trends of the Boulevard theaters—which in the 1820s had not infrequently featured silent characters mixed in with singing or speaking ones in vaudevilles, melodramas, pantomimes and comic operas. In this chapter I offer a brief description of each of these three hybrid works (including tables showing the general layouts), with the simple goal of demonstrating from a practical standpoint how their silent and singing characters talked to each other. Like the parody ballets described in Chapter Three, these works (particularly the later two) have sunk into obscurity. But all three of them, quite well known in their own day, offer a sense of the easy interaction that took place between singing and dancing characters, showing another way in which ballet and opera comfortably co-existed.

Figure 27. *La Muette de Portici,* Act V, Viceroy's palace with Mt. Vesuvius in the background. By permission of the Bibliothèque nationale de France.

LA MUETTE DE PORTICI

La Muette de Portici, the first of these three hybrid works, has attracted the attention of scholars for reasons other than its mixed casting of silent and singing artists. (See Figures 27–32). R. M. Longyear believes that it "inaugurated the epoch of French grand opera" (though Elizabeth Bartlet has shown more recently that Spontini and Méhul established important precedents in this regard).[2] Jane Fulcher has credited *La Muette* with ushering in "a new operatic politics" since it was intended to help control the dangerous impulses of the French public "both in terms of official rhetoric and subsequent political exchange through the works" themselves.[3] Anselm Gerhard has characterized it as the first opera to reflect the frenzied pace, striking juxtapositions and anxieties of Parisian urban life.[4]

How did the unorthodox casting of *La Muette* come about? Silent roles were nothing new, but they had not yet come up in grand opera. According to one of Eugène Scribe's early biographers, it was Scribe himself who conceived the idea, during a performance of the highly successful comic opera *Deux mots,* in which Emile Bigottini played a silent role.[5] "I have our subject," he said to Auber, who had recently asked him to come up with a plot for a grand opera and happened to be seated next to him. "The Opéra has no great soprano at the

Figure 28. *La Muette de Portici*, nondancing *figurantes*. By permission of the Bibliothèque nationale de France.

Figure 29. *La Muette de Portici*, *figurant*, chorus and *corps de ballet*. By permission of the Bibliothèque nationale de France.

Figure 30. *La Muette de Portici*, Neapolitan costume, *corps de ballet*. By permission of the Bibliothèque nationale de France.

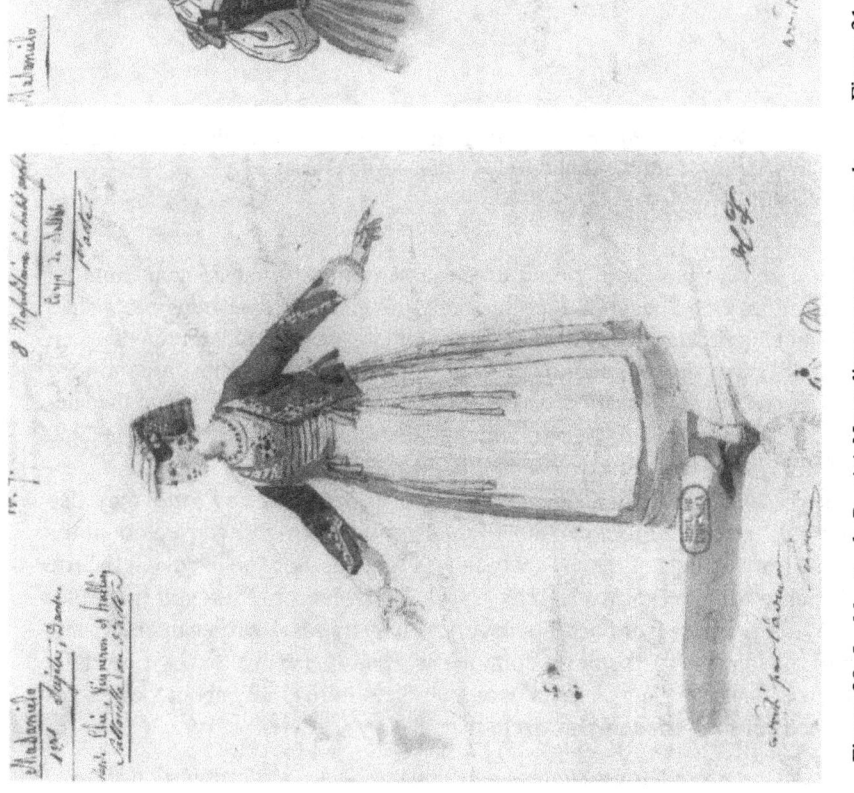

Figure 31. *La Muette de Portici*, women of the people, chorus, and *corps de ballet*. By permission of the Bibliothèque nationale de France.

Figure 32. *La Muette de Portici,* costumes for the *bolero* and *guarache*. By permission of the Bibliothèque nationale de France.

moment, and a mime role would create a sensation. What do you think?"[6] Moreover, as John Speagle has pointed out, the idea of a deaf-mute *per se* had fascinated the French since the turn of the century—this is apparent in the popularity of public demonstrations at the Institute for Deaf-Mutes, a continued public interest in the sensational case of the Wild Boy of Aveyron, and the success of the play *L'Abbé de l'Épée,* which dramatized a celebrated real-life legal controversy over the identity of a deaf child.[7]

The presence of the silent character Fénella in *La Muette de Portici* may also have made the opera more palatable to government censors worried about the political implications of the plot, which was based loosely on events in the life of Tomasso Aniello (known as "Masaniello"), the leader of a revolt in Naples in 1647. Parisian censors had objected strenuously to an earlier operatic version of the same story, the opéra comique *Masaniello* (with a text by Lafortelle and Moreau and music by Carafa[8]), but they felt more kindly about *La Muette.* One such censor, for example, wrote that:

> In the comic opera [*Masaniello*] the revolution of Naples was presented in all its crudity, if I may say so. The sovereign people and their hero Masaniello spoke too

much of insurrection, of liberty, of country and of all sorts of demagogic rubbish, and the tone of the work was generally sad and somber.

To the contrary, one distinguishes in the opera [*La Muette de Portici*] the fine and delicate touch of a skillful painter who knows the secrets of his trade. Nothing is more ingenious than the arrangement of the tableaux, nothing is more graceful than its construction. Masaniello is no longer in the forefront. The revolt of the Neapolitan peasants becomes nothing more more than an episode. The danger of legitimate authority, the popular tumult, the clamors of the rebellion, all is lost and forgotten, or rather blended into the interest inspired by a single person. It is a woman; this woman is mute and without being malicious one could say she is all the more interesting for that reason. Because of her, everything is enlivening and vivid; her presence always leads to a new turn of fortune. Ultimately everyone focuses on her; everyone feels warmly about her. It would be hard to find a better strategem for ameliorating the difficulties of the subject. The invention is not new—the deaf and mute of the *Abbé de l'Épée* was one of the first ones—but what is new, is to have steered attention away from a subject that is a little too serious . . . by using an artifice so cleverly.[9]

Whether or not the librettists used this "artifice" deliberately to blunt the potentially inflammatory impact of the work must remain a matter of conjecture. In any case, *La Muette* came to appeal far more to the public's growing anti-royalist fervor than the censors ever anticipated, and—ironically—the pathos excited by Fénella's silent victimhood may have helped it do so.

How precisely did Scribe fit Fénella, who mimes but never dances, into the action? As one can see in Table 5.1, Scribe included her in ten of the opera's eighteen numbers, having her perform a mimed soliloquy alone on the stage on two occasions but usually simply placing her (as miming interlocuter) in conversations with other characters, or having her stand by (making occasional gestures) as other characters sang.[10] Most of her miming occurred in scènes, recitatives, ensembles and finales (as opposed to arias or *pas de deux*)—types of numbers with a built-in formal elasticity that lent themselves more comfortably to the inclusion of a silent character and her requisite pantomime music than did set pieces of the air and cavatine type.

Fénella and her singing counterparts in *La Muette* also retained their characteristic "speaking" styles in these works and are thus easily distinguishable from one another in the libretto—prose for the ballet characters, and verse for opera characters. Consider this passage from Act Four, scene vi, for instance, in which the spurned Fénella is called upon by her rival Elvire to save Alphonse's life:[11]

ALPHONSE.

. . .

Ciel! que vois-je? c'est elle! O justice sévère!
Elle est maîtresse de mon sort!

TABLE 5.1 *La Muette de Portici,* THE UNFOLDING OF THE ACTION

[This table is based on a printed libretto, a printed full score, and the manuscript *livret de mise en scène*.[20]]
"Opéra in Five Acts,/ Words by Scribe and Delavigne;/ Music by Auber;/ Divertissements by Taglioni/ Performed for the first time in Paris at the Académie Royale de /Musique, 29 February 1828."

Principal Characters:

Masaniello, Neapolitan fisherman	M. Nourrit
*Fénella, his sister	Mlle Noblet
Alphonse, son of the Comte d'Arcos	M. Alex. Dupont
Elvire, fiancée of Alphonse	Mme Cinti-Damoreau
Pietro, Masaniello's companion	M. Dabadie
Moreno, Masaniello's companion	M. Pouilley
Borella, Masaniello's companion	M. Prévost
Lorenzo, Alphonse's confidant	M. Massol
Selva, an officer of the Viceroy	M. F. Prévost
A Lady in Elvire's suite	Mlle Lorotte

*mime role

Minor Characters:

	Dance	**Singing**
Act One	Spanish (4), corps (8), Neapolitans (8), pas de trois (3), bolero (6), nobles (30), pages (6)	In the chapel (28), soldiers (5), people (39)
Act Two	Children of the people (8), fishermen (7)	Fishermen and people (53) *[some are extras]*
Act Three	La Saltarello (6), corps (33), musicians (7)	Fishermen and people (53)
Act Four	Magistrates (4), pages (6)	Conspirators (9), people, the rest of the choir, and fishermen
Act Five	The *corps de ballet* of Act Three	Fishermen and people (entire chorus)

(*continued*)

TABLE 5.1 Continued

Note: Scenes without intoned text are in regular type. Scenes with singing are in italics and are marked with an asterisk if they feature nonsinging characters as well.

Act One

Naples, in the gardens of the palace of the viceroy, the Duke of Arcos. At the back, a colonnade; to the left, the entrance to a chapel; to the right, a throne prepared for a celebration.

	Plot	No. of measures
Overture		334
No. 1 Intro & Air	*The people anxiously celebrate Alphonse's upcoming marriage while he secretly agonizes with guilt over seducing Fénella [Choeur: "Du prince, objet de notre amour"; Air: "O toi, jeune victime"].*	227
No. 2 Choeur	*Elvire arrives as the crowd continues to celebrate [Choeur: "Du prince, objet de notre amour"].*	81
No. 3 Air	*Elvire tells of her love for Alphonse [Air: "Plaisirs du rang suprême"].*	200
Air de danse	To honor Elvire, dances of her native Spain are performed. First, the guarache.	238
Air de danse	Then, the bolero.	215
No. 4 Scène et Choeur de la chapelle	*Fénella arrives and explains that she has been wrongly imprisoned and her heart broken. Then she watches as Elvire enters the church to marry Alphonse [Choeur: "O Dieu puissant"].*	181 137
No. 5 Finale	*Fénella confronts the bridegroom upon his emergence from the chapel and astonishes one and all with her revelation that he is her traitorous lover [Finale: "Ils sont unis"]. Chaos ensues; Fénella disappears and Elvire expresses sympathy for her.*	278

(*continued*)

TABLE 5.1   Continued

Act Two

A picturesque site near Naples; the sea is in the background; fishermen repair their nets and play at various games.

	Plot	No. of measures
No. 6 Choeur des Pêcheurs	*The fishermen prepare for a day of work* *[Choeur: "Amis, amis, le soleil va paraître"]*	312
No. 7 Barcarolle	*Masaniello arrives; to boost their spirits in the face of their virtual enslavement, the fishermen sing a unifying barcarolle.*	244
No. 8 Duo	*Masaniello and Pietro swear vengeance against the Spanish for their oppression [Duo: "Mieux vaut mourir que rester misérable"].*	186
	*Suddenly Fénella appears, atop the rocks; she discloses that her seducer is a Spaniard Masaniello demands revenge ["Que vois-je"].	93
No. 9 Finale	**Masaniello summons his companions and rouses them to march upon Naples to rebel against the Spanish ["Venez, amis"]. The women join them ["Chantons gaîment la barcarolle"].*	250

Act Three

An apartment in the palace.

	Plot	No. of measures
No. 10 Duo	*Elvire expresses her fury then finally forgives her husband [Duo: "Ecoutez moi"]. Alphonse orders the guards to find Fénella.*	250

Scene change: the marketplace in Naples.

	Plot	No. of measures
No. 11 Choeur du Marché	**People sell their wares; young people dance. Fénella and her companions from Portici arrive [Choeur: "Au marché qui vient de s'ouvrir"].*	245
Tarentelle	*People dance the Tarantella.*	187
No. 12 Finale	*A guard recognizes Fénella and chases her. Masaniello arrives and his men drive the soldiers away. They pray for divine guidance and then prepare to conquer the city ["Non, je ne me trompe pas"].*	265

(*continued*)

TABLE 5.1 Continued

Act Four

The interior of Masaniello's cabin. The back door is covered by a sail; at the right a table and chair; at the left, a mat that serves as Masaniello's bed.

	Plot	No. of measures
No. 13 Air et Cavatine	*Masaniello laments that corruption has set in [Air et Cavatine: "Spectacle affreux"].*	179
	*Fénella arrives and tells him of the murder and pillaging she has witnessed in the city ["Et cependant pour eux"]. He sings her to sleep ["Du pauvre seul ami"].	84 53
No. 14 Choeur et Cavatine	**Pietro and his companions arrive to entreat Masaniello to lead them once more to victory [Choeur: "Mais on vient"]; Fénella eavesdrops.*	127
	*Fénella answers a knock at the door; to her shock it is Alphonse and Elvire; Fénella at first refuses to help them.	89
	*Elvire begs for mercy [Cavatine: "Arbitre d'une vie"] and Fénella softens.	98
No. 15 Scène et Choeur	** Masaniello enters and extends his hospitality, not recognizing his enemies ["Des étrangers dans ma chaumière!"].*	60
	* Pietro returns, recognizes his foes, and demands that they be killed; a bitter argument ensues and Fénella persuades her brother to adhere to his promise of hospitality ["Que vois-je"].	140
No. 16 Marche et choeur	*The people enter hailing Masaniello; he mounts the horse they have brought him as the furious Pietro and his followers swear vengeance on Masaniello.*	465

(*continued*)

134   HYBRID WORKS AT THE OPÉRA

TABLE 5.1   Continued

Act Five

The palace of the viceroy; to the left a large stone stairway leading to a terrace. In the back in the distance, Mount Vesuvius.

	Plot	No. of measures
No. 17 Barcarolle	*Pietro, corrupted by victory, has just debauched himself in the palace; the revellers proclaim their revolt a success; Pietro discloses that he has poisoned Masaniello [Barcarolle: "Voyez du haut de ces rivages"].*	194
No. 18 Finale	** Borella announces that Mt. Vesuvius is erupting and that Alphonse's army is marching against them; the people cry out for Masaniello but he is already dazed by the poison; he is momentarily spurred into action by Fénella and leads the troops into battle; his sister prays for his protection. Elvire and Alphonse arrive with the news of Masaniello's death; Fénella dashes up the stairs and throws herself down into the flowing lava of Mt. Vesuvius.*	610

FÉNELLA.
(Elle jette un regard sur Elvire, court vers elle, entr'ouvre son manteau, lui arrache le voile qui couvre son visage, s'éloigne d'elle avec colère, et semble dire: «Voilà donc celle que tu m'as préférée, et tu veux que je l'épargne»!)

[Alphonse: Heavens! Whom do I see? It's she! Oh severe justice!/ She is mistress of my fate! Fénella: (She casts a glance at Elvire, runs toward her, half-opens her mantle, takes off the veil which covers her face, withdraws from her angrily, and seems to say "There is the one whom you prefer to me, and you want me to save her!")]

(Note that Scribe and Delavigne use the term *semble dire* [seems to say] as it is so often used in ballet-pantomime libretti: to introduce the text rendered by silent characters.)

On several occasions, Fénella's music is interspersed with sung recitative; here she tells her brother of her wish for a private conversation with him in Act Two scene iii (Example 5.1). Occasionally, her music seems to match the

EXAMPLE 5.1. Fénella tells her brother of her wish for a private conversation.

speech-rhythm of her unsaid words—as in Act Two scene iv, when she resists answering her brother's query about the identity of her faithless lover. In the last four measures of this excerpt, the first violins match the phrase, "Il n'est plus d'espérance" (Example 5.2).

Another example of speech-rhythm in Fénella's pantomime music may be found in Act One scene v, when the suddenly suspicious Elvire anxiously questions Fénella (Example 5.3).

To lend extra emphasis to Fénella's crucial line ("c'est lui," plainly hearable as such even though the libretto merely explains that Fénella points Alphonse out at that moment), Auber has Elvire, and then the orchestra, echo it immediately. The phrase originates as Fénella's un-intoned "voice," bounces to Elvire who does intone it, and then winds up as a pianissimo orchestral reverberation, allowing everyone to absorb the impact of the shocking statement.

Thus Auber drew on the customary techniques for writing pantomime music—*parlante* and otherwise—but deftly interwove it with sung melodies and sung recitatives as the situation required, allowing Fénella plenty of opportunities for compelling "conversations" with other characters.

Critical Comments

How did newspaper critics take to the idea of having miming and singing characters converse together? Some critics, significantly, did not mention the hybrid nature of *La Muette* at all but simply commented upon the actors' skills.[12]

EXAMPLE 5.2. Fénella refuses to identify the offender.

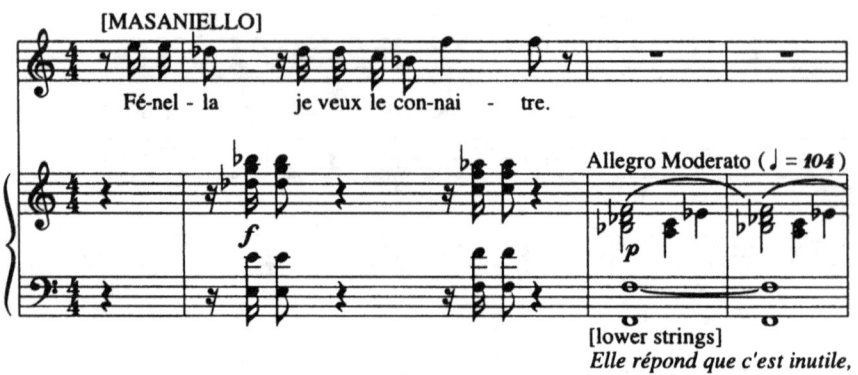

qu'il n'est plus d'espérance,
qu'il est uni à une autre.

[Fénella, I want to know who he is. / She answers that it's futile; that there is no more hope; that he is united with another.]
The text is printed as shown here in the full score, but in the piano-vocal score, the text reads simply "Elle répond que c'est inutile qu'il est uni à une autre" [She answers that it's futile; that he is united with another.] In the libretto the text is the same as in the full score.

Charles Maurice, for instance, in the first of his several articles about *La Muette*, put the primary focus on the question of whether or not Scribe had succeeded as a writer of grand opera, and of the performance says simply "all the actors played well."[13] Certainly, Lise Noblet's performance as Fénella was received with great enthusiasm, the *Moniteur* critic paying her the ultimate compliment by likening her to the beloved Emilie Bigottini, the brilliant mime who had inspired Scribe to create the role in the first place: "No more could have been expected," wrote this critic, "from the consummate talent and the great means of expression of Mlle Bigottini."[14]

Not every critique, however, overlooked the matter of *La Muette*'s hybridity.

EXAMPLE 5.3. Fénella accuses her betrayer.

[Out with it! / I tremble / (It's he who wronged me) (It's he who betrayed me) / Well! the guilty man? / (Fénella points out Alphonse) / It is he!]
In the printed piano-vocal score, Fénella's text is printed in parentheses, as shown here. (This was a common custom in printed hybrid scores.) I read the ascending pairs of eighth-notes in the pantomime music as Fénella's "voice" and the subsequent descending scale as accompaniment. The bracketed "c'est lui" is not printed in the score.

In a later review, Maurice reported that "the muteness of Fénella is more and more a subject of talk and curiosity. . . ."[15] Fétis also addressed the idea of a mute role directly, declaring his liking for it:

> The role of the mute is witty. Though it may seem as though I'm joking when I point out a nonsinging role as an asset [to this work], I declare that I am serious, and that the melodramatic music—which expresses what Fénella cannot say except through gestures—does the greatest honor to Mr. Auber. It would have been impossible for him to have rendered any better the delicate nuances of the sentiments that agitate this young woman's heart. The public does not appreciate this sort of merit, but despite themselves, they do feel these impressions. And even though they believe they are fully focused on the actress's gestures, in fact, the music guides them and moves [their emotions].[16]

Still others did find it incongruous to have the two different kinds of characters onstage together, Gautier, for instance, suggesting that "the role of Fénella, being set among a host of characters who are not dumb, seems somewhat out of place and tedious. It makes one think of the histrion in Roman farces who used to mime the speech being declaimed by an actor alongside, or those fairground shows at which only a single actor was permitted to speak."[17] This did not prevent him, however, from admiring Fanny Elssler's portrayal of Fénella in a revival of 1837: "Mlle Fanny Elssler . . . made the most of a thankless rôle [; she] . . . had one magnificent moment when, rejected by the guards of the chapel where her seducer's marriage is taking place, she sits down on the ground and lets her head fall into her hands as she dissolves into a flood of tears. . . . Her Neapolitan costume, which was completely authentic and severe, fell in large austere folds that were incomparably stylish."[18]

Whatever the comments of the critics, *La Muette de Portici* achieved enormous popularity, the public registering its approval in no uncertain terms at the box office. Indeed, it enjoyed a great following in Paris—reaching its hundredth performance with extraordinary speed (that is, within two years)—and was also quickly exported to numerous provincial and foreign houses, ultimately achieving the status of one of the most widely performed French operas of the nineteenth century.[19]

LE DIEU ET LA BAYADÈRE

The enormous popularity of *La Muette* and of Lise Noblet's affecting performance in the title role paved the way for *Le Dieu et la Bayadère,* which was conceived by Auber and Scribe with the express intent of giving a Fénella-like role to the young Marie Taglioni, whose career was just beginning to burgeon.[21] (See Figures 33, 34.) Taglioni's role as the bayadère Zoloé, however, called for dancing as well as miming because Taglioni, though already highly esteemed as a dancer, was not yet believed to possess the requisite skills for a dramatic

Figure 33. *Le Dieu et la Bayadère,* bayadere costume. By permission of the Bibliothèque nationale de France.

Figure 34. *Le Dieu et la Bayadère,* chorus costume. By permission of the Bibliothèque nationale de France.

role depending upon mime alone. The authors' wisdom was borne out by the critical response, which generally found Taglioni's miming to be lackluster but praised her dancing lavishly.[22] Consider, for example, this enthusiastic description of Taglioni by the American visitor Nathaniel Willis, which gives quite a keen sense of the powerful impact her dancing exerted upon spectators. It is worth quoting at some length:

> Taglioni . . . does not speak during the play, but her motion is more than articulate. Her first appearance was in a troop of Indian dancing girls, who performed before the prince in the public square. At a signal from the vizier, a side pavilion opened, and thirty or forty bayadères glided out together, and commenced an intricate dance. They were received with a tremendous round of applause from the audience; but, with the exception of a little more elegance in the four who led the dance, they were dressed nearly alike; and as I saw no particularly conspicuous figure, I presumed that Taglioni had not yet appeared. The splendor of the spectacle bewildered me for the first moment or two, but I presently found my eyes riveted to a childish creature floating about among the rest, and taking her for some beautiful young student making her first essays in the chorus, I interpreted her extraordinary fascination as a triumph of nature over my unsophisticated taste; and wondered to myself whether, after all, I should be half so much captivated with the show of skill I expected presently to witness. *This was Taglioni!* She came forward directly, in a *pas seul,* and I then observed that her dress was distinguished from that of her companions by its extreme modesty both of fashion and ornament, and the unconstrained ease with which it adapted itself to her shape and motion. She looks not more than fifteen. Her figure is small, but rounded to the very last degree of perfection; not a muscle swelled beyond the exquisite outline; and not an angle, not a fault. . . . No language can describe her motion. She swims in your eye like a curl of smoke, or a flake of down. Her difficulty seems to be to keep to the floor. You have the feeling while you gaze upon her, that, if she were to rise and float away like Ariel, you would scarce be surprised. And yet all is done with such a childish unconsciousness of admiration, such a total absence of exertion or fatigue, that the delight with which she fills you is unmingled; and, assured as you are by the perfect purity of every look and attitude, that her hitherto spotless reputation is deserved beyond a breath of suspicion, you leave her with as much respect as admiration; and find with surprise that a dancing girl, who is exposed night after night to a profaning gaze of the world, has crept into one of the most sacred niches of your memory.[23]

The charisma of Taglioni led Scribe and Auber to ensure that she hardly ever left the stage during *Le Dieu et la Bayadère:* she appeared in ten of the work's eleven numbers, including two *airs* that were sung directly to her (Olifour's "Sois ma bayadère" and the Unknown's "Tu ne peux connaître"), as well as both of the two extended dances of this work (the *pas de schall,* or "shawl dance," in Act 1 and the dance contest with Fatmé in Act 2).

Zoloé's inability to speak, like Fénella's, was carefully accounted for in the libretto. Quite like Fénella, in fact, Zoloé wished to speak but was prevented from doing so: newly arrived in a foreign land, she could understand but not yet speak the language. This meant that, as in *La Muette,* the silent character's miming was meant to be taken literally as such, both by the audience and by other characters on stage. It also meant, as one can see in this excerpt from Act One scene vii, that Zoloé (again, like Fénella) was less garrulous than characters in typical ballet-pantomimes. In keeping with the tenets of verisimilitude, the bayadère Zoloé's inability to speak forces her to restrict herself to short lines and simple concepts:

L'INCONNU, ZOLOÉ

(Zoloé a suivi les dernières personnes du cortège, et quand elle est bien certaine que tout le monde est éloigné, elle revient vivement vers l'inconnu qui est au bord du théâtre à droit, et lui dit: C'est toi que l'on cherche. . . .)

L'INCONNU

Eh bien! oui, j'en conviens, proscrit par le visir
Je suis cet étranger que poursuit sa vengeance.
Ce matin je l'ai vu condamner l'innocence;
Témoin de ce forfait, le ciel ne tonnait pas:
 A son défaut j'avais armé mon bras,
 Le tyran m'en punit en proscrivant ma tête. . . .
Courez la lui livrer. . . . la récompense est prête!

(Zoloé repousse cette idée avec horreur)

Aussi bien je ne puis échapper à leurs coups;
Sans appui; sans amis, où fuir?

(Elle lui montre les portes de la ville, et lui indique qu'il faut fuir hors des remparts.)

Que dites-vous?
Loin de ces lieux, hors des murs da la ville,
 Où puis-je espérer un asile?
(Chez moi! . . . lui dit vivement Zoloé.)
 O ciel! Chez vous! . . . ne savez-vous donc pas
Qu'un pareil dévouement vous expose au trépas?
 (N'importe . . . venez! . . . [. . .])

[THE UNKNOWN, ZOLOÉ

(Zoloé has followed the last people of the cortège, and when she is certain that everyone is gone, she comes back quickly to the Unknown who is on the side of the stage to the right and says to him: It is you whom they are seeking. . . .)

THE UNKNOWN
Well! Yes, I admit, banished by the Vizir
I am this stranger whom his vengeance pursues.
This morning I saw him condemn innocence;
Witness of this crime, the heavens did not thunder:
  To redress this silence I armed myself,
  The tyrant punished me for it by demanding my head. . . .
  Hasten to hand it over to him. . . . The reward awaits!

(Zoloé rejects this idea with horror)

Just as well I cannot escape their blows;
Without support, without friends, whither would I flee?

(She shows him the city gates and indicates to him that he must escape through the ramparts.)

What are you saying?
  Far from this place, outside the city walls,
  Where could I hope for asylum?

(In my home! . . . says Zoloé to him eagerly.)
  Oh heavens! In your home! . . . don't you know
  That you would risk death with such self-sacrifice?
  (It is of no consequence! Come! . . . [. . .])]

Like Fénella's pantomime music in *La Muette,* Zoloé's sometimes follows the speech rhythm of her words. Too, it frequently alternates with recitative, as in Act Two scene iii of *Le Dieu et la Bayadère,* in which The Unknown realizes that his flattering words to Ninka have hurt Zoloé's feelings (Example 5.4).

SINCE Zoloé (unlike Fénella) dances, however—both in the set dance pieces and in dramatic scenes—one finds a good deal of dance music interwoven with singing. For example, Auber and Scribe even made a point of incorporating a few intoned comments in one of the extended dance set pieces, the dance contest of Act Two scene iii, in which the dance numbers are interspersed with short comments by the Unknown (Example 5.5). More typical are scenes in which short bits of recitative and dance music alternate, as in Act One scene iii, in which the Bayadère responds to Olifour's questions by dancing (Example 5.6).

Critical Comments

Castil-Blaze, with a somewhat jaundiced eye, recounts the above-described scene as follows:

> The [judge] addresses his words to Zoloé, who does not respond at all. Then her singing companion advises the judge that Zoloé comes from a faraway country and

EXAMPLE 5.4. Zoloé cries. [Text is from the libretto.]

[Ah, my little test has gone too far. / Succumbing to her sadness, Zoloé withdraws to a corner of the cabin, sits down and melts in her own tears. / She is crying. Oh, ye Gods!]

EXAMPLE 5.5. The Unknown comments on the dancing.

[Not bad.]

> understands the Indian language but doesn't speak it. Alifour [sic] interrogates the lovely woman and asks her about her circumstances. She responds with a series of *jetés battus.* "Her consolation in sorrow [?]"—A rigaudon step. "Her resource in the face of misfortune [?]" A *pas de basque* seasoned with some pirouettes. "Am I so fortunate as to have you find me pleasing?" Negative gesture. "What must I do to have such luck?" Zoloé then points out the stranger who has taken her part against the capricious tyranny of the judge. Renewed anger of Alifour; Fatmé appeases him by advising her friend to be more responsive to the wishes of the old fellow.[24]

Indeed, despite the popular success of *Le Dieu et la Bayadère,* several critics seemed to lose patience with the notion of mixing mute and sung roles in a single work. Castil-Blaze also surmised that the prominence of Taglioni's role might have offended the singers: "Mute roles; pantomime mixed with singing and recitative, have a displeasing and cheap effect. Musicians feel spiteful and impatient when they see a ballerina meandering her way through an opera, to cripple the ensemble pieces, to hobble the duos, and show a *rond de jambe* in place of a missing note in the vocal harmony."[25] Fétis, too, suggested that the piece relied too heavily on the charms of Taglioni:

> The singular idea of making of a woman who doesn't speak the principal character in an opera succeeded for Scribe in *La Muette de Portici;* that was good for-

EXAMPLE 5.6. The bayadère answers a question by dancing.

[What is your refuge in times of trouble? / (Zoloé again begins to dance)]

tune from which he would have profited more had he not tried it a second time. . . . The misfortune of the young girl [Fénella] inspired pity, but the silence of a bayadère in love is something ridiculous, and this ridiculousness is all the more perceptible because she doesn't leave the stage and occupies such a prominent position there. What does it matter, they say, because it is Taglioni, and because Mlle Taglioni charms the public? However, they should have created a ballet in which Mlle Taglioni would be placed more fittingly, and in which the musician would never have to be ashamed of the secondary role they have made him play. A day will come where Mlle Taglioni will no longer dance; then the score of *Le Dieu et la Bayadère,* becoming a mere chapter in the history of music, will be utterly lacking in prestige.[26]

The role of the bayadère, it is true, remained closely associated with Taglioni, who chose to dance excerpts from this work for gala farewell performances before departing Paris for St. Petersburg in 1837, and again at the time of her retirement from the Opéra in 1844.[27] However, this work did flourish even with-

TABLE 5.2 *Le Dieu et la Bayadère,* The Unfolding of the Action

[This table is based on the printed libretto, a manuscript full score, and Auber's annotated copy of a printed score.[30]]

"Words by Scribe;/ Music by Auber; /Divertissements by Taglioni; /Sets by Ciceri; /*Mise en scène* by Solomé."

"Opera in two acts,/ Performed for the first time/ at the *Académie royale de Musique,*/ 13 October 1830."

Characters:

An Unknown	M. Nourrit
Olifour [a judge]	M. Levasseur
The Tchop-dar	M. Alexis
The Captain of the Guard	M. Ferd. Provot [sic]
The Chief of the Slaves	M. Pouilley
A Eunuch	M. Trevaux
Ninka	Mmes Cinti-Damoreau
*Fatmé	Noblet
*Zoloé	Taglioni

*mime/dance roles

Minor Characters:

	Dance	Singing
Act One	Bayadères (28) musicians (4), soldiers (6), other musicians (6), people and old people (no number given)	Bayadères (7), people (56), students (13)
Act Two	[none]	Soldiers (11), people and bayadères as in Act One

Scenes without intoned text are in regular type. Scenes with singing are in italics, and are marked with an asterisk if they feature nonsinging characters as well.

Act One

Plaza in the city of Cashmere; mountains in the distance.

	Plot	No. of measures
Overture		437
No. 1	*The people anxiously await the judge's arrival [Choeur: "Faut-il longtemps"].*	62
Intro &	Olifour arrives; he muses on the splendid	233

(*continued*)

HYBRID WORKS AT THE OPÉRA

TABLE 5.2 Continued

	Plot	No. of measures
Recitatif	repast he has just enjoyed [Air: "Je suis content"]. The people ask him to administer justice [Choeur: "Voilà donc la justice"].	
No. 2 Scène & Choeur	*He tries to sentence a wrongdoer; a band of bayadères interrupts [Choeur "Gaîté, plaisir"].	119
	Olifour orders their arrest; he questions Zoloé.	30
	She and her sister bayadères waltz.	26
	*[Choeur: Gaîté, plaisir"].	74
	Olifour orders their arrest; offers to pardon Zoloé if she will be kind to him.	4
No. 3	*Olifour asks Zoloé to be his bayadère [Air: "Sois ma bayadère"].	90
	She refuses him; Ninka counsels prudence; Olifour is angry.	8
	The Unknown and the people are angry at Olifour; he is angry at this challenge to his authority [Solo, Choeur: "Désormais je suis insensible!/ Ah! quelle tyrannie"]. Zoloé offers to accept Olifour's attentions if he will set free the Unknown; he agrees; Zoloé is escorted to his pagoda; Olifour departs.	180
No. 4 Scène, Air et Marche	*Zoloe seeks out the Unknown, who thanks her.	55
	*[Cavatine of the Unknown: "Tu ne peux connaître.]	58
	Slaves arrive and present jewels to Zoloé.	30
	*The Chief Eunuch presents a treasure chest.	23
No. 5 Air de Danse [Pas de schall]	The bayadères seize the lovely materials and drape them about their bodies.	255
No. 6 Scène et Choeur	The Captain and his soldiers enter; he announces a reward for the arrest of a stranger (the Unknown), who will be put to death [Solo, choeur: "Que la terreur succède . . . "]. The captain and his army depart.	71

(*continued*)

TABLE 5.2 Continued

	Plot	No. of measures
	*Zoloé tells the Unknown that she and her companions will protect him.	52
	*An entertainment begins; Ninka announces a contest; Olifour is in attendance.	227
No. 7 Final	*Olifour is called away momentarily the festivities continue; the Unknown joins Zoloé in the palanquin, shielded by the bayadères [Choeur: "Honneur à la plus belle!"].	340
Act Two		
Zoloé's hut.		
No. 8 Entr'acte, Scène and Air	Entr'acte *Zoloé and the Unknown enter cautiously; he is starving; she leaves to find food. He thinks of love [Cavatine: "Où trouver l'amitié sincère?"].	94 74 136
No. 9	*Zoloé, Fatmé and Ninka enter, carrying provisions [Air: "Tout ce que je possède . . . "].	198
No. 9 bis Scène and duo	*["Comment, aimables bayadères"] They eat eagerly, except Zoloé, who is sad.	144 37
	*The Unknown asks Ninka to sing; she obliges [Nocturne: "O bords heureux du Gange!"].	118
No. 10 Air de Danse et scène	Ninka asks Fatmé to dance. She does so. Zoloé is jealous. The Unknown praises Fatmé; Ninka suggests that Zoloé dance too.	16 192
No. 10 bis Duo/recit.	*Zoloé joins Fatmé in dancing. The Unknown scarcely notices and praises Fatmé's dancing.	205
No. 11	Zoloé cries; Ninka and Fatmé quickly depart; the Unknown is distressed.	9
	*[Ensemble: Ninka: "Oui, je crois . . . The Unknown: Combien dans mon âme . . . "]	52
	*Zoloé tells the Unknown of her love for him; she kneels; he begs her to rise and explains that he must rest; he sleeps in the hammock; Olifour knocks on the door.	129

(continued)

TABLE 5.2 Continued

	Plot	No. of measures
No. 11 bis Finale	*Olifour looks through window at the two; he is furious. The Captain and soldiers arrive; Zoloé hides the Unknown in a secret cave. The Captain breaks down the door; the Unknown is gone; Zoloé is arrested and a pyre is built and set alight. As she is about to die, the Unknown appears; he is the God Brama. Together the two rise toward the clouds [Chorus: "Malheur à celle dont l'audace/ Brama! Gloire! qu'à jamais elle reste"].	245

out Taglioni dancing the principal role, Julia de Varennes and Carlotta Grisi being among other dancers who succeeded as Zoloé.[28] *Le Dieu et la Bayadère* reached its hundredth performance within eight years of its première, was revived in 1866, and found an audience in other cities as well.[29]

LA TENTATION

La Tentation, the première of which followed twenty months after that of *Le Dieu et la Bayadère,* was surely expected likewise to capitalize on the public's proven taste for mixed-medium works.[31] (See Figures 35–42.) The primary practical consideration behind its conception, however, was the cholera epidemic. Louis Véron wrote:

> In those desolate days [of the cholera epidemic] I wished neither to make use of nor to jeopardize any of the important works of the repertory. We first of all busied ourselves with hastening the rehearsals of *La Tentation*. This five-act fairy tale was merely a series of tableaux, of which the chorus and corps de ballet were the stars. The chorus members and corps dancers can always be replaced, and scenery, at least, never falls ill! *La Tentation,* an opera-ballet, was thus a work always in readiness for presentation.[32]

In *La Tentation,* the scenes in which singing and nonsinging characters interact (of which at least one occurs in each of the five acts) are quite like those in *La Muette de Portici* and *Le Dieu et La Bayadère* in that the characters stick to their respective prose and verse styles and manage to understand each other perfectly well—for instance, Act One scene iii, in which Hélène visits the hermit, seeking to renounce her material life:

Figure 35. *La Tentation*, the hermit. By permission of the Bibliothèque nationale de France.

Figure 36. *La Tentation*, Miranda. By permission of the Bibliothèque nationale de France.

Figure 37. *La Tentation*, the sultan. By permission of the Bibliothèque nationale de France.

Figure 38. *La Tentation*, an angel. By permission of the Bibliothèque nationale de France.

Figure 39. *La Tentation*, amazon. By permission of the Bibliothèque nationale de France.

Figure 40. *La Tentation*, demon. By permission of the Bibliothèque nationale de France.

Figure 41. *La Tentation*, demon. By permission of the Bibliothèque nationale de France.

Figure 42. *La Tentation*, the angel Mizaël. By permission of the Bibliothèque nationale de France.

HÉLÈNE

Coquette repentante,
D'un monde qui me tente
Voulant tromper l'attente,
Je viens ici vers vous.
Pour vivre sage et pure,
Amour, plaisir, parure,
Ces biens, je les abjure,
Mon père, à vos genoux.

Le solitaire, qui admire sa jeunesse et sa beauté, semble la plaindre et cherche à la dissuader. Elle persiste.

—Eh bien! soit, dit-il; mais c'est aux pieds de la Vierge que vous devez déposer votre offrande; allez, ma fille, et puisse-t-elle vous accorder un bonheur qu'elle me refuse!

[HÉLÈNE
Repentant coquette
From a world that tempts me
Desiring to defy expectation
I have come to you.
To live virtuous and pure,
Love, pleasure, finery,
These good things I renounce,
My father, at your knees.

The hermit, who admires her youth and her beauty, seems to pity her and tries to dissuade her. She persists.
—Very well! So be it, he says, but it is at the Virgin's feet that you must make your offering; go, my child, and may she accord you the happiness she has refused me!]

Too, the pantomime music for the silent characters in *La Tentation* (like that in its two hybrid predecessors) sometimes supplied the proper speech rhythms for their unspoken words (see Example 2 in Chapter Four).

In general, however, *La Tentation* bears more characteristics of the typical ballet-pantomime than do *La Muette de Portici* and *Le Dieu et la Bayadère*. First, it features far more mime/dance characters in major roles (four out of six, while in *La Muette* and *Le Dieu et la Bayadère,* only one or two characters are portrayed by dancers). Second, its silent characters, like those in regular ballet-pantomimes, prove themselves capable of fairly long "speeches." Here is a typically talkative exchange between two such silent characters, Marie and the hermit, in which the former spurns the latter's advances (in Act One scene vi).

—Comment, ingrate, tu veux me quitter . . . et je le souffrirais? non, par pitié pour toi-même; écoute. (On entend le tonnerre.) L'orage gronde toujours, et le soleil descend à l'horizon.
(A ces mots, il tombe à ses genoux, lui presse et lui baise les mains.)
—Laissez-moi! laissez-moi! s'écrie la jeune fille, s'efforçant de lui échapper.
—Jamais! jamais! je meurs, si je te perds. Seul, ici, je souffre depuis long-temps le plus cruel martyre. Mais avec toi, ma compagne bien aimée, quel bonheur dans ces lieux solitaires! tu es nécessaire à ma vie autant que l'air que je respire. Tu resteras, tu seras à moi, je le veux, je le jure par cette vierge dont tu es l'image.

[—How could you leave me, you ingrate? . . . and would I withstand it? No, for yourself, listen. (*Thunder is heard.*)
The storm is still rumbling and the sun is setting.
(With these words, he falls to her knees, clasps her and kisses her hands.)
—Leave me alone! Leave me alone! cries the young woman, straining to escape.
—Never! never! I will die if I lose you. Alone, here, I have suffered the most cruel martyrdom. But with you, my beloved companion, such happiness in this

lonely place! You are as neccesary to my life as the air that I breathe. You will stay here, you will be mine; I wish it, and I swear it by the Virgin whom you so strongly resemble.]

La Tentation is also structured differently than *La Muette de Portici* and *Le Dieu et la Bayadère,* which take the shape of conventional operas with *scènes* that are simply expanded somewhat to accommodate the necessary pantomime and (in the case of *Le Dieu et la Bayadère*) dance music. Long stretches of *La Tentation,* by contrast, consist entirely of pantomime music designed to follow the action and gestures of the players (as one may see in Table 5.3).[33] Indeed,

TABLE 5.3 *La Tentation,* THE UNFOLDING OF THE ACTION

[This table is based on the libretto, an autograph piano-vocal score by Halévy, the manuscript full score, and manuscript violin parts.[a]]
"Music of the Opera, by Halévy, /Music of the Ballet, by Halévy and Gide; /Sets created by Ed. Bertin, Eugène Lamy, Camille Roqueplan, Feuchères, et Paul Delaroche."
"Ballet-opéra in five acts,/ by MM. *** [Hygin-Auguste Cavé and Edmond Duponchel] and Coralli./ Performed for the first time in Paris,/at the Académie royale de Musique,/20 June 1832."

Principal Characters:

*The hermit	M. Mazilier
*Marie, young pilgrim	Mlle Leroux
Hélène, young woman of Iconium	Mlle Dorus
Mizaël, angel	Mme Dabadie
*Astaroth, head demon	M. Montjoie
*Miranda, daughter of Hell	Mlle Duvernay
Diablesses	
Anubri, *Raca	Mlle Jawurek; Mme. Élie
Demons	
*Ditikan, Asmodée	M. Simon, M. Alexis Dupont
Drack, Bélial	M. Prévot, M. Massol
Baal, Samiel	M. Pouilley, M. Trévaux
Moloc, Mammon	M. Hurteaux, M. Vartel
Belzébuth, Urian	M. Dérivis, M. Sambet
Favorites of the sultan	
*Validé,	Mlle Noblet
*Léila,	Mme Montessu
*Amidé	Mlle Julia
Effémi,	Mlle Jawurek
*Gulléiaz	Mme Dupont
*A monster	Mlle Keppler
*Alaédan, Sultan of Iconium	M. Mérante

* Mime/dance role   (*continued*)

TABLE 5.3 Continued

Minor Characters:

	Dance	**Singing**
Act One	Fiancés (2), shepherds (11), peasants [female] (12), children (4)	Shepherds (25), demons (all the men in the chorus), angels (8), peasants [female] (15)
Act Two	*Pas de neuf, pas de deux,* the Capital Sins (7), Astaroth's Army—captains (14), drum-major (1), music conductor (1), gunners (10), men (23), little devils [male] (13), women (36), little devils [female] (12)	Demons (all the singers in the chorus)
Act Three	Whippers-in (12), pages of the hunt (18)	Huntsmen, trumpeters (3), lords (4), cooks (20), angels and pilgrims (13)
Act Four	Harem women (40), matrons (2), black eunuchs (6)	Icoglans (4), harem women (14)
Act Five	Astaroth's subjects (8)	All the singers in the chorus
Part One	Dancing master, fencing master, painter, poet, cook, ogre, female devil, page, merchant, female magician	
Part Two	Demons—all the dancers of the *corps de ballet.* Angels—all the women of the *corps de ballet.*	Demons—all the men in the chorus Angels—all the women in the chorus.

(Castil-Blaze, surely exaggerating, claims that seven hundred people participated in the scene of hell.[b])

Scenes without intoned text are in regular type. Scenes with singing are in italics, and are marked with an asterisk if they feature non-singing characters as well.

(continued)

TABLE 5.3 Continued

	Plot	No. of measures
Act One		
	A desert in the Orient; a hermitage at the foot of a hill.	
Overture		53
No. 1	The unhappy hermit prays; finds himself tempted even by the image of the Madonna.	84
No. 2	*Young peasants arrive with food and wine [Choeur: "C'est nous, ouvrez, bon père"].*	211
No. 3	*Hélène wishes to renounce worldly goods [Prière: "Coquette repentante" and choeur "Pour vivre sage et pure"].*	89
No. 4	A young couple asks the hermit to bless their marriage; dancing begins; it shocks the hermit.	30
No. 5	*Hélène tells of their innocence [Romance: En paix tous deux"].*	73
No. 6	The hermit blesses the couple; general joy *[Romance and choeur: "Leur noce s'apprête!"].* Dancing in celebration. *Celebration continues; a storm begins everyone leaves [Hélène and choeur: "Nous partons bien vite!/ Leur noce s'apprête"].*	93 174 130
No. 7	The hermit mourns his lost youth; a pretty young pilgrim, Marie, arrives.	96
No. 8	He chases her sinfully; lightning strikes him dead.	287
No. 9 [Final]	*Demons and angels argue; it is decided that the hermit will be granted another chance; he will be tempted again. [Choeurs of angels and demons, "Hâtez-vous!" and "Dieu puissant!"; prière "O bonté souveraine!"]* He awakens and sees the unconscious Marie; to avoid temptation, he quickly flees.	294

(continued)

TABLE 5.3 Continued

Act Two

Hell: the interior of a volcano.

Plot		No. of measures
Entr'acte		88
March	Astaroth summons the demons; an army of them descends the giant staircase.	122
No. 2 and No. 3 and No. 4	Joy; they drink a fiery brew; they dance, parodying human dances. [Valse, pas de 6, galop, branle]	72 604
No. 5	Astaroth consults the infernal book. He demands vengeance against heaven; they plan ways to tempt the hermit.	41
	Ditikan introduces seven diablesses: each one represents a capital sin.	186
No. 7	*The demons celebrate; a giant cauldron is placed on a giant stove [Grande scène de l'enfer: "Aux enfers triomphe"].	225
No. 7 (bis)	*Many ingredients are thrown into the bubbling cauldron to create a woman who can tempt the hermit [Choeur: "Obéissons à notre maître"]. An ugly monster appears instead.	71
	*The diablesses bring more feminine ingredients [Ballade: "Joyeux tissus couleurs"].	47
	*A beautiful fabricated woman appears [Choeur: "La violà! / Aux enfers triomphe et gloire"].	178
No. 8	Miranda is examined by everyone.	20
No. 9	Her senses are tested.	96
	A meteor, carrying the angel Mizaël and the hermit, zooms by. General alarm. The demons try to shoot them down; monsters howl; winged demons brandish flaming swords; Mizaël and the hermit take flight.	223
No. 10	Miranda follows the meteor with her eyes; she watches the combat.	339

(*continued*)

TABLE 5.3 Continued

Act Three

An old castle in a desolate forest near dusk; the ground is covered with snow.

	Plot	No. of measures
Entr'acte		66
[No. 1]	The earth opens up and vomits flames; Astaroth appears, summons Miranda	
No. 2	The hermit appears; he is starving.	62
No. 3	He knocks on the door of the castle; the châtelain receives him and says the hermit must destroy a cross if he wishes to eat; the hermit refuses.	92
No. 4	Hunters on horseback arrive and play the halali.	77
No. 5	The hermit begs them for food. They grant him any wish in exchange for his cross; he refuses.	16
	*He falls to the ground. Inside, one hundred cooks are cooking; the hunters eat happily [Choeur (a capella): "Allons, amis"]. Someone puts a plate of food outdoors in the snow; the hermit is tempted but refrains from eating it, afraid of being thought a thief.	140
	Miranda comes outdoors and promises to help him.	45
Terzettino	Several pilgrims arrive hungry [Choeur: "Riches chrétiens..."]. Meanwhile, diners inside continue to eat [Choeur: "Allons, amis"].	186
	Astaroth instructs Miranda.	13
No. 6	She offers the hermit entry to the castle if he will don party clothes. He refuses.	77
	The diners keep eating [Choeur: "O bruyante folie"].	210
	*The pilgrims applaud his courage and pray [Prière: "O puissance infinie"].	28
	[Choeur continues: "O bruyante folie"]	55
	Miranda is touched by the prayer; she crosses herself and kneels; she is torn.	88
	*The demons are furious with Miranda; angels sing her praises [Choeur: "Esclave	197

(continued)

TABLE 5.3 Continued

Plot	No. of measures
ingrate et perfide / Esclave douce et timide"]. The pilgrims turn into angels [Mizaël: "A cette épreuve . . . "].	20
Mizaël burns the castle [Choeurs of angels and demons: "Gloire au Très-Haut/ O misère!"].	95

Act Four

The interior of a magnificent harem near the beach, in a city in the Orient.

	Plot	No. of measures
Entr'acte and chorus	Odalisques bathe while slaves perfume them and braid their hair. *The odalisques sing [Choeur: "Amour, Amour"; Effémi: "O mes blanches amis"].	228
La Roméca	Dancers execute the Roméca; the hermit notices their beauty.	39
No. 3	Miranda arrives; she wants to join in the dancing but the odalisques are jealous. The dancing continues.	39
No. 4	Pas de Quatre	335
No. 5	Pas de Mlle Duvernay [Miranda]	83
Final	The hermit, jealous of the sultan, is told to murder him; thus he can acquire the harem. At the moment of committing the crime, Miranda stops him. The two escape by leaping into the sea.	260

Act Five

Near the hermitage of Act One.

	Plot	No. of measures
Entr'acte	The hermit is asleep in the grass; he wakes up, enters his hermitage, finds Marie, asleep. The demons plan to tempt him.	48
[No. 1]	*Three patrols of demons arrive, marching in an orderly and quiet fashion [Choeur: (whispered) "Démons, silence!"].	74

(*continued*)

TABLE 5.3 Continued

	Plot	No. of measures
No. 2	[Choeur of principal demons: "Sentinelles, sentinelles"]	208
No. 2 [sic]	Miranda talks to Marie; Marie says she believes in God.	55
	Suddenly light fills the stage; Miranda wants to join Marie in worshipping God; Marie gives her a cross.	65
	Astaroth appears; he causes will o' the wisps and nude dancing women to appear before the hermit.	25
No. 3	The hermit tries to flee; demons are everywhere, dancing, laughing, grimacing.	112
[No. 4]	*Astaroth, on his mountaintop, demands silence; crazed, the hermit believes himself a guest in the Act Three festivities and recalls the impious singing of the demons [Choeur; "Plaisir gaîte"/ "O bruyante folie"]. Astaroth commands a new diabolical round to deafen the hermit, calling up crocodiles, flying toads, etc.	106
No. 5	Miranda, under Astaroth's orders, approaches the hermit; he reaches to heaven to repent; Mizaël appears on a mountaintop with a flaming sword; the demons kill Miranda with an enormous cutlass.	129
No. 6	The scene changes; trees and mountains disappear; combat between demons and angels is carried out in the sky. The angels win; the hermit is taken to heaven [*Choeur at end: Gloire au Très-Haut / O colère!].	39

^a*La Tentation* libretto (Paris: J.-N. Barba, 1832), autograph piano-vocal score by Halévy, F-Po A.502, and violin parts (including F-Po 19 [303, 155–58 and 192–93). These scores are not heavily annoted, and in the nonvocal sections (which are many and lengthy), I have sometimes resorted to speculation when matching the music to the action.
^bCastil-Blaze, *L'Académie impériale de musique* vol. 2, 236.

twenty-two of its thirty-five numbers are ballet-pantomime-like scenes exclusive of intoned text.

The music written for these dance and mime passages even followed the ballet-pantomime convention of borrowing music from other sources, the composers Gide and Halévy showing a particular fondness for Beethoven, quoting

EXAMPLE 5.7. The hermit ("Antoine") and Miranda.

[Antoine hesitates anew / Miranda wrestles the dagger from Antoine's hands]

for example from the finale of the Fifth Symphony in Act Two no. 2 (the joyful assembly of demons), and turning several times to the piano sonata op. 13 (*Pathétique*) as a resource[34] (Example 5.7). The mime music for this work also uses a recurring melody (a technique favored far more by composers of ballet-pantomime than opera), which is identified with the temptation of the hermit, and which turns up in several guises (Examples 5.8 and 5.9).

La Tentation also made particularly extensive use of the chorus and *corps de ballet* in a way that ensured a frequent mingling of large singing and nonsinging groups. Consider, for example, one of *La Tentation*'s most talked-about scenes, in which Astaroth (portrayed by a dancer) conspires with the assembled demons, *diablotins* and *diablotines* of hell (portrayed by both singers and dancers) to formulate a foolproof plan to tempt the hermit. After Ditikan (a dancing character) introduces the Seven Capital Sins (impersonated by dancers), Astaroth (in mime) announces his intentions to the masses (accompanied by the opening melody of "Voi che sapete" from *Le Nozze di Figaro*):

> —Créons, dit-il, une femme plus belle que toutes les femmes, plus gracieuse, plus légère, qui sera notre esclave docile. Qu'elle ait en apparence la pureté et la pudeur d'un ange; mais que l'ange ait l'esprit rusé et le coeur pervers du démon son créateur.

EXAMPLE 5.8. The hermit prays for relief from temptation.

EXAMPLE 5.9. The hermit is tempted by Marie.

[The hermit is tempted by Marie]

This melody is that of "Malbrouck s'en va-t'en-guerre," a popular song about the downfall of Malborough. Perhaps the "downfall" idea led Halévy and Gide to deem it a fitting melody for representing a character so prone to temptation.

[—Let's create, he says, a woman more beautiful than all others, more graceful, lighter, who will be our docile slave. May she appear to possess the purity and the modesty of an angel, but may the angel have the crafty soul and the perverse heart of her creator, the Devil.]

All hell applauds with delight; the demons Bélial and Asmodée (portrayed by singers) echo his ideas with words:

BÉLIAL
[*recitative*]
Oui, le maître l'a dit; voici sa volonté:
　　Pour que l'ermite aux enfers soit jeté,
　　　Créons une femme plus belle,
　　　Plus légère qu'aucune mortelle,
　　Et pourtant à l'image de celle
　　　Qui déjà l'a tenté.

ASMODÉE
[*solo melody*]
Que d'une vierge elle ait la grace
Et la candeur d'un jeune enfant!

[BÉLIAL
Yes, the master has spoken; here is his desire:
　　For the hermit to be thrown into hell
　　　Let us create a women more beautiful
　　Lighter than any mortal
And, however, in the image of the one
　　　Who already tempts him.

ASMODÉE
May she have the grace of a virgin
And the ingenuousness of a child!]

EXAMPLE 5.10. Miranda appears.

As the chorus of demons sings in anticipation of hell's triumph, a huge cauldron is brought forward, and each principal demon (nine singers, one dancer) contributes his own ingredient—for example, blood and tears, a black cat, a proud peacock, a shrieking sea-eagle, a grimacing monkey, a lascivious goat, and a poisonous snake. Astaroth becomes enraged, however, when a grotesque blue-skinned monster (portrayed by a dancer) jumps forth from the cauldron. The monster is hastily thrown back in and the seething Astaroth orders the demons to recommence the process (an order repeated, in words, by Bélial). They send for the diablesse Anubri (portrayed by a singer), who prescribes a more feminine recipe, calling for such ingredients as cashmere in rich colors, jewels and precious stones, vases of exquisite perfumes, white doves, milk and honey, baskets of fruit and flowers. The onlookers are rapt, and the chorus sings in anticipation ("La nouvelle Eve prend naissance" [the new Eve is being born]). At long last, the lovely and truly feminine Miranda (a dancing character) appears, as the "temptation" theme is sounded (Example 5.10). The chorus bursts into a triumphant song, and the dancing demons and diablesses of the *corps de ballet* lift her high above them and dance around her.

Critical Comments

It was the spectacular *mise en scène* of *La Tentation* (featuring, among other attractions, a gigantic flaming staircase that rose and disappeared into the flies) that occupied the lion's share of the critics' attention. The *Courrier des Théâtres,* for instance, commented on the "luxury of the . . . costumes, the sets, the music, horses, the orchestra, the angels, the demons, the smoke, the spindrift, the clamor and the glory" and declared that "no description could convey the impact of the magnificence of this spectacle which ends in a Miltonian combat in the clouds, between the legions of heaven and hell."[35] Fétis compared it to the opera-ballets of Louis XV's day, adding that it enjoyed the advantage of "all the luxury of the singing, orchestra, costumes and decorations of our times."[36] But the idea of mixing media was not ignored; Castil-Blaze again voiced objections to it, this time with a metaphor: "The statue must be entirely of marble, stone or wood; it cannot be part marble and part cardboard." He also asked if the recitatives in *La Tentation* were "preferable to the *écriteaux* [texted signs] that choreographers sometimes use." (These *écriteaux* "at least are in accord with the adopted language; they are silent like the actors", he wrote.)[37] But despite his objections, he complimented the choreography, the music and the spectacle. And he made a grudging concession: "This mixture of sound and silence, these mute characters followed by an interpreter who speaks for them, is unsuccessful as far as I'm concerned, though I must admit that in two or three places the voices came in very cleverly, lending new life and irresistible action to the theatrical effect."[38] *La Tentation* found the box-office success that Véron had hoped for, even if it fell short of attaining the profits of the two hybrid works that preceded it. Gentil paid tribute to Véron's entrepreneurial skills in his *Chronique:*

> The most original work performed at the Opéra, and the one Véron has known how best to exploit, is without contradiction the ballet-opera *La Tentation.* To create an attractive spectacle without the aid of nary an opera or ballet star, to succeed for fifty performances, to fill the house with a full-length and not terribly interesting work, and then to use, successfully, its acts and smaller segments to keep the most trite works in the repertory alive—such is the mission of this work (. . . called a bastard by critics) which has contributed as much to the coffers of the Opéras *premier entrepreneur* as if it had been a masterpiece.[39]

THE shortcomings that prevented Zoloé in *Le Dieu et la Bayadère* and Fénella in *La Muette* from speaking were, of course, imposed so that the characters could communicate through dance and gesture. And their way of communicating, as Noverre might have argued had he lived long enough to see these works, constitutes an entirely separate (even a superior) language from that used by opera characters or even transcends language altogether; it goes beyond words and is capable of expressing the ineffable.[40] Therefore, the "disabled" characters Zoloé and Fénella, and the mime characters in *La Tentation* and the Opéra's ballet—pantomimes too, for that matter—were not restricted by their muteness but liberated by it.

Yet it would be wrong to contend that ballet characters of this age had fully differentiated themselves from opera characters by adopting a language that worked without words. Only after they had done so did they come to be cast in hybrid works as otherwordly spirits, or birds, or shades; as creatures incapable of and uninterested in language, instead of as regular humans able to understand but not, to their own regret, to speak. Clearly, it still made sense around 1830 at the Opéra to create ballet characters who occupied the same language-world as singing characters.[41]

Fétis's prediction about the downfall of *Le Dieu et la Bayadère* (that its score would become a mere "chapter in the history of music . . . utterly lacking in prestige") has certainly come true.[42] Indeed, the ill feelings of those taking umbrage at the mixed nature of all three of these hybrid works foreshadowed the current state of affairs, in which opera and ballet characters seem to occupy two very separate domains. But what is striking about these works—aside from whatever intrinsic interest they may hold—is not their continuing stageworthiness (or lack thereof) but the fact that they could have been created at all, could find box-office success, and could be reviewed by critics who, in some cases, saw no reason to say much (or anything) about their hybrid nature. They show that opera and ballet characters could communicate face to face, and could still partake in the same plot and understand the same language. The world they occupied was the same world, and the common heritage that bound them together as stage characters had not yet been forgotten.

CHAPTER SIX

Giselle

> "Yes," says Berthe, "it's foolish. She is always dancing." Bathilde smiles and asks her if she has a beau. "Yes!" answers Giselle. "We love each other. He is as handsome as the day is long. He will be my husband." She runs to find her mother. "Isn't it true that we shall be married?" Berthe says "Yes." Bathilde says, "She is charming." She summons Giselle and tells her that she, too, will soon be married—to a great nobleman. She asks if Giselle would like to come to her wedding. Giselle evinces her great joy. . . ."
>
> *Giselle* Parisian manuscript *répétiteur.* St. Petersberg

OF ALL THE dozens of popular and successful works created during the July Monarchy at the Opéra, *Giselle* (1841) is the only one to have survived as a regular staple in the current-day repertory. Performed every season by major companies on both sides of the Atlantic and the subject of several popular books, it is also widely available on commercial video, and some of its more famous scenes have even been featured in Hollywood films.[1] Yet one would not guess, by watching most of today's productions, how much the original *Giselle* behaved like opera. Its characters now engage far less frequently in emotional dialogues and soliloquies—comparable to recitatives and dramatic *scènes* in operas—than they used to. The nondancing ones, who originally helped convey the story in various ways (and added to the overall appeal by being interesting in themselves), have declined in number and relinquished quite a few stage minutes. Adolphe Adam's music, carefully wrought by the composer in close collaboration with the choreographers and dancers, no longer seems to participate moment-to-moment in getting the story across, as operatic music does.[2] The upshot of all this is that the story of *Giselle,* once so well served by the music tailor-made to bring it to life, and by numerous mime scenes, has been pushed into the background to make more room for dancing. The story still matters, but it is no longer—like so many of opera's stories—rife with details, colorful minor solo characters, and lengthy dramatic scenes enacted without dancing.

This streamlining is the price it has paid for survival, perhaps. And in this way, it serves as an emblem of the fate of the vital and famous repertory of which it was originally a part. For nearly all of these ballet-pantomimes, and their elaborate, detailed stories, have utterly vanished from the stage, to be replaced by ballets in newer styles which usually tell their stories in more abstract ways or tell none at all. (And, needless to say, the generic term "ballet-pantomime" has given way to "ballet.") Meanwhile, most operas performed nowadays continue to impart detailed stories, with an array of vivid major and minor characters.

To be sure, one may still find a few indications—in its characters, setting, and plot—that *Giselle* was created in an era in which ballet and opera more closely resembled one another. Opera afficianados today no doubt notice, for example, that this ballet dips into the same pool of popular theatrical motifs as three operas well known in Paris at the time of its première. Like *Der Freischütz* (1821), it transpires in a fantastic Germany and frames its scariest sequence of events—set in a dark forest clearing—with the ominous sound of tolling bells. Like *Robert le diable* (1831), it features a cross-clutching scene, a magical scepter that breaks, and a group of white-clad, ghostly virgins who emerge from their graves to dance by the light of the moon.[3] (See Figures 43, 44.) And like *Lucia di Lammermoor* (1835), its heroine loses her mind before a crowd of sympathetic onlookers in a lengthy and riveting mad scene.[4] (It was perhaps Lucia's delusional enactment of her own wedding that inspired Adolphe Adam to compose prayer music for *Giselle*'s mad scene so that she, too, could have a phantom wedding.[5])

One may also find a few specific musical likenesses to opera in the score of *Giselle,* the most obvious being the contemplative aria in the second act, in the expansive melodic style of Bellini, "sung" by solo oboe as the grief-stricken Albrecht mourns at the tomb of Giselle (Example 6.1).

Adolphe Adam himself pointed out another of *Giselle*'s analogies to opera, declaring that he had treated the Act 1 finale "like a finale of an opera."[6] Though it is unclear what precisely he meant by this, he may have been referring to his technique for drawing attention to the climactic moments: abject silence, followed by fortissimo tutti expressions of rage and despair. (Such is the musical treatment he renders at the two most disastrous moments of the *Giselle* finale: first, the confirmation of Giselle's worst fears when the Prince's retinue salutes Albrecht, and second, the moment of Giselle's death. This is closely akin to Meyerbeer's treatment of the breaking of the magic branch in the Act Four finale of *Robert le diable,* and of Raoul's refusal of Valentine in the Act Two finale of *Les Huguenots.*) Too, Adam might have been referring to the fact that this finale is graspable as a separate, self-sufficient entity—for he unifies it by returning repeatedly to particular segments of thematic material. (Such a thing was not unheard of in ballet composition, but the far more typical strategy for the end of an act was simply to continue reflecting the action, moment to moment, with through-composed music.) He also begins this finale with a bit of *parlante* music when Hilarion leaps into the crowd and yammers at the two

Figure 43. *Robert le diable*, Bertram and Alice. By permission of the Bibliothèque nationale de France.

Figure 44. *Giselle*, Albrecht and Giselle (Anton Dolin and Alicia Markova, photographed by Gordon Anthony). By permission of the Victoria and Albert Picture Library, London.

EXAMPLE 6.1. Albrecht mourns at Giselle's tomb.

young lovers; this is roughly analagous to the recitatives that often opened opera finales in that it ignites a fuse that burns steadily throughout the finale before finally detonating toward the end. Further, Adam places the longest number of consecutive fortissimo measures of the finale at the end, giving the effect of the final stretta chorus typical of French opera (though its tempo does not increase as so often happens in the operatic stretta).

IF these features of *Giselle* are noticed by today's audience as indications of the ballet's kinship with opera, however, a good many of its original narrative details, many of them designed to be communicated to the audience through careful co-ordination of gesture with music, have been lost, thereby hiding from the spectator its dedication to telling a story, perhaps the most fundamental feature shared by *Giselle* and the operas alongside which it was conceived and performed. Indeed, a close examination of the old *Giselle,* by revealing so many of these details, reminds us that by expecting so much dancing and so little miming from a ballet nowadays we have traveled a considerable aesthetic distance in the past century and a half. In this chapter I focus on the old *Giselle* (as revealed in archival materials[7]), comparing it to some of today's versions, and showing in particular how much care was taken in the old production to convey subtleties of the story to the audience with the use of music.

FIRST, a brief note on *Giselle*'s genesis is in order.[8] According to Théophile Gautier himself—one of the authors of the libretto—the story of *Giselle* was inspired by two literary works. One was a poem of Victor Hugo, "Fantômes,"

GISELLE

which includes a description of a Spanish girl whose love for dancing leads to her demise.

>Une surtout.—Une ange, une jeune Espagnole!
>Blanches mains, sein gonflé de soupirs innocents,
>Un oeil noir, où luisaient des regards de créole,
>Et ce charme inconnu, cette fraîche auréole
>   Qui couronne un front de quinze ans! [. . .]
>
>Elle aimait trop le bal, c'est ce qui l'a tuée.
>Le bal éblouissant! Le bal délicieux!
>Sa cendre encor frémit, doucement remuée,
>Quand, dans la nuit séreine, une blanche nuée
>   Danse autour du croissant des cieux. [. . .]
>
>Mais, hélas! Il fallait, quand l'aube était venue,
>Partir, attendre au seuil le manteau de satin.
>C'est alors que souvent la danseuse ingénue
>Sentit en frissonnant sur son épaule nue
>   Glisser le souffle du matin. [. . .]
>
>Elle est morte—A quinze ans, belle, heureuse, adorée!
>Morte au sortir d'un bal qui nous mit tous en deuil,
>Morte, hélas! et des bras d'une mère égarée
>La mort aux froides mains la prit toute parée,
>   Pour l'endormir dans le cercueil.
>
>[One above all, an angel girl of Spain—
>   White hands, a breast no sighs unholy swell,
>Black eyes, where did the South's bright languor reign—
>That untold charm and halo which pertain
>   To brows which fifteen summers tell.
>
>Dancing caused her death: with eager, boundless love,
>   Balls—dazzling balls—filled her with ecstasies;
>And now her ashes thrill and gently move,
>When, in a balmy night, white clouds above
>   Dance round the crescent of the skies.
>
>Alas! she had to quit when dawn displayed
>   Its light, and wait, exposed, her cloak to find.
>How often thus the giddy, thoughtless maid
>Feels, shivering, on her naked shoulderls laid,
>   The cold blast of a chilling wind!
>
>Dead at fifteen!—loved, lovely, happy, gay,
>   Leaving the ball; long, long to make us weep.

> Dead! from her frenzied mother torn away
> By Death's cold clutch; e'en in her ball array,
> And in a coffin put to sleep.[9]]

The other was a passage in Heinrich Heine's *De l'Allemagne* about Wilis, ghostly brides who rise from their graves at midnight to dance seductively by the light of the moon:

> In parts of Austria there exists a tradition . . . of slavic origin: the tradition of the night-dancer, who is known, in Slavic countries, under the name Wili. Wilis are young brides-to-be who die before their wedding day. The poor young creatures cannot rest peacefully in their graves. In their stilled hearts and lifeless feet, there remains a love for dancing which they were unable to satisfy during their lifetimes. At midnight, they rise out of their graves, gather together in troops on the roadside and woe be unto the young man who comes across them! He is forced to dance with them; they unleash their wild passion, and he dances with them until he falls dead. Dressed in their wedding gowns, with wreaths of flowers on their heads and glittering rings on their fingers, the Wilis dance in the moonlight like elves. Their faces, though white as snow, have the beauty of youth. They laugh with a joy so hideous, they call you so seductively, they have an air of such sweet promise, that these dead *bacchantes* are irresistable.[10]

As Gautier tells it, he responded to these words by saying aloud, "What a pretty ballet this would make!" Then, as he recalls (shrinking the true timetable somewhat):

> In a burst of enthusiasm, I . . . took up a large sheet of fine white paper and wrote at the top, in superb rounded characters, "*Les Wilis,* a ballet." But then I began to laugh, and I threw the sheet aside without giving it a further thought, saying to myself, with the benefit of my journalistic experience, that it was quite impossible to transpose onto the stage that misty, nocturnal poetry, that phantasmagoria that is so voluptuously sinister, all those makings of legend and ballad that have so little relevance to our present way of life. That same evening I was wandering backstage at the Opéra, with my mind still full of [Heine's] idea, when I met that amusing man [Saint-Georges] who has managed, while adding so much wit of his own, to make a ballet out of all the fantasy and whimsy of *Le Diable amoureux* of Cazotte, the great poet who foreshadowed Hoffmann in the eighteenth century when the Encyclopadeists held sway. I related the tradition of the Wilis, and three days later, the ballet of *Giselle* was written and accepted. In another week Adolphe Adam had sketched out the music, the scenery was nearly ready, and the rehearsals were in full swing.[11]

An unusual urgency did attend the production of *Giselle*. Léon Pillet, the director of the Opéra, was eager to capitalize on the popularity of young Carlotta Grisi, who had recently caused a sensation dancing in the divertissement of

Donizetti's *La Favorite*. At the very time that Adolphe Adam approached him with the *Giselle* scenario—sometime early in the spring of 1841—Pillet had been frustrated in his attempts to find a suitable ballet for her. Plans for casting her in the title role of a revival of *La Sylphide* had fallen through when the ballerina Adèle Dumilâtre, with the help of her powerful protector, reminded Pillet that she had been promised the role.[12] And Mlle Grisi was not enthusiastic about dancing the lead in *La Rosière de Gand*, a new ballet Adam was working on. She found it too long and wanted something *"plus dansante"* for her first big role.[13] So Adam's suggestion that they stage *Giselle* was welcome to Pillet, who soon engaged Jean Coralli to choreograph it and postponed *La Rosière de Gand*.[14]

Gautier's implication that Adam composed the score in a week's time is untrue, as is Adam's own oft-quoted statement that he finished it in three weeks.[15] The composer did, however, "come up with some music" soon after reading the scenario and said later that he had been "rushed, and that always fires my imagination."[16] But it took him approximately two months to complete the score; he signed and dated most of the numbers as he finished them, the earliest date being April 11, 1841, and the last June 8. (See Table 6.1.)

TABLE 6.1   TIMETABLE OF COMPOSITION OF THE *GISELLE* SCORE

Segment of Music	Date Completed
Overture	1 June 1841
Act One	
No. 1 (scenes i, ii)	1 June 1841
No. 2 (scene iii)	1 June 1841
No. 3 (scene iv)	1 June 1841
No. 4 (scenes v, vi)	11 April 1841
No. 5 (end of scene vi; scenes vii, viii)	11 April 1841
No. 6 (scenes ix, x)	14 April 1841
No. 7 (scene xi) [except for Galop]	28 April 1841
Galop	28 April 1841
Finale	17 April 1841
Act Two	
Introduction	17 April 1841
Scenes i - v	28 April 1841
Scenes vi - ix	8 June 1841
Scene x (through death of Hilarion)	5 May 1841
Scene x (end), xi, xii (to end of fugue)	14 May 1841
Scene xii (to end of Albrecht's variation)	30 May 1841
Scene xii (end), xiii	3 June 1841

Note that Adam does not use a numbering system consistently.

Gautier had never written a ballet scenario before, and his initial plan was simply to stage the Hugo poem for Act One, and the Heine passage about Wilis for Act Two. Act One, he said, "would be set in the ballroom of some prince":

> The chandeliers would have been lit, the flowers placed in vases, buffets laden with food, but the guests would not have arrived yet. The Wilis would be shown for an instant, attracted by the idea of dancing in a room sparkling with crystals and gilt, and the hope of ensnaring some new companions. The Queen of the Wilis would touch the floor and with her magic branch give the feet of the dancing ladies an insatiable desire for contredanses, waltzes, galops, and mazurkas. The arrival of the lords and ladies makes them fly away like airy shadows. Giselle, after having danced all night, spurred on by the dance floor and the desire to keep her lover from dancing with other women, would be surprised by the morning chill like the young Spanish girl [of Hugo's poem], and the pale Queen of the Wilis, invisible to everyone, would put her icy hand on Giselle's heart.[17]

Act Two was to be set in a "forest glade," at "a certain time of year," when

> The Wilis gather on the banks of a pond where large waterlilies spread their leaves on the viscous waters that have opened up to receive the drowned dancers. Moonbeams shine between the black cut-up hearts that seem to float like dead loves. Midnight sounds, and from every point on the horizon, led by will o' the wisps, come the ghosts of girls who died dancing. First, with the rattling of *castañets* and a swarming of white butterflies, wearing a large comb cut in the latest style like the interior of a Gothic cathedral, silhouetted against the moon, comes a cachucha dancer from Seville, a gitana, twisting her hips and wearing a skirt which is tight with flounces of cabalistic signs; a Hungarian dancer in a fur bonnet, making the spurs on her boots, like teeth, chatter in the cold; a *bibiaderi* [bayadère] in a costume like that of Amani, a bodice with a sheath of sandalwood, gold lamé pants, a belt and necklace of mirror-bright metal plates, . . . bizarre jewels, rings in her nose, bells around her ankles; and then the last, showing herself timidly, a small student from the Opéra in practice clothes, with a handkerchief around her neck, her hands in a little furry muff. All these costumes, exotic and otherwise, are discolored and they take on a sort of spectral uniformity. This solemn assembly takes place and ends with the scene in which the dead girl leaves her tomb and seems to come back to life in the embrace of her lover who believes he can feel her heart beating alongside his.[18]

This "plot" is almost completely devoid of action: in Act One, the Wilis cast a spell on a ballroom floor, Giselle dances and dies. In Act Two, Wilis of various nationalities dance in a gloomy woods, and Giselle emerges from her grave to embrace her lover. As Gautier admitted, "I was ignorant of the contrivances of the theater and the requirements of the stage." The final version of the libretto, crafted with the collaboration of the more experienced librettist Vernoi de Saint-Georges, is much more stageworthy.[19] In Act One (set in a "pleasant valley" in Thuringia), the peasant "Loys" woos the innocent young peasant girl, Giselle. Hilarion, unbeknownst to the rest of the villagers, ascertains that Loys is in fact the noble Albrecht, son of the Prince. Giselle, however, falls quite in love with the disguised nobleman. She is crowned Queen of the Vintage and is dancing gaily with her lover when, finally, Hilarion loses patience and exposes Albrecht as a deceiver. Though Albrecht denies the accusation, a noble hunting party (which includes his fiancée, Bathilde) soon arrives and confirms that Hilarion is right. Giselle, horrified and heartbroken, goes mad and dies. In Act Two (set in a "damp and chilly" forest on the banks of a pool), Hilarion warns his fellow gamekeepers away from the forest, explaining that the Wilis kill all men who dare stumble into their territory. Soon thereafter, Giselle, shrouded in white, emerges from her grave as a Wili. Her sister Wilis, led by their queen, Myrtha, dance by moonlight and attempt to kill a group of young village men. The villagers escape, but Hilarion is not so lucky; the Wilis exhaust him by forcing him to dance with them, and then drown him in the swamp. When the grief-stricken Albrecht arrives to visit Giselle's grave, however, Giselle re-emerges and saves his life despite the best efforts of Myrtha and her murderous band to dance him to death. The Wilis' power wanes at sunrise; as Giselle sinks back into her grave she gives her blessing to Albrecht and his union with his mortal fiancée, who has just arrived along with the Prince and several others. The exhausted Albrecht falls into the arms of his friends and reaches his hand out to Bathilde.[20] (See the libretto, Appendix Two.)

Now, to return to the topic at hand. How was the first *Giselle* more devoted to conveying the story than the versions we see today? What would today's ballet-goer, accustomed to current productions, find striking about it? There is a simple answer: it had more nondancing scenes. Roughly half of the ballet, in fact, was devoted to plot-propelling mime and action scenes—fifty-four minutes' worth, while sixty minutes were devoted to dancing.[21] (*Giselle* now has a far higher concentration of dancing, achieved through the years mainly by shortening or eliminating mime and action scenes—see Table 6.2.)

Yet it is not only the preponderance of mime and action that would jolt today's balletgoer. It is the way the gestures worked so closely with the music throughout the ballet, a tongue and groove fit that is revealed, in great detail, in the *répétiteur* (annotated, line by line, with descriptions of the gestures, "utterances," and actions of the characters). Most of the carefully wrought narrative details in the music, however, fall flat without the gestures and stage actions with which they once worked in such close accord. Though in its broad contrasts the music for *Giselle* is still considered serviceable, and sufficiently dramatic to use to quite good effect for today's purposes, many of the cues lying beneath its surface are denied their intended role. (And, of course, some of them are no longer played at all because of substantial cuts in the mime and action scenes.)

TABLE 6.2 *Giselle*— SCENES OFTEN CUT IN CURRENT PRODUCTIONS

Mime/Action Scenes in the 1841 Giselle	*Current Performance Customs*
Act One	
Scene v. Introduction to the waltz (mime and action among Giselle and her friends).	Often shortened
Scene vi. Giselle and her mother argue about the likelihood of Giselle's turning into a Wili. Berthe tells everyone who the Wilis are.	Often shortened; description of Wilis sometimes cut out entirely
Scene vii. Hilarion, alone, is sad and contemplative. Then he suddenly figures out Loys's true identity.	Often shortened
Scene ix. Hilarion emerges from Loys's cottage, anticipating revenge	Often shortened
Scene xi. (beginning of finale). Hilarion confronts Albrecht and accuses him of duplicity.	Often shortened
Act Two	
Scene i. Hunters appear in the forest.	Often eliminated
Scene ii. Hilarion shows the hunters Giselle's tomb.	Hunters usually eliminated
Scene vi. Villagers stumble into the Wilis' territory and (despite the best efforts of the Wilis to entice them) are warned away by an old man.	Usually eliminated
Scene vii. Albrecht visits Giselle's grave; Wilfride tries to talk him into fleeing.	Wilfride is often eliminated from this scene
Scene xii. The Wilis try to attack Albrecht, who is clinging to a cross.	Usually eliminated
Scene xiii. Wilfride, Bathilde, and many other of Albrecht's noble friends find the exhausted Albrecht. Giselle encourages Albrecht to return to Bathilde.	Usually eliminated

Note: See also Frank W. D. Ries, "In search of Giselle: Travels with a Chameleon Romantic," *Dance Magazine* 53 no. 8 (August 1979): 59–74, in which he compares the *Giselle* of 1841 with Petipa's 1888 St. Petersburg production (as revealed in a score in a private collection in England). Ries includes the *andante religioso* found in Adam's autograph score as part of the 1841 mad scene, though I have left it out of this table because it was not included in the full score copied in 1841 from Adam's autograph (F-Po A.533 I-III). I suspect this scene was cut before the première. It is sometimes performed in modern productions, however, including that of Carla Fracci (1981) at the Arena di Verona. My thanks to Giannandrea Poesio for pointing this out to me.

The overall effect of this modern, cut-back version, then—both visually and musically—is rather at variance with that of the old *Giselle*. Not only are many mime and action scenes shorter or missing, but in those that have survived, the performers execute fewer mime gestures and tend to stray from the music that was intended to express and describe their moment-to-moment emotions (and occasionally lend them a voice). The characters portrayed by these performers, therefore, behave far less like well-rounded linguistic people (that is, like opera characters who partook in recitatives) than they used to. They are not nearly as inclined, for example, to describe offstage action. They also tend to shy away from addressing the audience in monologues. And their sharp disagreements, once vividly seen and heard as such, are now reduced to milder little chats.

As a consequence both of the scene-cutting and the breaking up of the musical-gestural partnership—as well as our own new habits of expecting mere background accompaniment from *Giselle*'s music—we are less inclined (or able) to follow the threads that once held the story together, musical and otherwise. We perceive less of the characters' motivations and reactions to events; we understand less of their plans and of their ideas. Some of the crucial elements of the story are thereby sacrificed: conflict, suspense, depth of personality, buildup of tension, resolution. So *Giselle* seems less a mimed musical drama with dancing than a danced work with a modicum of miming in which the music plays only a minor dramatic role.

This is not to say, of course, that *Giselle* has lost its power to move the audience. Far from it. But it relies more heavily now upon dance to do so, having radically reduced the complexity of its plot and the demands upon its actors to convey ideas and demonstrate emotions through mime.

MISSING MIME SCENES IN ACT TWO

Let us now compare the old *Giselle* to the new in more detail. First, what are the effects of the scene-cutting in Act Two? Never as heavily laced as Act One with mime scenes, it is now virtually devoid of them, and everyday mortals of the type who populated Act One are now, for the most part, missing: gone are gamekeepers and peasants who wandered unknowingly into the Wilis' territory and then depart in terror; gone are Albrecht's noble friends, who appeared shortly before the final curtain to drag him away from Giselle's grave. (In fact, only two or three of the mortals from Act One—Albrecht, Hilarion, and sometimes Wilfride—ever venture onto the stage at all.) Without their presence, connections between the sunny daytime setting of Act One and the spooky nighttime setting of Act Two are all but severed.[22] So the second act seems even more distant from the first act than it was intended to be, becoming more abstract, more strange, more nearly a perfect "white" act, with the geometric patterns of tutu-clad Wilis dominating many scenes. Thus it better fulfills the ideal expressed early in the twentieth century by André Levinson in these glowing remarks about the *ballet blanc:*

> The dance instead of being subservient to expressive gesture, itself became the interpreter of the emotions and their symbolic equivalent. . . . In a constant approach to a geometric purity of design, making a pattern in space of straight lines and sweeping perfect curves, idealizing the dancer's body and dematerializing her costume, the *ballet blanc* is able to transmute the formal poses of the slow dance movement—the *Arabesques* of the *Adagio*—as well as those aerial parabolas outlined by seemingly imponderable bodies . . . into a mysterious and poetic language.[23]

Indeed, for some twentieth-century critics (Levinson among them), "pure dance" has taken something akin to a moral precedence over narrative and any sort of dance that expresses or portrays something outside itself. And the mysterious and poetic language of which he writes so laudatorily is harder to achieve in *Giselle* Act Two when the ethereal white-clad women are joined by the twenty-four nondancing performers (costumed as aristocrats, peasants, and hunters) called for in the original production (see Appendix Two).

WILFRIDE VS. ALBRECHT

Even more telling of our altered priorities, however, is the way the mime scenes that *do* survive are performed. For they have been so modified as to impart fewer details and, sometimes, to blunt the impact of the voices supplied by the orchestra. In some cases, the music is left intact but the mime and action rechoreographed—for instance, the argument between Wilfride and Albrecht that comprises Act One scene ii, a scene worth examining closely. Here, Wilfride questions the wisdom of his superior's plan to woo the peasant Giselle; at the end of the scene he finally leaves at Albrecht's behest (and salutes him, to the astonishment of Hilarion, who is spying from his nearby hiding-place). Adam composed forty-five measures of music for this scene, in ABA form, providing the contrasting moods that the interlocutors needed (see Table 6.3).

Adam does not grant exclusive ownership of any musical motif or idea to one character alone here. Instead, he unifies the scene by opening and closing it with the same music, which means that some of the same melodies are used first for one character's utterances and then for the other's. A single phrase of sweet music "c," for example (which is slower and quieter than what immediately precedes it), works as well for Loys's declaration of love in measures 9–11 as it does for the softening of Wilfrid's resistance in measures 38–40. But the music does follow the men's discussion scrupulously, fluctuating widely from one moment to the next, mirroring the characters' shifting moods—from skeptical to sweet to passionate to peevish.

Little of Adam's carefully wrought dialogue for this scene, however, is

TABLE 6.3 ARGUMENT BETWEEN LOYS AND WILFRIDE

Measure numbers	Music	Action
	[A]	
1–4	a—excited (M-m)	*Entrance of L. and W.*
4–8	b—resistant (m)	*W. says to L., . . . what are you planning to do?*
9–10	c—slower, softer, sweeter (M)	*L. answers, pointing to G's house, she is so pretty . . .*
	[B]	
11–12	d—1° tempo; higher energy (M)	*I love her like a fool*
13–14	d—rising sequence (M)	W. counters, telling L. to come
15	e—(m)	with him
16	f—(m)	L. resists
17	e—(m)	[W. argues back?]
18	f—(m)	*L. says, "I want to stay"*
19–25	g—softer, sweeter (~)	W. asks if he should
	h—(m–M)	love a peasant girl
26–28	h—(M)	*L. responds yes*
29	i—(preparation)	He grows passionate
	[A]	
30–33	a—excited (M-m)	He loves her; he orders W. away
34–35	b—resistant (m)	*W. resists*
36–37		*L. again orders him to withdraw*
38–40	c—slower, softer, sweeter (M)	W. acquiesces, salutes, withdraws
41–45	cadential (M)	*L. says finally he is gone*

Italicized words are quoted verbatim from the *répétiteur*; other descriptions of the action are paraphrased from the *répétiteur* for the sake of brevity, except for the one in brackets. M = major; m = minor

heeded in today's productions. Even the starkest musical contrast in this 45-measure scene—that between conflict and sweetness—can be neutralized by choreographers. In David Blair's production, for example, Wilfride gallantly ushers Albrecht into his cottage even as his musical voice expresses *resistance* to his employer's ruse. Musical voices can also be patently ignored—in the same production, Albrecht fails to point toward Giselle's cottage telling his squire "I love her" as tender music is played, but instead leaves the stage for a moment (to hide his cape and sword) leaving his interlocutor standing entirely alone. Thus Albrecht's voice can still be heard, but his body is out of sight.[24]

What Adam composed as *parlante* music, then, can be taken just as easily nowadays as some sort of voiceless background music; as meaningless, bland musical wallpaper. And latter-day audiences are likely to be unfazed even by performances that blatantly turn a deaf ear to such voices because they don't expect them to be there in the first place.

One could protest, of course, that even the Blair production succeeds in imparting the gist of the disagreement between these two men—or at the very least, in showing that they *are* having a dispute about *something*. Indeed, a measure-by-measure matching of music to gesture (one could argue further) might too closely resemble old-fashioned melodrama for today's audiences. Nonetheless, the effect of a staging that pays so little attention to the music—to the point that the voice speaks while the body is off the stage—is startling to anyone aware of the care Adam took to supply the interlocutors' voices. The emotional content of this scene has been obscured and the crispness of its dialogue lost, compromising the critical message that Albrecht—overruling objection—is embarking on a reckless course of action.

BERTHE VERSUS GISELLE

The rough contours of disagreement are similarly smoothed down in Berthe's confrontation with her daughter (Act One scene vi), a crucial scene in which the elder woman forecasts her daughter's future as a Wili, and Giselle dismisses her mother's fears. Here, the impact of the scene is lessened not only by rechoreographing the mime, but by deleting a few critical moments of music and miming.

The original scene opened with Berthe bustling onto the stage to upbraid Giselle and her friends (to a syncopated *parlante* melody) for waltzing instead of harvesting grapes. Here is an outline of the exchange between mother and daughter, as the *répétiteur* describes it (Table 6.4).

Anyone familiar with current stagings of *Giselle* will immediately notice several differences between the *répétiteur*'s version of this famous exchange and that performed today. Berthe's opening monologue (measures 1–25) about grape harvesting and the throwing down of the harvesting tools, first of all, is nearly always replaced by a simple action scene in which she works her way through the crowd of villagers confusedly searching for her daughter, who is playfully hiding behind her friends. This hide-and-seek business obviates the need for mime gestures (in keeping with modern-day tastes), for it is acted out and not "spoken"—though the *parlante* music composed for it is still played.[25] And it makes Berthe seem slightly ineffectual (Example 6.2). The dialogue between mother and daughter then begins in earnest, but it is usually shortened: though Berthe and Giselle originally were allocated eight measures of waltz music *apiece* in which to debate the wisdom of Giselle's leading the villagers in a dance (measures 26–41), this waltz passage has been cut in half and the dialogue usually reduced to convey something much simpler, along the lines of "I am worried,"/ "I love to dance" or, even more simply, "I dance." Moreover,

TABLE 6.4 ARGUMENT BETWEEN BERTHE AND GISELLE

Measure numbers	Music	Action
1–25	a—active, syncopated, parlante (Berthe's monologue) (M-m-M)	Berthe asks Giselle and her friends why they have thrown down their harvesting tools; the girls explain that Giselle led the waltzing; Berthe grabs her daughter by the apron, touches her heart, and says, "You will exhaust yourself"
26–41	b—16 measures from the waltz that Berthe just brought to a close (M)	*B: When you dance, you don't think it could kill you. G: It's true; my dancing, and him, and you, that's all that I love*
42–49	a'—tense rising sequence (m)	B: *"wings will grow on your back"* G: *"I won't notice the wings . . ."*
50–51	a"—emphatic (m)	B: *"listen well"*
52–72	c—dark, scary (m)	B. gathers the girls around her and tells them about the Wilis, who rise from their graves in shrouds
	d—seductive oboe (m)	and force men to dance with them
73–76	e—dance music (m)	G: *"I don't believe any of that."* She crosses the stage dancing
77–86	f—sad, resigned (m, with a hint of Phrygian)	B. expresses fears for her daughter's health; A. comforts her; he and G. go upstage; B. says to her daughter, "Come with me;" G. answers, "No, no."

Italicized words are quoted verbatim from the *répétiteur*; other descriptions of the action are paraphrased from the *répétiteur* for the sake of brevity. M = major; m = minor.

the tense exchange in the next segment—in which Berthe warns her daughter that she will grow wings and Giselle retorts that she will ignore them—is ususally boiled down to Berthe's solo expression of nervousness (measures 42–49).[26] Nor does Giselle dance across the stage toward the end of the scene in a display of nonchalance—so the perky dance music Adam wrote for the occasion sometimes serves simply as background music for Berthe's static worried postures (measures 73–76).[27] Just as Berthe is less spunky and assertive, her daughter seems far less defiant these days.[28] The heat of their disagreement has

EXAMPLE 6.2. Berthe's parlante music.

[Berthe to Giselle: what are you doing there, and you girls over there? Cutting the grapes / and you girls . . .]

cooled considerably, and with it, the impact of the message that Giselle, like Albrecht, is embarking on a foolhardy course of action.

An even more drastic alteration, however, may be found in the occasional deletion of the very climax of this sequence—Berthe's riveting twenty-two-measure solo mime scene, in which she explains to a group of rapt village girls who the Wilis are.[29] Passages of this type, of course, were familiar to Opéra audiences of the July Monarchy, who were accustomed to seeing both opera and ballet characters describe offstage phenomena to enthralled onstage listeners. Though it is still performed in several productions today—including those of the Royal Ballet and the Hartford Ballet—this virtuosic mime scene is absent in a good many others, a fact that surely reflects the discomfort felt by many of today's audiences and performers when confronted with pantomime.[30] In such altered productions, in fact, Berthe and Giselle also cut out their talk about the growing of wings, and Berthe sums up her fears quite quickly in one pose signifying death (straight arms, crossed at the wrist), which she holds for about five seconds during the emphatic fortissimo music that originally underscored the words "bien écoute" [listen well] and led into the mime scene.[31]

What are the ramifications for the audience of eliminating Berthe's explicit revelation of the substance of her fears: that her daughter could die and turn into a Wili? First, quite simply, it makes the plot harder to understand, for without it one cannot be sure of what exactly poor Berthe is so afraid *of*—merely that the specter of death is somehow haunting her. This vagueness, in turn, puts a different spin on Berthe's personality, making her seem more an overwrought worrywart than a wise mother with deep insight into the shadow world. It also deprives the audience of the foreknowledge—and therefore heightened suspense—that a prediction can bring, leaving them officially unacquainted with the notion of Wilis until the creatures actually appear in Act Two. And by leaving the Wilis largely out of the picture in Act One, it makes shallower all the pointed references to Giselle's dire fate. When Berthe puts her hand on Giselle's heart and says, "You will exhaust yourself," for instance, the uninformed balletgoer could get the impression that Berthe fears, at most, that Giselle will die from dancing too much; not that she will turn into a Wili. The latter concept is far more worthy of a Romantic ballet.

One of Adam's intended second-act effects is also nullified by the chopping out of Berthe's mime scene in Act One: his signification that Berthe's dire prediction is coming true in Act Two, which he accomplishes by quoting Berthe's Wili-describing music note for note at the precise moment that the Wilis' scary domain is revealed to the audience as such.[32] When this single passage of music ("c" in Berthe's mime scene, Table 6.4), designed to be heard twice by the audience, is only heard once, what was intended as evocative recalling music is heard for the first and only time in Act Two as mere descriptive music unconnected to the past.[33] Though it works perfectly well to set the mood for the Wilis in Act Two, this music is far more powerful when also perceived, simultaneously, as a recollection of Berthe's scary story, for it drives home the point that her fears are being realized. Adam may even have *intentionally* designed it to give the effect of a disembodied voice; of Berthe's voice retelling the story in Act Two (somewhat like the flashback voice in film in which prophetic words are repeated verbatim as a voice-over at an appropriate juncture, perhaps treated with electronic echo to make them sound as if they are reverberating from the past). In any case the ramifications of eliminating Berthe's mime scene in Act One are felt in Act Two as well, for it incidentally peels away the recollective layer of meaning in the music.

ONE could cite many more examples of revisions to the choreography that play havoc with Adam's well-thought-out musical contributions to the drama. In some productions, for example, the curtain is brought up early on Act One so that the dreamy lilting adagio of the overture now accompanies the peasants' joyous arrival instead of the robust curtain-up musette intended to do so. (This of course breaks up Adam's matching of country music with country people.) The same dreamy music also announces Hilarion a few moments later instead of the petulant and sneaky "Hilarion" motif intended to do so—thus offering quite a different musical characterization of the gamekeeper than Adam and the original choreographers had intended.[34] Too, many *parlante* details tend to go by without acknowledgment in the choreography (and indeed are so subtle that it is difficult to detect them without knowing of the *parlante*-music tradition Adam inherited). It is difficult to guess, for instance, that Adam twice intended to echo the sound of women's laughter:[35] Giselle's crazy giggle in the mad scene, and the Wilis' satanic laughter in Act Two as they menace Albrecht (Examples 6.3 and 6.4).[36] The custom of shortening Hilarion's long speech at the opening of the first-act finale also makes it harder to hear his voice in the yammering *parlante* melody Adam wrote for him. Here, he leaps into the crowd and launches his long-planned verbal attack on the young lovers (Example 6.5).

Choreographers today also tend to overlook bits of music that seem to have been written intentionally to match the characters' words; for example,

EXAMPLE 6.3. Giselle's crazy giggle in the mad scene.

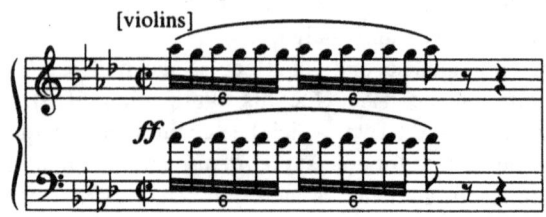

EXAMPLE 6.4. The Wilis's satanic laughter.

EXAMPLE 6.5. Hilarion yammers at the lovers.

[To Loys with irony: You chased me away, then to Giselle: and you too, you and him, you are planning to marry.]

EXAMPLE 6.6. "Il est parti."

[Loys says finally he has left.]
These measures are often eliminated, probably because they can sound like a meaningless cadential extension to anyone unaware of the conventions of parlante music.

Albrecht's contented observation that his pesky squire has finally left him alone ("il est parti") in Act One scene iii; Berthe's admonition to her daughter to listen to the story of the Wilis ("bien ecoute") in Act One scene vi; Albrecht's irate orders to Hilarion ("va-t-en, va-t-en"), in Act One scene iv.[37] All three of these lines of text are written into the *répétiteur* and match the music well (Examples 6.6, 6.7, and 6.8). Adam also seems to have incorporated the portentous line "on verra" [we shall see] in his music for the end of Act One scene iv to match the threatening utterance of Hilarion, who is being chased away by Giselle and Hilarion. This scene is described as follows in the libretto:

> Loys le repousse et le menace de sa colère, s'il ne cesse pas ses poursuites amoureuses près de Giselle. *C'est bon,* dit Hilarion avec un geste de menace, *plus tard, on verra.*[38]
>
> [Loys repulses him and threatens him with his anger, if he doesn't cease his amorous pursuits of Giselle. *That's fine,* says Hilarion with a menacing gesture. *Later, we'll see what happens.*]

The dotted speech rhythm of the words "on verra" [literally, "we'll see"] is heard four times in the closing moments of the scene, and the anger with which

EXAMPLE 6.7. "Oui, et bien écoute."

[Yes, and listen well.]
The choreography here now sometimes calls for the mime gesture for "death."

EXAMPLE 6.8. "Va-t'en, va-t'en."

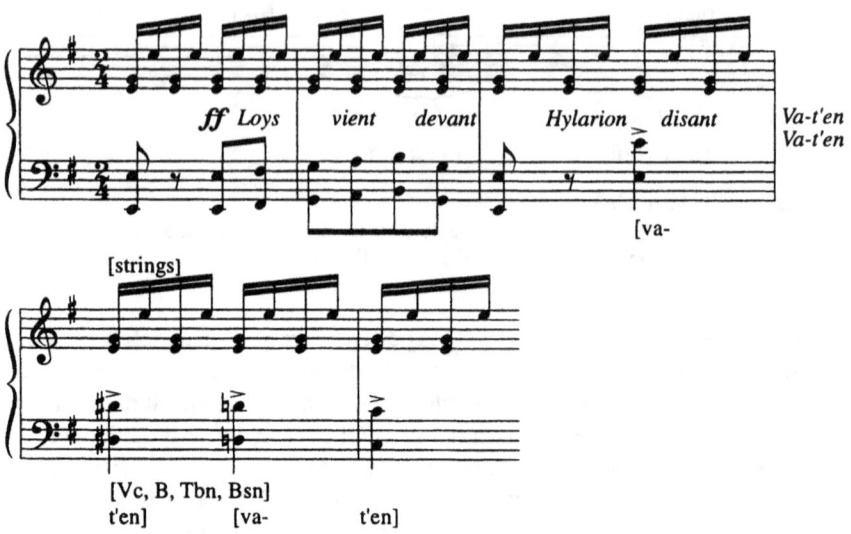

[Loys comes before Hilarion saying Go away, go away!]

Hilarion "speaks" is brought out with accents, a *forte* dynamic level, and the heavy sound of the full string section. In one widely used modern arrangement of this scene, however, the anger is neutralized by a slowing of the tempo, a softening of the dynamic level, a smoothing out of some of the dotted rhythms, and a change in scoring that gives the melody to a plaintive oboe.[39] The arranger of this version, surely unaware of the *parlante* implications of this passage, may have picked up on its intensity, found it strange, and felt a need to neutralize it (Example 6.9). Hearing the new arrangement, one would be most unlikely to discern that Hilarion is hotly saying "on verra." This scene of open anger and dispute, instead, ends on an oddly tender note.

EXAMPLE 6.9. "On verra."

[We'll see what happens.]

HILARION

Given the latter-day emphasis on dancing in *Giselle,* it is hardly surpring that the non-dancing characters in this piece are now reduced in prominence. Wilfride, as noted above, is often entirely cut out of Act Two, wherein he once accompanied his master to Giselle's gravesite and then, at the very end, led him to Bathilde. (His music is given over to Albrecht in the first of these scenes and simply deleted in the second.) Bathilde, who once made her first entrance on horseback and chatted at length with the peasant Giselle, now arrives on foot and speaks more perfunctorily with the title character.[40] (And recall that she is usually denied the opportunity to appear at the end of the ballet to retrieve her philandering fiancé.) Even the vital role of Hilarion the gamekeeper (largely a nondancing one, though he does dance in Act Two when the Wilis force him to), is considerably reduced.[41] His more limited duties today provide perhaps the best illustration of the less story-oriented sensibilities that govern many current productions of *Giselle.*

Hilarion, the odd man out in the love triangle, originally spent a good deal of the first act scheming to discern and then to expose Albrecht's true identity, appearing in no fewer than eight of the thirteen scenes of this act. The librettists clearly intended him to serve as a narrator of sorts, witnessing events and musing to himself in solo mime scenes. He also acted as sparkplug, bringing the conflict out in the open and finally instigating the crisis that led to Giselle's death at the end of Act One. Nowadays Hilarion still serves fairly well as the sparkplug (still castigating the two lovers in Act One scene iv, and still setting in motion the fatal chain of events of the first-act finale). But he is no longer allowed to do as much onstage witnessing or narrating as he once did. His overall stage minutes are cut, and he says less when he *is* on stage.

Let us examine briefly his three first-act solo mime scenes. In the first of these, scene ii, he was originally charged with setting up the major conflict of the first act, and given a substantial chunk of music (fifty-three measures' worth) in which to do so. He prepared the audience for the imminent appearance of the two lead characters by pointing out their respective cottages (recall that opera characters at the Paris Opéra during this period, too, had the habit of pointing at houses).[42] He also conveyed his feelings about both Giselle and Albrecht, along with the crucial bit of information about their plan to marry and his own determination to thwart it. (In the playing of this scene, the original Hilarion surely executed several specific mime gestures, including those for "I," "love," "me," "you," "young," "man," "there," "married," "never.") By listening at the door, too, he displayed his own curiosity about Albrecht.

Giselle Act One scene ii, *répétiteur,* 4–5

["Loys" is Albrecht's "peasant" name. Note that the annotations are instructions for mime gestures; if read as regular prose of the sort one would find in a libretto, the grammar and syntax would seem awkward. Note further that when quoting the *répétiteur* here and elsewhere in this chapter, I retain the original spellings and punctuation, but in the English translation, I add punctuation marks and capitalize some words.]

Hylarion entre il dit personne ne me voit il regarde de tous côtés et répete encore personne ne me voit en designant la maison de Giselle il dit c'est la qu'habite celle qu j'aime et en faisant une menace il approche de la maison de Loys et il ecoute il dit: ici est un jeune homme toi et elle vous vous aimez et vous compter vous épouser mais moije jure que cela ne sera paselle sera à moiil s'approche de la maison du jeune homme et il ecoutemais on vient sortons! Il se sauve du côté de la maison de Loys.

Hilarion enters; he says "nobody sees me"; he looks all around him and repeats again "nobody sees me." [*Hilarion motif*] Pointing to the house of Giselle, he says "the one I love lives there" [*sweet minor-key music*] and making a sign of menace he approaches Loys's house [*threatening music*] and he listens [*major-key cadence*]. He says, "Here is a young man. You and she love each other and you plan to get married [*Hilarion motif*] but me, I say this will never happen. She will be mine." He approaches the house of the young man and he listens. "But they're coming. We must go!" He hides himself by the side of Loys's house. [*Major-key cadential material based on last three notes of the Hilarion motif*]

Though the music for this scene remains intact in most current productions of *Giselle,* Hilarion conveys substantially less information than he used to. He usually just gravitates toward Giselle's cottage and mimes his love for its occupant. (In some productions he leaves a gift at her door or greets other people who have been brought on stage for the occasion—actions that keep him busy but require few, if any, conventional mime gestures.[43]) The sweet and then harsh music Adam wrote specifically to convey Hilarion's tenderness for Giselle and his distaste for Albrecht (as the gamekeeper indicated, one after another, their two cottages), is usually used for tender gestures alone. Hilarion explains little about the general state of affairs; he is mainly there to display his affection for Giselle. He makes fewer mime gestures, neglecting to "say," for instance, that "nobody sees me," and leaving out the business about Giselle's marriage plans and his desires to sabotage them.[44]

Hilarion's next solo miming takes place in scene vii, which he originally began in a reflective and disconsolate frame of mind. Giselle has just rejected him outright, and Albrecht has ordered him away. The audience has freshly witnessed Hilarion's defeat at the hands of his rival; all is despair for the poor gamekeeper. Midway through this scene, however, his mood changes radically, for upon hearing distant hunting horns he suddenly realizes that Albrecht is a *grand Seigneur;* Hilarion even slaps his head at his moment of epiphany. The noblemen's music, it seems, has stirred the memory of Wilfride saluting Albrecht, a gesture Hilarion and the audience witnessed together in scene 3. All at once, Hilarion is energized, and he breaks in to Albrecht's cottage to look for damning evidence, the diegetic hunting music still sounding off stage.

Giselle Act One scene vii, *répétiteur,* 28–29

Hilarion parait, regarde si personne ne le voit il médite fait un geste de vengeance il marche vers la maison de Giselle il soupire et il dit sous ce toît est celle que j'aime mais elle me repousse ah que je suis malheureux misérable que faire que devenir il reste absorbé dans ses reflections retourne et regarde la maison de Loys s'en approche et il écoute Les fanfares se rapprochent il court voir sur la montagne qu'ils sont encore loin bien loin et je suis ce que c'est ici qui vu un Seigneur qui le saluait lui la renvoyé il s'est incliné en le saluant ah j'y suis dit il en se frappent la fronde est un grand Seigneur Penetrons ce mystère entrons dans la maison et si quelqu'un vient et me voit ah c'est égal il court vers la porte de la maison qu'il essaye d'ouvrir elle est fermée que faire cette croisée [forçons?] la il prend son couteau de chasse le [?] si personne ne le voit et l'introduit par la on apperçoit la chasse la chasse entre les seigneurs arrivent.

Hilarion appears, looks about to see if anyone sees him; he meditates; he makes a gesture of vengeance; he goes toward Giselle's cottage [*Hilarion motif*]. He sighs and says, "under this roof is the one I love, but she has rejected me. Ah, but I am so unhappy, so miserable. What will happen? What will be?" He remains absorbed in his reflections. [*Sad, lethargic, resigned music*] He returns and looks at Loys's cottage. Approaching, he listens. [*Sad but slightly more active music*] The fanfares are returning. He runs toward the mountain to see that they are still far away, very far, and "I am the one, it was here that I saw a Seigneur who was saluted; he sent him away; he bowed while saluting him. Oh, I say," he says, slapping his forehead; "he is a grand Seigneur! Let us solve this mystery. Let us enter his house, and if anyone sees me, I don't care." He runs toward the door of the cottage, which he tries to open. It is locked. What to do with this door frame? Let's force it [?]. He takes his hunting knife, [looking to see?] if anybody sees him, and over there one can see the hunters. [*Fanfares and busy music signifying the hunters' approach.*] The hunting party enters, the seigneurs arrive. [*Hunters' motif*]

This pivotal scene is often cut drastically in today's productions—reduced, for example, from sixty-three to nine measures in one production.[45] Indeed, it is not atypical today for the first half (the sad contemplative part) to be left out entirely. In many cases, Hilarion simply dashes onto the stage (to the sound of hunting horns and without benefit of his own motif), takes a brief look around, and then hides in Albrecht's cottage. Yet even when the contemplative opening is retained, few of the scene's salient ideas (requiring mime gestures) are retained. For instance, it is rare today for Hilarion to harken back to Wilfride's fateful salute of Albrecht of scene iii, or to force the door with his hunting knife, or to slap his head at the moment of epiphany. Thus, according to the wishes of the choreographer today, Hilarion might lose the opportunity to display his sorrow, his resourcefulness, his determination. And the diegetic hunting call that once so providentially sparked his memory, enabling him to figure out Albrecht's identity, now often signals nothing more than the hunters' return.

The third of Hilarion's solos (scene ix) shows him triumphantly exiting his rival's cottage with the booty: the sword and gold chain, which he hides in a bush.[46] Reiterating a threat he first uttered in his opening scene, he tells Giselle and Albrecht (who are in absentia of course) that their cozy domestic plans will be thwarted. With the evidence at his disposal, he is now loaded for bear and prepared for a confrontation:

Giselle Act One scene ix, *répétiteur,* 41–42

Hilarion parait à la fenêtre il se retire vivement il sort de la maison précipitament et avec précaution tout content de ce qu'il vient de trouver il tient sa vengeance prête il dit j'étais sûr que c'était un Grand seigneur j'en ai la preuve toi Loys toi Giselle vous comptez vous aimer cela ne sera pas il indique l'épée la collier qu'il vient de voler Je me vengerai il entend du bruit et regarde ou il pourra cacher les insignes du Prince ah sous ce buisson il y court lui il sort du côté gauche de l'acteur

Hilarion appears at the window. He withdraws quickly; he exits the house with haste but carefully, quite pleased with what he has just discovered. [*Hilarion motif*] He feels vengeance to be close at hand [*sweet minor-key music*]. He says, "I was certain that he was a nobleman and now I can prove it. [*threatening music*] You, Loys, and you Giselle, you two are planning to love each other but that will not be." He indicates the sword and the gold chain that he has just stolen. "I will find vengeance." He hears a noise [*Hilarion motif*] and looks for a place to hide the insignia of the Prince. "Ah, under this bush." He rushes there; he exits stage left. [*Major-key cadential material based on last three notes of Hilarion motif*]

Though this scene is sometimes kept at its original length nowadays, it is made shallower in depth: the current-day Hilarion usually refrains from addressing the absent lovers to reiterate his earlier plan to thwart their marriage plans; he usually fails to refer again to Albrecht's noble status. In most cases he simply exits the cottage with the sword, looking triumphant; sometimes he crosses the stage with the intention of knocking on Giselle's door to show her, only to be interrupted by the unexpected arrival of newcomers.[47]

One could even argue that the story of Act One is now mainly told by the principal dancing characters, Giselle and Albrecht, whose love affair is made clear in their first scene together, and whose disastrous breakup is plainly demonstrated when Giselle goes mad and dies at the end of Act One. Indeed, in many productions today, the whys and wherefores have been jettisoned, and only the broadest outlines of the first-act story are still apparent: that Giselle is in love with Albrecht, despite Hilarion's best efforts, and that Albrecht betrays her. And this much is clear, of course, whether Hilarion's three solo mime scenes (or any other mime scenes) hit their mark or not. For many of the details Hilarion and other miming characters were assigned to convey have been deemed irrelevant, and much of the burden of imparting the first-act story has been shifted to scenes transpiring in the here and now: Giselle shows her affection for Albrecht in their first scene together; the two lovers display their disdain for Hilarion when they send him away; Albrecht is exposed as a cad when Bathilde claims him as her fiancé; Giselle goes mad and dies upon learning of this betrayal. Hilarion's job as narrator is reduced in scope, and many of the details that he once supplied in his monologues through mime gestures —about everything from the lovers' wedding plans to his own sadness to Albrecht's true social rank—fall by the wayside. Thus, as Hilarion is given far fewer chances to recollect, to reflect, to reason, to anticipate, so too is the audience.

Many more instances could be cited of deletions of nondancing characters from scenes, erased voices, scaled-down dialogues, and shortened soliloquies. But the point, I hope, is clear: that the characters in *Giselle* today mime less and therefore disclose fewer details of the story than they used to. The messages they once conveyed are allowed to disintegrate to varying degrees and the story is stripped to its bare bones, and told without benefit of the narration that a wide vocabulary of mime gestures, an eleven-page libretto, and a carefully wrought score could supply. So the story—though still compelling in its new simplicity—is narrowed in scope.

ETHNIC MUSIC AND NATIONAL DANCE

Just as audiences in 1841 were far more likely than we to discern the niceties of such details in *Giselle*'s music as the title character's crazed giggle in the mad scene, they were accustomed to listening for dance music "characteristic and analogous to the place where the action takes place."[48] But what in the *Giselle* score might they have heard in this regard? Today, this ballet is often considered devoid of the sorts of strong national or ethnic characterizations (musical and choreographic) to be found in, say *Don Quixote,* or in the character-variety divertissement of *Nutcracker.* Yet in 1841 critics did remark on the Germanic quality of *Giselle*'s setting and characters ("Albrecht" and "Gisela" of course being decidedly German names). For, just as Gautier found himself inspired by Heinrich Heine's tales of "delicious apparitions . . . encountered in the Harz mountains and on the banks of the Ilse, in a mist softened by German moonlight . . . " when he wrote the libretto, so did Adam admirably perform his duty of providing geographically appropriate music by composing three waltzes (two for the leading character and a third for the Wilis), the waltz being a dance very strongly associated at the time with German-speaking lands.[49] (Any German character appearing in a ballet divertissement, in fact, was likely to perform a waltz, just as French characters in such divertissements tended to dance a minuet. For example, when four European women are introduced into the harem in Act One of *La Péri,* the Scot dances a jig, the German a waltz, the Frenchwoman a minuet, and the Spaniard a bolero.[50]) This may seem odd, since the ethnic connotations of the waltz have all but disappeared in the twentieth century (particularly in the United States). Yet the Opéra audience of 1841 would instantly have recognized its geographic connotations. This is why Giselle enters waltzing in her first scene, and it is why she leads her friends in now-famous "Giselle Waltz" later in the act. Of this waltz, Adam said, rather proudly, that it had "all the German color indicated by the locality"[51]—an idea echoed by critics. Escudier, for example, called it "an enchanting waltz, in the Germanic spirit of the subject. . . ."[52] It was also said that Adam's score demonstrated the "grace, the suavity and the vaporous poetry of the Germanic deities that inspired the composer."[53]

Audiences of the nineteenth century, further, would have grasped the ethnic references in the brief snippets of Spanish- and Indian-sounding music that Adam wove into the waltz for the "fantastic ball" scene of Act Two, presumably to accompany the foreign Wilis' execution of "the figures of their native dance."[54] As the libretto explains: "Several Wilis present themselves, in turn, before their sovereign. First there is Moyna, the Odalisque, executing an oriental dance-step; then Zulmé, the Bayadere, who displays her Indian poses, then two French women, dancing a sort of bizarre minuet; then the German women, waltzing among themselves."[55] When one listens to the music closely, one can plainly hear eight measures of Indian-sounding music, surely intended for the Odalisque and the bayadère. And shortly thereafter one can hear music that might be interpreted as the minuet and waltz danced (respectively) by the French and German Wilis.[56] Too, this musical passage opens with eight bars of distinctly Spanish-sounding music (Examples 6.10, 6.11, 6.12, and 6.13).[57]

EXAMPLE 6.10. Music for the Bayadère and Odalisque Wilis.

EXAMPLE 6.11. Music for the French Wilis.

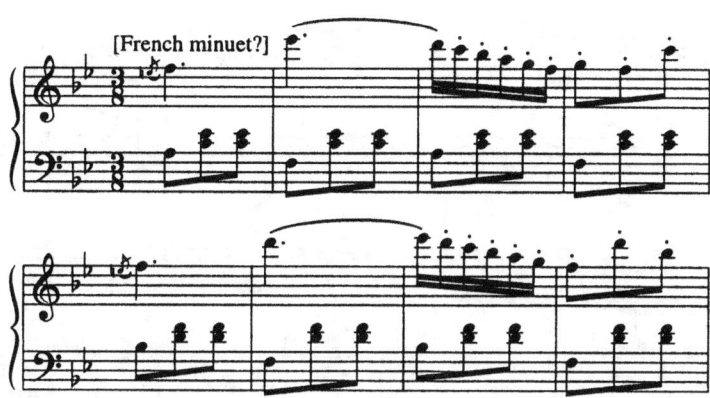

EXAMPLE 6.12. Music for the German Wilis.

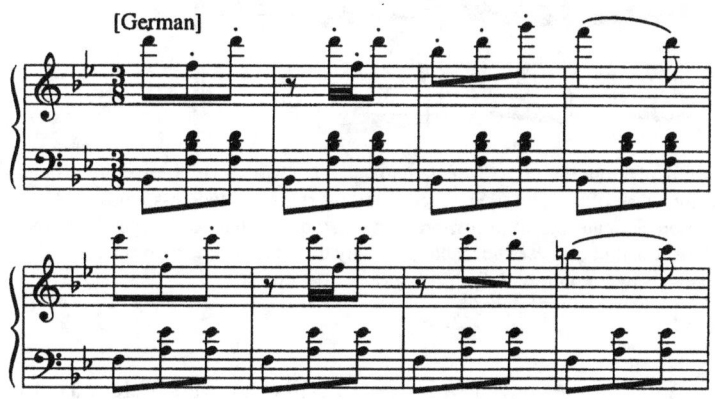

THIS somewhat startling burst of Spanish music can surely be attributed to the fact that Gautier had told Adam of his earlier idea of including a Wili in Spanish garb who arrives "with the rattling of *castañets* and a swarming of white butterflies." (Adam even wrote the words "group général de Wilis—papillons" [general group of Wilis—butterflies] in the score at the beginning of the scene in which the Wilis arrived.) Recall that in Gautier's initial plans for the second act of *Giselle,* he had envisioned Wilis of different lands, including one from Spain, one from India, and one from Hungary, all wearing "exotic" costumes.[58]

Though Gautier's original idea of putting the Wilis in national costumes was discarded before the ballet's première, the evidence of the music and the libretto strongly suggests that a handful of solo Wilis—the Odalisque Wili, the

EXAMPLE 6.13. Music for the Spanish Wilis.

It is something of a tour de force that Adam managed to work all of these ethnic connotations into the framework of a waltz—Spanish-sounding rhythms, Indian-sounding instrumentation, and a more delicate and slightly more fussy melody in what I am suggesting is the French minuet. Note, too, that of these four melodies, only the German one comes back in this scene. This of course is in keeping with the setting of the ballet.

Bayadère Wili, and the German and French Wilis who *were* included in the final version of the libretto—did perform a few measures of national steps during this fantastic ball scene, and perhaps a Spanish wili did so as well; her presence is certainly suggested by the music. Though nothing is known of the original choreography of this scene, one tantalizing clue, perhaps, may be seen in the *renversé* danced by a solo Wili in most productions today to the strains of the Spanish music—an off-balance turn that requires "wrapping yourself around your own center" (in the words of one dancer experienced in the part).[59] This unusual movement displays the salient Spanish characteristic of turning off one's vertical axis. (Peter Appel of the Zurich Ballet has even instructed performers in this role to "sweep the floor with your hand," faintly echoing the words of Gautier in his descriptions of Spanish dance: "Her body curves back ... that hand ... skims over the dazzling barrier of the footlights ..."[60]) Might this sequence be a latter-day version of a choreography originally intended to suggest the Spanish character of one of the Wilis, as its music still does?

In any case Adam made sure to include "ethnic" bits in the music for this ball scene, and they would probably not pass unrecognized today as such if national steps were danced to them, nor if ballet audiences were in the habit (as Parisians in *Giselle*'s era were) of hearing such music regularly, and associating it (just as regularly) with national costumes and choreography. Our failure to recognize these ethnic connotations makes it all the easier for us to see the second act of *Giselle* as a *ballet blanc* in which geometric design supercedes character and story in importance.

THE CLOSING SCENES OF ACT TWO

Let us consider, finally, the closing scenes of the ballet, in which Albrecht comes under the Wilis' attack and is saved by Giselle. This famous sequence of events, which entails both the climax of the second act and the melancholy denouement, falls into three distinct formal segments: the action scene and set piece in which the Wilis attempt to kill Albrecht, the *pas de deux* in which Giselle, against her will, furthers this murderous attempt even as she expresses her love for Albrecht, and the finale, in which the Wilis sink back into their graves and Albrecht returns to Bathilde. The action of these closing scenes may be described as follows (I have drawn this description from both the *répétiteur* and the libretto):

Action scene and set piece: [*Action scene*] Albrecht finds himself in the clutches of the Wilis, who laugh satanically. He is frightened and the Wilis try to make him dance (44 mm.). The Wilis chase him (15 mm.). But at the moment Myrtha reaches out to touch him with her magic branch, Giselle intervenes, imploring her lover to flee. He is frozen with terror; Giselle grabs his hand and the two of them hasten to the marble cross, which serves as a shield against the Wilis' evil. When Myrtha tries to touch Albrecht with her magic branch, it breaks in her very hand (26 mm.). [*Set piece*] The band of Wilis then tries to attack Albrecht but is repelled because he holds fast to the holy cross (53 mm.). *Total of 113 measures*

Pas de deux: Finally Myrtha, determined to draw Albrecht away from his safe post at the cross, stretches out her hand toward Giselle, whose wings open immediately, and who begins to dance so beautifully that Albrecht cannot help but forsake the cross. He would rather die than be separated from Giselle. He dances with her a quick, airy, and frenzied dance; now and again they pause to fall into each other's arms. His strength is beginning to be exhausted. The queen forces Giselle to "take flight anew" and Albrecht continues to dance, nearly to the point of death. *Total of 213 measures*

Finale: Albrecht falls, exhausted; Myrtha orders Giselle and the other Wilis to keep dancing with him until he dies; they dance with him; he falls (42 mm.); the clock chimes (12 mm.). The sun begins to rise; Myrtha announces that the Wilis must return to their tombs, and disappears into her own grave. Meanwhile, Giselle tells Albrecht to flee (24 mm.). The hunting party can be heard approaching. As Giselle sinks into her grave, she tells Albrecht to marry Bathilde; Albrecht protests as Wilfride appears (23 mm.). Wilfride begs his master to flee with him; Albrecht, in despair, falls onto Giselle's tomb. Wilfride summons "everyone" (16 mm.). Bathilde, the Prince, and others arrive; Wilfride leads Albrecht to Bathilde (23 mm.). *Total of 140 measures*

Most productions in the present day take an approach quite at variance with the scenes as described above, drastically shortening both the opening and closing segments, lengthening the *pas de deux,* and eliminating the appearance of the nondancing characters altogether—Wilfride, Bathilde, and all the other mortals who arrive in the woods at sunrise:

Action scene and set piece: Albrecht finds himself in the clutches of the Wilis, who laugh satanically (7 mm.). He is frightened and the Wilis try to make him dance (12 mm.). The Wilis chase him (15 mm.). But at the moment Myrtha reaches out to touch him with her magic branch, Giselle intervenes, imploring her lover to flee. He is frozen with terror; Giselle grabs his hand and the two of them hasten to the marble cross, which serves as a shield against the Wilis' evil. When Myrtha tries to touch Albrecht with her magic branch, it breaks in her very hand (ca. 22 mm.[61]). *Total of ca. 60 measures in most current productions* (ca. 53 measures shorter than in 1841).[62]

Pas de deux: Finally Myrtha, determined to bring about Albrecht's demise, stretches out her hand toward Giselle, who begins to dance so beautifully that Albrecht cannot help but join in, forsaking the cross. He would rather die than be separated from Giselle. He dances with her a quick, airy, and frenzied dance; now and again they pause to fall into each other's arms. His strength is beginning to be exhausted. The Queen forces Giselle to "take flight anew" and Albrecht continues to dance, nearly to the point of death. *Total of 273 measures* (60 measures longer than 1841 because of the addition of a solo variation for Giselle).[63]

Finale: Albrecht falls, exhausted; Myrtha orders Giselle and the other Wilis to keep dancing with him until he dies; they dance with him; he falls (42 mm.); the clock chimes (12 mm.). The sun begins to rise; Myrtha announces that the Wilis must return to their tombs, and disappears into her own grave. Meanwhile, Giselle tells Albrecht to flee (24 mm.). Giselle goes back to her grave; Albrecht is overcome with emotion (ca. 20 mm.[64]). *Total of 74 measures* (over 60 measures shorter than in 1841)

This streamlining neatly expunges many details of the plot and narrows the spectators' focus to the lead couple and their *pas de deux,* which has itself been altered in ways that detract from its narrative potency but boost its strength as an episode of abstract dancing.

Indeed, the power of this *pas de deux* as a dramatic episode—as opposed to a set piece of dancing that takes place during a respite from the action—is now compromised before it even begins, because the 53-bar cross-clutching scene that helps sets up its dramatic *raison d'être* has been eliminated entirely in most productions today.[65] In the set-up scene, Albrecht holds fast to the cross while angry Wilis, bent on killing him, are magically repulsed. For fifty-three long measures, the cross's power and the frustration of the Wilis are shown plainly, making utterly clear why an infuriated Myrtha, in the ensuing *pas de deux,* should finally resort to the "diabolically feminine ruse" of making Giselle dance so appealingly as to inveigle Albrecht away from his protective shield to dance to the point of exhaustion.[66] Yet without the clear presentation of the reason for Myrtha's renewed wrath, the *pas de deux*—which is brought about solely at Myrtha's behest, against the wills of its protagonists—cannot be seen for what it is: Myrtha's last resort.[67]

Pas de Deux

[*Entrance*[68]]—Andante, 5 mm. Myrtha orders Giselle to dance. Giselle begs for mercy. Myrtha tells her: you must dance.[69]

[*Adagio*]—Larghetto, 38 mm. Giselle poses so fetchingly that Albrecht leaves the cross. Then, Myrtha touches Giselle's hand to make her dance.[70]

[*Variations*]—Andantino, 63 mm.—Giselle dances. Andante, 26 mm. Myrtha touches Albrecht's hand to force him to dance; he dances.[71]

[*Coda*]—Allegro moderato, 81 mm. Despite Giselle's entreaties, Myrtha forces her to continue dancing. Albrecht dances. He becomes exhausted.[72]

Given the absence of the cross-clutching scene, it follows that Myrtha's role in this *pas de deux* is now scaled back. Originally—having been riled up by Giselle's success at protecting Albrecht—she served as an ever-present mistress of ceremonies for the *pas de deux,* ordering Giselle to dance during the Entrance, exhorting her to keep dancing in both the Adagio and the Coda despite Giselle's overt pleas for clemency, and touching the hands of the two lovers at the beginnings of their respective Variations to force them to dance. Her malevolent presence is still felt, to be sure, but the latter-day Myrtha is inclined to stay close to the wings and to refrain from physically touching the principal characters.

What these principal characters dance nowadays more closely resembles the formulaic *grand pas de deux* of the late nineteenth century (familiar to us from the Tchaikovsky ballets), a lengthy set piece in which the advancement of the plot was not usually a primary consideration. This difference may be attributed to the addition of a 60-measure variation for Giselle (in bold, below)—an addition made in Russia in the latter half of the 19th century:[73]

Pas de Deux, Old Version	*Pas de Deux, Current Day*
Entrance—Andante, 5 mm.	Entrance—Andante, 5 mm.
Adagio—Larghetto, 38 mm.	Adagio—Larghetto, 38 mm.
Variations—Andantino, 63 mm. (feminine)	Andantino, 63 mm.
—Andante, 26 mm. (masculine)	Variations—Andante, 26 mm. (masculine)
Coda—Allegro moderato, 81 mm. probably not calling for the *corps de ballet*	**[Allegro], 60 mm. (feminine)**[74]
	Coda—Allegro moderato, 81 mm. calling for the *corps de ballet* as well as the two principals
Total: 213 mm.	Total: 273 mm.

One crucial effect of this interpolated variation is to draw attention momentarily away from the story of Albrecht's plight—actually granting him a respite from the deadly dancing—and place the emphasis instead on the ballerina's virtuosity. It also endows the *pas de deux* with the spacious proportions of *Nutcracker* and *Sleeping Beauty* by allowing an expansion of the adagio, and closes out the variations segment (in keeping with the conventions of the late-nineteenth-century *pas de deux*) with the female soloist instead of the male. These considerations have to do less with plot than with form; less to do with sharpening the narrative than with making the dancing last longer. And though this *pas de deux* is still considered programmatic—and still presented as an episode of attempted murder combined with a display of transcendent love—its increased emphasis on the ballerina's virtuosity, its greater length, its whittling away of Myrtha's presence, and its interruption of Albrecht's forced dancing, all serve to dilute the original story considerably. Though this *pas de deux* remains now, as it was in 1841, a dramatic high point in the ballet, these revisions clearly made it match up more closely to late-nineteenth-century formal conventions, and served to bring more attention to the ballerina and her skills as a dancer than to deepen the impact of the story.

THE FINALE

The finale, in which the Wilis lose their magical powers and withdraw from sight as the noble hunting party arrives, is nowadays reduced in length and in population. In the old *Giselle,* it supplied a faint echo of the first-act finale in that a crowd of concerned onlookers framed a fallen figure (in Act One, the dead Giselle; in Act Two, the exhausted Albrecht). It also called for a fair amount of "talking": Myrtha ordering the Wilis to continue dancing and then to return to their tombs, Giselle admonishing Albrecht to return to Bathilde, Albrecht protesting this suggestion, Wilfride begging his master to flee the gravesite. In today's productions, however, the curtain falls soon after the Wilis vanish. Albrecht is left alone on the stage for only a minute or so of emotional farewell— a farewell not requiring conventional mime gestures. All references to first-act characters (not to mention the characters themselves) are expunged and the focus is left upon Albrecht and Giselle's redeeming love for him. Indeed, the memory of the *pas de deux* is allowed to loom a bit larger in the audience's mind as the curtain falls, for very little has intervened in the moments since its conclusion. It is a fitting end for this "white" act, for a long nondanced scene featuring mime characters would spoil the reverie, according to latter-day standards.

BRINGING BACK THE OLD *GISELLE?*

What would happen if an attempt were made to mount a *Giselle* that conforms as nearly as possible to the version described in the libretto and the *répétiteur?* It would require, among other things, eliminating Giselle's much-beloved solo in the second-act *pas de deux,* reinstating the horses in the first act, bringing back to life several nondancing minor characters and elevating Hilarion to the role of "narrator" again. It would also call for the restoration of lengthy and detailed mime scenes. And it would require co-ordinating the stage action and mime to the music with great exactitude—an exactitude that would require far more mime gestures than are usually performed now, would liberate the musical voices so they could be heard again as such, and would re-establish the important place of Adam's score as a storytelling agent in this ballet.

The difficulty audiences might have with swallowing such radical changes to *Giselle* as they know it, of course, serves as an apt gauge of just how much this ballet-pantomime has changed in the century and a half since its premiere. The mere notion of allotting roughly equal time to dancing and mime/action scenes might alone be enough to sink it. Yet if such a production were successfully mounted, it could allow us to become reacquainted, at a deeper level, with the varied cast of characters in *Giselle,* and reflect in new ways upon this ballet's narrative depth and gestural beauty. It could show us a world in which the audience not only took for granted the notion that stories were told in instrumental music, and that voices were likely to emanate from the orchestra, but assumed that the story was central to ballet; that ballet, like opera, should have "a logical dramatic development, a moral, a clearly defined ending. . . ."[75] In so doing, it could bring to life the sort of ballet-pantomime that made perfect sense when performed alongside opera, as *Giselle* always was. And it could offer us, in the most graceful way, persuasive beyond words, a taste of something the Opéra's audiences habitually felt when they attended ballet-pantomimes and operas: the sheer pleasure of seeing, and hearing, a good story unfolding before them.

APPENDIX ONE[1]

Ballet-Pantomimes and Operas Produced at the Paris Opéra, 1825–1850

Date of lst Opéra perf.	Title No. of acts	Genre[2]	Librettist	Composer[3]	Choreographer[4]	Scene designer	Costume designer
1825							
2 March	La Belle au Bois Dormant (3)	Opéra-féerie	Planard	Carafa	Gardel	Ciceri	Garnerey père
10 June	Pharamond (3)[5]	Opéra	Ancelot, Guiraud, Soumet	Boieldieu, Berton, Kreutzer, Daussoigne	Gardel	Ciceri	Lecomte
17 Oct.	Don Sanche (1)	Opéra	Théaulon, de Rancé	Liszt	*no ballets*	Ciceri	Lecomte
1826							
29 May	Mars et Venus, ou les Filets de Vulcain* (4)	Ballet-pantomime	none named[6]	Schneitzhoeffer	Blache	Ciceri	Lecomte
10 June	Le Siège de Corinthe* (3)	Tragédie lyrique	Soumet, Balocci	Rossini	Gardel	Ciceri	Lecomte
1827							
29 Jan.	Astolphe et Joconde, ou les Coureurs d'aventures (2)[7]	Ballet-pantomime	none named	Hérold	Aumer	Ciceri	Lecomte
26 March	Moïse* (4)	Opéra	Balocchi, de Jouy	Rossini	Gardel	Ciceri	Lecomte
1 June	Le Sicilien, ou l'Amour peintre (1)[8]	Ballet-pantomime	none named	Sor, Schneitzhoeffer[9]	Anatole Petit	none named[10]	Lecomte
29 June	MacBeth (3)	Tragédie lyrique	de l'Isle, Hix	Chelard	Gardel	Ciceri	Lecomte

(continued)

APPENDIX ONE

Date of 1st Opéra perf.	Title No. of acts	Genre[2]	Librettist	Composer[3]	Choreog- rapher[4]	Scene designer	Costume designer
19 Sept.	La Somnambule ou L'Arrivée d'un Nouveau Seigneur (3)	Ballet- pantomime	Scribe	Hérold	Aumer	Ciceri	Lecomte
1828							
29 Feb.	La Muette de Portici (5)	Opéra	Scribe, Delavigne	Auber	Aumer	Ciceri	Lecomte
2 July	Lydie (1)	Ballet- pantomime	none named	Hérold	Aumer	Ciceri	Lecomte
20 Aug.	Le Comte Ory (2)[11]	Opéra	Scribe, Delestre- Poirson	Rossini	[dancers featured[12]]	Ciceri	Lecomte
17 Nov.	La Fille mal gardée* (2)[13]	Ballet- pantomime	none named	Hérold	Aumer	Ciceri	Lecomte
1829							
27 April	La Belle au bois dormant (4)	Ballet- pantomime- féerie	Scribe	Hérold	Aumer	Ciceri	Lecomte
3 Aug.	Guillaume Tell (4)	Opéra	Bis, de Jouy	Rossini	Aumer	Ciceri	Lecomte
1830							
15 March	François I à Chambord (2)	Opéra	Saint-Yon, Fougeroux	de Ginestet	Vestris	Ciceri	Lecomte
3 May	Manon Lescaut (3)	Ballet- pantomime	Scribe	Halévy	Aumer	Ciceri	Lecomte
13 Oct.	Le Dieu et la Bayadère (2)	Opéra	Scribe	Auber	Taglioni	Ciceri	Lecomte
1831							
6 April	Euryanthe* (3)	Opéra	von Chézy, tr. Castil- Blaze	Weber	*no ballets*	Ciceri	unknown[14]

(continued)

APPENDIX ONE 203

Date of 1st Opéra perf.	Title No. of acts	Genre[2]	Librettist	Composer[3]	Choreographer[4]	Scene designer	Costume designer
20 June	Le Philtre (2)	Opéra	Scribe	Auber	[dancers featured]	Ciceri	unknown[15]
18 July	L'Orgie (3)[16]	Ballet-pantomime	Scribe	Carafa	Coralli	Ciceri	Lami
21 Nov.	Robert le diable (5)	Opéra	Scribe, Delavigne	Meyerbeer	Taglioni	Ciceri	Lapaulle
1832							
12 March	La Sylphide (2)[17]	Ballet-pantomime	Nourrit	Schneitzhoeffer	Taglioni	Ciceri	Lami
20 June	La Tentation (5)	Ballet-Opéra	Cavé, Duponchel	Halévy, Gide	Coralli	Bertin, Lami, Feuchère, Delaroche, Roqueplan	Boulanger, Lormier
1 Oct.	Le Serment, ou les Faux Monnayeurs (3)	Opéra	Scribe, Mazères	Auber	[dancers featured]	Ciceri	Lami
7 Nov.	Nathalie, ou la Laitière suisse* (2)[18]	Ballet	none named	Gyrowetz, Carafa[19]	Taglioni	Ciceri	Lami
1833							
27 Feb.	Gustave III ou la bal masqué (5)	Opéra historique	Scribe	Auber	Taglioni	Feuchère, Dieterle, Alfred, Ciceri, Philastre, Cambon	Lami, Lormier
22 July	Ali-Baba ou les Quarante voleurs (4)[20]	Opéra	Scribe, Mélesville	Cherubini	Coralli	Ciceri, Philastre, Cambon	Lami, Lormier

(*continued*)

APPENDIX ONE

Date of 1st Opéra perf.	Title No. of acts	Genre[2]	Librettist	Composer[3]	Choreographer[4]	Scene designer	Costume designer
4 Dec.	La Révolte au Sérail (3)[21]	Ballet-féerie	none named	Labarre	Taglioni	Ciceri, Feuchère, Despléchin, Léger	Lormier, Duponchel
1834							
10 March	Don Juan* (5) [Don Giovanni]	Opéra	DaPonte, trans. Deschamps, Blaze, and Castil-Blaze[22]	Mozart, arr. Castil-Blaze	Coralli	Ciceri, Feuchère, Despléchin, Philastre, Cambon	Duponchel
15 Sept.	La Tempête, ou l'ile des génies (2)	Ballet-féerie	Nourrit	Schneitzhoeffer	Coralli	Ciceri, Feuchère, Dieterle, Despléchin, Séchan	unknown[23]
1835							
23 Feb.	La Juive (5)	Opéra	Scribe	Halévy	Taglioni	Ciceri, Feuchère, Dieterle, Despléchin, Philastre, Cambon	Lormier
8 April	Brézilia, ou la Tribue des Femmes* (1)	Ballet	none named	Gallenberg	Taglioni Cambon	Philastre,	Lormier
12 Aug.	L'Ile des Pirates (4)	Ballet-pantomime	Nourrit	Carlini, Gide[24]	Henry, Bonnachon[25]	Séchan, Feuchère, Dieterle, Despléchin, Philastre, Cambon	Fleury?

(continued)

APPENDIX ONE   205

Date of 1st Opéra perf.	Title No. of acts	Genre[2]	Librettist	Composer[3]	Choreog- rapher[4]	Scene designer	Costume designer
1836							
29 Feb.	Les Huguenots (5)	Opéra	Scribe, Deschamps	Meyerbeer	Taglioni	Séchan, Feuchère, Dieterle, Despléchin	Delaroche
1 June	Le Diable boiteux (3)	Ballet- pantomime	de Burgy, Nourrit	Gide	Coralli	Feuchère, Despléchin, Dieterle, Séchan, Philastre, Cambon	Orschwiller
21 Sept.	La Fille du Danube (2)	Ballet- pantomime	none named	Adam	Taglioni	Ciceri, Dieterle, Feuchère, Despléchin, Séchan	Orschwiller
14 Nov.	La Esméralda (4)	Opéra	Hugo	Bertin	[dancers featured]	Philastre, Cambon	Boulanger
1837							
3 March	Stradella (5)	Opéra	Deschamps, Pacini	Nieder- meyer	Coralli	Séchan, Feuchère, Dieterle, Despléchin	Orschwiller
5 July	Les Mohicans (2)[26]	Ballet- pantomime	L. Halévy	Adam	Guerra	Devoir, Pourchet	Lormier
16 Oct.	La Chatte Metamorphosée en femme (3)	Ballet- pantomime	Duveyrier	Montfort	Coralli	Devoir, Philastre, Cambon	Lormier
1838							
5 March	Guido et Ginevra ou la Peste de Florence (5)	Opéra	Scribe	Halévy	Mazilier	Philastre, Cambon	Lormier

(*continued*)

Date of 1st Opéra perf.	Title No. of acts	Genre[2]	Librettist	Composer[3]	Choreographer[4]	Scene designer	Costume designer
5 May	La Volière ou les Oiseux de Boccace (1)	Ballet-pantomime	Scribe	Gide	T. Elssler	Philastre, Cambon	Lormier
10 Sept.	Benvenuto Cellini (2)	Opéra	Wailly, Barbier	Berlioz	[dancers featured]	Philastre, Cambon	Lormier
1839							
28 Jan.	La Gipsy (3)	Ballet-pantomime	St.-Georges	Benoist (I), Thomas (II), Marliani (III)	Mazilier	Philastre, Cambon	Lormier
1 April	Le Lac des Fées	Opéra	Scribe, Mélesville	Auber	Coralli	Philastre, Cambon	Lormier
24 June	La Tarentule (2)	Ballet-pantomime	Scribe	Gide	Coralli	Séchan, Feuchère, Dieterle, Despléchin	Lormier
11 Sept.	La Vendetta (3)	Opéra	Pillet, Vannois	de Ruolz	Mazilier	Philastre, Cambon	Lormier
28 Oct.	La Xacarilla (1)	Opéra	Scribe	Marliani	[dancers featured]	Philastre, Cambon	Lormier
1840							
6 Jan.	Le Drapier (3)	Opéra	Scribe	Halévy	[dancers featured][27]	Philastre, Cambon	Lormier
10 April	Les Martyrs* (4)[28]	Opéra	Scribe	Donizetti	Coralli	Devoir, Pourchet, Séchan, Feuchère Dieterle, Despléchin	Lormier
23 Sept.	Le Diable Amoureux (3)	Ballet-pantomime	St.-Georges	Benoist (I, III), Reber (II)	Mazilier	Philastre, Cambon	Lormier

(*continued*)

Date of 1st Opéra perf.	Title No. of acts	Genre[2]	Librettist	Composer[3]	Choreographer[4]	Scene designer	Costume designer
2 Dec.	La Favorite (4)	Opéra	Royer, Vaez	Donizetti	Albert[29]	Philastre, Cambon, Séchan, Feuchère, Dieterle, Despléchin	Lormier
1841							
9 April	Le Comte de Carmagnola (2)	Opéra	Scribe	Thomas	no ballets	Ciceri	Lormier
June	Le Freyschutz (3)	Opéra romantique	Kind	Weber (ed. by Pacini, Berlioz)	Mazilier	Philastre, Cambon	Lormier
8 June	Giselle ou les Wilis (2)	Ballet fantastique	Gautier, St.-Georges	Adam	Coralli, Perrot	Ciceri	Lormier
2 Dec.	La Reine de Chypre (5)	Opéra	St.-Georges	Halévy	Mazilier	Philastre, Cambon	Lormier
1842							
2 June	La Jolie Fille de Gand (3)	Ballet-pantomime	St.-Georges	Adam	Albert	Ciceri, Philastre, Cambon	Lormier
2 June	Le Guérillero (2)	Opéra	Anne	Thomas	[dancers featured]	Séchan, Dieterle, Despléchin	Lormier
Nov.	Le Vaisseau-Fantôme (2)	Opéra	Foucher, Révoil (after Wagner)	Dietsch	no ballets	Philastre, Cambon	Lormier
1843							
5 March	Charles VI (5)	Opéra	C. & G. Delavigne	Halévy	Mazilier	Ciceri, Philastre, Cambon, Séchan, Dieterle, Despléchin	Lormier

(continued)

APPENDIX ONE

Date of 1st Opéra perf.	Title No. of acts	Genre[2]	Librettist	Composer[3]	Choreog- rapher[4]	Scene designer	Costume designer
17 July	La Péri (2)	Ballet-pantomime	Gautier	Burgmuller	Coralli	Séchan, Dieterle, Despléchin, Philastre, Cambon	Lormier, Orschwiller
13 Nov.	Dom Sébastien, Roi de Portugal (5)	Opéra	Scribe	Donizetti	Albert	Séchan, Dieterle, Despléchin, Philastre, Cambon	Lormier
1844							
21 Feb.	Lady Henriette ou la Servante de Greenwich (3)	Ballet-pantomime	St.-Georges	Flotow (I), Burgmuller (II), Deldevez (III)	Mazilier	Ciceri, Rubé	Lormier
29 March	Le Lazzarone (2)	Opéra	St.-Georges	Halévy	[dancers featured]	Dieterle, Séchan, Despléchin, Philastre, Cambon	Lormier
7 Aug.	Eucharis (2)	Ballet-pantomime	none named	Deldevez	Coralli	Ciceri, Séchan, Dieterle, Despléchin	Lormier
2 Sept.	Othello* (4)	Opéra	Berio di Salsa	Rossini	Mazilier	[Borrowed from other produc- tions]	Lormier
7 Oct.	Richard en Palestine (3)	Opéra	Foucher	Adam	Mazilier	Séchan, Dieterle, Despléchin, Ciceri	Lormier
6 Dec.	Marie Stuart (5)	Opéra	Anne	Nieder- meyer	Coralli	Séchan, Dieterle, Despléchin, Philastre, Cambon	Lormier

(*continued*)

APPENDIX ONE 209

Date of 1st Opéra perf.	Title No. of acts	Genre[2]	Librettist	Composer[3]	Choreographer[4]	Scene designer	Costume designer
1845							
11 Aug.	Le Diable à Quatre (2)	Ballet-pantomime	deLeuven	Adam	Mazilier	Ciceri, Séchan, Sieterle, Despléchin	Lormier
17 Dec.	L'Etoile de Séville (4)	Grand opéra	Lucas	Balfe	Coralli	Philastre, Cambon, Séchan, Dieterle, Despléchin	Lormier
1846							
1 April	Paquita (2)	Ballet-pantomime	Foucher	Deldevez	Mazilier	Philastre, Cambon, Séchan, Dieterle, Despléchin	Lormier, Orschwiller
20 Feb.	Lucie de Lammermoor* (4)	Opéra	Cammarano	Donizetti	[dancers featured][30]	Ciceri[31]	Bianchini[32]
3 June	David (3)	Opéra	Soumet, Mallefille	Mermet	Coralli	Séchan, Dieterle, Despléchin, Ciceri, Rubé	Lormier
29 June	L'âme en peine (2)	Ballet-fantastique	St.-Georges	Flotow	Coralli	Thierry, Martin Wagner, Ciceri, Rubé	Lormier
10 July	Betty (2)	Ballet-pantomime	none named	Thomas	Mazilier	Séchan, Dieterle, Despléchin, Ciceri, Rubé, Philastre, Cambon	Lormier

(*continued*)

Date of 1st Opéra perf.	Title No. of acts	Genre[2]	Librettist	Composer[3]	Choreographer[4]	Scene designer	Costume designer
30 Dec.	Robert Bruce (3)	Opéra	Royer, Vaez	Rossini, arr. Niedermeyer	Mazilier	Thierry, Cambon, Dieterle, Deschéplin, Philastre, Cambon	Lormier
1847							
26 April	Ozaï, ou l'insulaire (2)	Ballet-pantomime	none named	Gide	Coralli	Ciceri, Rubé	Lormier
31 May	La Bouquetière (1)	Opéra	Lucas	Adam	no ballets	Cambon, Thierry	Lormier
20 Oct.	La Fille de Marbre (2)	Ballet-pantomime	none named	Pugni	St.-Léon	Cambon, Thierry	Lormier
26 Nov.	Jérusalem (4)	Opéra	Royer, Vaez	Verdi	Mabille	Séchan, Dieterle, Despléchin, Cambon, Thierry	Lormier
1848							
16 Feb.	Griseldis ou les Cinq Sens (3)	Ballet-pantomime	Dumanoir	Adam	Mazilier	Cambon, Thierry	Lormier
16 June	L'Apparition (2)	Opéra	Delavigne	Benoist	Mabille	Séchan, Dieterle, Despléchin	?[33]
21 Aug.	Nisida ou les Amazones des Açores (2)	Ballet-pantomime	Delavigne	Benoist	Mabille	Ciceri, Philastre, Cambon, Thierry	Lormier
20 Oct.	La Vivandière (1)	Ballet-pantomime	none named	Pugni	St.-Léon	Séchan, Dieterle, Despléchin	Lormier

(continued)

APPENDIX ONE 211

Date of 1st Opéra perf.	Title No. of acts	Genre[2]	Librettist	Composer[3]	Choreographer[4]	Scene designer	Costume designer
6 Nov.	Jeanne la Folle (5)	Opéra	Scribe	Clapisson	Mabille	Séchan, Dieterle, Despléchin, Cambon, Thierry	Lormier
1849							
19 Jan.	Le Violon du Diable (2)	Ballet fantastique	none named	Pugni	St.-Léon	Despléchin, Thierry	Lormier
16 April	Le Prophète (5)	Opéra	Scribe	Meyerbeer	Mabille	Cambon, Thierry Séchan, Despléchin	Lormier
8 Oct.	La Filleule des Fées (3)	Ballet-féerie	St.-Georges	Adam	Perrot	Cambon, Thierry, Despléchin	Lormier
24 Déc.	Le Fanal (2)	Opéra	St.-Georges	Adam	no ballets	?[34]	?[35]
1850							
22 Feb.	Stella ou les Contrebandiers (2)	Ballet-pantomime	none named	Pugni	St.-Léon	Cambon, Thierry	Lormier
6 Dec.	L'Enfant Prodigue (5)	Opéra	Scribe	Auber	St.-Léon	Despléchin, Séchan, Cambon, Thierry	Lormier

*Created at a house other than the Paris Opéra.

[1] I consulted the following sources in compiling this table: first-, second-, and third-edition libretti for many of the works in question (from the *livret* collection at the Bibliothèque nationale and at the Blbiothèque de l'Opéra), the manuscript *Journal de l'Opéra* (F-Po Usuels, Réserve), costume lists in F-Pan AJ13 184, 185, 214, 215, and 223; Castil-Blaze, *L'Académie Impériale de Musique;* Gustave Chouquet, *Histoire de la Musique Dramatique en France;* A. Soubies, *Soixante-sept ans à l'Opéra en unge page du "Siège de Corinthe" à "La walkyrie" (1826–1893)* (Paris: Fischbacher, 1893); Franz Stieger, *Opernlexicon* (Tutzing: Schneider, 1975–83); Théodore LaJarte, *Bibliothèque musicale du Théâtre de l'Opéra—Catalogue;* Ivor Guest, *Le Ballet de l'opéra de Paris,* tr. Paul Alexandre; Ivor Guest, *The Romantic Ballet in Paris;* and Nicole Wild, *Décors et Costumes du XIXe Siècle a l'Opéra de Paris.*

Oratorios and cantatas performed at the Opéra during this period are *Loyse de Montfort,* with text by Pacini and Deschamps and music by Bazin, first performed 7 Oct. 1840 (performed in costume and designated as an opera in its libretto); *Le Renégat* (de Pastoret/Massé, 21 Feb. 1845); *Lionel Foscari* (Maillart and de Pastoret, 13 Oct. 1841); *Moïse au Sinaï* (St.-Etinne/David, 21 March 1846) and *L'Éden,* a "mystère en 2 parties" (Méry/David, 25 Aug. 1848).

[2] I have listed the genre as designated in the earliest available edition of the libretti at the Bibliothèque nationale and the Bibliothèque de l'Opéra.

(*continued*)

³Note that the task of the ballet composer often included arranging borrowed music in addition to providing original music.

⁴Libretti and newspaper reviews tend to name the person responsible for ballets without using the terms "choreographer" or "ballet master."

⁵Composed in honor of the coronation of Charles X.

⁶It may usually be assumed, when no author is mentioned by name, that the author is the choreographer.

⁷Based on the opéra comique *Joconde, ou les coureurs d'aventures* (3 acts), with text by Étienne, music by Isouard, first performed at the Opéra-comique 28 Feb. 1814.

⁸Based on Molière's comédie-ballet of the same name.

⁹Schneitzhoeffer wrote the overture and several dance airs for this work.

¹⁰There is no inventory number for décorations for this ballet, and the total value of accessories in 1848 was very low. It seems likely that décorations for this work were borrowed from other works. (F- Pn AJ 13 223)

¹¹This work was an updated version of a vaudeville originally written by Scribe and Poirson in 1816.

¹²For most of the Opéra's shorter operas of this period (i.e., those of 3 acts or fewer) there exists evidence—for example, rehearsal scores for ballet, or mention of dancers in newspaper reviews, costume inventories, or librettis—indicating that dancers were included in the performance, though no choreographer is named. (Perhaps the choreography devised was not elaborate enough to warrant attribution. In some cases, perhaps, the dancers did not dance but carried out some sort of stage business that required special skills lacked by chorus members and extras.) For each such opera in this table, I have simply indicated in the "choreographer" column that dancers were featured.

¹³The first version of this ballet, *Le Ballet de la Paille*, was created by Dauberval in Bordeaux and first performed 1 July 1789 (Guest, *The Romantic Ballet in Paris*, 88, 288).

¹⁴It is likely that costumes for this production were borrowed from other works. See AJ 13 214 and 215.

¹⁵Though the designer is unnamed, 144 costumes for this work were listed in an inventory of 1838 (AJ13 215).

¹⁶This work, called *Léocadie* in its earliest stages, is based on the opéra comique *Léocadie* by Scribe and Auber, first performed at the Opéra-comique 4 Nov. 1824.

¹⁷This work was preceded by Louis Henry's *La Silfide*, at La Scala, Milan, in 1828. On Elise Henry's accusations of Taglioni of plagiarism of her brother's work, see Guest, *The Romantic Ballet in Paris*, 116, 123, 126, 289.

¹⁸Filippo Taglioni had staged an earlier version of this ballet at the Court Opera in Vienna (first performed 18 July 1821), with a score by Gyrowetz, as *Das Schwiezer Milchmädchen*. It was then restaged by Titus in Paris at the Théâtre de la Porte-Saint-Martin in September 1823 as *La Latière suisse*.

¹⁹According to Chouquet, Carafa retouched and augmented Gyrowetz's Viennese score (*Histoire de la Musique Dramatique en France*, 397).

²⁰According to Castil-Blaze, this is based on a play of 1791 by Duveyrier-Mélesville père called *Koukourgi* (*L'Académie Impériale de Musique*, 240).

²¹Filippo Taglioni had staged an earlier version of this ballet, *Die Neue Amazon*, at the Royal Opera in Berlin (first performed 4 May 1830), with a score by Kramer, arranged by Henning. Labarre wrote new music for the Paris production. Taglioni's *Die Neue Amazon* was preceded by Louis Henry's *Die Amazonen*.

²²Blaze was the son of Castil-Blaze.

²³Two unsigned *maquettes de costumes* exist; see Wild, *Décors et costumes*, 262.

²⁴Carlini wrote the music for Act One and the pas de deux of Act Three; Gide provided the rest.

²⁵The libretto names "Henry et * * *" as choreographers.

²⁶According to Gautier, a set depicting a North American forest in this ballet was a retouched version of one used to depict a South American forest in *Brézilia*. Guest, *Gautier on Dance*, 10.

²⁷It is known that the ballet soloists Louise and Nathalie Fitzjames and Eugene Coralli appeared in this opera (Guest, *The Romantic Ballet in Paris*, Appendix C).

²⁸An earlier version of *Les Martyrs*, *Poliuto* (Cammarano after Corneille, Donizetti), was first performed in Naples 30 Nov. 1848.

²⁹"Albert" was the name often used by François Decombe.

³⁰Ballet soloists in this opera were Plunkett, Robert, L. Petipa, and Hilariot. (Guest, *The Romantic Ballet in Paris*, Appendix C.)

³¹No new décors were created for this revival; borrowings were made from *Sigurd, Freischütz, Henri VIII, Le Prophète, La Korrigane, Robert le diable, le Roi de Lahore, Françoise de Rimini, Don Juan,* and *Faust*. (Wild, *Décors et costumes,* 164–65).

³²Approximately 180 costumes were refurbished for this production, and six were newly created (AJ13 215).

³³Only two new costumes were made for this production (AJ13 215).

³⁴Décors were borrowed from *Moïse* and *La Muette de Portici* (AJ13 185).

³⁵Of the 137 costumes for this work only fourteen were new (F-Pa AJ13 185). See also Wild, *Décors et costumes,* 99.

APPENDIX TWO

GISELLE[1]
OU
LES WILIS,

Ballet fantastique en deux Actes,
par

MM. DE SAINT-GEORGES, THÉOPHILE GAUTIER ET CORALY;
MUSIQUE DE M. ADOLPHE ADAM,
Décorations de Mr Cicéri.
REPRÉSENTÉ POUR LA PREMIÈRE FOIS SUR LE THÉÂTRE DE L'ACADÉMIE
ROYALE DE MUSIQUE, LE LUNDI 28 JUIN 1841.
PARIS.
MME VVE JONAS, ÉDITEUR, LIBRAIRIE DE L'OPÉRA
1841.

ACTE PREMIER.

PERSONNAGES.		ACTEURS.
LE DUC ALBERT DE SILÉSIE, sous les habits de villageois	MM.	PETIPA.
LE PRINCE DE COURLANDE		QUÉRIAU.
WILFRIDE, Ecuyer du Duc		CORALLI.
HILARION, Garde-Chasse		SIMON.
UN VIEILLARD PAYSAN.		L. PETIT.
BATHILDE, Fiancée du Duc	Mlles	FORSTER.
GISELLE, Paysanne		CARLOTTA GRISI.
BERTHE, Mère de Giselle		ROLAND.
MYRTHA, Reine des Wilis		ADÈLE DUMILATRE.
ZULMÉ ⎫ Wilis		SOPHIE DUMILATRE.
MOYNA ⎭		CARRÉ.

---

[1] All ellipses are to be found in the original text; I have deleted nothing. Note also that, if two or more of the Opéra's dancers shared the same surname, they were listed in the order in which they had been hired there (for instance, Dabas 1re, Dabas 2me, etc.).

PAS DÉTACHÉS.

PAS DE 2. M. Mabille; Mlle Nathalie Fitzjames.
PAS DE 2. M. Petipa; Mlle Grisi.

CORYPHÉES.

M. Desplaces 2me.

Mmes	Dimier.	Mmes	Marquet 1re.
	Breistroff.		Laurent 1re.
	Wiéthof.		Fleury.
	Caroline.		Robert.

VIGNERONS.

MM.	Isambert.	MM.	Renauzy.
	Millot.		Chatillon.
	Lefevre.		Constant.
	Célarius.		Gourdoux.
	Duhan.		Cornet 2me.
	Dugit.		Rouyet.
	Fromage.		Souton.
	Dimier.		Scio.
Mmes	Saulnier 1re.	Mmes	Dubignon.
	Leclercq.		Galby.
	Lacroix.		Rénard 1re.
	Marivin.		Athalie.
	Colson.		Dabas 1re.
	Gougibus.		Josset.
	Robin.		Courtois.
	Bouvier.		Marquet 2me.

MUSICIENS.

MM.	Ernest.	MM.	Maujin.
	Petit-Alix.		Wiéthof 1er.

ENFANS VILLAGEOIS.

MM.	Hardy.	MM.	Peaufert.
	Liger.		Albrié.
	Minart.		Wiéthof 2me.
Mlles	Masson.	Mlles	Toulain.
	Cassan.		Vioron.
	Devion.		Hunter.
	Debas 2me.		Favre.
	Franck.		Passerieux.
	Jeunot.		Jeandron 2me.
	Laurent 2me.		Vaudras.
	Chambret.		Voisin.
	Cluchar.		Feugère.

SEIGNEURS.

MM.	Lenfant.	MM.	Darcour.
	Cornet 1er.		Feltis.
	Grénier.		Jesset.
	Martin.		Lénoir.

DAMES.

Mmes	Rodriguez.	Mmes	Léoni.
	Cartembert.		Petit.
	Clément.		Deuénil.
	Richard.		Coupotte.

PAGES.

Mmes	Pèche.	Mmes	Bourdon
	Julien.		Pézée.

CHASSEURS, PIQEURS, VALETS.

ACTE DEUXIÈME.

WILIS.

Mmes Carré.   Sophie Dumilatre.   Adèle Dumilatre.

CORYPHÉES.

Mmes	Dimier.	Mmes	Marquet 1re.
	Breistroff.		Laurent 1re.
	Wiéthof.		Fleury.
	Caroline.		Robert.
Mmes	Robin.	Mmes	Saulnier 1re.
	Athalie.		Gougibos.
	Galby.		Bouvier.
	Dubignon.		Colson.
	Marivin.		Leclercq.
	Bénard 1re.		Toussaint.
	Courtois.		Danse.
	Josset.		Lacoste.
	Dabas 1re.		Jeandron 1re.
	Chévalier.		Drouet.
	Perés.		Potier.

Les Acteurs du 1er acte.—LES VIGNERONS, LES SEIGNEURS.

TRADITION ALLEMANDE
Dont est tiré le sujet du Ballet de Giselle ou les Wilis.

Il existe une tradition de la danse nocturne connue dans les pays slaves sous le nom de Wili.—Les Wilis sont des fiancées mortes avant le jour des noces; ces pauvres jeunes créatures ne peuvent demeurer tranquilles sous leur tombeau. Dans leurs coeurs éteints, dans leurs pieds morts, est resté cet amour de la danse qu'elles n'ont pu satisfaire pendant leur vie, et à minuit elles se lèvent, se rassemblent en troupes sur la grande route et malheur au jeune homme qui les rencontre, il faut qu'il danse avec elles jusqu'à ce qu'il tombe mort.

Parées de leurs habits de noce, des couronnes de fleurs sur la tête, des anneaux brillants à leurs doigts, les *Wilis* dansent au clair de lune comme les *Elfes;* leur figure quoique d'un blanc de neige est belle de jeunesse. Elles rient avec une joie si perfide, elles vous appellent avec tant de séduction, leur air a de si douces promesses, que ces bacchantes mortes sont irrésistibles.

Henri HEINE (de l'Allemagne).

Les WILIS.
ACTE PREMIER.

Le théatre représente une riant Vallé de l'Allemagne. Au fond, des collines couvertes de vignes, une route élevée conduisant dans la Vallé.

SCÈNE Ire

Un tableau des vendanges sur les côteaux de la Thuringe, il fait à peine jour. Les vignerons s'éloignent pour continuer leur récolte.

SCÈNE II.

Hilarion paraît, regarde autour de lui, comme pour chercher quelqu'un: puis, il indique la chaumière de Giselle avec amour, et celle de Loys avec colère. *C'est là qu'habite son rival. S'il peut jamais s'en venger, il le fera avec bonheur.* La porte de la chaumière de Loys s'ouvre mystérieusement, Hilarion se cache pour voir ce qui va se passer.

SCÈNE III.

Le jeune duc Albert de Silésie, sous les habits et le nom de Loys, sort de sa maisonnette, accompagné de son écuyer Wilfride. Wilfride semble conjurer le Duc de renoncer à un projet secret; mais Loys persiste, il montre la demeure de Giselle; ce simple toit couvre celle qu'il aime, l'objet de son unique tendresse . . . Il ordonne à Wilfride de le laisser seul. Wilfride hésite encore, mais sur un geste de son maître, Wilfride le salue respectueusement, puis s'éloigne.

Hilarion est resté stupéfait, en voyant un beau seigneur comme Wilfride, témoigner tant d'égards à un simple paysan son rival. Il paraît concevoir des soupçons qu'il éclaircira plus tard.

SCÈNE IV.

Loys, ou plutôt le duc Albert, s'approche de la chaumière de Giselle, et frappe doucement à la porte. Hilarion est toujours caché. Giselle sort aussitôt et court dans les bras de son amant. Transports, bonheur des deux jeunes gens. Giselle raconte son rêve à Loys: Elle était jalouse d'une belle dame que Loys aimait, qu'il lui préférait.

Loys, troublé, la rassure: il n'aime, il n'aimera jamais qu'elle. *C'est que si tu me trompais,* lui dit le jeune fille, *je le sens, j'en mourrais.* Elle porte la main à son coeur comme pour lui dire qu'elle en souffre souvent. Loys la rassure par de vives caresses.

Elle cueille des marguerites, et les effeuille pour s'assurer de l'amour de Loys.—L'épreuve lui réussit et elle tombe dans les bras de son amant.

Hilarion n'y résistant plus, accourt près de Giselle et lui reproche sa conduite. Il était là; il a tout vu!

Eh! que m'importe, répond gaîment Giselle, *je n'en rougis pas; je l'aime, et je n'aimerai jamais que lui* . . . puis elle tourne brusquement le dos à Hilarion, en lui riant au nez, tandis que Loys le repousse et le menace de sa colère s'il ne cesse pas ses poursuites amoureuses près de Giselle. *C'est bon,* dit Hilarion avec un geste de menace, *plus tard, on verra.*

SCÈNE V.

Une troupe de jeunes vigneronnes viennent chercher Giselle pour les vendanges. Le jour paraît; c'est le moment de s'y rendre; mais Giselle, folle de danse et de plaisirs, retient ses compagnes. La danse est, après Loys, ce qu'elle aime le mieux au monde. Elle propose aux jeunes filles de se divertir au lieu d'aller au travail. Elle danse seule d'abord, pour les décider. Sa gaîté, sa joyeuse ardeur, ses pas pleins de verve et d'entraînement, qu'elle entremêle de témoignages d'amour pour Loys, sont bientôt imités par les vendangeuses. On jette au loin les paniers, les hottes, les instruments de travail, et grâce à Giselle, la danse devient bientôt bruyante et général. Berthe, la mère de Giselle, sort alors de sa chaumière.

SCÈNE VI.

—*Tu danseras donc toujours,* dit-elle à Giselle . . . *Le Soir . . . . . le matin. . . . . c'est une véritable passion . . . et cela, au lieu de travailler, de soigner le ménage.*

—*Elle danse si bien!* dit Loys à Berthe.

—*C'est mon seul plaisir,* répond Giselle, *comme lui,* ajoute-t-elle en montrant Loys, *c'est mon seul bonheur!!!*

—*Bah!* dit Berthe. *Je suis sûre que si cette petite folle mourait, elle deviendrait Wili, et danserait même après sa mort, comme toutes les filles qui ont trop aimé le bal!*

—*Que voulez-vous dire?* . . . s'écrient les jeunes vendangeuses avec effroi, en se serrant les unes contre les autres.

Berthe alors, sur une musique lugubre, semble dépeindre une apparition des morts revenant au monde, et dansant ensemble. La terreur des villageoises est à son comble. Giselle seule en rit; et répond gaîment à sa mère: qu'elle est incorrigible, et que, morte ou vivante, elle dansera toujours.

—*Et pourtant,* ajoute Berthe, *cela ne te vaut rien . . . il s'agit de ta santé, de ta vie, peut-être!!!*

Elle est bien délicate, dit-elle à Loys, *la fatigue, les émotions lui seront funestes, le médecin l'a dit, cela peut lui porter malheur.*

Loys, troublé par cette confidence, rassure la bonne mère; et Giselle, prenant la main de Loys, la presse sur son coeur, et semble dire qu'avec lui *elle n'a jamais de dangers à craindre.*

Des fanfares de chasse se font entendre au loin. Loys, inquiet à ce bruit, donne vivement le signal du départ pour les vendanges, et entraîne les paysannes; tandis que Giselle, forcée de rentre dans la chaumière avec sa mère, envoie un baiser d'adieu à Loys, qui s'éloigne suivi de tout le monde.

SCÈNE VII.

A peine Hilarion se voit-il seul, qu'il explique son projet. Il veut à tout prix, *pénétrer le secret de son rival, savoir ce qu'il est* . . . S'assurant que personne ne peut le découvrir, il entre furtivement dans la chaumière de Loys . . . A ce moment, les fanfares se rapprochent, et l'on voit paraître des piqueurs et des valets de chasse sur la colline.

SCÈNE VIII.

La Prince et Bathilde, sa fille, paraissent bientôt, à cheval, accompagnés d'une nombreuse suite de seigneurs, de dames, de fauconniers le faucon au poing. La chaleur du jour les accable; ils viennent chercher un endroit favorable pour se reposer: un piqueur indique au prince la chaumière de Berthe; il frappe à la porte, et Giselle paraît sur le seuil, suivie de sa mère. Le Prince demande gaîment l'hospitalité à la vigneronne; celle-ci lui offre d'entrer dans sa chaumière, quoique bien pauvre pour recevoir un si grand seigneur!

Pendant ce tems, Bathilde fait approcher Giselle; elle l'examine et la trouve charmante. Giselle lui fait de son mieux les honneurs de sa modeste demeure; elle engage Bathilde à s'asseoir et lui offre du laitage et des fruits. Bathilde, ravie des grâces de Giselle, détache de son cou une chaîne d'or, et la passe à celui de la jeune fille, toute fière et toute honteuse de ce présent.

Bathilde interroge Giselle sur ses travaux, sur ses plaisirs.

—*Elle est heureuse! elle n'a ni chagrins ni soucis; le matin, le travail; le soir, la danse!* . . . *Oui!* dit Berthe à Bathilde, *le danse surtout . . . c'est là sa folie.*

Bathilde sourit, et demande à Giselle si son coeur a parlé, si elle aime quelqu'un? . . . —*Oui! oui!* s'écrie la jeune fille en montrant la chaumière de Loys: *celui qui demeure là! mon amoureux, mon fiancé . . . ! Je mourrais s'il ne m'aimait plus!* Bathilde semble s'intéresser vivement à la jeune fille . . . leur position est la même, car elle aussi, va se marier à un jeune et beau seigneur. . .! elle dotera Giselle, qui semble lui plaire de plus en plus. . . . . Bathilde veut voir le fiancé de Giselle, et elle rentre dans la chaumière, suivie de son père et de Berthe, tandis que Giselle va chercher Loys.

Le Prince fait signe à sa suite de continuer la chasse; il est fatigué, et désire se reposer quelques instans. Il sonnera du cor quand il voudra les rappeler.

Hilarion, qui parait à la porte de la chaumière de Loys, voit le Prince et entend les ordres qu'il donne. Le prince entre avec sa fille dans la chaumière de Berthe.

SCÈNE IX.

Tandis que Giselle va regarder sur la route s'il elle n'aperçoit pas son amant, Hilarion ressort de la chaumière de Loys, tenant une épée et un manteau de chevalier; il connaît enfin son rival! c'est un grand seigneur! Il en est sûr à présent . . . c'est un séducteur déguisé! il tient sa vengeance, et veut le confondre en présence de Giselle et de tout le village. Il cache l'épée de Loys dans une buisson, en attendant que tous les vignerons soient rassemblés pour la fête.

SCÈNE X.
Loys parait au fond . . . il regarde autour de lui, avec inquiétude, et s'assure que la chasse s'est éloignée.

Giselle l'aperçoit et vole dans ses bras! en ce moment une joyeuse musique se fait entendre.

SCÈNE XI.
Une marche commence. La vendange est faite. Un char, orné de pampres et de fleurs, arrive lentement, suivi de tous les paysans et paysannes de la vallée avec leurs paniers pleins de raisin. Un petit Bacchus est porté triomphalement à cheval sur un tonneau, selon la vieille tradition du pays.

On entoure Giselle. On la déclare Reine des vendanges . . . On la couronne de fleurs et de pampres. Loys est plus amoureux que jamais de la jolie vigneronne. La plus folle joie s'empare bientôt de tous les paysans.

On célèbre la fête des vendanges! . . . Giselle peut se livrer maintenant à son goût favori; elle entraîne Loys au milieu de la troupe des vendangeurs, et danse avec lui, entourée de tout le village, qui se joint bientôt aux jeunes amants dont le pas se termine par un baiser que Loys donne à Giselle . . . A cette vue, la fureur, la jalousie de l'envieux Hilarion, n'ont plus de bornes . . . il s'élance au milieu de la foule, et déclare à Giselle que Loys *est un trompeur, un suborneur,* UN SEIGNEUR DÉGUISÉ! . . . Giselle, émue d'abord, répond à Hilarion qu'il ne sait ce qu'il dit; qu'il a rêvé cela . . . Ah! je l'ai rêvé, continue le garde-chasse . . . Eh bien! voyez vous-même, s'écrie-t-il en découvrant aux yeux des villageois, l'épée et le manteau de Loys. Voilà ce que j'ai trouvé dans sa chaumière . . . ce sont là des preuves, j'espère.

Albert, furieux, s'élance sur Hilarion, qui se cache derrière les villageois.

Giselle, frappée de surprise et de douleur, à cette révélation, semble recevoir un coup terrible, et s'appuie contre un arbre, chancelante et prête à tomber.

Tous les paysans s'arrêtent consternés! Loys, ou plutôt Albert, court à Giselle, et croyant encore pouvoir nier son rang, cherche à la rassurer, à la calmer par les protestations de sa tendresse. *On la trompe,* lui dit-il, *il n'est pour elle que Loys, un simple paysan, son amant, son fiancé!!!*

La pauvre fille ne demande pas mieux que de le croire. Déjà même l'espoir semble lui revenir au coeur; elle se laisse aller, heureuse et confiante, dans les bras du perfide Albert, lorsqu'Hilarion, poursuivant sa vengeance, et se rappelant l'ordre du Prince à sa suite, de revenir au son du cor, saisit celui d'un des seigneurs, appendu à un arbre, et en sonne avec force . . . A ce signal on voit accourir toute la chasse, et le Prince sort de la chaumière de Berthe. Hilarion désigne à la suite du Prince, Albert aux genoux de Giselle; et chacun en reconnaissant le jeune duc, l'accable de saluts et de respect. Giselle, en voyant cela, ne peut plus douter de son malheur et du rang élevé d'Albert.

SCÈNE XII.
Le Prince s'approche à son tour, reconnaît Albert, et se découvrant aussitôt lui demande l'explication de son étrange conduite et du costume qu'il porte.

Albert se relève, stupéfait et confondu de cette rencontre.

Giselle a tout vu! Elle est sûre alors de la nouvelle trahison de celui qu'elle aime, sa douleur est sans bornes; elle semble faire un effort sur elle-même, et s'éloigne d'Albert avec un sentiment de crainte et de terreur. Puis, comme atterrée par ce nouveau coup qui la frappe, elle court vers la chaumière et tombe dans les bras de sa mère, qui en sort en ce moment, accompagnée de la jeune Bathilde.

SCÈNE XIII.

Bathilde s'avance vivement vers Giselle, et l'interroge avec un touchant intérêt sur l'agitation qu'elle éprouve. Celle-ci, pour toute réponse, lui montre Albert accablé et confondu.

Que vois-je? . . . dit Bathilde . . . *Le Duc sous ce costume!* . . . *Mais c'est lui que je dois épouser* . . . *C'est mon fiancé!* . . . ajoute-t-elle, en désignant l'anneau des fiançailles qu'elle porte à son doigt.

Albert s'approche de Bathilde, et veut en vain l'empêcher d'achever ce terrible aveu; mais Giselle a tout entendu, tout compris! La plus profonde horreur se peint sur les traits de la malheureuse enfant; sa tête se trouble, un horrible et sombre délire s'empare d'elle, en se voyant trahie, perdue, déshonorée! . . . Sa raison s'égare, ses larmes coulent . . . puis elle rit d'un rire nerveux. Elle prend la main d'Albert, la pose sur son coeur, et la repousse bientôt avec effroi. Elle saisit l'épée de Loys, restée à terre, joue d'abord machinalement avec cette arme, puis va se laisser tomber sur sa pointe aiguë, quand sa mère se précipite sur elle et la lui arrache. L'amour de la danse revient à la mémoire de la pauvre enfant: elle croit entendre l'air de son pas avec Albert . . . . elle s'élance et se met à danser avec ardeur, avec passion. Tant de douleurs subites, tant de cruelles secousses, jointes à ce dernier effort, ont enfin épuisé ses forces mourantes . . . la vie semble l'abandonner . . . sa mère la reçoit dans ses bras . . . un dernier soupir s'échappe du coeur de la pauvre Giselle . . . elle jette un triste regard sur Albert au désespoir, *et ses yeux se ferment pour toujours!*

Bathilde, bonne et généreuse, fond en larmes. Albert, oubliant tout, cherche à ranimer Giselle sous ses brûlantes caresses . . . Il met la main sur le coeur de la jeune fille, et s'assure avec horreur qu'il a cessé de battre.

Il saisit son épée pour s'en frapper; le prince l'arrête et le désarme. Berthe soutient le corps de sa malheureuse fille. On entraîne Albert, fou de désespoir et d'amour.

Les paysans, les seigneurs, toute la chasse, entourent et complètent ce triste tableau.

FIN DU PREMIER ACTE

ACTE DEUXIÈME.

Le théâtre représente une Forêt sur le bord d'un étang. Un site humide et frais où croissent des joncs, des roseaux, des touffes de fleurs sauvages et de plantes aquatiques; des bouleaux, des trembles et des saules-pleureurs inclinent jusqu'à terre leurs pâles feuillages. A gauche, sous un cyprès, se dresse un croix de marbre blanc où est gravé le nom de Giselle. La tombe est comme enfouie dans un végétation épaisse d'herbes et de fleurs des champs. La lueur bleue d'une lune très vive éclaire cette décoration d'un aspect froid et vaporeux.

SCÈNE I.

Quelques gardes-chasse arrivent par les avenues de la forêt; ils semblent chercher un endroit favorable pour se mettre à l'affût, et vont s'établir sur le bord de l'étang, lorsque Hilarion accourt.

SCÈNE II.

Hilarion témoigne la plus vive terreur en devinant les projets de ses camarades. *C'est un endroit maudit,* leur dit-il, *c'est le cercle de danse des Wilis!* Il leur montre la tombe de Giselle . . . de Giselle qui dansait toujours. Il la désigne par la couronne de pampres qu'on lui mit sur le front pendant la fête, et qui est appendue à la croix de marbre.

A cet instant, on entend sonner minuit dans le lointain: c'est l'heure lugubre où, selon la chronique du pays, les Wilis se rendent à leur salle de bal.

Hilarion et ses compagnons écoutent l'horloge avec terreur; ils regardent en tremblant autour d'eux, s'attendant à l'apparition des légers fantômes. *Fuyons,* dit Hilarion, *les Wilis sont impitoyables; elles s'emparent des voyageurs et les font danser avec elles, jusqu'à ce qu'ils meurent de fatigue ou soient engloutis dans le lac que vous voyez d'ici.*

Une musique fantastique commence alors; les gardes-chasse pâlissent, chancellent et s'enfuient de tous côtés, avec les signes du plus grand effroi, poursuivies par des feux follets qui apparaissent de toutes parts.

SCÈNE III.

Une gerbe de jonc marin s'entrouvre alors lentement, et du sein de l'humide feuillage on voit s'élancer la légère Myrtha, ombre transparente et pâle, *la Reine des Wilis.* Elle apporte avec elle un jour mystérieux qui éclaire subitement la forêt, en perçant les ombres de la nuit. Il en est ainsi toutes les fois que les Wilis paraissent sur les blanches épaules de Myrtha, palpitent et frémissent des ailes diaphanes dans lesquelles la Wili peut s'envelopper comme avec un voile de gaze.

Cette apparition insaisissable ne peut rester en place, et s'élançant tantôt sur une touffe de fleurs, tantôt sur une branche de saule, voltige çà et là, parcourant et semblant reconnaître son petit empire, dont elle vient chaque nuit prendre de nouveau possession. Elle se baigne dans les eaux du lac, puis se suspend aux branches des saules et s'y balance.

Après un pas dansé par elle seule, elle cueille une branche de romarin, et en touche alternativement chaque plante, chaque buisson, chaque touffe de feuillage.

SCÈNE IV.

A mesure que la sceptre fleuri de la reine des Wilis s'arrête sur un objet, la plante, la fleur, le buisson s'entr'ouvrent, et il s'en échappe une nouvelle Wili qui vient, à son tour, se grouper gracieusement autour de Myrtha, comme les abeilles autour de leur reine. Celle-ci, étendant alors ses ailes azurées sur ses sujettes, leur donne ainsi le signal de la danse. Plusieurs Wilis se présentent alors alternativement devant la souveraine.

C'est Moyna, d'Odalisque, exécutant un pas oriental; puis Zulmé, la Bayadère, qui vient développer ses poses indiennes, puis deux Françaises, figurant une sorte de menuet bizarre; puis des Allemandes, valsant entr'elles. . . . Puis enfin la troupe entière des Wilis, toutes mortes pour avoir trop aimé la danse, ou mortes trop tôt, sans avoir assez satisfait cette folle passion, à laquelle elles semblent se livrer encore avec fureur sous leur gracieuse métamorphose.

Bientôt, sur un signe de la reine, le bal fantastique s'arrête. . . . Elle annonce une nouvelle soeur à ses sujettes. Toutes se rangent autour d'elle.

SCÈNE V.

Un rayon de lune vif et clair se projette alors sur la tombe de Giselle, les fleurs qui la couvrent se relèvent et se dressent sur leurs tiges, comme pour former un passage à la blanche créature qu'elles recouvrent.

Giselle parait enveloppée de son léger suaire. Elle s'avance vers Myrtha, qui la touche de sa branche de romarin; le suaire tombe . . . Giselle est changée en Wili. Ses ailes naissent et se développent . . . ses pieds rasent le sol. Elle danse, ou plutôt elle voltige dans l'air, comme ses gracieuses soeurs, se rappelant et indiquant avec joie les pas qu'elle a dansé, au premier acte, avant sa mort.

Un bruit lointain se fait entendre. Toutes les Wilis se dispersent et se cachent dans les roseaux.

SCÈNE VI.

De jeunes villageois revenant de la fête du hameau voisin traversent gaiment la scène, conduits par un vieillard; ils vont s'éloigner, lorsqu'une musique bizarre, l'air de la danse des Wilis se fait entendre, les paysans semblent éprouver, malgré eux, une étrange envie de danser. Les Wilis les entourent aussitôt, les enlacent et les fascinent par leurs poses voluptueuses.

Chacune d'elles, cherchant à les retenir, à leur plaire, avec les figures de leur danse native. . . . Les villageois émus, vont se laisser séduire, danser et mourir, lorsque le vieillard se jette au milieu d'eux, leur dit avec effroi le danger qu'ils courent, et ils se sauvent tous, poursuivis par les Wilis, furieuses de voir cette proie leur échapper.

SCÈNE VII.

Albert parait suivi de Wilfride, son fidèle écuyer. Le Duc est triste, pâle; ses vêtemens sont en désordre; sa raison s'est presqu'égarée à la suite de la mort de Giselle. Il s'approche lentement de la croix, semble chercher un souvenir, et vouloir rappeler ses idées confuses.

Wilfride supplie Albert de le suivre, de ne pas s'arrêter près de ce fatal tombeau, qui lui retrace tant de chagrins . . . Albert l'engage à s'éloigner . . . Wilfride insiste encore; mais Albert lui ordonne avec tant de fermeté de la quitter, que Wilfride est forcé d'obéir, et sort, en se promettant bien de faire une dernière tentative pour éloigner son maître de ce lieu funeste.

SCÈNE VIII.

A peine resté seul, Albert donne un libre cours à sa douleur; son coeur se déchire, il fond en larmes. Tout-à-coup il pâlit, ses regards se fixent sur un objet étrange, qui se dessine devant ses yeux .. Il reste frappé de surprise et presque de terreur, en reconnaissant Giselle qui le regarde avec amour.

SCÈNE IX.

En proie au plus violent délire, à la plus vive anxiété, il doute encore, il n'ose croire à ce qu'il voit; car ce n'est plus la jolie Giselle, tel qu'il l'adorait, mais Giselle la Wili, dans sa nouvelle et bizarre métamorphose, toujours immobile devant lui. La Wili semble seulement l'appeler du regard. Albert, se croyant sous l'empire d'une douce illusion, s'approche d'elle à pas lents, et avec précaution, comme un enfant qui veut saisir un papillon sur une fleur. Mais au moment où il étend la main vers Giselle, plus prompte que l'éclair, celle-ci s'élance loin de lui, et s'envoie en traversant les airs comme une colombe craintive, pour se poser à une autre place, d'où elle lui jette des regards pleins d'amour.

Ce pas, ou plutôt ce vol se répète plusieurs fois, au grand désespoir d'Albert, qui cherche vainement à joindre la Wili fuyant quelques fois au-dessus de lui comme une légère vapeur.

Par fois pourtant, elle lui fait un geste d'amour, lui jette un fleur, qu'elle enlève sur sa tige, lui adresse un baiser; mais, impalpable comme un nuage elle disparaît dès qu'il croit pouvoir le saisir.

Il y renonce enfin! s'agenouille près de la croix, et joint les mains devant elle, d'un air suppliant. La Wili, comme attirée par cette muette douleur, si pleine d'amour, s'élance légèrement près de son amant: il la touche; déjà, ivre d'amour, de bonheur, il va s'en emparer, lorsque glissant doucement entre ses bras, elle s'évanouit au milieu des roses, et Albert, en ferment les bras, n'embrasse plus que la croix du tombeau.

Le désespoir le plus profond s'empare de lui, il se relève et va s'éloigner de ce lieu de douleur, lorsque le plus étrange spectacle s'offre à ses yeux et le fascine au point qu'il est en quelque sorte arrêté, fixe, et forcé d'être témoin de l'étrange scène qui se déroule devant lui.

SCÈNE X.

Caché derrière un saule pleureur, Albert voit paraître le misérable Hilarion, poursuivi par la troupe entière des Wilis.

Pâle, tremblant, presque mort de peur, le garde-chasse vient tomber au pied d'un arbre, et semble implorer la pitié de ses folles ennemies! Mais la Reine des Wilis le touchant de son sceptre, le force à se lever, et à imiter le mouvement de danse qu'elle commence elle-même autour de lui. . . . Hilarion, mû par une force magique, danse, malgré lui, avec la belle Wili, jusqu'à ce que celle-ci le cède à une de ses compagnes, qui le cède, à son tour, à une autre, et ainsi de suite jusqu'à la dernière!

Dès que le malheureux croit son supplice terminé avec sa partenaire fatiguée, une autre la remplace avec une nouvelle vigueur, et lui, s'épuisant en efforts inouïs, sur des rythmes de musique toujours plus rapides, finit par chanceler et se sentir accablé de lassitude et de douleur.

Prenant enfin un parti désespéré, il cherche à s'enfuir; mais les Wilis l'entourent d'un vaste cercle, qui se rétrécit peu à peu, l'enferme, et se convertit en une valse rapide, à laquelle une puissance surnaturelle l'oblige à se mêler. Un vertige alors s'empare du garde-chasse, qui sort des bras d'une valseuse pour tomber dans ceux d'une autre.

La victime, enveloppée de toutes parts dans ce gracieux et mortel réseau, sent bientôt ses genoux plier sous lui. Ses yeux se ferment, il n'y voit plus . . . et danse pourtant encore avec une ardent frénésie. La reine des Wilis s'en empare alors et le fait tourner et valser une dernière fois avec elle, jusqu'à ce que le pauvre diable, arrivé sur le bord du lac, au dernier anneau de la chaîne des valseuses, ouvre les bras, croyant en saisir une nouvelle et va rouler dans l'abîme! Les Wilis commencent alors une bacchanale joyeuse, dirigée par leur reine triomphante, lorsque l'une d'elles vient à découvrir Albert, et l'amène au milieu de leur cercle magique, encore tout étourdi de ce qu'il vient de voir.

SCÈNE XI.

Les Wilis semblent s'applaudir de trouver une autre victime: leur troupe cruelle s'agite déjà autour de cette nouvelle proie; mais au moment où Myrtha va toucher Albert de son sceptre enchanté, Giselle s'élance et retient le bras de la reine levé sur son amant.

SCÈNE XII.

Fuis, dit Giselle à celui qu'elle aime, *fuis, ou tu est mort, mort comme Hilarion,* ajoute-t-elle, en désignant le lac.

Albert reste un instant frappé de terreur, à l'idée de partager le sort affreux du garde-chasse. Giselle profite de ce moment d'indécision pour s'emparer de la main d'Albert; ils glissent tous deux par la force d'un pouvoir magique vers la croix de marbre, elle lui indique ce signe sacre comme son seul salut! . . .

La reine et toutes les Wilis le poursuivent jusqu'au tombeau; mais Albert, toujours protégé par Giselle, arrive ainsi jusqu'à la croix qu'il saisit; et au moment où Myrtha va le toucher de son sceptre, la branche enchantée se brise entre les mains de la reine, qui s'arrête, ainsi que toutes les Wilis, frappées de surprise et d'épouvante.

Furieuses d'être ainsi trahies dans leurs cruelles espérances, les Wilis tournent autour d'Albert, et s'élancent plusieurs fois vers lui, toujours repoussées par une puissance au-dessus de la leur. La reine, alors, voulant se venger sur celle qui lui ravit sa proie, étend la main sur Giselle dont les ailes s'ouvrent aussitôt, et qui se met à danser avec la plus gracieuse et la plus étrange ardeur, et comme emportée par un délire involontaire.

Albert, immobile, la regarde, accablé, confondu de cette scène bizarre!!! mais bientôt les grâces et les poses ravissantes de la Wili, l'attirent malgré lui, c'est ce que voulait la reine: il quitte la croix sainte qui le préserve de la morte, et s'approche de Giselle, qui s'arrête alors avec épouvante, et le supplie de regagner son talisman sacré; mais la Reine la touchant de nouveau, la force à continuer sa danse séductrice. Cette scène renouvelle plusieurs fois, jusqu'à ce qu'enfin, cédant à la passion qui l'entraîne, Albert abandonne la croix, et s'élance vers Giselle . . . Il saisit la branche enchantée, et veut mourir, pour rejoindre la Wili, pour n'en plus être séparé!!! . . .

Albert semble avoir des ailes, il rase le sol, et voltige autour de la Wili, qui parfois essaie encore de le retenir.

Mais bientôt entraînée par sa nouvelle nature, Giselle est forcée de se joindre à son amant. Un pas rapide, aérien, frénétique, commence entr'eux. Ils semblent tous deux lutter de grâce et d'agilité: parfois ils s'arrêtent, pour tomber dans les bras l'un de l'autre, puis la musique fantastique leur rend de nouvelles forces et une nouvelle ardeur!!! . . .

Le corps entier des Wilis se mêle aux deux amans, en les encadrant dans des poses voluptueuses.

Une mortelle fatigue s'empare alors d'Albert. On voit qu'il lutte encore, mais que ses forces commencent à l'abandonner. Giselle s'approche de lui, s'arrête un instant, les yeux baignés de pleurs; mais un signe de la reine l'oblige à s'envoler de nouveau. Encore quelques secondes, et Albert va périr de lassitude et d'épuisement, lorsque le jour commence à paraître . . . les premiers rayons du soleil éclairent les ondes argentées du lac.

La ronde fantastique et tumultueuse des Wilis se ralentit à mesure que la nuit se dissipe.

Giselle semble renaître à l'espoir, en voyant s'évanouir le prestige terrible qui entraînait Albert à sa perte.

Peu à peu, et sous les vifs rayons du soleil, la troupe entière des Wilis se courbe, s'affaisse, et tour à tour on les voit chanceler, s'éteindre et tomber sur la touffe de fleurs ou sur la tige qui les a vu naître, comme les fleurs de la nuit qui meurent aux approches du jour.

Pendant ce gracieux tableau, Giselle subissant, comme ses légères soeurs, l'influence du jour, se laisse aller lentement dans les bras affaiblis d'Albert; elle se rapproche de la tombe, comme entraînée vers elle par sa destinée.

Albert, devinant le sort qui menace Giselle, l'emporte dans ses bras loin du tombeau, et la dispose sur un tertre, au milieu d'une touffe de fleurs. Albert s'agenouille près d'elle, et lui donner un baiser, comme pour lui communiquer son âme et la rappeler à la vie.

Mais Giselle, lui montrant le soleil, qui brille alors de tous ses feux, semble lui dire qu'elle doit obéir à son sort et le quitter pour jamais.

En ce moment des fanfares brayantes retentissent au sein des bois. Albert les écoute avec crainte, et Giselle avec une douce joie.

SCÈNE XIII.

Wilfride accourt. Le fidèle écuyer précède le prince, Bathilde et une suite nombreuse; il les ramène près d'Albert, espérant que leurs efforts seront plus puissans que les siens pour l'arracher à ce lieu de douleur.

Tous s'arrêtent en l'apercevant. Albert s'élance vers son écuyer pour le retenir. Pendant ce tems, la Wili touche à ses derniers instans; déjà les fleurs et les herbes qui l'entourent se relèvent sur elle, et la couvrent de leurs tiges légères . . . une partie de la gracieuse apparition est déjà cachée par elles.

Albert revient, et reste frappé de surprise et de douleur en voyant Giselle s'affaisser peu à peu et lentement au milieu de ce vert tombeau; puis, du bras qu'elle conserve libre encore, elle indique à Albert la tremblante Bathilde, à genoux à quelques pas de lui, et lui tendant la main d'un air suppliant.

Giselle semble dire à son amant de donner son amour et sa foi à la douce jeune fille . . . c'est là son seul voeu, sa dernière prière, à *elle* qui ne peut plus aimer en ce monde, puis, lui adressant un triste et éternel adieu, elle disparaît au milieu des herbes fleuries qui l'engloutissent alors entièrement.

Albert se relève avec un vive douleur; mais l'ordre de la Wili lui semble sacré . . . Il arrache quelques-unes des fleurs qui recouvrent Giselle, les presse sur son coeur, sur ses lèvres, avec amour; et faible et chancelant, il tombe dans les bras de ceux qui l'entourent en tendant la main à Bathilde!!!

Tableau.

FIN DU BALLET.

GISELLE[2]
OR
THE WILIS,

Fantastic Ballet in Two Acts,
by

MM. DE SAINT-GEORGES, THÉOPHILE GAUTIER AND CORALY;
MUSIC BY M. ADOLPHE ADAM,
Sets by Mr Cicéri.
PERFORMED FOR THE FIRST TIME ON THE STAGE OF THE ROYAL ACADEMY
OF MUSIC, MONDAY THE 28th OF JUNE 1841.
PARIS.
MME WIDOW JONAS, PUBLISHER, OPÉRA BOOKSTORE
1841.

FIRST ACT.

CHARACTERS		ACTORS
DUKE ALBERT OF SILESIA, in the attire of a villager	MM.	PETIPA.
THE PRINCE OF COURLAND		QUÉRIAU.
WILFRIDE, the Duke's squire		CORALLI.
HILARION, the game-keeper		SIMON.
AN OLD PEASANT MAN		L. PETIT.
BADHILE, the Duke's fiancée	Mlles	FORSTER.
GISELLE, a peasant girl		CARLOTTA GRISI.
BERTHE, Giselle's mother		ROLAND.
MYRTHA, Queen of the Wilis		ADÈLE DUMILATRE.
ZULMÉ ⎫ Wilis		SOPHIE DUMILATRE.
MOYNA ⎭		CARRÉ.

DANCE NUMBERS.

PAS DE DEUX. M. Mabille; Mlle Nathalie Fitzjames.
PAS DE DEUX. M. Petipa; Mlle Grisi.

CORYPHÉES.
M. DESPLACES 2ME.

Mmes	Dimier.	Mmes	Marquet 1re.
	Breistroff.		Laurent 1re.
	Wiéthof.		Fleury.
	Caroline.		Robert.

---

[2]This translation, while not as poetic as that of Cyril Beaumont (*The Ballet Called Giselle,* Chapter Four), is more complete, more literal, and more faithful to the original in its details.

VINEGATHERERS.

MM.	Isambert.	MM.	Renauzy.
	Millot.		Chatillon.
	Lefevre.		Constant.
	Célarius.		Gourdoux.
	Duhan.		Cornet 2me.
	Dugit.		Rouyet.
	Fromage.		Souton.
	Dimier.		Scio.
Mmes	Saulnier 1re.	Mmes	Dubignon.
	Leclercq.		Galby.
	Lacroix.		Rénard 1re.
	Marivin.		Athalie.
	Colson.		Dabas 1re.
	Gougibus.		Josset.
	Robin.		Courtois.
	Bouvier.		Marquet 2me.

MUSICIANS.

MM.	Ernest.	MM.	Maujin.
	Petit-Alix.		Wiethof 1er.

VILLAGER CHILDREN.

MM.	Hardy.	MM.	Peaufert.
	Liger.		Albrié.
	Minart.		Wiéthof 2me.
Mlles	Masson.	Mlles	Toulain.
	Cassan.		Vioron.
	Devion.		Hunter.
	Debas 2me.		Favre.
	Franck.		Passerieux.
	Jeunot.		Jeandron 2me.
	Laurent 2me.		Vaudras.
	Chambret.		Voisin.
	Cluchar.		Feugère.

LORDS.

MM.	Lenfant.	MM.	Darcour.
	Cornet 1er.		Feltis.
	Grénier.		Jesset.
	Martin.		Lénoir.

LADIES.

Mmes	Rodriguez.	Mmes	Léoni.
	Cartembert.		Petit.
	Clément.		Deuénil.
	Richard.		Coupotte.

PAGES.

Mmes	Pèche.	Mmes	Bourdon.
	Julien.		Pézée.

HUNTERS, WHIPPERS-IN, VALETS.

SECOND ACT.

WILIS.

Mmes	Carré.	Sophie Dumilatre.	Adèle Dumilatre.

CORYPHÉES.

Mmes	Dimier.	Mmes	Marquet 1re.
	Breistroff.		Laurent 1re.
	Wiéthof.		Fleury.
	Caroline.		Robert.
Mmes	Robin.	Mmes	Saulnier 1re.
	Athalie.		Gougibos.
	Galby.		Bouvier.
	Dubignon.		Colson.
	Marivin.		Leclercq.
	Bénard 1re.		Toussaint.
	Courtois.		Danse.
	Josset.		Lacoste.
	Dabas 1re.		Jeandron 1re.
	Chévalier.		Drouet.
	Perés.		Potier.

The Actors of the first act.—THE VINEGATHERERS [male], THE NOBLEMEN.

GERMAN TRADITION
FROM WHICH THE PLOT OF THE BALLET GISELLE OR THE WILIS IS TAKEN

There exists a tradition of the night-dancer, who is known, in Slavic countries, under the name Wili.—Wilis are young brides-to-be who die before their wedding day. The poor young creatures cannot rest peacefully in their graves. In their stilled hearts and lifeless feet, there remains a love for dancing which they were unable to satisfy during their lifetimes. At midnight they rise out of their graves, gather together in troupes on the roadside, and woe be unto the young man who comes across them! He is forced to dance with them until he dies.

Dressed in their wedding gowns, with wreathes of flowers on their heads and glittering rings on their fingers, the Wilis dance in the moonlight like *Elves*. Their faces, though white as snow, have the beauty of youth. They laugh with a joy so hideous, they call you so seductively, they have an air of such sweet promise, that these dead *bacchantes* are irresistible.

Henrich HEINE (*On Germany*).

The WILIS.

ACT ONE

The setting represents a pleasant Valley in Germany. In the distance, vine-covered hills, across which runs a road leading into the Valley.

SCENE I.
A tableau of grape-harvesting on the Thuringian slopes in the early morning. The vinegatherers depart to continue the harvest.

SCENE II.
Hilarion appears, and glances around, as though looking for someone: then, he points lovingly at Giselle's cottage, and angrily at Loys's cottage. *It's there that his rival lives. If he can ever avenge himself, he will do so gladly.* The door to Loys's cottage opens mysteriously; Hilarion hides himself so he can see what will happen next.

SCENE III.
The young Duke Albert of Silesia, under the name Loys and wearing humble attire, emerges from his cottage, accompanied by his squire Wilfride. Wilfride seems to be imploring the Duke to renounce some secret project; but Loys persists, pointing to Giselle's dwelling place. This simple roof shelters the one he loves, the object of his unique affection . . . He orders Wilfride to leave him alone. Wilfride is still hesitant, but at a gesture from his master, Wilfride salutes him respectfully and then departs.

Hilarion is left stupefied by seeing a fine lord like Wilfride evince such high regard for his rival, a simple peasant. He seems to conceive suspicions that he will clear up later.

SCENE IV.
Loys, or rather the duke Albrecht, approaches Giselle's cottage and knocks lightly on the door. Hilarion remains hidden. Giselle immediately emerges and runs into the arms of her beloved. Transports of delight and happiness of the two young people. Giselle recounts her dream to Loys: She was jealous of a beautiful lady whom Loys loved; whom he preferred to Giselle.

Loys, troubled, reassures her: he doesn't—he will never—love anyone but her. *If you ever betrayed me,* the young girl says to him, *I can feel it, I would die.* She places his hand over her heart as though to tell him that she often suffers from this. Loys reassures her with spirited caresses.

She picks some daisies, and strips away the petals, to assure herself of Loys's love.—The test succeeds, and she falls into her beloved's arms.

Hilarion, no longer able to restrain himself, runs up to Giselle and reproaches her for her conduct. He was there; he saw everything!

Ah—what does it matter to me? Giselle airily responds. *I'm not ashamed, and I will never love anyone but him* . . . then she brusquely turns her back to Hilarion, laughing in his face, while Loys pushes him, threatening him with his wrath if he doesn't cease his amorous pursuit of Giselle. *Fine,* says Hilarion with a menacing gesture. *Later, we'll see.*

SCENE V.
A troupe of young vinegatherer girls comes to fetch Giselle for the vintage. Day has broken and duty calls; but Giselle, passionately fond of dancing and diversion, forestalls her companions. Dancing is, after Loys, the thing she loves most in the world. She proposes to the young girls that they indulge in pastimes instead of going to work. She dances alone at first, in order to persuade them. Her gaiety, her joyous ardor—her steps, so full of joy and enthusiasm, and infused with her love for Loys, are soon imitated by the vinegatherers. They throw down the baskets, the staffs, the instruments of their labor, and thanks to Giselle, everyone joins in boisterously. Berthe, Giselle's mother, then emerges from her cottage.

SCENE VI.

—*You will always dance,* she says to Giselle . . . *Evening . . . . . morning . . . . . it's truly a passion . . .* and all that, instead of working, instead of doing household chores.

—*She dances so well!* says Loys to Berthe.

—*It's my only pleasure,* Giselle responds, *just as he,* she adds, pointing out Loys, *he is my sole happiness!!!*

Bah! says Berthe. *I am sure that if this foolish little thing died, she would become a Wili, and dance even after her death, like all the girls who love dancing too much!*

—*What do you mean? . . .* the young village girls cry out with fright, pressing closely to one another.

Berthe then, to a lugubrious music, seems to depict an apparition of dead people returning to the world and dancing together. The terror of the village girls is at its height. Giselle alone laughs, and responds gaily to her mother that she is incorrigible and that, dead or alive, she will always dance.

Nevertheless, Berthe adds, *it's not good for you . . . It concerns your health, and your life, perhaps!*

She is very fragile, she says to Loys, *fatigue and excitement could be fatal to her, the doctor has told her; it could do her harm.*

Loys, troubled by this disclosure, reassures her good mother; and Giselle, taking Loys's hand, presses it to her heart, and seems to say that as long as she is with him *she is never in fear of danger.*

The fanfares of the hunt are heard in the distance. Loys, worried by this sound, quickly gives the signal to depart for the harvest and hurries the peasant girls away. Meanwhile Giselle, forced to return to her cottage with her mother, blows a farewell kiss to Loys, who departs, following everyone else.

SCENE VII.

As soon as Hilarion find himself alone, he explains his project. He wishes, at any price, *to discover the secret of his rival; to find out what it is.* . . . Assuring himself that no one can discover him, he furtively gains entry to Loys's cottage. . . . At this moment, the fanfares come near again, and the whippers-in and valets of the hunt appear on the hillside.

SCENE VIII.

The Prince and Bathilde, his daughter, soon appear on horseback, accompanied by a numerous suite of lords, ladies, and falconers with falcons on their fists. The heat of the day is overpowering them; they have come to find a favorable spot for repose. A huntsman points out Berthe's cottage to the Prince; he knocks on the door, and Giselle appears at the threshold, followed by her mother. The Prince gaily calls for hospitality from the young vine-gatherer; she invites him into the cottage, though it is a poor place in which to receive so fine a lord!

During this time, Bathilde approaches Giselle; she observes her and finds her charming. Giselle exerts herself to the utmost to do the honors of her modest dwelling; she bids Bathilde be seated, and offers her fruit and milk. Bathilde, charmed by Giselle's graces, removes a gold chain from her own neck and clasps it around that of the young girl, who is both proud and shy at this gift.

Bathilde asks Giselle about her work and her pleasures.

—*She is happy! she has neither sorrows nor cares; in the morning, work; in the evening, dancing! . . . Yes!* says Berthe to Bathilde, *especially dancing! . . . It is her obsession.*

Bathilde smiles and asks Giselle if her heart has spoken; if she loves someone? . . . —*Yes! yes!* cries the young girl while pointing out Loys's cottage: *the one who lives there! my beloved, my fiancé . . . ! I would die if he loved me no more!* Bathilde seems to take a lively interest in the young girl. . . . They are in the same situation, because she too will soon be married, to a young and handsome lord. She will give a dowry to Giselle, who seems to please her more and more. . . . Bathilde wants to see Giselle's fiancé, and she goes back into the cottage, followed by her father and Berthe, while Giselle goes to find Loys.

The Prince makes the sign for his retinue to continue the hunt; he is tired and desires to rest for awhile. He will sound the horn when he wishes them to return.

Hilarion, who appears at the door of Loys's cottage, sees the Prince and hears the orders he gives. The Prince goes with his daughter into Berthe's cottage.

SCENE IX.

While Giselle goes to look down the road to see if she can find her beloved, Hilarion re-emerges from Loys's cottage, holding a nobleman's sword and mantle; he finally knows who is rival is! It's a great lord! Now he is sure of it. . . . he is a seducer in disguise! He can now take revenge and wants to destroy his rival in the presence of Giselle and the entire village. He hides Loys's sword in a bush, waiting until all the vinegatherers are assembled for the feast.

SCENE X.

Loys appears in the distance . . . he looks worriedly about, and assures himself that the hunt is far away.

Giselle sees him and flies into his arms! At this moment a joyous music is heard.

SCENE XI.

A march commences. The harvest is over. A wagon, decorated with palms and flowers, slowly comes into view, followed by all the peasants of the valley, their baskets full of grapes. A little Bacchus is carried triumphally astride a cask, in keeping with an old country tradition.

Giselle is surrounded. She is named Queen of the vintage . . . They crown her with flowers and palms. Loys is more in love than ever with his pretty vinegatherer. All the peasants are soon possessed with a most joyous abandon.

It is the festival of the vintage! . . . Giselle can now abandon herself to her favorite pastime; she leads Loys to the middle of the troupe of vine-gatherers and dances with him, surrounded by the entire village, who soon join in with the young lovers, whose dance ends with a kiss that Loys bestows on Giselle . . . At this sight, the fury, the jealousy of the envious Hilarion knows no bounds . . . he throws himself into the middle of the crowd and declares that Loys *is a deceiver, a seducer, A NOBLEMAN IN DISGUISE!* . . . Giselle, at first taken aback, responds to Hilarion that he knows not what he is saying; that he has dreamed it all up . . . Ah! I dreamed it, continues the gamekeeper . . . Well! See for yourself, he cries while revealing Loys's sword and mantle for the villagers to see. Here is what I found in his cottage . . . this is sufficient proof, I trust.

Albrecht, furious, lunges toward Hilarion, who hides behind some villagers.

Giselle, struck with surprise and sadness at this revelation, appears to have sustained a terrible blow, and leans against a tree, unsteady and on the verge of collapse.

All the peasants pause, in a state of consternation! Loys, or rather Albrecht, rushes up to Giselle, and still believing he can deny his rank, tries to reassure her; to calm her with protestations of tenderness. *This is a mistake,* he says to her, *he is just her Loys, a simple peasant, her sweetheart, her fiancé!!!*

The poor girl asks nothing more than to believe him. Already hope seems to return to her heart; happy and confident, she accepts the embrace of the perfidious Albrecht, when Hilarion, seeking his vengeance, and recalling the Prince's order to his suite to return at the sound of the horn, seizes a horn belonging to one of the noblemen, attached to a tree, and blows it forcefully . . . At this signal the entire hunting party is seen rushing in, and the Prince exits Berthe's cottage. Hilarion points out to the Prince's suite the sight of Albrecht on his knees before Giselle. Everyone, upon recognizing the young duke, overwhelms him with salutations and deference. Giselle, on seeing this, can no longer doubt her misfortune nor Albrecht's high station.

SCENE XII.

The Prince steps forward in his turn, recognizes Albrecht, doffs his hat in salutation, and immediately asks him for an explanation of his strange conduct and the costume he is wearing.

Albrecht rises, stupefied and confounded by this encounter.

Giselle has seen everything! She is sure then of fresh betrayal by the one she loves; her sorrow is boundless; she seems to make an effort to control herself, and withdraws from Albrecht with feelings of fear and terror. Then, as though horror-stricken by this new blow, she runs toward the cottage and falls into the arms of her mother, who emerges therefrom at this moment, accompanied by the young Bathilde.

SCENE XIII.

Bathilde advances briskly toward Giselle and questions her with a touching interest about the agitation she feels. Giselle's sole response is to point out Albrecht, distressed and confounded.

What do I see? . . . says Bathilde . . . *The Duke in this costume! . . . But he is the one I am going to marry . . . It's my fiancé!* . . . she adds, pointing out the engagement ring she wears on her finger.

Albrecht approaches Bathilde and tries in vain to prevent her from finishing this terrible avowal; but Giselle has heard everything and understood all! The deepest horror is now manifested on the features of the poor child; her mind becomes confused, a horrible and dark delirium consumes her, as she sees herself betrayed, lost, dishonored! . . . Her reason is lost, tears begin to fall . . . then she laughs a nervous laugh. She takes Albrecht's hand, places it on her heart, and then quickly pushes it away with fear. She seizes Loys's sword, resting on the ground, first of all playing mechanically with this weapon, and is about to let herself fall on its sharp point, when her mother hurries toward her and grabs it away. The love of dance returns to the poor girl's memory: she believes she hears the music of her dance with Albrecht . . . She lunges forward and begins to dance with ardor, with passion. So many sudden sorrows, so many cruel blows, together with this latest effort, have finally exhausted her dwindling resources . . . Life seems to abandon her . . . Her mother takes her in her arms . . . A last sigh escapes from the heart of poor Giselle . . . She glances sadly at Albrecht in despair, *and her eyes close forever!* Bathilde, kind and generous, melts in tears. Albrecht, forgetting everything, tries to revive Giselle with burning caresses . . . He puts his hand on the young girl's heart and with horror assures himself that it has ceased to beat.

He seizes his sword to kill himself; the Prince stops him and takes his weapon. Berthe embraces the body of her ill-starred daughter. Albrecht is led away, crazed with love and despair.

The peasants, the noblemen, the entire hunting party, gathers round and completes this sad picture.

END OF ACT ONE

ACT TWO

The setting represents a forest on the banks of a pond. A damp and chilly spot where rushes, reeds, clumps of wild flowers, and aquatic plants grow. Birch trees, aspens and weeping willows droop their pale foliage to the ground. To the left, beneath a cypress, stands a white marble cross on which Giselle's name is engraved. The tomb is overgrown with the thick vegetation of grasses and wildflowers. The bluish gleam of a very bright moon gives a cold and misty appearance to the scene.

SCENE I.

Several gamekeepers arrive by different paths in the forest; they seem to be seeking a favorable spot for setting up an observation post and are about to do so by the bank of the pool when Hilarion comes rushing in.

SCENE II.

Hilarion evinces the liveliest fear upon divining the plans of his comrades. *It's a cursed spot,* he tells them, *it's the circle where the Wilis dance!* He shows them the tomb of Giselle . . . of Giselle who was always dancing. He points it out by the wreath of palms Giselle wore on her brow during the festival, and which is attached to the marble cross.

At this moment, midnight is heard striking in the distance: it is the gloomy hour when, according to local tradition, the Wilis gather in their ballroom.

Hilarion and his companions listen to the chimes with terror; trembling, they look about, expecting to see the apparition of the airy phantoms. *Let us flee,* says Hilarion, *the Wilis are pitiless; they surround travellers and force them to dance with them, until they die of exhaustion or are engulfed in the lake that you see here.*

A fantastic music then commences; the gamekeepers grow pale, staggering and fleeing on all sides, showing the greatest fright, pursued by will-o'-the-wisps that appear all around them.

SCENE III.

A sheaf of bullrushes slowly opens, and from the depths of the humid foliage the airy Myrtha, *the Queen of the Wilis,* a pale and transparent shade, is seen darting forth. She carries with her a mysterious radiance that suddenly illuminates the forest, piercing the shadows of the night. It is thus every time the Wilis appear; on the white shoulders of Myrtha, trembling and fluttering, are the diaphanous wings in which the Wili can envelop herself as though in a gauzy veil.

This intangible apparition cannot stay in place and leaps now to this tuft of flowers, now to a willow branch, flying here and there, traversing and seeming to explore her tiny empire whither she comes each night to reclaim possession. She bathes herself in the water of the lake, then suspends herself from the willow branches and swings to and fro.

After a solo dance, she plucks a branch of rosemary and in turn touches it to each plant, each bush, each tuft of foliage.

SCENE IV.

Scarcely has the Wili queen's flowery scepter rested on an object, a plant, a flower, a bush than it opens up, letting escape a new Wili who joins, in her turn, the graceful group that surrounds Myrtha, like bees around their queen. This last named, hearing the azure wings of her subjects, then gives them the signal to dance. Several Wilis present themselves, in turn, before their sovereign.

First Moyna, the Odalisque, executing an oriental step; then Zulmé, the Bayadere, who displays her Indian poses, then two French women, dancing a sort of bizarre minuet; then the German women, waltzing among themselves . . . Then, finally, the entire troupe of Wilis, all of whom died for loving dancing too much, or perished too early in life before sufficiently gratifying this foolish passion, to which they appear to surrender themselves furiously in their new graceful metamorphosis.

Before long, at a sign from the queen, the fantastic ball comes to a close . . . She announces to her subjects the arrival of a new sister. All arrange themselves around the queen.

SCENE V.

A vivid, bright ray of moonlight shines on Giselle's tomb; the flowers that cover it rise up and straighten themselves on their stems, as if to form a passageway for the pale creature they cover.

Giselle appears, wrapped in her thin shroud. She advances toward Myrtha, who touches her with her rosemary branch; the shroud falls off . . Giselle is transformed into a Wili. Her wings grow and unfold . . . her feet skim the ground. She dances, or rather she flutters in the air, like her graceful sisters, joyfully recalling and showing the steps that she danced in the first act before her death.

A sound is heard in the distance. All the Wilis disperse and hide themselves in the rushes.

SCENE VI.

Young villagers returning from a festival in the neighboring village gaily cross the scene, led by an old man. They are going to depart when a bizarre music, the Wilis' dance music, is heard. The peasants, in spite of themselves, seem to feel a strange desire to dance. The Wilis soon surround them, twine about them, and fascinate them with their voluptuous poses.

Each of the Wilis seeks to detain the men, to please them with the figures of their native dance . . . The villagers, deeply affected, are about to succumb to this seduction, to dance and die, when the old man throws himself in their midst and tells them with fright of the risk they run and rescues them all, chased by the Wilis, who are furious at seeing their prey escape.

SCENE VII.

Albrecht appears, followed by Wilfrid, his faithful squire. The Duke is sad and pale; his garments are in disorder; his reason is nearly gone, as a result of Giselle's death. He slowly approaches the cross as if seeking a memory, as though he wished to collect his confused thoughts.

Wilfrid entreats Albrecht to accompany him, and not to linger near the fatal tomb, which recalls so many sorrows . . . Albrecht bids him depart . . . Wilfrid again insists, but Albrecht orders him away with such vigor that Wilfrid is forced to obey. He departs, promising himself to make one last effort to induce his master to leave this fatal spot.

SCENE VIII.

Scarcely is he left alone than Albrecht gives vent to his sorrow. His heart is torn to pieces; he melts in tears. All of a sudden he grows pale; his gaze fixes on a strange object that takes shape before his eyes. He remains stricken with surprise and very nearly with terror, on recognizing Giselle, who looks lovingly at him.

SCENE IX.

A prey to the most violent delirium, the most lively anxiety, he still doubts and dares not believe in what he sees. For it is no longer the pretty Giselle, the one he adored, but Giselle the Wili, in her new and strange metamorphosis, who remains motionless before him. The Wili seems only to invite him with a look. Albrecht, believing himself in the thrall of a sweet illusion, approaches her with slow steps and cautiously, like a child wishing to capture a butterfly poised on a flower. But at the moment when he extends his hand toward Giselle, quicker than lightning, she darts far away from him, to take flight and traverse the air like a frightened dove; to alight elsewhere, whence she throws him loving glances.

This dance, or rather this flight, is repeated several times, to the great despair of Albrecht, who vainly attempts to join with the Wili, who flees several times above him like a wisp of mist.

Sometimes, however, she makes him a loving gesture, throws him a flower, which she plucks from its stem, throwing him a kiss; but, as intangible as a cloud, she disappears just as he thinks she is in his grasp.

At last he gives up! He kneels before the cross and joins his hands together before her, in a prayerful attitude. The Wili, as if attracted by this mute sorrow, so full of love, bounds lightly alongside her lover: he touches her; already drunk with love and delight, he goes to embrace her. But when he is gliding gently between her arms, she vanishes among the roses; while Albrecht clasps his arms together, embracing nothing more than the cross of the tomb.

The deepest despair seizes him; he rises and is about to leave this place of sorrow, when the strangest spectacle appears before his eyes and fascinates him to the point that he is transfixed, frozen, and forced to witness the strange scene that unfolds in front of him.

SCENE X.

Hidden behind a weeping willow, Albrecht sees the wretched Hilarion, pursued by the entire band of Wilis.

Pale, trembling, frightened nearly to death, the gamekeeper collapses at the foot of a tree, and seems to implore the pity of his demented foes! But the Queen of the Wilis touches him with her scepter and forces him to rise and imitate the dance movement which she herself begins to dance around him . . . Hilarion, impelled by a magic force, dances despite himself with the beautiful Wili until she gives way to one of her companions, who in turn cedes her place to another, and so on, up to the last of all!

Just when the hapless wretch believes his torment ended with his wearied partner, she is replaced with another, more vigorous one. Exhausted by unimaginable effort, to the rhythms of an ever-quickening tempo, he finishes by staggering and feeling overwhelmed by weariness and woe.

He takes a desperate action, finally, and tries to flee; but the Wilis surround him in a vast circle, which contracts little by little, closing in on him and then changing into a fast waltz movement, in which a supernatural power obliges him to partake. A giddiness seizes the gamekeeper, who leaves the arms of one waltzing Wili only to fall into those of another.

The victim, completely enmeshed in this graceful and deadly web, soon feels his knees giving way beneath him. His eyes close, he can no longer see . . . and he dances, however, with an ardent frenzy. The queen of the Wilis seizes him and makes him turn and waltz one last time with her, until the poor devil, the last link in the chain of waltzers, arrives at the water's edge, opens his arms, expecting to find the next waltzer, and goes tumbling into the abyss! The Wilis commence a joyous bacchanale, led by their triumphant queen, when one of them comes to discover Albrecht, still stunned by what he had just seen, and leads him to the center of their magic circle.

SCENE XI.

The Wilis seem to applaud the discovery of another victim: their cruel troupe has already begun to hover around this new prey; but at the moment when Myrtha is about to touch Albrecht with her magic scepter, Giselle darts forward and restrains the queen's arm, which is raised toward Giselle's lover.

SCENE XII.

Flee, says Giselle to the one she loves, *flee, or you will die, as Hilarion has,* she adds, pointing toward the lake.

Albrecht is frozen with terror for an instant at the idea of sharing the frightful fate of his gamekeeper. Giselle profits from this moment of indecision to seize Albrecht's hand; they glide together by the force of a magical power toward the marble cross, and she indicates this sacred symbol as his only salvation! . . .

The queen and all the Wilis chase him up to the tomb; but Albrecht, ever protected by Giselle, arrives at the cross, which he embraces; and at the moment when Myrtha is about to touch him with her scepter, the enchanted branch breaks in the hands of the queen, who stops short, as do all the Wilis, struck with surprise and dismay.

Furious at thus having their cruel hopes dashed, the Wilis encircle Albrecht, and frequently dart toward him, each time repelled by a power greater than their own. The queen, then, wishing to avenge herself on the one who robbed her of her prey, extends her hand toward Giselle, whose wings soon open, and who begins dancing with strangest, most graceful ardor, as though transported by an involuntary delirium.

Albrecht, motionless, watches her, overwhelmed and astounded at this bizarre scene!!! but soon the Wili's graces and ravishing poses attract him despite himself; this is what the queen wanted: he leaves the holy cross that protects him from death, and approaches Giselle, who pauses with dismay, and begs him to go back to the sacred talisman. But the Queen touches her anew, forces her to continue her seductive dance. This scene is replayed several times, until finally, ceding to the passion that consumes him, Albrecht abandons the cross and rushes toward Giselle . . . He seizes the enchanted branch and wishes to die, so he can rejoin the Wili and never again be separated from her!!! . . .

Albrecht seems to have wings; he skims the ground and hovers around the Wili, who from time to time tries to restrain him.

But soon compelled by her newfound nature, Giselle is forced to join her lover. A rapid, airborne, frenetic dance begins between them. They seem to vie with each other in grace and agility: at times they pause, to fall into each other's arms, then the fantastic music lends them new strength and a fresh ardor!!! . . .

The entire groups of Wilis intermingles with the two lovers, framing them in voluptuous poses.

A deadly weariness seizes Albrecht. It is clear that he still struggles, but his powers are beginning to abandon him. Giselle approaches him, stops for an instant, her eyes full of tears; but a sign from the queen obliges her to take flight anew. After a few seconds, Albrecht is about to perish from weariness and exhaustion, when dawn begins to break . . . the first rays of the run illuminate the silvery ripples of the lake.

The fantastic and tumultuous round of the Wilis slows down as the night fades away.

Giselle seems inspired by new hope on seeing the disappearance of the terrible enchantment that was leading Albrecht to his doom.

Little by little, and under the bright rays of the sun, the entire band of Wilis sinks and collapses; one by one they can be seen staggering, expiring, and falling in a tuft of flowers, or on the stem that witnessed their birth, like flowers of the night that die at the approach of dawn.

During this graceful tableau, Giselle, subject like her airy sisters to the influence of daylight, slowly gives herself up to Albrecht's enfeebled embrace; she goes back to her tomb, as though drawn toward it by fate.

Albrecht, conscious of the doom that threatens Giselle, carries her in his arms far from her tomb and puts her down on a knoll, amidst a clump of flowers. Albrecht kneels by her and gives her a kiss, as though to infuse her with his spirit and restore her to life.

But Giselle, pointing to the sun, which is now shining brightly, seems to tell him that she must obey her fate and leave him forever.

At this moment, loud fanfares are heard from the depths of the woods. Albrecht hears them with fear, and Giselle, with a sweet joy.

SCENE XIII.

Wilfrid comes running up. The faithful squire is ahead of the Prince, Bathilde, and a numerous retinue; he leads them to Albrecht, hoping that their efforts will be more effective than his own in inducing Albrecht to leave this place of sadness.

Everyone stops on seeing him. Albrecht leaps toward his squire to hold him back. During this time, the Wili nears her last moments; already the flowers and the grasses that surround her have begun to rise and cover her with their tender stems . . . already partly concealing the graceful apparition.

Albrecht comes back, and remains spellbound with surprise and sorrow on seeing Giselle sink slowly, little by little, into this verdant tomb; then, with the arm that she still keeps free, she points Albrecht toward the trembling Bathilde, on her knees a few steps away and stretching out her hand in a gesture of entreaty.

Giselle seems to tell her lover to give his heart and soul to this sweet young girl . . . it's her only wish, her last prayer, from *her* who can no longer live in this world, then, wishing him a sad and eternal adieu, she disappears in the midst of the flowery grasses which now completely engulf her.

Albrecht rises heartbroken; but the Wili's command to him seems sacred . . . He gathers some of the flowers that cover Giselle, and lovingly presses them to his heart, to his lips. Weak and staggering, he falls into the arms of those who surround him, and reaches out his hand to Bathilde!!!

Tableau.

END OF THE BALLET.

APPENDIX THREE

Sources for Musical Examples

ALL SCORES are unpublished manuscripts unless otherwise indicated. A *répétiteur* is a rehearsal score.

Chapter One

1. *La Sylphide*, full score, F-Po A.501
2. *La Sylphide*, full score, F-Po A.501
3. *La Sylphide*, full score, F-Po A.501
4. *La Somnambule*, autograph composing score, F-Pn Vm6 250
5. *La Somnambule*, autograph composing score, F-Pn Vm6 250
6. *Le Diable a Quatre*, full score F-Po A.547
7. *Le Diable boiteux*, *répétiteur*, F-Po Mat 19e [314 (9)]
8. *Le Diable boiteux*, *répétiteur*, F-Po Mat 19e [314 (9)]
9. *Giselle répétiteur*, RU-SPtob 7114/8
10. *Giselle* full score, F-Po A.533
11. *Giselle* full score, F-Po A.533
12. *Giselle* full score, F-Po A.533
13. *La Volière*, full score, F-Po A.520
14. *La Revolte au sérail*, *répétiteur*, F-Po Mat 19e [310 (21)]

Chapter Three

1. *Le Page Inconstant*, full score, F-Po A.474
2. *Le Page Inconstant*, full score, F-Po A.474

Chapter Four

1. *Psiché*, full score, F-Po A.337a
2. *La Tentation*, full score, F-Po A.502
3. *La Gipsy*, *répétiteur*, F-Po Mat 19 [321 (40)]
4. *Le Diable boiteux*, *répétiteur*, F-Po Mat 19 [314 (14)]
5. *La Sylphide*, full score, F-Po A.501
6. *Le Diable boiteux*, *répétiteur*, F-Po Mat 19 [314 (9)]
7. *La Fille du Danube*, autograph composing score, F-Pn MS 2641
8. *L'Orgie*, *répétiteur*, F-Po Mat 19 [287 (21)]
9. *La Gipsy*, *répétiteur*, F-Po Mat 91e [321 (40)]
10. *La Somnambule*, autograph composing score, F-Pn Vm6 250
11. *Giselle*, full score, F-Po A.533, with annotations from *répétiteur*, RU-SPtob 7114/8

Chapter Five

1. *La Muette de Portici*, piano-vocal score (Paris: La Haye, n.d).
2. Music from *La Muette de Portici*, piano-vocal score, published by La

Haye; text from *La Muette de Portici*, full score (Paris: Troupenas, n.d.), 332.
3. *La Muette de Portici*, piano-vocal score (Paris: La Haye, n.d.).
4. *Le Dieu et la Bayadère*, piano-vocal score (Paris: Brandus, n.d.) Text is from the libretto.
5. *Le Dieu et la Bayadère*, piano-vocal score (Paris: Brandus, n.d.)
6. *Le Dieu et la Bayadère*, piano-vocal score (Paris: Brandus, n.d.)
7. *La Tentation, répétiteur*, F-Po Mat 19e [303 (157)]
8. *La Tentation, répétiteur*, F-Po Mat 19e [303 (155) and full score, F-Po A.502
9. *La Tentation, répétiteur*, F-P Mat 19e [303 (192) and full score, F-Po A.502
10. *La Tentation, répétiteur*, F-Po Mat 19e [303 (192) and full score, F-Po A.502

Chapter Six

1. *Giselle* full score, F-Po A.533
2. *Giselle* full score, F-Po A.533, with text from *répétiteur*, RU-SPtob 7114/8
3. *Giselle* full score, F-Po A.533
4. *Giselle* full score, F-Po A.533, with text from *répétiteur*, RU-SPtob 7114/8
5. *Giselle* full score, F-Po A.533e, with text from *répétiteur*, RU-SPtob 7114/8
6. *Giselle* full score, F-Po A.533, with text from *répétiteur*, RU-SPtob 7114/8
7. *Giselle* full score, F-Po A.533, with text from *répétiteur*, RU-SPtob 7114/8
8. *Giselle* full score, F-Po A.533, with text from *répétiteur*, RU-SPtob 7114/8
9. *Giselle* full score, F-Po A.533
10. *Giselle* full score, F-Po A.533
11. *Giselle* full score, F-Po A.533
12. *Giselle* full score, F-Po A.533
13. *Giselle* full score, F-Po A.533

NOTES

Preface

1 Jean Georges Noverre, *Lettres sur la Danse et les Ballets* (Stuttgart, 1760) tr. Cyril Beaumont (London: Cyril W. Beaumont, 1930; rpt. Brooklyn: Dance Horizons, 1975), 51–53.

2 Among those interested in a wordless, self-standing theater art relying on dance and mime are John Weaver, Louise, Duchesse de Maine, Marie Sallé, Franz Hilverding, Gasparo Angiolini, Jean-Baptiste François Dehesse and Auguste-Frédéric-Joseph Ferrère. See, for example, Marian Hannah Winter, *The Pre-Romantic Ballet* (London: Pitman Publishing, 1974), 164; Carol Marsh, "Lumberjacks and Turkish Slaves," *Choreologica* 2 (1995): 37–45; and Ivor Guest, *The Ballet of the Enlightenment* (London: Dance Books, 1996), 1–11.

The bitter relationship between Angiolini and Noverre is of particular interest. On Angiolini's ballets, his dismay with Noverre's use of printed programs, the rivalry between the two men, the reluctance of the Paris Opéra to accept the *ballet d'action,* Noverre's later disillusionment with the new genre, his determination to improve ballet's status within opera, and other related matters, see Bruce Brown, *Gluck and the French Theatre in Vienna* (Oxford: Oxford University Press, 1991), chs. 5 and 8, and Kathleen Kuzmick Hansell, "Opera and Ballet at the Regio Teatro of Milan, 1771–1776: A Musical and Social History" (Ph.D. dissertation, University of California at Berkeley, 1980), especially chs. 9, 10, and epilogue.

Nineteenth-century French accounts of ballet history tended to ignore the achievements of Angiolini and Hilverding. See, for example, Adolphe Ledhuy and Henri Bertini, *Encyclopedia Pittoresque de la Musique* (Paris: Delloye, 1835), 40; and P. L. Jacob, *Bibliothèque Dramatique de Monsieur de Soleinne* (Paris: Administration de l'Alliance des Arts, 1844), vol. 3, 117–18. Jacob writes that "Avant cette époque (1776), les ballets ne différaient guère des opéras que par des entrées de danse qui entrecoupaient les scènes de chant. Noverre et Gardel introduisèrent à l'Académie royale de musique la pantomime, qui n'était plus admise que sur des théâtres inférieurs, après avoir fait longtemps les délices de la cour sous Henri IV et sous Louis XVIII." [Before this epoch (1776), ballets scarcely differed from operas except for the danced *entrées* which interrupted the sung scenes. Noverre and Gardel introduced pantomime to the Académie royale de musique; pantomime had not been allowable anymore except in the lower theaters, after having brought delight for quite some time to the courts of Henri IV and Louis XVIII.] By contrast, Pietro Lichtenthal writes, in his *Dizionario e Bibilografia della Musica* (Milan: A Fontana, 1826), 81: "Il Ballo pantomimico, il quale nella Francia deve la sua gloria a Noverre e Gardel, e in Italia a Salvatore Viganò, è la prima, e la più importante specie" [of ballet]. [Pantomime ballet, which in France owes its glory to Noverre and Gardel, and in Italy to Salvatore Viganò, is the first and the most important type (of ballet).]

3 Louis de Bachamount, *Mémoires secrets pour servir à l'histoire de la République des Lettres en France depuis MDCCLXII jusqu'à nos jours, ou Journal d'un observa-*

teur contenant les Analyses des Pièces de Théâtre (London [1778–91]), vol. 9, 264 (13 October 1776), tr. and quoted by Hansell, *Opera and Ballet at the Regio Teatro of Milan,* 913. It must be noted, however, that independent *ballets d'action* were performed on other stages (in Stuttgart, Versailles, and at the Comédie-Italienne in Paris for example), well before they first appeared at the Opéra in 1776.

4 Like many lyric theaters of that day in Paris (including the Opéra-Comique, the Théâtre Italien, and the smaller boulevard theaters), the Opéra maintained a ballet company and enhanced its sung works by incorporating danced divertissements within them. Among other theaters in Paris presenting ballet dancing were the Gaîté, the Porte Saint-Martin, the Opéra-Comique (which employed a ballet master for most of the nineteenth century, and a small troupe of dancers), the Ambigu-comique (which maintained a *corps de ballet* of roughly twenty dancers and an *école de danse,* and employed ballet masters from ca. 1797 to 1831, and again in 1853), and the Théâtre Italien, where students from the Opéra's *école de danse* performed. Also, the Odéon, under the direction of Bocage in 1849–1850, presented ballets and pieces *mêlées de chant et de danses,* and the Théâtre des Bouffes-Parisiens was authorized in 1855 to present *pas* for five dancers or more. See Nicole Wild, "La Musique dans le Mélodrame des Théâtres Parisiens," *Music in Paris in the Eighteen-Thirties,* ed. Peter Bloom, introduction by Jacques Barzun, *Musical Life in 19th-Century France,* vol. 4 (Stuyvesant, New York: Pendragon Press, 1987), 589–610, and Nicole Wild, *Dictionnaire des Théâtres Parisiens au XIXe Siècle,* 38–39, 174, 294, 334–35, 367.

Ballet-pantomime scores from the Théâtre de la Porte Saint-Martin are now kept at the Bibliothèque de l'Opéra and have recently been catalogued by Pauline Girard of the Bibliothèque nationale.

On the melodrama in Paris, see Emilio Sala, *L'opera senza canto—Il mélo romantico e l'invenzione della colonna sonora* (Venice: Marsilio, 1995). On vaudeville, see Herbert Schneider, ed., *Das Vaudeville—Functionen eines multimedialen phänomens* (Hildesheim: Georg Olms, 1996). Forthcoming studies concerning the performance of musical drama in France in the nineteenth century include Mark Everist's work on the Théâtre de l'Odéon (*Music Drama at the Paris Odéon, 1823–28*) and Janet Johnson's on the Théâtre Italien (*Rossini and the Italian Opera in Paris*). See also Janet Johnson, "The Théâtre Italien and Opera and Theatrical Life in Restoration Paris 1818–1827" (Ph.D. dissertation, University of Chicago, 1988).

5 See Lillian Moore's foreword to Ivor Guest, *The Romantic Ballet in Paris* (London: Dance Books, 1966, 2nd rev. ed., 1980), ix. In the "white ballet" (or *ballet blanc*), dancers perform in white filmy tutus, often portraying ghosts, often in dim light.

On the subject of ballet in other cities in the nineteenth century, see for example Ivor Guest, *The Romantic Ballet in England* (Middletown: Wesleyan University Press, 1972); Janina Pudelek, *Warszawski balet romantyczny (1802–1866)* (Cracow: Polskie Wydawn. Muzyczne, 1968); Janina Pudelek, "The Warsaw Ballet under the Directorships of Maurice Pion and Filippo Taglioni, 1832–1852," tr. and intro. Jadwiga Kosicka, *Dance Chronicle* 11 no. 2 (1988): 219–73; Kathleen Kuzmick Hansell, "Il ballo teatrale e l'opera italiana," *Storia dell'opera italiana,* vol. 5, ed. Lorenzo Bianconi and Giorgio Pestelli (Turin: Edizioni di Torino, 1988); and Lynn Garafola, ed., *Rethinking the Sylph—New Perspectives on the Romantic Ballet,* Studies in Dance History series (Hanover and London: Wesleyan University Press, 1997).

6 There are important exceptions to the rule. Musicological studies of Paris in the nineteenth century entailing both dance and music include Karen Pendle, *Eugène Scribe and French Opera of the Nineteenth Century* (Ann Arbor: UMI Research Press, 1979), 378–79, 455; Ralph Locke, "Paris: Centre of Intellectual Ferment," *The Early Romantic Era—Between Revolutions: 1789 and 1848,* ed. Alexander Ringer, Music and Society series (Englewood Cliffs, NJ: Prentice Hall, 1991), 32–83; Karin Pendle and Stephen Wilkins, "Paradise Found: The Salle le Peletier and French grand opera" in *Opera in Context,* ed. Mark A. Radice (Portland: Amadeus Press, 1998), 171–207; Maribeth Clark, "Understanding French Grand Opera Through Dance" (Ph.D. dissertation, University of Pennsylvania, 1998); and Sarah Hibberd, "Magnetism, Muteness, Magic: Spectacle and the Parisian Lyric Stage circa 1830" (Ph.D. dissertation, Univ. of Southampton, 1999). Ballet and opera are accorded equal treatment in two recent books about sets and costumes at the Opéra in the nineteenth century: Nicole Wild, *Décors et costumes du XIXe Siècle a l'Opéra de Paris* (Paris: Bibliothèque nationale, 1987) and Catherine Join-Diéterle, *Les Décors de Scène de l'Opéra de Paris à l'Epoque Romantique* (Paris: Picard, 1988). The dance historians Ivor Guest and Stephanie Jordan have also made crucial contributions to the study of ballet music and its role in dance. See, for example, Guest, *The Romantic Ballet in Paris,* 10–13 (and his many quotations of nineteenth-century critical commentary on particular ballet scores in this volume); Guest and John Lanchbery, "The Scores of 'La Fille Mal Gardée.' I—The Original Music," *Theatre Research/Recherches Théâtales,* 3 (1961): 32–42, "II—Hérold's Score," 121–34, and "III—The Royal Ballet's Score," 191–204; and Stephanie Jordan, "The Role of the Ballet Composer at the Paris Opéra: 1820–1850," *Dance Chronicle* 4 no. 4 (1982): 374–88. See also Stephanie Jordan, *The Listening Eye: Dialogues with Music in 20th-century Ballet* (forthcoming).

7 Wagner actually first arrived in Paris 17 September 1839.

8 Ulrich Weisstein, review of *Pipers Enzyklopädie des Musiktheaters: Oper-Operette-Musical-Ballett,* ed. Sieghart Döhring and Carl Dahlhaus, vol. 1 (Munich: Piper, 1986) in the *Cambridge Opera Journal* 1 no. 2 (July 1989): 196.

9 Members of the Jockey Club (young aristocrats known for their puerile behavior and fondness for the Opéra's ballerinas) attended the première of *Tannhäuser* in Paris in March 1861 and ruined it with their prolonged and coordinated outburst of catcalls. On the second night, they blew dog whistles. After they disrupted the third performance as well, Wagner withdrew the production. One reason for the club members' behavior was their distaste for Wagner's patron the Princess Metternich, wife of the Austrian ambassador. On the Paris production of *Tannhäuser* in 1861, see, for example, Carolyn Abbate, "The Parisian 'Vénus' and the 'Paris' *Tannhäuser*," *Journal of the American Musicological Society* 36 no. 1 (Spring 1983): 72–123. See also Susan Trites Free, "Dance of the Demi-Monde—Paris Opera Ballet Dance and Dancers in the Social Imagination of the Second Empire" (M.F.A. Thesis, York University, 1986), 46.

10 Humphrey Searle, *Ballet Music* (London: Cassell, 1958, rev. ed. New York: Dover, 1973), 56–58. Searle also reports, wrongly, that French ballets of this period took an entire evening to perform.

11 Roland John Wiley, *Tchaikovsky's Ballets* (Oxford: Oxford University Press, 1985), 6. See also Wiley's discussion of *simfonizm* (the Russian term for the use of symphonic procedures in ballet), 64.

12 Carolyn Abbate, "Opera as Symphony, a Wagnerian Myth," *Analyzing Opera—Verdi and Wagner* (Berkeley: University of California Press, 1989), 92–124; Arthur

Groos, introduction to *Reading Opera* (Princeton: Princeton University Press, 1988), 1–11; and Carolyn Abbate, "Wagner, 'On modulation,' and *Tristan*," *Cambridge Opera Journal* 1 no. 1 (March 1989): 33–58.

13 See Roger Parker and Carolyn Abbate, introduction to *Analyzing Opera—Verdi and Wagner*, 1–24.

14 Ivor Guest, *Le Ballet de l'Opéra de Paris*, tr. Paul Alexandre (Paris: Théâtre National de l'Opéra, 1976), 302.

15 Undated letter from the Théâtre Impérial de l'Opéra, Louis Palianti *dossier d'artiste*, F-Po. Louis Palianti, a singer and assistant régisseur at the Opéra-Comique, published over two hundred staging manuals for plays and operas. See Marian Smith, "The *Livrets de Mise en scène* of Donizetti's Parisian Operas," *L'Opera Teatrale di Gaetano Donizetti*, ed. Francesco Bellotto (Bergamo: Comune di Bergamo, 1993), 375.

16 For specific evidence of the steps executed in ballet classes, see the work of Sandra Noll Hammond, including "Clues to Ballet's Technical History from the Early Nineteenth-Century Ballet Lesson," *Dance Research* 3 no. 1 (Autumn 1984): 53–66; "Steps through Time: Selected Dance Vocabulary of the Eighteenth and Nineteenth Centuries," *Dance Research* 10 no. 2 (Autumn 1992): 93–108; and "A Nineteenth-Century Dancing Master at the Court of Württemberg: The Dance Notebooks of Michel St. Léon," *Dance Chronicle* 15 no. 3 (1992): 291–312. As Hammond reports, St. Léon's notebooks also include choreographies by François Decombe (known as "Albert") for a *pas de deux* for *La Muette de Portici* and a *pas de deux* for *La Vestale*. See also Lisa C. Arkin, "The *Mazurka* and the *Krakovia*: Two Polish National Dances in Michel St. Léon's Dance Notebooks, 1829–1830," *Proceedings—Society of Dance History Scholars—Reflecting our Past; Reflecting on Our Future* (Riverside: Society of Dance History Scholars, 1997), 129–36. See Knud Arne Jürgensen, *The Bournonville Heritage: A Choreographic Record* (London: Dance Books, 1990) for choreographies by August Bournonville reconstructed by Jürgensen and notated by Ann Hutchinson Guest.

A NOTE TO THE READER

1 The Opéra was housed at the rue le Peletier from 16 August 1821 until 28 October 1873. Its official name changed fairly frequently. From 5 April 1814 until 21 March 1815, it was known as the Académie royale de musique; until 8 July 1815 it was known as the Académie impériale de musique, at which time it once again came to be called the Académie royale de musique. On 4 August 1830 it became known as the Théâtre de l'Opéra, but the name was changed back six days later to the Académie royale de musique. On 26 February 1848 it was renamed as the Théâtre de la Nation. Nowadays it is called the Théâtre national de l'opéra. See Nicole Wild, *Dictionnaire des Théâtres Parisiens au XIXe Siècle* (Paris: Aux Amateurs de Livres, 1989), 299–321.

2 "Le mot *ballet* désigne quatre différents genres de spectacles; savoir: le *ballet*, la *comédie-ballet*, l'*opéra-ballet;* et le *ballet d'action* ou *ballet-pantomime*. Dans le premier, la danse est une partie accessoire de l'action représentée: dans le second et le troisième, elle est partie principale: la poésie et la musique vocale sont alors accessoires à leur tour: dans le quatrième enfin, la danse est tout; et pour représenter une action, les hommes ne parlent pas, ils ne chantent pas; ils jouent la pantomime et dansent." [The word *ballet* designates four different types of spectacle, namely: ballet, comédie-ballet, opéra-ballet, and ballet d'action or ballet-pantomime. In the first, dance is an accessory to the action performed. In the second and third, it is the principal part: the poetry and the vocal music are accessory. Finally, in the fourth type, the dance is everything, and to perform a plot, the actors don't speak or sing; they pantomime and dance.] Castil-Blaze [François Henri Joseph Blaze], *Dictionnaire de musique moderne* (Brussels: L'Académie de Musique, 1828), 18.

"Ballet-pantomime" was the official term used in the Opéra directors' contracts to denote self-standing dramatic work calling for pantomime and dance. Yet as Appendix One shows, other appellations were sometimes used as well.

Chapter One: Introduction: Music and the Story

1 *La Presse*, 23 October 1848, tr. Ivor Guest, *Gautier on Dance* (London: Dance Books, 1986), 204.

2 As George Dorris has pointed out, the *Giselle* score is a vital source for research on the first production of that ballet. George Dorris, "The Music of *Giselle*," *Ballet Review* 4 no. 2 (Summer 1972): 61–67.

3 "Les *airs* de danse ne sont plus calqués sur un modèle connu, le compositeur s'accorde avec le chorégraphe pour les formes, le caractère et l'extension qu'il convient de leur donner." Castil-Blaze, *Dictionnaire de musique moderne*, 10. *Chronique de l'Académie Royale de Musique* (F-Po Rés. 658), qu. by Robin-Challan, *Danse et Danseuses à l'Opéra de Paris, 1830–1850* (Thèse de Troisième Cycle de l'Université de Paris VII, 1983), 284. This *Chronique*, also known as the *Manuscrit Gentil, Les cancans de l'Opéra,* and *Extraite du Journal tenu par une habilleuse,* is a manuscript account of activities at the Opéra, in the house, on the stage, and behind the scenes. It exists in two segments, one at the Bibliothèque de l'Opéra and one at the Dance Collection at the New York Public Library. Jean-Louis Tamvaco has identified its author as Louis Gentil, the *contrôleur de matériel* at the Opéra. Tamvaco has transcribed, annotated and supplemented this chronicle with illustrations and additional information in his doctoral thesis, the full title of which is "Les Cancans de l'Opéra, Première édition critique intégrale du manuscrit dit: 'Les Cancans de l'Opéra' ou 'Les Mémoires d'une Habilleuse,' de 1836 à 1845, accompagnée d'une histoire sommaire de la salle Le Peletier, de la chronologie théâtrale des années 1836/37/38, de l'édition de la correspondance des frères Louis et Joseph Gentil, et d'un lexique biographique des personnages cités dans le manuscrit et dans la chronologie." Université de la Sorbonne Nouvelle (Paris III), 1992.

4 Adolphe Adam, however, felt himself a true collaborator on *Giselle*. He said, for instance, that it was his idea for Giselle to be carried to a bed of flowers and slowly sink into the ground at the very end of the ballet (instead of returning to her tomb, as originally planned), and he describes with pleasure his work on this ballet with the ballerina Carlotta Grisi and the choreographer Jules Perrot "in my salon." See Arthur Pougin, *Adolphe Adam* (Paris: G. Charpentier, 1877), 162, and Guest, *The Romantic Ballet in Paris,* 207.

5 "Il n'y a pas de tâche plus pénible et plus ingrate à la fois que celle imposée nécessairement au compositeur d'une musique de ballet. Quand il a fini, on le fait recommencer. Est-il content d'un morceau, dont il a sagement ménagé la conduite et le développement, le maître chorégraphe arrive, il faut couper ceci, allonger cela, supprimer entièrement une période ou même refaire le morceau. Puis aux répétitions les danseurs demandent une autre instrumentation, qui des trombones, qui de la grosse caisse, là où l'auteur avait peut-être mis des flûtes avec un accompagnement en pizzicato. Pauvre compositeur! . . . quand le musicien est un artiste distingué, comme M. Schneitzoeffer [sic], alors il faut sincèrement le plaindre de se trouver placé dans une semblable position; elle est affreuse." *La Gazette Musicale de Paris,* 21 Sept. 1834. Another instance of the exigencies of ballet composition is given by Gentil, who reports that an elderly male patron of the Opéra solicited the choreographer and the composer of a certain ballet to lengthen a number for Nathalie Fitzjames. *Chronique de l'Académie royale de Musique,* vol. 1, 2nd redaction, 8.

6 *L'Art du Théâtre* (Jan. 1903) 14, tr. and qu. by Guest, *The Romantic Ballet in Paris,* 11.

7 Letter to "The Times", 6 July 1914, reprinted in Roger Copeland and Marshall Cohen, *What Is Dance? Readings in Theory and Criticism* (New York: Oxford University Press, 1983), 260.

8 *Tantsy voobshche, baletnye znamenitosti i natsional'nye tantsy* [*Dances in General, Ballet Celebrities, and National Dances*] (Moscow: Lazarevsk, 1864), 46, tr. and qu. by Wiley, *Tchaikovsky's Ballets,* 5. The long career of Carlo Blasis (1797–1878), who lived in Marseilles, Bordeaux, Paris, Milan, London, and St. Petersburg, entailed dancing, choreographing, and theoretical writing.

9 My emphasis. "[La] musique . . . a mission d'expliquer ou de traduire [les scènes]." *La Sylphide,* 26 Sept. 1840.

10 "Par leur caractère, par leur expression et par leur style, les mélodies peuvent and doivent compléter la signification du geste et du jeu de la physionomie." Gustave Chouquet, *Histoire de la Musique Dramatique en France* (Paris: Librairie Firmin Didot Frères, 1873), 170.

11 "La musique des ballets a son caractère particulier; elle sera plus accentuée, plus parlante, plus expressive que la musique d'opéra, car elle n'est pas destinée seulement à accompagner et à rehausser les paroles du poète, mais à être elle-même le poème tout entier." Auguste Baron, *Lettres et Entretiens sur la Danse* (Paris: Dondey-Dupré Père et Fils, 1824), 296.

12 "En général, ce n'est pas de la musique qu'on demande à un compositeur de ballet-pantomime; c'est un orchestre qui soit la traduction, le commentaire du texte qu'on aurait pu ne pas saisir." *Le Moniteur universel,* 21 Sept. 1827.

13 "Si la musique n'exprime pas les sentimens des acteurs, qu'y a-t-il pour les exprimer? Les grands mouvemens de bras sont une pauvre langue." *Le Siècle,* 23 Sept. 1836.

14 "Le compositeur est presque chargé de raconter l'action." *Le Constitutionnel,* 11 Aug. 1845. Gustave Chouquet, in 1873, wrote that "at the Opéra . . . it was Noverre who created the *ballet d'action* and made a certain type of musical drama out of it, since instrumental music in it took the place of the word and of singing." [A l'Opéra . . . ce fut Noverre qui créa le ballet d'action et en fit un drame musical d'un genre particulier, puisque la symphonie instrumentale y tient lieu de la parole et du chant.] Chouquet, *Histoire de la Musique Dramatique,* 170.

15 "Chaque situation, chaque passion qui vient momentanément à prédominer, demande un nouveau rythme, de nouveaux motifs, des changements de ton et des périodes. L'habile compositeur, malgré ces exigences, sait former de ce mélange un ensemble agréable. Cette musique doit être imitative, capable de peindre les images et d'exciter tous les sentiments qui conviennent aux diverses circonstances de l'action. Cette imitation peut être, il est vrai, *objective,* c'est-à-dire, cette musique peut peindre les phénomènes physiques de la nature, par exemple une tempête, mais elle doit être surtout *subjective,* afin de réveiller dans l'âme du spectateur les sentiments qu'il éprouverait s'il se trouvait dans des circonstances semblables à celles qu'on représente. Quant aux airs de danse, on conçoit facilement qu'ils doivent être caractéristiques et analogues au lieu où se passe l'action; ainsi les airs de danse des Indiens, des Écossais, des Hongrois, doivent avoir le caractère de la musique de leur pays." Peter Lichtenthal, *Dictionnaire de musique,* tr. (into French) and augmented by Dominique Mondo (Paris: Troupenas, 1839), vol. 1, 115–16 [tr. from *Dizionario e Bibliografia della Musica* (Milan, 1826)]. Newspaper reviews, too, occasionally refer to both types. "La partie dramatique a été fort bien traitée par [Halévy]. . . . Les airs de danse sont jolis. . . ." [The dramatic part was treated very well by (Halévy). . . . The dance airs are pretty.] *La Revue Musicale,* review of *Manon Lescaut,* 1830, 11–15.

16 "Dans un ballet pantomime, la symphonie, destinée à peindre l'action et les sentiments des personnages, diffère beaucoup des airs destinés aux pas exécutés par les danseurs; ces airs représentent les cavatines, les duos, les trios des chanteurs placés au milieu des récitatifs." Léon and Marie Escudier, *Dictionnaire de Musique Théorique et Historique* (Paris: Bureau Central de Musique, 1844), 113–14. The word *symphonie* was often used to identify instrumental music, as opposed to vocal music. Here it refers to instrumental music as opposed to airs played for danced numbers, which are likened to vocal music.

As another observer wrote of this music, it is "sans formes arrêtés, . . . jamais ne finit et toujours recommence" [without stopped forms, [it] never finishes and always recommences]. *La Revue Musicale,* 9 Dec. 1835.

17 See beginning of note 15. In ballet music as opposed to symphonic music, as Wiley explains, "the structure is shaped by the libretto. . . . The coherence of the ballet is maintained as it goes along by the principle of 'through-development'—that is, the score is continuously responsive to the narrative and to the emotional states of the characters." Wiley also notes that "Simfonizm," the Russian term for the use of symphonic procedures in ballet, is characterized by Boris Asafiev as "the continuity of the musical current." The concept of the continuous musical current, apt in discussions of Tchaikovsky's ballets, is also applicable to the dramatic music in this Parisian repertory. See Wiley, *Tchaikovsky's Ballets,* 64.

See also Carolyn Abbate, *Unsung Voices: Opera and Musical Narrative in the Nineteenth Century* (Princeton: Princeton University Press, 1991), especially 10–29 and 122–55; and Anne Dhu Shapiro, "Action Music in American Pantomime and Melodrama," *American Music* 2 (1984): 49–72.

18 Gide was no doubt aware of the jumble of sound and a mixing of meters and styles one could hear at the Opéra's own masked balls by going back and forth from foyer to *salle,* and of earlier dramatic music designed to re-create the sensation, the most famous of which is found in *Don Giovanni.*

19 See Chapter Four, Examples 4.3 and 4.4.

20 Instances may be found, respectively, in *La Sylphide* (Act Two scene iv), *Giselle* (Act One scene xiii), and *La Somnambule* (Act Two scene iii). Of the term "reminiscence theme" (or *Erinnerungsmotiv*), Joseph Kerman has written, "I think we would do a little better with the term 'recalling theme,' since opera is a form of drama, and of all

memory verbs 'to reminisce' seems the most undramatic." "Verdi's Use of Recurring Themes," *Studies in Music History—Essays for Oliver Strunk,* ed. Harold Powers (Princeton: Princeton University Press, 1968), 495.

21 Roger Fiske guesses that this new variation may have been composed by Tcherepnin, Minkus, or Drdla. See his *Ballet Music* (London: George G. Hurrap, 1958), 21. See below, Chapter Six, note 74.

22 See Wagner's review of *Giselle* for the *Abendzeitung* in Dresden in Wagner, *Richard Wagner's Prose Works,* tr. William Ashton Ellis (1899; repr. St. Clair Shores, Michigan: Scholarly Press, 1972), vol. 8, 141–48.

23 On recurring motifs in *Giselle,* see, for example, Roger Fiske, *Ballet Music* (1958), 14–21.

24 See Appendix One. *Le Corsaire,* first performed at the Opéra 23 January 1856 (libretto by Mazilier and Saint-Georges, choreography by Mazilier, music by Adam), was restaged by Petipa at the St. Petersburg Maryinsky Theater, with additional music by Drigo, Minkus, and Pugni. The music for the famous *pas de deux* so often performed without the rest of the ballet is by Drigo. (There was an earlier *Corsaire* by François Decombe, also known as "Albert," with music by Boscha, premiered at the King's Theatre in London in 1837.) *Don Quixote* (libretto and choreography by Petipa, music by Minkus) was first performed in Moscow 26 December 1869, and then drastically revised by Petipa for a production in St. Petersburg; it has undergone many revisions since. *Coppélia* (libretto by Nuitter and Saint-Léon, choreography by Saint-Léon, music by Délibes) was first performed at the Opéra 25 May 1870.

The ballet music of opera composers has also been used by twentieth-century choreographers for ballets danced outside the confines of opera, for example, *Donizetti Variations* (Balanchine, 1960), and the *Four Seasons* from Verdi's *Vêpres siciliennes* (which has been choreographed by Violette Verdy, 1970, and Kenneth MacMillan, 1975, to name only two).

25 Castil-Blaze credits the dancer Françoise Prévost (c. 1680–1741) with having popularized the practice of dancing to a solo melody (most likely in a special solo performace at the Opéra). In 1720, he reports, she danced to a popular and difficult violin caprice composed by Rebel. "Mlle. Prévôt mit les solos d'instrumens à la mode, et c'est depuis lors, que l'on a introduit des concertos ou des récits d'apparat, exécutés par un ou plusieurs virtuoses de l'orchestra, tandis que le danseur règle ses pas sur les traits brillants du violon, de la mandoline, du violoncelle, de la flûte, de la clarinette, du hautbois, de la harpe, et même de la trompette à clés. C'est Rodolphe, qui, le premier, a placé des solos de cor dans les ballets. M. Gardel, jouant le rôle du maître de danse de *la Dansomanie,* exécutait un concerto de violon, qu'une de ses élèves dansait. Je citerai le solo de violon des *Pages du Duc de Vendôme,* le solo des harpes de *La Caravane,* celui de cor d'*Hécube,* celui de flûte des *Filets de Vulcain,* celui de trompette à piston de *La Sylphide.*" [Mlle. Prévôt brought these instrumental solos into vogue and since that time, concertos or *récits d'apparat,* played by one or several virtuosos of the orchestra, have been introduced, while the dancer arranges his *pas* to the brilliant flourishes of the violin, the mandoline, the cello, the flute, the clarinet, the oboe, the harp, and even the keyed trumpet. It is Rodolphe who first put horn solos in his ballets. Gardel, in the role of the dancing-master in *Dansomanie,* played a violin concerto while one of his students danced. I will also cite the violin solo from *Les Pages du Duc de Vendôme,* the harp solo in *La Caravane,* the horn solo in *Hécube,* the flute solo in *Les Filets de Vulcain,* and the

trompette à piston solo in *La Sylphide.*] Castil-Blaze, *La Danse et les Ballets depuis Bacchus jusqu'à Mlle Taglioni* (Paris: Paulin, 1832), 325.

26 This music was composed as Giselle's variation for a *pas de deux* that took place during a *divertissement* directly before the Act One finale; however, this *pas de deux* has been subjected to considerable alterations. The music for Giselle's variation now only occasionally crops up, and when it does it is often used in the peasant *pas de deux*. See Poesio, "Giselle—Part III," 689. See also note 28 below.

27 Wiley, *Tchaikovsky's Ballets,* 127.

28 Ibid., 18. The first-act *pas de deux* for Giselle and Albrecht originally followed this format, though it has been altered since; the music composed for Giselle's variation is occasionally used in the peasant *pas de deux,* and the coda is now danced immediately after the waltz, much earlier in the act.

29 Some were brought to the Opéra's stage as soon as possible after gaining currency in the ballroom, in turn boosting their popularity as social dances, and others were probably introduced to Paris from the Opéra's stage. See Arthur Loesser, *Men, Women and Pianos—A Social History* (New York: Simon and Schuster, 1954), 393–96; G. Matoré, "Cancan et chahut, termes de danse (1829–1845)," *Mélanges Bruneau* (Genève: Librairie E. Droz, 1954), 177–83; François Gasnault, *Guinguettes et lorettes—bals publics à Paris au XIXe siècle* (Paris: Aubier, 1986); Ivor Guest, *The Romantic Ballet in Paris,* 229; Cyril Beaumont, *The Complete Book of Ballets* (New York: Garden City Publishing, 1941), 122; Lisa C. Arkin and Marian Smith, "National Dance in the Romantic Ballet," in *Rethinking the Sylph: New Perspectives on the Romantic Ballet,* ed. Lynn Garafola (Hanover: Wesleyan University Press, 1998), 11–68; and Marian Smith, "Noisy Audiences and Masked Balls in Paris" (forthcoming). The polka, which was according to Guest (*The Romantic Ballet in Paris,* 229) "all the rage in the ballrooms and public balls" in the early 1840s, is said to have made its first appearance on the stage of the Opéra in the ballet *Lady Henriette* (first performed 21 February 1844). The cachucha was popularized in Paris by Fanny Elssler (as Florinde) in *Le Diable boiteux,* though there is some indication that it might have appeared in the ballroom somewhat earlier. It became so popular that it soon came to be included in other ballets, both new and old (e.g., *Beniowsky,* revived in London 16 March 1837), and it caused great sensations in the ballroom as well.

30 *Le Journal des Débats,* 17 March 1834.

31 See notes 13 and 14.

Chapter Two: A Family Resemblance

1 On the Opéra's audience, see Steven Huebner, "Opera Audiences in Paris, 1830–1870," *Music and Letters* 70, no. 2 (May 1989): 206–25 and James Johnson, *Listening in Paris—Cultural History* (Berkeley: University of California Press, 1995), 239–56. See also Patrick Barbier, *La Vie quotidienne: L'opera au temps de Rossini et de Balzac: Paris (1800–1850),* Series *La vie quotidienne* (Paris: Hachette, 1987), and Jean Mongrédien, *La Musique en France des Lumières au Romantisme* (Paris: Flammarion, 1986).

2 "Il ne pourra être exploité sur la scène de l'Opéra que les genres attribués jusqu'à ce jour à ce théâtre: 1° Le grand ou le petit opéra, avec ou sans ballet; 2° Le ballet-pantomime" [On the stage of the Opéra, only the genres allocated to this theater up to the present day will be performed: 1° Great or small opera, with or without ballet; 2° ballet-pantomime]. Quoted in Véron, *Mémoires d'un bourgeois de Paris* (Paris: G. de Gonet, 1853–55), 6 vols. vol. 3, 174. It must be noted that, though "grand" operas were not officially obliged to include ballet, all operas of four acts or more (and some of three acts) performed at the Opéra during the July Monarchy did so. Shorter operas sometimes included dancers but it is not clear that they featured danced segments. See Appendix One.

The expense records also show that the director spent prodigious amounts of money to meet material costs for productions of both genres, and to maintain in his employ a good many singers and dancers. Expenditures for ballet-pantomimes sometimes exceed those of particular operas in a given season. For example, the material cost of the ballet *La Gipsy,* produced in the 1838–39 season, was 44,199.33 francs; Berlioz's *Benvenuto Cellini,* in production at the same time, cost 22,599.64. *Le Diable amoureux,* a ballet produced in the 1840–41 season, cost 61,530.66; Donizetti's *La Favorite,* produced the same season, cost 48,741.58. *Giselle,* produced in the 1841–42 season, cost 20,182.81; Weber's *Le Freyschutz,* 16,582.98. F-Pn AJ13 228, 229, and 230.

In the season of 1838–39 (a fairly typical one), the Opéra retained the services of twenty-two principal singers and thirty-one principal dancers, seventy-three choristers and an equal number of *corps de ballet* dancers. Their ranks were often swelled with students, children, and supernumeraries.

3 See, for example, Théophile Gautier, *Les Beautés de l'Opéra* (Paris: Soulié, 1845), and the *Album de l'Opéra* (Paris, Challamel, n.d.). The lithographs published in both of these books were made available to customers on a work-by-work basis. See also the *Album des Théâtres* (Paris: Chez Buyot, 1837) and the *Galerie dramatique ou Receuil de différents costumes d'Acteurs des Theatres de la Capital* (Paris: chez Martinet Hautecoeur, frères, n.d.), which features hand-colored prints of costumed actors from these theaters: the Académie royale de musique, the Théâtre Français, the Theatre Feydeau, the Odéon, the Vaudeville, the Variétés, the Molière, the Porte-Saint-Martin, the Gaité, the Ambigu-comique, the Franconi.

4 For example, Castil-Blaze, *L'Académie Impériale de Musique—histoire litteraire, musicale . . . politique et galant de ce theatre, de 1645 à 1855,* 2 vols. (Paris: Castil-Blaze, 1855); Chouquet, *Histoire de la Musique Dramatique en France,* P. L. Jacob, ed., *Bibliothèque dramatique de Monsieur de Soleinne* (Paris: Alliance des Arts, 1843–44), vol. 3, 117–18; and Albert Soubies, *Soixante-sept ans à l'Opéra en une page* (Paris: Fischbacher, 1893).

5 This is the format: verbose preamble on a topic periphally related to the performance at hand; "analyse" retelling the plot in great detail; comments about individual performances.

6 See, for example, *Le Constitutionnel, La Revue musicale, Le Courrier des Théâtres, La France musicale, Le Ménestrel, La Revue et Gazette musicale* and *La Presse.*

7 "Nouvelles: . . . Demain lundi, a l'Opéra, *Stradella,* suivi du *Diable amoureux;* au second acte M. Coralli et Mlle Maria danseront *la Polka.* Pendant toute la semaine on a répété généralement *le Lazzarone,* dont la première représentation est fixée a mercredi prochain. Aujourd'hui dimanche aura lieu la dernière répétition générale. . . . Deux danseuses célébrés à diverse titres, Mmes Cerrito et Lola Montès, se sont trouvées ensemble à Paris. La première est déjà partie pour Bruxelles." *La Revue et Gazette Musicale,* 24 March 1844. Recall, too, that critics acknowledged the importance of ballet to the success of opera. One critic, for instance, wrote of *Le Lac des Fées:* "Qu'on y ajoutât

un pas pour la Carlotta Grisi, et nous garantirions à l'Opéra un succès très grand et de longue durée" [Add a *pas* for [Carlotta] Grisi and we would guarantee a great success and a long run.] *La France Musicale,* 3 July 1842. Of the 1837 revival of *La Muette de Portici,* Gautier wrote: "A triple attraction drew a large crowd ... first, the début of Duprez in the rôle of Masaniello, formerly played by Nourrit; then that of Fanny Elssler, to whom Mlle Noblet, with a generosity that may have been a trifle perfidious, has yielded the rôle of Fénella; and in addition to that, the titbit of a new Spanish *pas* danced by Mme Alexis Dupont and her sister.... The great success of the evening was the Spanish dance...." *La Presse,* 2 October 1837, tr. Guest, *Gautier on Dance,* 17. Even Berlioz, whose anti-Terpsichorian sentiments are well known, asserted that "le ballet des patineurs est une de ces jolies choses qui assurent la vogue d'un opéra" [The skaters' ballet in *Le Prophète* was "one of the fine things that assure the popularity of an opera"]. *Le Journal des Débats,* 20 April 1849.

8 The nine special performances given by Paganini in March and April of 1831 constitute a rare exception; most of these were followed by a ballet-pantomime but not an opera.

9 In attendance at these meetings (in 1837), according to Gentil, were the director, Duponchel; the administrator, de la Baume; the singing director Halévy; two other directors; Schneitzhoeffer; the librarian Benoit; the chief copyist, Le Borne; the head orchestra conductor, Habeneck; the ballet master, Coralli, or his assistant, Mazilier; the two *inspecteurs* of the chorus and *corps de ballet* Trevaux and Desplaces; the head machinist, Contant; the head of the costume department, Géré; and the *inspecteur* of the theatre, Picard. *Chronique de l'Académie royale de Musique,* vol. 2, 310. Gentil maintains that Halévy dominated this "tribunal of elders" (*sanhédrin*) entirely.

10 This is not to overlook the direct influence on *La Sylphide* of the ballet of the nuns in *Robert le diable* (1831), and possibly of Louis Henry's *La Silfide.* Castil-Blaze, *La Danse et les Ballets Depuis Bacchus Jusqu'à Mlle Taglioni,* 202. *Medée et Jason,* a ballet *d'action* first performed at the Opéra on 26 January 1776, is called by Ivor Guest the first ballet "in the modern sense of the term" to appear there. *Le Ballet de l'Opéra de Paris,* 302. See Preface, note 5.

11 "[L]es ballets ... depuis un demi-siècle à peu près, ont pris leur place à côté des opéras, et ... partagent avec eux l'empire de Polymnie et de Terpsychore ..." *Le Journal des Débats,* 22 September 1827.

12 My emphasis. "L'exécution de la musique est entièrement confiée à l'orchestre." Peter Lichtenthal, *Dictionnaire de musique,* vol. 1, 115.

13 My emphasis. "Le *chant instrumental* n'a plus de rival dans les ballets ... Tout est du ressort de l'orchestre et c'est lui qui doit tout exprimer." Castil-Blaze, *Dictionnaire de Musique moderne,* vol. 1, 121–22.

14 On the use of Spanish themes in French ballet, see Joellen A. Meglin, "*Le Diable Boiteux:* French Society behind a Spanish Facade," *Dance Chronicle* 17, no. 3 (1994): 263–302, and Lisa C. Arkin, "The Context of Exoticism in Fanny Elssler's Cachucha," in *Dance Chronicle* 17, no. 3 (1994), 303–25.

15 Libretti of both types also reflected, to a certain extent, the influence of literary works so beloved of nineteenth-century readers, including the writings of Goethe, Scott, Heine, and Shakespeare; for instance, *La Tempête, Othello, Le Dieu et la Bayadère* (based on Goethe's ballad *Der Gott und die Bajadere*), *Giselle* (inspired in part by Heine's *De l'Allemagne*), and several works set in Scotland, inspired directly or indirectly by Sir Walter Scott, including *La Gipsy, Lucie de Lammermoor, Marie Stuart,* and *La Sylphide.*

16 Steven S. Stanton identifies six structural features of the well-made play: "(1) a delayed-action plot whose point of attack occurs at the climax of the story of which it is a part and whose central character struggles to overcome obstacles (usually to love and marriage); (2) a pattern of increasingly intense action and suspense, carefully prepared by exposition which establishes certain facts for the spectator and causes him to anticipate each significant event (this pattern is supported throughout the play by contrived exits and entrances, letters, and other devices for conveying these facts to certain characters while keeping them secret from others); (3) a teeter-totter arrangement of incidents to create successive ups and downs in the fortunes of the hero caused by his conflict with one or more opponents and leading to his ultimate triumph or failure; (4) the counterpunch of peripeteia or upset followed by a *scène à faire* or obligatory scene, in which the hero is victorious because of the release to his opponent of the formerly withheld secrets (these have on the latter a devastating effect); (5) a central misunderstanding or *quiproquo,* made obvious to the spectator but withheld from the participants; and (6) the reproduction in miniature of the overall delayed-action pattern in the individual acts." *English Drama and the French Well-Made Play, 1815–1915* (Ann Arbor: University Microfilms, 1955), 41–42. Oscar G. Brockett writes that the "well-made play" merely perfected dramatic devices current since the time of Aeschylus. Brockett, *History of the Theatre* (Boston: Allyn and Bacon, 1968), 371. See also Patti P. Gillespie, "Plays: Well-complicated," *Speech Monographs* 42 (March 1975): 20–28, and Karin Pendle, *Eugène Scribe and French Opera of the Nineteenth Century,* especially 85–102 and 345–415. As Anselm Gerhard has pointed out, some of the structural features of the "well-made play" identified by Stanton are owed to traditions in comedy and comic opera. *Die Verstäderung der Oper: Paris und das Musiktheater des 19.Jahrhunderts* [*The Urbanization of Opera: Paris and the Musical Theater of the Nineteenth Century*] (Stuttgart: J. B. Metzler, 1992), 122–26.

17 See Philip Gossett, "Verdi, Ghislanzoni, and *Aida*: The Uses of Convention," *Critical Inquiry* vol. 1 (1974): 391–34; Harold Powers, "'La solita forma' and 'The Uses of Convention,'" *Acta musicologica* 59 (1987): 65–90, and Steven Huebner, "Italianate duets in Meyerbeer's grand opera," *Journal of Musicological Research* 8, nos. 3–4 (March 1989): 203–58.

18 On the solo instrument in ballet, see Chapter One, note 25.

19 *La Sylphide,* 26 Sept. 1840. See Chapter One, note 9.

20 This is not to overlook such operas as *Jérusalem,* which was remade for the Paris Opéra by Verdi. But the accepted practice in ballet of drawing from a variety of outside musical sources was not followed in the composition of opera.

21 "La musique domine dans un opéra, elle n'occupe que le second rang dans une composition chorégraphique; le danseur est l'objet intéressant, et l'on fait peu d'attention à la mélodie qui règle ses pas." Léon and Marie Escudier, *Dictionnaire de la musique Théorique et historique* , 5th ed. (rev., cor., "considerablement augm.," Paris: E. Dentu, 1872), 113–14.

22 "Le compositeur a trouvé une idée naïve et simple; un motif pompeux et solennel, une phrase d'une mélancolie gracieuse, un passage martial, fier et marqué; tous ces motifs différens sont remarquables par leur élégance et leur originalité. Croyez-vous que le compositeur, peu soigneux de sa gloire, va sacrifier les fruits de son génie et enfouir ses perles et ses diamans dans un fatras chorégraphique?" *Le Journal des Débats,* 28 Sept. 1822.

23 Gautier, *Histoire de l'art dramatique en France* (Paris, 1858), vol. 2, 67, translated and quoted by Crosten, *French Grand Opera—An Art and a Business* (New York: King's Crown Press, 1948), 68. The Théâtre-Français, too, was slow to adopt the new fashion for more realistic stagings. Pichat's tragedy *Léonidas* (first performed 27 Nov. 1825) represented the first breakthrough for the new fashion, according to Crosten, and the audience responded favorably to the decorations, the costumes and the *mise en scène,* the likes of which it had never seen in that theater. See Crosten, *French Grand Opera,* 54 et seq.

On the *mise en scène* at the Opéra, see, for example, Marie-Antoinette Allévy, *La Mise en scène en France dans la première moitié du dix-neuvième siècle* (Paris: E. Droz, 1938); Catherine Join-Diéterle, *Les Décors de Scène de l'Opéra de Paris à l'Époque Romantique,* Nicole Wild, *Décors et Costumes du XIXe Siècle à l'Opéra de Paris,* and Rebecca Wilberg, "The mise-en-scène at the Paris Opéra Salle le Peletier and the staging of the first French grand opera: Meyerbeer's *Robert le diable*" (Ph.D. dissertation, Brigham Young University, 1990); and Karin Pendle and Stephen Wilkins, "Paradise Found: the Salle le Peletier and French grand opera."

24 This mobile panorama served as a backdrop to a scene depicting a rowboat trip, and was drawn at varying speeds to create the illusion of a boat alternately drifting and moving forward. This effect, designed by Contant, is ably described by Crosten who, however, does not mention that *La Belle* was a ballet-pantomime. See Crosten, *French Grand Opera,* 60. (This ballet-pantomime is not to be confused with the opéra-féerie of the same name, by Planard, Carafa, and Gardel, first performed at the Opéra on 2 March 1825.) Contant also received a special commendation for the effect he created in the last act of *Manon Lescaut:* the Governer's ship became larger and larger, making it appear as though it were nearing the shore. F-Pa AJ13 135. See also Guest, *The Romantic Ballet in Paris,* 97.

25 When the Opéra failed to provide a *mise en scène* of suitable opulence, the critics complained. For example: "All we ask for is the refurbishment of the first set, which is showing its age. In many places the backcloth has lost its paint and can be seen through like a worn-out dish cloth. It is not worthy of the Opéra's reputation for splendour." Gautier, *La Presse,* 24 Sept. 1838, tr. Guest, *Gautier on Dance,* 54.

26 The exact number of flying sylphides is unknown; it is said to have been between twelve and fifteen. Véron mentions the flights of the Sylphides in his memoirs: "The better to justify the title numerous flights of sylphides were devised, and, above all, a circling flight; there was fantasy in this ballet; the first act . . . diverted the spectator by more than one surprise." Véron, *Mémoires d'un bourgeois de Paris,* tr. and qu. by Beaumont, *Complete Book of Ballets,* 84. Véron paid the flying dancers a special bonus of ten francs per performance and personally inspected the flying apparatus before every performance of *La Sylphide* during his tenure as director. Guest, *The Romantic Ballet in Paris,* 114, 159.

27 "La scène change, et représente la salle de l'opéra, où Manon se trouve en grande loge avec le marquis de Gerville. Suivant l'usage du temps, des banquettes sont rangées sur le théâtre pour les jeunes étourdis de la cour. On joue le ballet de l'*Amour vainqueur.* Des bergers frisés et poudrés, des bergères en polonaises de satin, des fleuves en habit de drap d'argent, des naïades en vertugadins et des amours en culottes de satin rose, offrent les costumes de théâtre de l'époque. Les célèbres danseuses Petitpas, Camargot [sic] et Sallé étalent leurs grâces sur les airs de Rameau. . . ." [The scene changes and represents the opera house, where Manon finds herself in the *grande loge* with the marquis of Gerville. According to the custom of the time, benches are set up on the stage for the young blades of the court. [The orchestra] is playing the ballet *l'Amour vainqueur.* Shepherds in powdered wigs, shepherdesses in satin dresses, river-gods garbed in silver drapes, naiads in hoop skirts and Cupids in rose-colored satin breeches—everyone is wearing theatrical costumes of that age. The famous ballerinas Petitpas, Camargot, and Sallé display their charms as the orchestra plays Rameau. . . .] *La Revue Musicale,* 1830, 12–13.

28 *Le Journal des Débats,* 1 March 1833, tr. and qu. by Guest, *The Romantic Ballet in Paris,* 124–25.

29 "Dans Gustave, il se révéla tout à fait; il se posa comme l'Alexandre de la mise en scène du monde, comme le César du costume." Charles de Boigne, *Les Petits Mémoires de l'Opéra* (Paris: Librairie Nouvelle, 1857), 72.

30 "N'est-ce pas, en effet, depuis l'intronisation de M. Halévy à l'Opéra que les chevaux ont été élevés à la dignité d'acteurs indispensables, ni plus ni moins que M. Duprez? Eh bien! voici que les chevaux font également irruption dans le ballet" [Isn't it so that, since Halévy's enthronement at the Opéra, horses have been elevated to the office of indispensible actors, no more and no less so than M. Duprez? Well! Here the horses equally invade the ballet]. *La France musicale,* 25 August 1839.

31 Backdrops and sets were sometimes shared as well, though the practice was viewed with ambivalence because of the Opéra's official policy of providing a new and fresh *mise en scène* for every new work. Rules governing the reuse of costumes were made stricter in 1840 (perhaps because of Véron's perceived abuse of the practice). Pillet expressed his dismay about the new regulations thus: "Quand on voit dans *La Juive* un homme du peuple a vêtu d'un pourpont jaune et d'un pantalon rouge, et que dans *Charles VI* on voit un autre homme du peuple vêtu d'un pourpont noir et d'un pantalon rouge, se le demande-t-on si le pantalon rouge est neuf ou s'il est déjà été employé avec un pourpont jaune?" [When you see a man of the people in *La Juive* wearing a yellow pourpont and red pantalons, and in *Charles VI* you see another man of the people in a black pourpont and red pantalons, will you ask if the red pantalon is new or if it was already used with a yellow pourpont?] F-Pa AJ13 184.

32 F-Pn, AJ13 215. Among other borrowings are these: costumes for sailors from *La Muette de Portici,* and for pirates from *Ali-Baba,* were used in *L'Ile des Pirates;* pantalons worn by guards in *La Juive* were used in *La Fille du Danube;* costumes for shepherds and ambassadors in *Manon Lescaut* were used in *Gustave III.*

33 The evidence for opera is found in the staging manuals, libretti, scores, lithographs and drawings and newspaper accounts; the evidence for ballet (which is far scantier, in part because no staging manuals were written for ballet) is found in libretti, occasional annotations in scores, lithographs and drawings, and newspaper accounts. The ballet scores most likely to be annotated are the autograph composing scores, the orchestral parts, the *répetiteurs,* and the scores prepared by copyists at the Opéra for export to other houses. I owe a debt of gratitude to David A. Day, who has unearthed several exemplars of this latter type at the Archives de la Ville de Bruxelles and brought them to my attention. See his forthcoming "Bibliographie Théâtre Royal de la Monnaie" (prepared with the collaboration of Malou Haine), and his forthcoming doctoral dissertation, "Early Romantic Ballet in Brussels, 1816–1830" (New York University).

34 Ballet-pantomime performers probably had at their disposal a vocabulary of conventional mime gestures (specific gestures for such words as "love," "marriage," "pledge," "death," "I," "you," etc.), though, as Giannandrea Poesio has pointed out, they relied on spontaneity and their own artistry, and their performances of mime scenes could vary from night to night. While it seems unlikely that opera singers mimed and gestured as extensively as ballet dancers did, the connection between their styles of acting is well worth exploring further. Recall, for example, Stendhal's discussion of Giuditta Pasta's debt to Pallerini: "J'ai entendu dire à madame Pasta qu'elle a les plus grandes obligations . . . à la sublime Pallerini, l'actrice formée par Viganò pour jouer dans ses ballets les rôles de Myrrha, de Desdemona et de la Vestale." [I've heard it said to Mme Pasta that she owes much . . . to the sublime Pallerini, the actress taught by Viganò to perform in his ballets the roles of Myrrha, Desdemona and la Vestale.] Stendhal, *Vie de Rossini* (Paris: A. Boulland, 1824), 492, quoted in Hansell, "Il ballo teatrale e l'opera italiana," 271.

35 For example, the banner is inclined as Jean passes in *Le Prophète* Act Three; onlookers wave their hats and cry "vivat!" when Fernand offers to buy wine for everyone in *L'Orgie* Act One. *Le Prophète* livret de mise en scène (Paris: Supplément à la Revue et Gazette des Théâtres, 1849), repr. in Cohen, ed., *The Original Staging Manuals for Twelve Parisian Operatic Premières,* preface by Marie-Odile Gigou (Stuyvesant, N.Y.: Pendragon Press, 1991), 91 [165]; *L'Orgie* libretto (Paris: Bezou, 1831), 2-3.

36 See M. Elizabeth C. Bartlet, "Staging French Grand Opera: Rossini's *Guillaume Tell*" in *Gioachino Rossini, 1792-1992: il testo e la scena,* ed. Paolo Fabbri (Pesaro: Fondazione Rossini, 1994), 623-48. See also Bartlet, *Guillaume Tell di Gioachino Rossini: Fonti iconografiche* (Pesaro, Fondazione Rossini, 1996).

37 See Marian Smith, "Ballet, Opera and Staging Practices at the Paris Opéra," in *La realizzazione scenica dello spettacolo verdiano,* ed. Pierluigi Petrobelli and Fabrizio Della Seta (Parma: Istituto nazionale di studi verdiani, 1996), 273-318.

38 *La France musicale,* 3 Feb. 1839; *Le Prophète livret de mise en scène,* 98 [172]. For a fuller (and rather sarcastic) description of mime in *La Gipsy,* see Chapter Four. Gautier may also be referring to ensemble miming in his review of *Gemma,* in which he remarks that "[i]t is a difficult task to set five big scenes, in which the stage is often filled with more than a hundred people whose gestures have to be designed and co-ordinated from the coryphee before the footlights to the humblest supernumerary fluttering obscurely at the back. To discipline and manoeuvre such a crowd the choreographer has to be poet, painter, musician and drill-sergeant all at the same time." *La Presse,* 13 June 1854, tr. Guest, *Gautier on Dance,* 265. Ensemble miming may be encountered occasionally in current productions of nineteenth-century works. In *Giselle* Act Two, for instance, the corps de ballet all make the same gesture of disdain at the same time in some productions (for example, David Blair's production of *Giselle* performed by American Ballet Theatre, directed by Robert Schwarz, 1977, issued by Lincoln Center Video/ Bel Canto Paramount Home Videos, 1989). In Pierre Lacotte's staging of *La Sylphide,* members of the *corps* render the mime gesture for "dancing" simultaneously in Act One (performed by the Paris Opéra Ballet and issued on video by Kultur Inc., 1971).

39 "Jonas, au milieu du théâtre, bat le briquet qu'il a pris sur la table. (Il faut battre le briquet en mesure, sur les notes du triangle.)" [Jonas, at the middle of the stage, strikes the *briquet* which he has taken from the table. (One must strike the *briquet* in measured fashion, on the notes of the triangle.)] *Le Prophète livret de mise en scène* 89 [163]. A critic refers to "pantomime mesurée" in a review of *La Chercheuse d'Esprit* in

1778: "[L]e danseur pantomime doit toujours régler ses gestes et ses pas sur la musique, et s'il s'abandonne quelquefois à une marche libre et non mesurée; il trahit alors son art; il devient un Pantomime de Comédie; son jeu, défiguré par cette négligence, n'a plus le même intérêt ni le même agrément. C'est un défaut que nous révélons ici, parce que nous l'avons remarqué dans plusieurs Ballets Pantomimes, où ce mélange de Pantomime libre avec la Pantomime mesurée, faisoit longueur, et un disparate sensible" [The pantomime dancer must always regulate his gestures and his steps to the music, and if he sometimes abandons himself to a free and unmeasured movement, he thus betrays his art; he becomes a Comedy Pantomime; his playing, marred by this negligence, is no longer as interesting nor as pleasing. We reveal this fault here because we have noted it in several ballet-pantomimes, where this mixture of free pantomime with measured pantomime created boredom, and an obvious incongruity]. *Le Mercure de France* (April 1778), 166. Baron F. M. von Grimm also provides valuable information about pantomime mesurée: "In the ballets of Noverre dancing and rhythmical walking are kept very distinct. Dance is used only in great passionate movements, at decisive moments, whereas in the [mimed] scenes the performers walk—in time, it is true, but without dancing. The transition from rhythmical walking to dancing, and from dancing to rhythmical walking, is as indispensable in this form of spectacle as the transitions in opera from recitative to aria and from aria to recitative; but dancing for the sake of dancing can only take place when the danced action has come to an end." *Mémoires historiques* (London: Colburn, 1813–14), tr. and qu. by Guest, *The Ballet of the Enlightenment*, 48.

Lincoln Kirstein, drawing from the work of Prunières and Ritorni before him, writes of "rhythmic pantomime" or "cadenced figuration of the several plastic groups" and "dancers and supers . . . trained to make the same gestures in choral unison." He quotes (without clear attribution) this description of Viganò's *Prometheus:* "The apple passed from hand to hand, always seized by the strongest. One could see as in the palæstra, a thousand varied attitudes of these savage athletes, the interlacings, the numerous contrasts . . . at each measure the picture shifted and the same elements competed to compose an entirely new painting." Kirstein, *Dance—A Short History of Classic Theatrical Dancing* (New York: G. P. Putnam's Sons, 1935; rev. edition, Garden City, NY: Garden City Publishing Co., 1935; repr. Brooklyn: Dance Horizons, 1969), 232–35. More recent scholarship on the subject of Italian pantomime includes Ezio Raimondi, ed., *Il sogno del coreodramma. Salvatore Viganò, poeta muto* (Bologna: Mulino, 1984) and Giannandrea Poesio, "The Language of Gesture in Italian Theatre Dance, from the Commedia dell'arte to Blasis" (Ph.D. dissertation, the University of Surrey, 1993).

The "pas en avant" and the "pas général en avant" often called for in the staging manuals for opera and often used to express the increasing stress of a situation, might also strike the present-day audience as strange or amusing. See Roger Parker's review of H. Robert Cohen, *The Original Staging Manuals,* in *The Opera Quarterly* 10 no. 1 (Autumn, 1993): 120–25, and my "The Livrets de Mise en Scène for Donizetti's Parisian Operas," 375.

40 As William Crosten reports, Louis Daguerre (1789–1851) invented the "Diorama," a "species of painting, partly opaque and partly transparent, which depended for its effects of illusion on the play of light and color." It was shown in a circular room seating about 350 people on a movable floor. *French Grand Opera,* 56.

Tableaux vivants were not commonly staged at the Opéra; an exception may be found in a work called *Le Concert à la cour,* performed there for a benefit for the Elssler sisters 5 May 1838. Fanny Elssler portrayed the principal figure in Baron Gérard's painting *Corinne au cap Mysène*. Guest, *Gautier on Dance*, 33n.

41 *Gemma* libretto (Paris: Michel Levy Frères, 1854), tr. Beaumont, *Complete Book of Ballets*, 377.

Gautier himself, who together with Cerrito wrote the libretto, describes the *pas du tableau* as follows: "The *pas du tableau*, danced by Gemma when she has escaped from the vulture's clutches and taken refuge with the painter, is extremely graceful. Never has the celebrated ballerina [Fanny Cerrito] performed *poses penchées* more sensual or more deliciously conceived. There are moments when she recalls Canova's statue of Psyche leaning over Cupid; her white muslin skirt gives the illusion of white marble, and certainly no sculptor ever fashioned out of Paris or Carrara marble arms more supple, more caressing or more beautifully moulded." Gautier, *La Presse*, 13 June 1854, tr. Guest, *Gautier on Dance*, 267. The statue to which Gautier refers, *Cupid and Psyche*, was sculpted in 1793 and is in the Louvre.

42 *La Révolte au sérail* libretto (Paris: J.-N. Barba, 1833), tr. Beaumont, *Complete Book of Ballets*, 94.

43 *Le Dieu et la Bayadère*, libretto, tr. and ed. by Beaumont, *Complete Book of Ballets*, 75.

44 *Le Corsaire-Satan*, 14 July 1846, tr. Beaumont, *Complete Book of Ballets*, 195.

45 Emphasis in the original. Bronislava Nijinska, choreographic notebook, "Theory of Movement", n.d., Nijinska archives. (This essay appears in the notebooks dated 1919–25, but she may have revised it later.) Trans. from the Russian by Anya Lem and Thelwall Proctor with assistance from Simon Karlinsky and Robert Hughes. Edited by Joan Ross Acocella and Lynn Garafola. Nancy Van Norman Baer, *Bronislava Nijinska, a Dancer's Legacy*, exhibition catalogue (San Francisco: The Fine Arts Museums of San Francisco, 1986), 85–88.

46 *Le Diable amoureux* libretto (Paris: Henriot et Cie, 1840), 18; *Giselle* (Paris: Mme Vve Jonas, 1841), 16. [Miranda's] poses, whether decent or voluptuous, excited the applause of all hell." [. . . ses poses décentes ou voluptueuses, excitent les applaudissemens de tout l'enfer.] *La Tentation* libretto (Paris: J.-N. Barba, 1832), Act Two, scene vii, p. 27. See Gautier's description of Indian dancers "stopping abruptly in their tracks," *La Presse*, 20 August 1838, tr. Guest, *Gautier on Dance*, 39–46. In the *Giselle* libretto, the wili Zulmé is described as a bayadere who displays Indian poses.

47 To name five examples among many:

Manon Lescaut, 1830. Ciceri's sets are "exact reproductions of Boucher and Watteau." *Le Constitutionnel*, 5 May 1830, tr. Guest, *The Romantic Ballet in Paris*, 97.

La Tempête, 1834. "Les groupes son dessinés avec goût, les pas réglés d'une manière neuve et originale, rien n'égale la richesse des costumes et l'illusion des décors" [The groups are drawn with taste, the *pas* devised in a new and original manner; nothing equals the richness of the costumes, the illusion of the sets]. *La Revue Musicale*, 21 Sept. 1834. This remark of a London critic is also telling: "The ballet [*La Tarentule*] should end more effectively; a postillion walks in to tell the doctor that his carriage is ready, and the curtain falls without anything like a *groupe* being formed. This was a kind of damper, the audience scarcely knew whether all was over or not, and for fear of applauding in the wrong place, at first did not applaud at all." Qu. in Beaumont, *Complete Book of Ballets*, 127–28.

(*La Fille du Danube,* 1836) "Pas un group élegant, pas un tableau gracieux . . . " [not an elegant grouping, not an elegant *tableau* . . .]. *La Presse,* 26 Sept. 1836.

(*La Fille du Marbre,* 1847) "Le ballet, le ballet! à quoi bon vous raconter les détails de cette *Fille du Marbre;* un ballet ne s'analyse pas. Il faut voir les groupes, il faut voir les décors. . . ." [Ballet, ballet! what good does it do to recount the details of *La Fille du Marbre;* a ballet can't be described. You must see the groups, the sets . . .]. *La France Musicale,* 24 Oct. 1847. The original verb was *analyser,* which in this case meant to give an abstract or summary of the ballet.

Fanny Elssler in the role of Fénella in *La Muette de Portici* "could have been a figure by Bendemann, the painter of *Jeremiah,* or of one of the Trojan women of Euripides. She was as beautiful as an antique statue." *La Presse,* 2 Oct 1837, tr. Guest, *Gautier on Dance,* 19.

48 The visual orientation of the Opéra's audience is frequently confirmed in the newspaper reviews and broadsheet descriptions of operas and ballets, wherein a great deal of attention is devoted to detailed and evocative descriptions of the performers, the sets, costumes, effects. Consider, for instance, the stark difference between the plot synopsis of *Les Martyrs* given in the Garland edition (New York: Garland, 1982) and the broadsheet description circulated in Paris in the nineteenth century ("Académie Royale de Musique—Argument." F-Pn, ThB 2164A). The Garland description, while excellent as an exposition of plot events, discloses hardly anything of the opera's appearance. See Appendix A of my "Ballet, Opera and Staging Practices at the Paris Opéra," 296–97.

49 Louis Véron, *Mémoires d'un bourgeois de Paris,* vol. 3, tr. Victoria Huckenpahler as "Confessions of an Opera Director: Chapters from the *Memoires* of Dr. Louis Véron," *Dance Chronicle* 7 no. 1 (1984): 89.

50 Dahlhaus, *Die Musik des 19.Jahrhunderts* (Neues Handbuch der Musikwissenschaft, vol. 6), Wiesbaden: Akademische Verlagsgesellschaft Athenaion 1980), published in English as *Nineteenth-Century Music,* tr. J. Bradford Robinson (Berkeley: University of California Press 1980), 126.

51 My emphasis. Crosten, *French Grand Opera,* 100–1, 104. See also Anselm Gerhard, *Die Verstäderung der Oper,* 113–36.

52 Crosten, *French Grand Opera,* 104. I use the term *metteur en scène* loosely, because especially in the case of opera it is not clear who precisely was responsible for the blocking of characters' movement on stage; among those who had an influence at the Opéra were librettists (especially Scribe), *chefs de chant, chefs des choeurs,* singers, set designers, *directeurs de la mise en scène,* composers, and *régisseurs.* Note, however, that there is no record of a *directeur de la mise en scène* at the Opéra in the period in question except for Edmond Duponchel (who held the post from June 1, 1840, to October 12, 1841), nor is there a record of a *régisseur de la scène* between June 1, 1831 (when Solomé left the post) to March 1, 1856 (when Alexis Colleuille père took it up). See Nicole Wild, *Dictionnaire des Théâtres Parisiens au XIXe Siècle,* 316. See also Gerardo Guccini, "Direzione scenica e regìa," in *Storia dell'opera italiana,* vol. 5, ed. Lorenzo Bianconi and Giorgio Pestelli (Turin: Edizioni di Torino, 1988), 125–74; and Karin Pendle and Stephen Wilkins, "Paradise Found: The Salle le Peletier and French grand opera," 181–84.

53 Among the reactions prescribed in the staging manual for *La Juive* are these: "Mouvement géneral d'indignation et de colère" (140); "Surprise génerale."

TABLEAU." (141); "Ils reculent épouvantés. TABLEAU." (144); "Mouvement d'effroi" (146). Also, the word *tableau* (denoting in some cases "frozen shock") appears no fewer than nine times as an instruction in this manual. *La Juive livret de mise en scène*, repr. in Cohen, *The Original Staging Manuals*, 137–50.

54 "Chacun reste étonné," *Nathalie, ou la Laitière Suisse* (Paris: D. Jonas, 1832), 29; "Surprise de tous," *Le Prophète livret de mise en scène*, 97 [171]; "Surprise générale," *La Juive livret de mise en scène* (reprinted in Cohen, *The Original Staging Manuals*), 5 [141].

55 The word *stupéfaction* sometimes appeared in the score; it is more likely to appear in autograph-composing scores and *répétiteurs* than in published scores.

56 Beatrix is "glacée d'effroi"; the crowd is "frappée de terreur." *La Jolie Fille de Gand* libretto (Paris: Mme Vve Jonas, 1842), 16–17.

57 *La Juive* libretto (Paris: Mme Vve Dondey-Dupré, 1835), and *La Juive livret de mise en scène*, 8 [144].

58 This particular ballet-pantomime in its entirety might be read as something of a voyeuristic fantasy. Cleophas is also allowed (through the devil's magical powers) to 1) see the normal everyday clothing worn by three women beneath their dominoes so that he can learn of their identities; 2) gain entrance to Florinde's dressing room by drifting through its walls; 3) visit the *foyer de la danse* at the Madrid Opera to watch the ballerinas preparing for a performance and greeting their male admirers. Another ballet featuring the disrobing of females is *Le diable amoureux* (in which, after Urielle's "page's costume vanishes and her true female form is discerned beneath a gauze dress . . . [, s]he dances before the Count in the most captivating manner imaginable, while Frédéric, still asleep, shows evidence of his delight." These descriptions are in Beaumont, *Complete Book of Ballets*, 125, 171.

French Grand Opera may have sought to allay the anxiety generated by the influx of new types of not readily identifiable people into Paris; disrobings of characters in disguise, which revealed their true identity, may have appealed to audiences at least partly because of the same anxiety (though Lauretta's striptease, of course, was not a shedding of a disguise). On the anxiety generated by sartorial anonymity in Paris and the care taken by the Opéra's costume designers to distinguish between character types, see Gerhard, *Die Verstäderung der Oper*, 135. See also Richard Sennett, *The Fall of Public Man—On the Social Psychology of Capitalism* (New York: Random House, 1974; repr. Vintage Books, 1978), 176.

59 This observations is Dahlhaus's, *Nineteenth-Century Music*, 133.

60 *La Gipsy* served as the model for *The Bohemian Girl* (composed by Michael William Balfe, with a libretto by Alfred Bunn, first performed 27 November 1843).

61 On contemporary interpretations of *Le Prophète*, see Fulcher, *The Nation's Image—French Grand Opera as Politics and Politicized Art* (Cambridge: Cambridge University Press, 1987), especially 146–62.

62 On the subject of pointing at houses, see Smith, "Ballet, Opéra and Staging practices at the Paris Opera" as well as Chapter Six and Appendix Two of the present volume. On the use of objects in opera, see Reinhard Strohm, "The Earl of Essex, s*ervitore di due padrone*" (forthcoming). On the use of objects in ballet-pantomime, see Susan Leigh Foster, *Choreography and Narrative—Ballet's Staging of Story and Desire* (Bloomington: Indiana University Press, 1996), 191.

63 *La Sylphide* libretto (Paris: J. N. Barba, 1832), 11–12, and *La Favorite livret de*

mise en scène (reprinted in Cohen, *The Original Staging Manuals*), 139 [83]. To name a few more examples: the soon-to-be enemies of Dom Sébastien shrug their shoulders to demonstrate their lack of sympathy when he addresses the poet Camoëns kindly in *Dom Sébastien;* two groups of courtiers in *La Favorite* show their jealousy of Fernand by refusing to shake his hand; Nevers displays his refusal to join in the conspiracy against the Huguenots by yielding his sword to St. Bris in *Les Huguenots.*

64 See "Quelques Indications sur La Mise en scène de Robert-le-Diable," reprinted in Cohen, *The Original Staging Manuals,* 3 [186]. See also my comparison of the staging manuals for *Le Trouvère* and *Les Vêpres siciliennes* in "Ballet, Opera and Staging practices at the Paris Opéra," in which I argue that the latter piece (which was conceived for the French stage) offers many more visual cues about the plot than the former piece (which was not).

65 Pérignon, *Rosine Stoltz* (Paris, 1847), p. 25, quoted by Mary Ann Smart, "The Lost Voice of Rosine Stoltz," *Cambridge Opera Journal* 6 no. 1 (March 1994): 48.

66 Louis Véron, *Mémoires d'un bourgeois de Paris,* vol. 3, 89 (quoted above), and Crosten, *French Grand Opera,* 104 (quoted above).

67 André Levinson makes the argument that *La Sylphide* (thanks in part to its ethereal dancing *en pointe*) helped liberate ballet from storytelling. See his remarks on the *ballet blanc* in Chapter Six of the present volume.

68 The Opéra's patrons in the 1830s and 1840s practiced many of the same mundane rituals of the audience in the *salle,* regardless of the type of the work being performed. Before both operas and ballet-pantomimes, they occasionally requested renditions of the *Marseillaise* and showed their eager impatience by clapping rhythmically. They were equally accustomed, in both kinds of works, to being subjected to the hired applause of the *claqueurs* whom both singers and dancers employed. And for both kinds of works, they shouted disapproval when they saw fit.

CHAPTER THREE: A LIGHTER TONE OF BALLET-PANTOMIME

1 Gérard de Nerval, *La Vie du théâtre,* ed. Jean Richer (Paris: M. H. Minard, 1961), 146, tr. and qu. by John Chapman, "An Unromantic View of Nineteenth-Century Romanticism," *York Dance Review* 7 (Spring, 1978): 34.

2 Véron, *Mémoires d'un bourgeois de Paris,* vol. 3, 224–25. This translation is based on those of Guest in *The Romantic Ballet in Paris,* 107, and Huckenpahler in "Confessions of an Opera Director 73. Note that Véron is writing retrospectively; *La Sylphide* and *Le Diable boiteux* were both created after Véron's arrival in 1831. Ivor Guest suggests that *Manon Lescaut* was removed from the Opéra's repertory as part of the general expunging of Aumer's ballets from the Opéra after his departure in 1831, and not because of weakness at the box office as Véron implies. Guest, *Le Ballet de l'Opéra de Paris,* 89–93. See also *The Romantic Ballet in Paris,* 97.

3 *La Sylphide* and *Giselle,* neither of which ends happily, constitute exceptions to this rule. So does *La Gipsy* (1839), which is the only one of these ballets to end bloodily: Stenio is mortally wounded by Mab's gypsy gunman shortly before the final curtain. *La Péri* (1843), too, included a scene—later removed—in which a character (an escaping slave) was shot. See Guest, *The Romantic Ballet in Paris,* 225.

4 Choreographers and librettists were quite resourceful in finding ways to demonstrate such contrasts. For instance, Giselle openly marvels at the richness of Bathilde's gown; the title character in *Ozaï,* ignorant of Western ways, commits a series of *faux pas,* including throwing away a bottle of perfume, toying with a Frenchman's epaulettes, accidently firing a musket, and drinking liquor to the point of passing out.

5 On the setting of *L'Africaine,* see Steven Huebner, "L'Africaine," *The New Grove Dictionary of Opera,* vol. 1.

6 Characters based on real people are featured in only four ballets from this era: King Alfred in *Alfred le Grand* (1822), which depicts the struggle between the Saxons and Danes; the dancers Marie Camargo and Marie Sallé, who give the title character a dancing lesson in *Manon Lescaut* (1830); the French explorer de Bougainville (1729–1814), whose voyages serve as a basis for the ballet *Ozaï* (1847); and Prince Charles (later Charles II), who was a central character in the ballet *Betty* (1846), the light subject matter of which is actually based on the play *La Jeunesse d'Henri V* by Alexandre Duval and has nothing to do with the execution of Charles's father, the Civil War, or any of the other events that marked the life of Charles II.

Historical figures portrayed in operas performed in Paris during this period include Dom Sebastien, the sixteenth-century Portuguese king who led a crusade against the Moslems in Morocco (*Dom Sebastien,* Donizetti, 1843), Masaniello, the Neopolitan fisherman who led an insurrection against the Spanish governors in 1647 (*La Muette de Portici,* 1828), Charles VI (in the opera of the same name, 1843), and Marguerite de Valois in *Les Huguenots.* Catherine de' Medici, too, was to be portrayed in *Les Huguenots* (in the scene of the blessing of the daggers), but the censors forbade it.

7 See Fulcher, *The Nation's Image,* esp. 1–10, and Dahlhaus, *Nineteenth-Century Music,* 128.

8 To be precise: principal male characters in opera outnumbered those of the opposite sex by a ratio of 2.8 to 1, as opposed to 1.4 to 1 in ballet-pantomime. These figures are based on a count of male and female characters listed in libretti published from *Moïse* in 1827 to *Jérusalem* in 1847, excepting three hybrid works (*La Muette de Portici, La Tentation,* and *Le Dieu et la Bayadère;* see Chapter Five). In opera libretti, 307 male characters and 109 female characters were listed, while 160 males and 113 females were listed in ballet-pantomime libretti. To be sure, many such male characters were rather insignificant and spent little time on stage. But it is nonetheless striking that opera libretti consistently listed so many more males than females, and that male characters in ballet-pantomime—no matter how insignificant—outnumbered female characters even though it is clear that, as Ivor Guest has put it, "[t]he Romantic Ballet was wonderfully rich in ballerinas, and their brilliance, which was enhanced by the exciting discovery of the *pointes,* quite eclipsed all but a few outstanding male dancers." *The Dancer's Heritage,* 5th ed. (London: Dancing Times Ltd., 1977), 41. These figures suggest that male dancers did maintain a presence, in minor nondancing roles, well into the period in which women were outshining them technically as dancers.

Ballets in urban settings were not unheard of—for instance, *Le Diable boiteux,* set in Madrid and featuring seven interior scenes and two exterior scenes, and *La Jolie Fille de Gand* (see Table 3.2).

9 One could argue that the vengeful Wilis provide an exception to the rule, though their Queen, Myrthe, directs their actions.

10 Anselm Gerhard views Jean in *Le Prophète* as the harbinger of the modern dictator. *Die Verstäderung der Oper,* 255.

11 Dahlhaus, *Nineteenth-Century Music,* 125.

12 Gerhard, *Die Verstäderung der Oper.*

13 "Rarement les personnages historiques sont des personnages dansants... la danse est tellement essentielle à un ballet, que tout acteur qui ne danse point y paraît déplacé, surtout lorsque l'action même appelle sur lui l'intérêt. Il en est du théâtre comme de nos bals de société; l'attention y est concentrée sur les danseurs; on ne s'occupe point des grand'mamans et des vieillards parce qu'ils ne dansent point; et s'ils dansaient, ils seraient ridicules. Faire sauter les héros de l'histoire moderne est tout-à-fait contraire à l'illusion; la gravité romaine se prêterait encore moins aux pirouettes et aux entrechats." A. Baron, *Lettres et Entretiens sur la danse,* 282.

14 "Ce chorégraphe [Noverre] a-t-il eu raison de croire que son art se prête à la représentation des fables les plus sérieuses et de traduire en gestes, en pas nobles et en attitudes les actions les plus tragiques? Nous pensons qu'il ne faut pas trop demander à la mimique et qu'il est imprudent de changer le ballet en une sombre tragédie qui resterait incompréhensible, sans le secours d'un livret.... Il importe d'éviter soigneusement tout ce que exige de longues expositions, tout ce qui ressemble à des raisonnements profonds, tout ce que le meilleur mime ne saurait rendre clairement: les sujets dramatiques les plus simples, les plus courts, les plus pittoresques et les plus animés nous paraissent... ceux qui conviennent le mieux à la chorégraphie." Gustave Chouquet, *Histoire de la Musique dramatique en France,* 169–71. This opinion, however, was not universal. Salvatore Viganò (1769–1821), who created ballets about Richard Coeur de Lion and Joan of Arc (among others) was one of many choreographers who like Noverre found history to be an appropriate source for ballet subjects.

15 See Susan Trites Free, "Dance of the Demi-Monde," 68–75.

16 Many of the dramatic scenes entailing dancing in these ballet-pantomimes, in fact, played upon the stark differences between high-class and low-class dancing. For example, in *Manon Lescaut,* Act Two scene iv, Manon takes a dancing lesson from Mlles Camargo and Petit-Pas; she fares poorly, however, and when the orchestra strikes up, simultaneously, a menuet and a fast country dance, Manon dances in the rustic manner while Camargo and Petit-Pas and their two seigneurs dance the menuet. In *Le Diable boiteux,* Paquita's simple country dance is laughed at by snobbish ballerinas at the Madrid Opera. In *Le Diable à Quatre,* Mazourka, magically transformed into a countess, baffles her dancing master by doing a rustic dance. Further, as Susan Manning points out, Albrecht's noble fiancée Bathilde doesn't dance at all and this demonstrates her social superiority over Giselle. See her "Borrowing from Feminist Theory," in *Proceedings—Society of Dance History Scholars,* "Retooling the Discipline: Research and Teaching Strategies for the 21st Century" (Riverside: Society of Dance History Scholars, 1994), 331–34.

17 "... ces éternelles leçons qui semblent faire du coryphée un maître de danse." *Le Journal des débats,* 20 October 1820.

18 Act One scene vi: "*C'est mon seul plaisir,* répond Giselle, *comme lui,* ajoute-t-elle en montrant Loys, *c'est mon seul bonheur.*" Act One scene viii: "Bathilde interroge Giselle sur ses travaux, sur ses plaisirs. —*Elle est heureuse! elle n'a ni chagrins ni souris; le matin, le travail, le soir, la danse!... —Oui!* dit Berthe à Bathilde, *la danse surtout... c'est là sa folie. Giselle* libretto, 1841. [Act one scene vi: "It's my only pleasure," responds Giselle; "like him," she adds, pointing out Loys, "he's my only happiness." Act One scene viii: Bathilde asks Giselle about her work and her pastimes: *She is fortunate! She has neither woes nor cares; in the daytime—work. In the evenings—*

dance! Yes, says Berthe to Bathilde, *especially dance. She is mad about it.*] *Giselle* libretto.

19 *Giselle* libretto; Gautier in *La Presse,* 25 July 1843; *La Fille du Danube* libretto (Paris: D. Jonas, 1836), *La Sylphide* libretto; all tr. and qu. by Beaumont, *Complete Book of Ballets,* 142, 101, 79. See Susan Leigh Foster, *Choreography and Narrative—Ballet's Staging of Story and Desire,* 199.

20 Gautier *La Presse,* 11 July 1837, tr. Guest, *Gautier on Dance,* 9–10.

21 See note 20.

22 Some contemporary testimony suggests that it was customary for female ballet dancers to play flirtatiously to the audience. According to Gautier, Fanny Elssler's Fénella (in the 1837 revival of *La Muette de Portici*) was unusual because of her refusal to follow the fashion of relating in a coquettish way to the spectators: "Mlle Fanny plays her rôle without any show of coquetry towards the audience, concentrating entirely on her desperate situation, and this conscientious approach might have prejudiced her success, which was not uncontested." *La Presse,* Oct. 2, 1837, tr. Guest, *Gautier on Dance,* 19. In his review of the début of Sofia Fuoco in *Betty* (1846), Gautier writes "[a] few months hence, Mlle Fuoco will know how to dress her hair better, to put on her clothes more tastefully; she will have acquired French coquetry, and her worth will be doubled." *La Presse,* 20 July 1846, tr. Beaumont, *Complete Book of Ballets,* 196. Gautier, in a review of Nathalie Fitzjames's début in *Nathalie, ou la Laitière suisse,* also suggests that ballerinas were expected to smile much of the time (at least in divertissements): "Mlle Nathalie [Fitzjames] ... wears a sad and cross expression when dancing that detracts from the charm of her features. Ballerinas' smiles are undoubtedly stupid and more horrible than the emaciated grin of death itself, but a merrier, more serene physiognomy would be much more appropriate in a simple, playful girl like a little Swiss milkmaid." *La Presse,* 16 Oct. 1837 (tr. Guest, *Gautier on Dance,* 20).

23 *La Presse,* July 25, 1843, tr. and qu. by Beaumont, *Complete Book of Ballets,* 143. It should be noted that Gautier and Grisi knew each other personally.

24 Charles de Boigne, *Les Petits Mémoires de l'Opéra,* tr. and qu. by Beaumont in *Complete Book of Ballets,* 121. The cachucha was founded in the technique of the Escuela bolera (the eighteenth and nineteenth century discipline that blended Andalusian dance elements with the classical style of Italian and French ballet). It distinguished itself from the French classical school by such nonclassical elements as (to quote Lisa Arkin) "rhythmically accented footwork, inward rotation of the legs, relaxed knees, hyper-extension of the spine, and a spiraling effect around the body core through the opposition of the arms, legs and upper torso." And as Arkin points out, "The entrance of the Escuela Bolera canon into the theatrical and popular dance forms of nineteenth century France corresponds to the arrival of Spanish art in France following Napoleon's Peninsular campaign." Though the kinds of movements characteristic of the Escuela Bolera style were not necessarily intended to be erotic, they were taken as such by many of the Opéra's patrons. Arkin, "The Context of Exoticism in Fanny Elssler's *Cachucha,*" 316, 318.

25 "Social Conditions of Ballet Dancers at the Paris Opera in the 19th Century," "Dance and Society in France," *Choreography and Dance* 2, Part 1 (1992): 25. See also Robin-Challan, *Danse et Danseuses à l'Opéra de Paris, 1830–1850* (Thèse de Troisième Cycle de l'Université de Paris VII, 1983); Lynn Garafola, "The Travesty Dancer in Nineteenth-Century Ballet," *Dance Research Journal* 17, no. 2 (1985–86):

35–40; Susan Trites Free, *Dance of the Demi-Monde;* Martine Kahane, ed., *Le Foyer de la danse,* Exhibition catalogue (Paris: *Les Dossiers du Musée d'Orsay* 22, 1988); and Susan Manning, "Borrowing from Feminist Theory."

Though not every ballet-pantomime produced at the Opéra was light-hearted in spirit, the comments of newspaper critics (favorable and otherwise) bespeak an approach aimed at satisfying the public taste for pleasing and light entertainment: "Ce ballet, il est presque superflu de la dire, orné de détails charmants, de danses variées . . . a obtenu un de ces succès garans a la vogue" [Needless to say, this ballet, with its charming details and varied dances . . . has earned much success . . .]. Review of *La Somnambule* in *Le Constitutionnel,* 21 Sept. 1827. " . . . ravissantes de détails, d'expression, de vérité et d'esprit. Ce sont les usages, les modes, d'une époque étudiée avec un goût parfait" [. . . ravishing in its details, expression, realism, and wit . . . the customs, modes, and epoch were studied with perfect taste]. Review of *Manon Lescaut, Le Moniteur universel,* 5 May 1830. " . . . des scènes intéressantes et conduites avec art, des danses charmantes, un mise en scène très soignée, des costumes vrais et frais, de belles décorations, un ensemble fort satisfaisant" [Interesting scenes conducted with art; charming dances, a very carefully executed *mise en scène,* authentic and fresh costumes, beautiful decorations, a satisfying ensemble . . .]. Review of *L'Orgie, La Revue Musicale,* 23 July 1831. " . . . rien, dans le spectacle, dans la mise en scène, dans l'élégance, la variété des costumes, le prestige des décors, le dessin des pas, des enchâinemens, des tableaux, ne dédommage de l'absurdité, du mauvais goût, du mauvais ton, de l'indulgence de l'ouvrage" [. . . nothing in the spectacle, in the mise-en-scène, in the elegance, the variety of costumes, the prestige of the decors, the enchainments, or the tableaux compensated for the absurdity, the bad taste, the bad tone, the indulgence of the work]. Review of *Les Mohicans, Le Moniteur Universel,* 15 July 1837. "The choice of subject is most unfortunate. Soldiers and savages have little to offer choreography. Naked redskins and other characters in buffalo skins provide nothing for the eyes to feast upon. A ballet demands brilliant scenery, sumptuous festivities and magnificent courtly costumes." Review of *Les Mohicans, La Presse,* 11 July 1837, tr. Guest, *Gautier on Dance,* 9. "[A ballet must have] splendid settings, cleverly composed music, and some *pas* danced with considerable grace and ethereal lightness. . . . In addition, it is essential to have an ingenious plot and simple and expressive miming. . . ." Review of *La Fille du Danube, Le Tam Tam,* 25 Sept. 1836, tr. Beaumont, *Complete Book of Ballets,* 103. "Les groupes sont dessinés avec goût, les pas réglés d'une manière neuve et originale, rien n'égale la richesse des costumes et l'illusion des décors." [The groups are drawn with taste, the *pas* devised in a new and original manner; nothing equals the richness of the costumes, the illusion of the sets.] Review of *La Tempête, La Revue Musicale,* 21 Sept. 1834. "Prenez un feuilleton, un roman le premier venu; faites un, deux paysages, jetez-y quelques personnages déguisés; prenez une jeune fille et un chevalier à Venise, à Rome, en Suisse, en Espagne; priez tous ces personnages de se regarder en riant, de sauter comme des cigales, de se quereller, de se rapprocher, de se faire toutes sortes de signes; accompagnez tout cela de musique gaie ou triste, selon la situation; enfin couronnez tous ces divertissemens par un hyménée, et vous aurez fait un ballet d'action, un ballet-pantomime, comme il vous plaira de l'appeler." [Take a *feueilleton* or any old common novel, make one or two landscapes, throw in some disguised people, take a young girl and a chevalier to Venice, Rome, Switzerland, or Spain. Ask all of these people to look at each other laughingly, to jump around like cicadas, to quarrel and make up, to make all sorts of signs to each other. Accompany all of this with music that is sad or happy, according to the situation. Then crown it all with a wedding and you'll have a *ballet d'action* or a ballet-pantomime, as it pleases you to call it.] Review of *La Jolie Fille du Gand, La France Musicale,* 10 July 1842.

26 In 1830 dancers' salaries constituted 53% of onstage performers' salaries; in 1831, 58%; from January through May, 1832, 51%; in 1832–33, 49%; in 1833–34, 46%; in 1834–35, 47%; in 1835–36, 44%; in 1836–37, 44%; in 1837–38, 38%, in 1838–39, 35%; in 1839–40, 38%. (The theatrical year was reckoned, beginning in June 1832, to run from June 1 to May 31.) It was Véron's idea to retain a large *corps de ballet* but to cut its members' salaries. F-Pa AJ13 187, 228, 229 and 230. It must be noted that the foyer de la danse had been opened to male patrons in the eighteenth century, according to Bachaumont (see Kahane, *Le Foyer de la Danse,* 5) but that the practice was expressly forbidden by the early nineteenth century.

27 Tr. and qu. by Louise Robin-Challan, "Social Conditions of Ballet Dancers at the Paris Opera in the 19th Century," 25–26. Gentil refers to "cannon-sized" binoculars in the *Chronique de l'Academie Royale de Musique,* vol. 3, 273–81. Margaret Miner, in "Phantoms of Genius: Women and the Fantastic in the Nineteenth-Century Musical Press" (conference paper, American Musicological Society National Conference, Pittsburgh, 1992), argues that "[e]ven by the male-oriented standards of the nineteenth century, the Paris Opéra was notorious as a miniature world created by and for men." She cites a passage from Alberic Sécond's *Les Petits Mystères de l'Opéra* (Paris: Kagelman, 1844): "After sleeping in his seat well past the end of a performance one night, Sécond's narrator wakes up in total darkness. Spooked, he decides that he will be able to feel his way out of the building only by finding the stage. He evokes his path in the following suggestive manner:

> Aided by my memories and spurred by fear, I then undertook the most perilous voyage that any man could dream of. At every step, I encountered some obstacle. While climbing the railing into the orchestra, I broke the membranes (*peau*) of the 2 tympanies and I disappeared into the vast flanks of M. Mathieu's double bass, like Jonah formerly disappearing into the belly of the whale. After thousands and thousands of detours in the corridors—a new labyrinth, considerably enlarged, where Theseus in person would infallibly have lost himself—I arrived at the stage. That was where all my desires were directed."

The narrator finally finds a ballerina named Leila who expertly guides the narrator through still another labyrinth of corridors to her beautifully decorated studio. See also Margaret Miner, "Phantoms of Genius: Women and the Fantastic in the Opera-House Mystery," *Nineteenth Century Music* 18 no. 2 (Fall, 1994): 121–35.

28 "[Il étendit cette faveur à] des députés, à des pairs, aux employés supérieurs des ministères, aux journalists, aux artistes distingués, en un mot, à toutes les personnes dont les rapports pourraient lui être utiles ou seulement agréables. . . ." Nestor Roqueplan, writing under the name Jules Vernières, *Les Coulisses de l'Opéra,* in *La Revue de Paris* (1836), qu. by Martine Kahane, ed., *Le Foyer de la danse,* 5–6. See also Susan Leigh Foster, "The Ballerina's Phallic Pointe," in *Corporealities—Dancing Knowledge, Culture and Power,* ed. S. L. Foster (London: Routledge, 1996), 1–24.

29 This unattributed phrase is quoted by Louise Robin-Challan, "Social Conditions of Ballet Dancers at the Paris Opera in the 19th Century," 28.

30 Kahane refers to "prostitution légère" in *Le Foyer de la Danse,* 8, 13. See also Felicia M. McCarren, "The Female Form: Gautier, Mallarmé and Céline Writing Dance" (Ph.D. dissertation, Stanford University, 1992).

31 See Susan Manning, "Borrowing from Feminist Theory," 331–34.

32 On the use of the female body to promote orientalistic values and the effects upon ballet-pantomime of perceived threats to women's traditional roles, see Joellen Meglin, "Fanny Elssler's Cachucha and Women's Lives: Domesticity and Sexuality in France in the 1830s," *Proceedings—Dance Reconstructed: Modern Dance Art Past, Present, and Future* (New Brunswick: Rutgers University Press, 1993), 73–96, and Lisa Arkin, "The Context of Exoticism in Fanny Elssler's Cachucha." See also Linda Nochlin, *Women, Art and Power* (New York: Harper and Row, 1988), and Ralph Locke, "Constructing the Oriental 'Other': Saint-Saëns's *Samson et Dalila,*" *Cambridge Opera Journal* 3, no. 3 (1991): 261–302.

33 Pointing out that the hero of *Le Diable boiteux* chooses an illiterate, unsophisticated country girl over Florinda, "whose threat of sexual allure and liaisons would constantly intrude on domestic happiness," Meglin posits that the libretto of this ballet-pantomime "enshrines dependency, illiteracy and selfless desire to please in women, at the same time as it is a moral lesson in men's prerogatives," and that "whether as threat to or embodiment of domestic happiness, Romantic ballerinas carried the same message of middle class morality and gender difference." Joellen Meglin, "Fanny Elssler's Cachucha and Women's Lives: Domesticity and Sexuality in France in the 1830s," 76, 87. See also Susan Leigh Foster, *Choreography and Narrative—Ballet's Staging of Story and Desire,* 243–51.

34 Rationales permitting men sexual contact with inappropriate women were often provided: Omopathetico in *La Tarentule* truly believed that his wife was dead when he married the charming young Lauretta and watched as her wedding garments fell to the floor; Surville in *Ozaï* truly believed that he would never be rescued from the South Sea Island and returned to his fiancée in France when he married Ozaï.

35 In *Giselle,* the title character, as she sinks into her grave, blesses Albrect's union with a woman of his own station, Bathilde (who is present). In *Ozaï,* the title character releases Surville from his vow to her so he can marry his French fiancée; she hands him back his ring and cross and then kneels before her lover's future father-in-law shortly before leaping aboard the boat that will take her back to her South Sea island. In *Le Diable boiteux,* the sexy cachucha-dancing Florinde gives up all thoughts of Cleophas and generously presents her more demure successor, Paquita, with a purse of gold. In the opera *La Muette de Portici,* Fénella, a peasant girl with whom a prince has dallied, tearfully joins her lover's hands together with his noble fiancée's immediately before committing suicide.

36 See Susan Manning, "Borrowing from Feminist Theory" and *Ecstasy and the Demon* (Berkeley: University of California Press, 1993), 33–34; and Lynn Garafola, "The Travesty Dancer in Nineteenth-Century Ballet."

This sort of sexual empowerment of male spectators may have in some sense compensated for the powerlessness imparted by the notoriously weak male protagonists in French grand opera (see, for example, Crosten, *French Grand Opera,* 97). As Steven Huebner has written, "A world of common denominators does not easily admit larger-than-life figures. Grand opera is not peopled by grand heroes. . . . Raoul in *Les Huguenots,* for example, is . . . relatively ordinary and identified strongly with a collectivity (Protestants) into which he does not fit comfortably because of his love for Valentine. At a crucial moment in the opera he vacillates between love and duty, allowing the massacre of his brethren to proceed apace. In the end, grand opera protagonists like Raoul cannot shape history. They are engulfed by it, like thousands of victims—Girondins, Dantonists, Robespierrists—caught up in the sweep of the Revolution in the streets of Paris. Raoul is ultimately shot, in the city and in relative anonymity." Huebner, review of Anselm Gerhard, *Die Verstäderung der Oper: Paris und das Musiktheater des 19. Jahrhunderts, Nineteenth Century Music* 18 no. 2 (Fall, 1994): 168–74. See also John Chapman, "An Unromantic View of Nineteenth-Century Romanticism", 34–37.

37 [L]e corégraphe [*sic*] ... traduire ... dans le langage propre à son art des situations déjà familières ... " *Le Journal des Débats,* 22 June 1820.

38 Such cross-generic parodies were common in European opera houses of the late-eighteenth and early-nineteenth centuries, ballet-to-opera parodies (including, for instance, Bellini's *La Sonnambula*) sometimes achieving as much success as the opera-to-ballet parodies. On the relationship between opera and mélodrame, see Janet Johnson's forthcoming "French Melodrama, Italian Opera, and the Rossinian *Quadro di Stupore.*"

39 Pantomimes on more serious subjects were were also performed at other venues in Paris; see David Charlton, *Grétry and the Growth of Opéra-comique* (Cambridge: Cambridge University Press, 1986), 212.

40 Bitter because the Opéra was able to profit at their expense, shareholders at the Opéra Comique sought to enjoin choreographers at the Opéra from taking any more of the "subjects and melodies that belong to them, to make *ballets d'action* out of them" [... prendre les sujets ni les airs que leur appartiennent, pour en former des Ballets d'action] shortly after the practice had begun (*Le Mercure,* 3 March 1787). By 1787 they had temporarily dropped their opposition, perhaps—as a critic for *Le Mercure* speculated—to squelch a counter-campaign by the Opéra to ban the performance of foreign works at the Opéra Comique, or because they realized that "après avoir vu un sujet traité en pantomime, on n'en est que plus curieux de la revoir traité en dialogue & en chant" [after having seen a subject treated in pantomime, one is only more curious about seeing it treated in dialogue and song]. (*Le Mercure,* 3 March 1787.) But there is no evidence that anyone at the Opéra Comique ever welcomed the practice, and in fact, the shareholders angrily counted it among the principal causes of their financial woes in a strongly worded letter of 1823, addressed to the Maison du Roi:

> En effet, le Vaudeville, les Variétés, le Gymnase, la Porte Saint-Martin, la Gaîté, l'Ambigu, au mépris de tous règlements, ont intercalé, depuis nombre d'années, dans les pièces de leur Répertoire des Airs, Duos, Trios, Morceaux d'ensemble, et représente journellement de petites Pièces qu'ils intitulent Vaudevilles, et pour lesquelles on fait de la musique, et même des partitions presque complètes, ce qui les rend bien réellement des Opéras Comiques, genre exclusivement réservé, et par privilège, à la Société actuelle.
>
> Si l'on regarde plus haut, on voit le sujet de *Cendrillon* porté à l'Opéra-Buffa; on le trouve à l'Académie Royale de Musique, qui le représente en grand ballet d'action, et qui s'est également emparée des sujets de *Nina,* de l'*Épreuve villageoise,* de beaucoup d'autres ouvrages, et qui, en ce moment même, s'occupe de mettre en scène *Aline* et *Zémire et Azore.*

Les grands et les petits théâtres empiètent donc sur le genre de l'Opéra-Comique, et détruisent toutes ses ressources... (Declaration des sociétaires du Théâtre Royal de l'Opéra Comique, Paris, 22 July 1827, 6–7, F-Pa, AJ13 1053).

[... the Vaudeville, the Variétés, the Gymnase, the Porte Saint-Martin, the Gaîté, the Ambigu, in defiance of all the rules, have for several years intercalated Airs, Duos, Trios, and ensemble pieces into works in their repertories, and daily performed small pieces that they call Vaudevilles, for which they write music and even nearly complete scores. This really makes them comic operas, a genre exclusively reserved, by privilege, for the present society.

If one looks at the higher theatres, the plot of *Cendrillon* is seen carried to the Opera-Buffa; one finds it at the Académie Royale de Musique, which performs it as a grand *ballet d'action,* and which, likewise, has taken over the plots of *Nina,* and l'*Épreuve villageoise,* and many other works; even now, they are occupied with staging *Aline* and *Zémire et Azore.*

Both the big and small theatres thus encroach upon the Opéra Comique's genre, and destroy all of its resources....]

An incident that occurred in 1829 further exemplifies the endless wrangling over rights that the state's policy of allocating specific genres to specific theaters engendered. The Nouveautés, a vaudeville theater, provoked the wrath of the Opéra Comique when one of its new works, *Isaure,* enjoyed a great success. The Opéra Comique requested that the Nouveauté's directors be prohibited from performing any works which included unpublished (and therefore new) music, and even tried to halt further performances of *Isaure.* Representatives of the Nouveautés responded with a counter-assignation, declaring, "Attendu que, si les théâtres de vaudeville n'ont pas le droit de faire représenter des drames et comédies avec de la musique nouvelle, les théâtres d'opéra-comique ne peuvent avoir le privilège de jouer des ouvrages nouveaux avec d'ancienne musique" [... if the vaudeville theatres don't have the right to put on dramas and comedies with new music, the Opéra Comique theatres shouldn't have the right to put on new works with old music]. They demanded that the comic opera *Jenny* be withdrawn from the repertory on the grounds that its music was old—"Que de ce fait, QUI NE PEUT ÊTRE IMPUTÉ AU HASARD, RÉSULTE LA PREMÉDITATION BIEN ÉVIDENTE D'ANTICIPER SUR LES DROITS DU VAUDEVILLE" [... a fact THAT CANNOT BE IMPUTED TO MERE CHANCE [AND FROM WHICH] RESULTS THE VERY EVIDENT PREMEDITATION OF ENCROACHING ON THE RIGHTS OF VAUDEVILLE]. They cite as further proof of the Opéra Comique's machinations against the Nouveautés "la manière dont l'orchestre dudit a exécuté cette prétendue partition nouvelle, râclant, détonnant, jouant à contre-mesure, ainsi qu'on le faisait dans le vaudeville primitif, au temps des AMOURS D'ÉTÉ et d'ARLEQUIN AFFICHEUR" [the manner in which the aforementioned orchestra executed this alleged new score, rasping, playing out of tune, off the beat, as they did in primitive vaudeville in the time of AMOURS D'ÉTÉ and ARLEQUIN AFFICHEUR]. See Pougin, *Adolphe Adam,* 63–80.

On the shareholders (*sociétaires*) of the Opéra Comique, see M. Elizabeth C. Bartlet, "Etienne Nicolas Méhul and Opera during the French Revolution, Consulate and Empire: A Source, Archival and Stylistic Study," Ph.D. diss. (University of Chicago, 1982), 2–55.

41 "Tout le monde connaît le joli opéra de Grétry qui donne son nom au ballet nouveau: M. Milon en a suivi assez fidèlement la marche.... l'auteur de la musique a placé très-à-propos la plupart des morceux de Grétry. . . . Tout fait croire que ce ballet, très-gai et fort bien exécuté, attirera beaucoup de monde à l'Académie impériale de musique." *Le Mercure,* April 1815, 368.

42 Original emphasis. "Il seroit donc parfaitement inutile de faire l'analyse d'un ballet que savent par coeur tous ceux qui ont vu l'opéra de *Joconde;* et qui n'a pas vu l'opéra de *Joconde?* De l'esprit traduit en pirouettes, la grâce des pas cadencés substituée aux grâces du style, des situations qui ne diffèrent que par le langage; l'échange du médaillon et de l'écharpe, l'apparition des deux femmes en bohémiennes, leur stratagème malicieusement concerté pour paroître infidèles, et pour confondre l'infidélité trop constante de leurs amans, la scène nocturne du double baiser, le couronnement de la rosière, la pédanterie jalouse du bailli, tout cela se retrouve également dans les deux ouvrages. Une ressemblance aussi complète justifie pleinement le mot d'un homme d'esprit qui disoit en sortant de la représentation: «Je viens *d'entendre* un ballet dont les paroles sont charmantes.»" *Journal des Débats,* 14 Feb. 1827.

43 This piece is also known under the name *Le Coq au Village.* ". . . l'on doit savoir beaucoup de gré à M. Gardel l'aîné, Auteur de ce Ballet, de rappeler ainsi à la vie ces petites Pièces, presque oubliées à force d'avoir été connues, qu'on ne peut plus voir sous leur première forme, parce qu'on les sait par coeur, & qui, sous cette forme nouvelle, semblent avoir quelque chose de plus vif & de plus piquant" [. . . we should be grateful to the elder Gardel, author of this ballet, for thus calling to life these little plays which by dint of having been so well known, have nearly been forgotten; one can no longer see them in their original form because we know them by heart, and, under this new form, they have something more lively and more piquant about them]. *Le Mercure,* 3 March 1787, 40.

44 " . . . la Pantomime, obligée, à défaut de paroles, d'exagérer l'expression, a des moyens plus puissants de nous électrifier." *Le Mercure,* 26 January 1788, 177.

45 The Opéra Comique was housed at the Théâtre Feydeau from 2 Sept. 1805 to 12 April 1829. Wild, *Dictionnaire des Théâtres Parisiens au XIXe siècle,* 328. "La pièce de Feydeau, malgré la suavité de sa mélodie, et l'extrême talent des deux actrices qui y ont brillé tour-à-tour, ne m'a jamais fait la moitié de l'impression que j'ai ressentie en voyant celle de l'Opéra." A. Baron, *Lettres et Entretiens sur la Danse,* 285.

46 "Cette traduction chorégraphique, brillante de luxe et de fraîcheur, rendra pâle et froid l'Opéra Comique, qui renferme aussi des fêtes et des danses nécessairement inférieurs à celles de l'Académie royale." A. Delaforest, *La Gazette de France,* 3 Oct. 1823, in *Cours de Littérature Dramatique,* 2 vols. (Paris: Allardin, 1836), vol. 1, 252–56.

47 Some Parisian pantomime of the eighteenth century entailed dialogue. See Charlton, *Grétry and the Growth of Opéra-Comique,* 212–13.

48 "Il seroit inutile de donner ici l'analyse de ce Ballet. . . . C'est un très-grand avantage pour le Pantomime de ne représenter que des sujets déjà bien sus des Spectateurs, & de leur laisser le plaisir de faire eux-mêmes l'interprétation des airs, des gestes & les danses." *Le Mercure,* April 1778, Ière partie, 164–67.

49 " . . . une action connue d'avance, on prévient ainsi l'obscurité, le plus grand inconvénient de cet Art." *Le Mercure,* 3 March 1787, 40.

50 *Le Journal des Débats,* 20 July 1831.

51 On the *timbre,* see Nicole Wild, "La Musique dans le mélodrame des théâtres parisiens." On the *ariette,* see Charlton, *Grétry and the Growth of Opéra-Comique,* 7.

52 I draw this information from Elizabeth Bartlet and Richard Langham Smith,

"Opéra comique," *The New Grove Dictionary of Opera*, vol. 3; Philippe Vendrix, Introduction to Vendrix, ed., *L'Opéra-Comique en France au XVIIIe Siècle* (Liège: Pierre Mardaga, 1992), 11; and Charlton, *Grétry and the Growth of Opéra-Comique*, 3–18.

53 See Charlton, *Grétry and the Growth of Opéra-Comique*, and Bruce Alan Brown, *Gluck and the French Theatre in Vienna*, especially chapters 6 and 10.

54 Sometimes the original score was even taken over nearly wholesale, as in the case of *Le Déserteur*. A copyist—possibly unaccustomed to copying ballet-pantomime scores from opera scores—even included Sedaine's text for *Le Déserteur* in three numbers of the violin rehearsal score, perhaps before realizing it was unnecessary. See F-Po, Mat 18[84] (1).

55 The libretto I have consulted, *La Chercheuse d'Esprit* (Paris: Duchesne, 1768), includes precisely seventy known airs, but we may assume that at various times over the long life of this work, it may have included more or fewer than this number. Favart's *La Chercheuse d'Esprit* is called an "opéra comique" in the published libretto; this term was common then for what are now sometimes referred to as "vaudevilles", i.e., works that make use of known airs. See, for example, Martin Cooper, "Early opéra comique," in Stanley Sadie, ed., *History of Opera* (New York: W. W. Norton, 1989), 115, and Bartlet and Smith, "Opéra comique," *The New Grove Dictionary of Opera*, vol. 3, 689.

Maximilien Gardel (1741–1787), the elder brother of Pierre Gardel (1758–1840), was a successful choreographer and dancer who favored dancing without wearing the painted mask that had long been customary on the stage of the Opéra. See Guest, *Ballet of the Enlightenment*, 50–52.

56 The scenes are not marked as such in the libretto, which consists of eleven paragraphs, each one describing a new action and in most cases, a change in stage personnel. For this reason I am interpreting them as "scenes" (like scenes in operas and plays of this period, and in ballet-pantomimes over the next few decades).

Many ballet scores used at the Paris Opéra (for parodied and original works alike) during the earliest years of the *ballet d'action*'s existence were unattributed. The choreographers of the works compiled many of these scores themselves, usually borrowing music from a variety of sources and incorporating in some cases only a modest amount of original music. A set of over sixty manuscript volumes of musical excerpts at the Bibliothèque de l'Opéra, known as the "Receuil de ballet," was probably used as a source for borrowing. Annotations of some of the excerpts from Haydn symphonies in these manuscripts indicate that they were copied from music owned by Gardel (probably Pierre, who was a musician and is believed to have arranged many of his own scores). After 1800 at the Opéra, the task of furnishing a ballet score was more likely to be assumed by a composer than a choreographer. The emergence of the ballet composer is reflected in two trends: the Opéra administration, after 1800, paid most of the composers who furnished ballet scores (whether by composing or arranging them or both), and copyists, around the same time, began to include the composer's name on the score much more consistently. See F-Po CO 289 for a list of attributions and honoraires paid.

57 See Guest, *Ballet of the Enlightenment*, 118.

58 Later, when Mme Madré launches into her flirtation with the hopelessly thickheaded Alain she sings to him "Où allez vous/ Avec cette innocent?" to the tune of "Je n'lui, je n'lui donne pas; mais je lui laisse prendre."

59 LA/CHERCHEUSE /D'ESPRIT,/ OPERA-COMIQUE;/ PAR M. FAVART:/ Représenté pour la premiere foir sur le Théâtre de/ la Foire Saint Germain, le 20 Février 1741 (Paris: Duchesne, 1768).

60 "Des Feuillantines," "Je ne vous ai vu qu'un seul petit moment," and "Si la jeune petit Iris a pour moi du mépris." The airs named in the footnotes in this summary of *La Chercheuse* are those of the known airs to which Favart's song texts were sung, according to the libretto of 1786.
61 "Tes beaux yeux ma Nicole."
62 "Que je suis à plaindre en cette débauche."
63 "J'offre ici mon sçavoir faire"; "Je voudrais bien me marier."
64 "C'est fort bien fait à vous."
65 "Si cela est, hé bien! Tant pis."
66 "L'éclat de mon bonheur."
67 "Ces filles sont si sottes!"
68 "A sa voisine"; "Dormir est un temps perdu."
69 "Ma femme est femme d'honneur."
70 "Ce qui n'est qu'enflure."
71 "Pourquoi vous en prendre à moi?"
72 Though it is difficult to determine with complete assurance what music was meant to accompany what action in the cases of ballet scores lacking detailed annotations, likely conjecture is possible. In the case of *La Chercheuse,* there are penciled titles in the violin rehearsal score (F-Po Mat 18 [65]):

1. Nicette	5. Alain
2. Subtil	6. [ ]
3. Mme. Madré	7. Nicette, Subtil,
4. [ ]	Madré

73 Subtil's enthusiasm for Nicette, for instance, is demonstrated definitively at the moment of his first appearance in the ballet when he kneels before his beloved's feet; in the opera he mentions it in the opening dialogue and then reinforces it by singing songs about Nicette's beauty, her sweetness, her virtue, and his enthusiasm for bringing her forth from innocence.
74 " ... paroît en dansant un pas qui caractérise sa simplicité." *La Chercheuse d'Esprit* libretto (Paris: Ballard, 1777), 5.
75 This novel is noted today for its antislavery sentiments and its detailed descriptions of nature. See Philip Robinson, *Bernardin de Saint-Pierre: Paul et Virginie* (London: Grant and Cutter, 1986), 58–61, and Isabelle Vissiere, "Esclavage et Négritude chez Bernardin de Saint-Pierre," in Jean-Michel Racault, ed., *Études sur Paul et Virginie et l'oeuvre de Bernardin de Saint-Pierre* (Paris: Diffusion, Didier-Erudition, 1986), 64–79. Among the other stage works this novel inspired was Jean Aumer's *les Deux Créoles,* produced at the Porte-Saint-Martin and first performed 28 June 1806. See Marian Hannah Winter, *The Pre-Romantic Ballet,* 194. On the topic of the representation of people of color in French ballet, see Joellen Meglin's forthcoming study; her paper on the subject, "Beauties and Benefactresses, Barbarians and Buffoons: Representations of Blacks in French Ballet 1779–1806," was presented at the 1996 conference of the Society of Dance History Scholars.
76 This character is called Domingue in the opera and Domingo in the ballet.
77 In the ballet the servant Domingo swims to her rescue with Paul and Zabi. The Virginie of the novel drowns, having balked at a naked sailor's admonitions to disrobe and dive into the water. See Philip Robinson, "Virginie's Fatal Modesty: Thoughts on Bernardin de Saint-Pierre and Rousseau," *British Journal for Eighteenth-Century Studies* 5 (1982): 35–48. In the opera a black man aboard ship tries to save her but she is

swept overboard (and ultimately saved by Paul and Zabi). In the ballet a black man offers to save her, but she refuses (and Paul, witnessing this event from onshore, dives in the sea and—with Zabi's and Domingo's assistance—saves her from drowning). The librettist of the ballet may have reasoned that an acceptable dramatic equivalent for Virginie's refusal to remove her clothes in the presence of an unfamiliar naked white sailor was her refusal to receive help from an unfamiliar fully clothed black man.

78 Gardel also simplified and deleted characters: the Pasteur of the opera is far more active than the Pasteur of the ballet, who serves mainly to gather wedding guests together; the little boy of the opera, in whom the heartbroken Virginie confides, disappears altogether in the ballet.

79 Domingo's rescue of Paul and Virginie in the jungle is fragmented as well: at the end of Act One, the mothers express their concern for their missing children and dispatch Domingo to find them. Domingo shows his dog Fidèle an article of Paul's clothing before setting forth into the jungle (a scene from the novel not found in the opera), and finally finds the pair in the middle of Act Two.

80 The only divertissement (of four) derived from a set piece in the opera is the jungle rescue celebration, in which Virginie is placed on a litter fashioned of tree branches and carried by two black men.

81 The bamboula, believed to be an African dance, became popular in the United States, especially New Orleans, in the late nineteenth and early twentieth centuries. In the ballet, the only actions of Domingo's wife Marie (who appeared in the novel but not in the opera), aside from spying with her husband on the young lovers and then dancing the bamboula, is to express chagrin along with the other islanders at times of crisis.

82 The second divertissement is occasioned by the arrival of the Pasteur (an event met unceremoniously in the opera) and entails eating, drinking, the distribution of fruits, and a country dance by Creole revelers. The impetus for the last divertissement comes when Virginie presents the blacks with a gift of *tambours de basque*. In the opera she simply gave them rings and a mirror.

83 There were exceptions to the rules implied here for eighteenth-century ballet music. However, discrete binary-form pieces were frequently used.

Kreutzer, best remembered as the dedicatee of Beethoven's violin Sonata op. 47, provided five ballet-pantomime scores at the Opéra between 1806 and 1820, one of which, *Paul et Virginie,* was based on the comic opera by de Favrières (1791), for which Kreutzer himself had composed the music. Kreutzer's ballet-pantomime scores, aside from *Paul et Virginie,* were *Les Amours d'Antoine et de Cléopatre* (Aumer, 1808); *La Fête de Mars* (P. Gardel, 1809); *La Servante Justifiée* (P. Gardel, 1818); and *Clari* (Milon, 1820). He also contributed (with Persuis and Berton) music to the occasional work, *L'Heureux Retour* (Milon, P. Gardel, 1815) and (with Persuis) to *La Carnaval de Venise* (Milon, 1816).

84 "L'origine de cet ouvrage remonte à l'époque où le *Mariage de Figaro* obtint tant de succès. *Dauberval* était à Bordeaux. Cette comédie fut jouée et défendue. Les Bordelais ne pouvant cacher les regrets que leur causait cette défense, *Dauberval* crut pouvoir, pour les dédommager, convertir cette *comédie* en *ballet*. En effet, la gaîté, le comique de l'ouvrage original se reproduiserent dans des situations dessinées avec art, et le *ballet* eut le succès de la *comédie*." *Le Mariage de Figaro* libretto (Paris: Chez J.-N. Barba, 1824), Avant-propos.

85 "Le Conte, la Comtesse et plusieurs seigneurs invités sont à table: le Page sert la

Comtesse, en la regardant très-attentivement. Antonio et Fanchette apportent des fleurs à leurs maîtres; Suzanne marche autour de la table; Bazile joue sur sa guitare un air bachique; des musiciens sont sur une estrade; tout respire de plaisir. . . . le Page admire la beauté de la Comtesse, les charmes de Suzanne et les grâces de Fanchette; Bazile ne perd pas un des regards de Chérubin."

86 Marcelline's desire to marry Figaro is also made clear to the eye when she abruptly interrupts the celebration of the Count's renunciation of his *droit de seigneur,* showing her the *promesse de mariage* and claiming rights to her beloved. Marcelline returns a few scenes later to reproach and then caress Figaro, an action (not found in the play) demonstrating effectively both her feistiness and her fondness for Figaro. (Beaumarchais's audience learned of her intentions when she spoke of them to Bartholo.) And Chérubin's affection for the Countess, unsubtly presented in the play, is even more overt in the ballet-pantomime. Alone with her for a few moments in the scene when the page is being dressed as a girl, he actually kisses one of her ribbons and then holds another against his heart; in the play, he wistfully relinquishes the precious ribbon during this scene without kissing it.

Another prop from the play, the diamond, is also used in a more explicitly visual fashion in the ballet-pantomime: the Count offers it to Suzanne during the armchair scene, demonstrating early in the action his ardor and wealth, instead of waiting until the darkness and confusion of the chestnut grove scene and giving it mistakenly to his wife, as he does in the play. ("My Suzanne—a Castilian's word is his bond. . . . Here is . . . this brilliant to wear for love of me.") Caron de Beaumarchais, *Le Mariage de Figaro,* tr. John Wood (London: Penguin, 1964), 206–7.

87 Its first act requires three sets and entails not only the action from Beaumarchais's first act, but two divertissements and the two newly devised scenes set in the Count's dining room and in Antonio's cottage. Its second act (which includes two divertissements) covers the action of Acts Two, Three and Four from Beaumarchais's play. Its final act follows, fairly closely, Beaumarchais's final act.

88 This brings to mind another scene from the ballet version of a Beaumarchais play-turned-opera: the singing lesson, which was turned into a dancing lesson in the Opéra's *Le Barbier de Séville* ballet. This was done at the behest of the censors, who frequently made helpful suggestions. AJ13 66.

89 The earliest ballet version of this story (Dauberval's, based closely on the Beaumarchais play and first performed in Bordeaux in 1786 only a few weeks after the première of *Le Nozze di Figaro* in Vienna) presumably featured none of Mozart's music. It was restaged by Aumer at the Theatre Porte Saint-Martin in Paris in 1805. Many questions about the provenance of the extant sources for this ballet remain unanswered, but Prud'homme offers useful information in "Le Page Inconstant," *La Revue de Musicologie* 21 (1935): 205–12. For a study of three early French versions of the opera *Le Nozze di Figaro* (two performed at the Opéra in 1793 and one at the Opéra-Comique in 1807), see Sherwood Dudley, "Les Premières Versions Françaises du *Mariage de Figaro* de Mozart," *La Revue de Musicologie* 69 (1983): 55–83.

90 "En ressuscitant cet ouvrage d'un grand-maître, j'ai cru devoir rajeûnir la musique. Des compositeurs m'ont aidé à puiser dans des sources nouvelles, et la musique, entièrement refaite, ne peut qu'être plus d'accord avec le goût du public." [In reviving this work of a great master, I believed it was necessary to rejuvenate the music. Composers have helped me borrow from new sources and the music, entirely remade,

cannot be more in accord with the taste of the public.] Aumer, *Le Mariage de Figaro* libretto, Avant-propos. Habeneck, named as the arranger in the payment records of the Opéra, was not paid for his services; see F-Po, CO 289.

See also Prud'homme, "Le Page Inconstant," 208, and James H. Johnson "Beethoven and the Birth of Romantic Musical Experience in France," *Nineteenth Century Music* 15, no. 1 (Summer, 1991): 24–25.

91 See Prud'homme, "Le Page Inconstant," 208, 211.

92 The scene in which the Countess of *Le Nozze* sings "Dove sono" is of Mozart's and DaPonte's own invention; her situation is less poignantly depicted by Beaumarchais, and by Aumer as well (whose ballet libretto, as noted above, is based on a Dauberval's, which derived from the play and not DaPonte's libretto). The Countess in the ballet expresses her chagrin fairly quickly and then dictates the letter to Suzanne. Thus, in the ballet score, the quotation from the sad, contemplative "A" section of "Dove sono" is limited to seven measures. This is followed by nineteen measures from the defiant "B" section, as "Suzanne la supplie . . . de ne s'occuper qu'à jouer son époux" [Suzanne begs her . . . to occupy herself only with tricking her spouse]. *Le Page inconstant* libretto, 22.

93 I am speculating about how precisely these motifs were matched to the action, though at the beginnings of scenes in particular these matchups seem clear. David A. Day has recently discovered an annotated score for this ballet at the Archives de la Ville de Bruxelles; it will allow a more accurate reading of how these motifs were co-ordinated to the action.

94 "Les Maîtres de ballet ont grandement raison de choisir les sujets de leurs compositions dans des faits en quelque sorte populaires. C'est épargner aux spectateurs la contention d'esprit nécessaire pour deviner et suivre le fil d'une action qui ne peut s'-expliquer des gestes, car on peut appeler la pantomime une énigme dramatique. . . . L'intelligence de tous les spectateurs n'est pas telle qu'elle puisse, sans effort, comprendre rapidement et parfaitement les désirs, les passions, les intérêts des personnages dont elle ne sait pas même les noms. . . . On évite ces inconvéniens en ne mettant en scène que les sujets connus de la mythologie ou de la féerie . . . ; ils traduisent en geste les pièces joués sur d'autres théâtres. Le public a accueilli ces traductions mimiques. . . . *le Barbier de Séville, Nina, les Pages du duc de Vendôme,* . . . n'étaient que des imitations d'ouvrages plus ou moins considérables. . . . Mais le public cependant n'accepte ces traductions qu'à de certaines conditions. Il faut que de jolis tableaux, des incidens, un personnage nouveau viennent jeter quelque diversion, quelque fraîcheur dans les effets et les couleurs usés de l'action, et ranimer une intrigue qui, sans cela, n'aurait plus rien de piquant." *La Gazette de France,* 4 Nov. 1824, in Delaforest, *Cours de Littérature Dramatique,* vol. 1, 408–15.

95 "Traduire en pantomime les opéras les plus saillans et les plus usés, n'est pas un moyen d'exciter la curiosité publique. . . . N'aurait-on pu trouver d'autres sujets à reproduire à l'Opéra, que ceux de *Zémire et Azore,* de *Cendrillon* et de *Joconde,* de *Nina,* des *Pages du duc de Vendôme?* Faut-il toujours marcher dans la même ornière? et le public, qui a raison de demander de nouveau, ne sera-t-il jamais satisfait? . . . ce n'est qu'avec des ouvrages originaux qu'on peut se rendre digne de la faveur du public." *La Pandore,* 6 Feb. 1827.

96 "Après avoir taillé nos plus belles tragédies en livrets d'opéras, l'Académie royale de Musique eut recours aux opérettes du Théâtre Feydeau, pour se former un répertoire de ballets. Vous avez déjà vu défiler un grand nombre d'opéras comiques traduits en en-

trechats.... *Cendrillon* ... ne sera pas le dernier emprunt de ce genre." Castil-Blaze, *L'Académie impériale de Musique de 1645 à 1855,* vol. 2, 175.

97 "Les chorégraphes avaient abusé de la patience du public, en lui montrant des comédies anciennes et fait un répertoire de vieux opéras comiques, de vaudevilles même, adornés d'entrechats et de pirouettes. Les faiseurs de ballets, depuis longtemps fort pauvres d'esprit et d'idées, montraient à nu leur indigence complète. Un riche capitaliste, un financier opulent et libéral, prend pitié de leur misère, ouvre son coffre-fort, son écrou, et sur-le-champ le ballet, cette silencieuse contre-épreuve des pièces les plus connues, et souvent les plus triviales, devient un drame spirituel, palpitant d'intérêt, d'une originalité précieuse et piquante." Castil-Blaze, *L'Académie impériale de Musique de 1645 à 1855,* vol. 2, 205. The idea of employing a scenarist was at first not wholeheartedly accepted by choreographers, who after all were accustomed to having a say in the creation of the story to be depicted. François Decombe (known as "Albert"), for example, refused to choreograph *La Somnambule* because the plot was not to be of his own devising; he was replaced by Jean Aumer. Aumer, who accepted the collaboration of scenarists on several ballets, was reproached by other choreographers for having done so. See Guest, *The Romantic Ballet in Paris,* 99.

It is surely no coincidence that the Opéra sought to improve the literary merit of its ballet libretti by hiring them out to writers (instead of always leaving the task in the hands of the choreographer, as had long been the custom), in the late 1820s, precisely the time that critics were beginning to dismiss opera libretti as "no longer on the margins of literature, but beneath it." Arthur Groos, introduction to *Reading Opera,* 5.

98 "Était-il bien nécessaire, on pourrait ajouter même, est-il bien loyal de prendre la pièce d'un auteur vivant que chaque semaine on applaudit? de suivre littéralement cette pièce dans ses principaux effets, dans ses situations les plus piquantes, et de nuire probablement, par le succès qu'on obtient de cette manière, aux intérêts de l'ouvrage qu'on a calqué?" *La Gazette de France,* 3 October 1823, in Delaforest, *Cours de Littérature Dramatique,* vol. 1, 252–56.

99 "Jamais la république des lettres n'a mieux mérité le nom de *république de loups* que lui donnait Beaumarchais! Voilà, en huit jours, deux pièces de M. Étienne qui, à peine déguisées sous d'autres titres, servent à faire de la réputation, et du bénéfice à ceux qui recherchent sans doute encore plutôt l'un que l'autre." *La Gazette de France,* 30 January 1827, in Delaforest, *Cours de Littérature Dramatique,* vol. 2, 280–83.

100 "... trop occupé du soin de piller l'Opéra Comique, pour en composer ce qu'on nomme bizarrement *ballet d'action.*" *La Pandore,* 9 Dec. 1823.

101 "Nous avons déjà blâmé cette habitude ... de rehabiller des opéras comiques, des mélodrames ou des comédies en ballets. Le ballet est un genre spécial, qui exige des sujets d'une nature toute particulière.... Un pièce traduite en signes mimiques et accompagnée d'un divertissement n'est pas un ballet." *La Presse,* 20 July 1846.

102 "Vous avez déjà vu défiler un grand nombre d'opéras comiques traduits en entrechats...." Castil-Blaze, *L'Académie impériale de Musique de 1645 à 1855,* vol. 2, 175. See note 96, above.

103 Any modern assessment of the distinctions between different kinds of operas of the late-eighteenth and early-nineteenth centuries in Paris, or of the never-ceasing wrangling over theater directors' compliance with laws governing the allotment of genres to the three main Parisian opera houses (the Opéra, Opéra-Comique, and the Théâtre Italien) should take ballet into account. More attention has been paid to the interchange between lyric genres; for instance, the short operas in the comic style that were occasionally produced at the Opéra (including *Le Comte Ory* and *Benvenuto Cellini*). See Philip Gossett's introduction to the Garland reprint of *Le Comte Ory* (New York and London: Garland Publishing Company, 1978). These operas were performed, in keeping with the theater regulations, with recitatives and not spoken dialogue.

104 The ballet-pantomime's connection with comic opera can also help explain why the most successful ballet composers in the 1830s and 1840s also succeeded as composers of comic opera. Adolphe Adam (1803–1856), for example, the most highly respected ballet composer of the age, provided melodies for vaudevilles gratis early in his career and went on to write twenty-six works for the Opéra-Comique, many of which, including *Le Chalet* (1834), *Le Postillon de Longjumeau* (1836) and *Le Brasseur de Preston* (1838), earned enormous success. Yet his serious operas failed. The same may be said of Ferdinand Hérold (1791–1833), who, aside from composing ballet scores, served as *chef du chant* at the Opéra and accompanist and talent scout for the Théâtre Italien. He wrote such popular comic operas as *Zampa* (1831) and *Le Pré aux clercs* (1832), both of which had over a thousand performances. But he did not, before his early death, achieve his goal of succeeding as a composer of serious operas. Henri Reber (1807–1880), Alexandre Montfort (1803–1856), and Casimir Gide (1804–1868) were among the others who found fairly equal success as composers of ballet and comic opera but made no mark as composers of more serious opera.

105 See note 14. For descriptions of pre-1830 ballets at the Opéra, see Guest, *Ballet of the Enlightenment;* Judith Chazin-Bennahum, *Dance in the Shadow of the Guillotine* (Carbondale: Southern Illinois University Press, 1988); Marian Hannah Winter, *The Pre-Romantic Ballet;* and Susan Leigh Foster, *Choreography and Narrative—Ballet's Staging of Story and Desire.*

106 It must be recalled that Véron's tenure at the Paris Opéra ended in 1835. Directors of the Paris Opéra (under various titles) during this period are as follows: Véron (1 March 1831–1 June 1835, with the assistance of Aguado and Las Marismas from 1 June 1831); Edmond Duponchel and Léon Pillet (1 Sept. 1835–1 Dec. 1839); Duponchel and Edouard Monnais (1 Dec. 1839–1 June 1840); Pillet, Duponchel, Monnais (1 June 1840–1 June 1842); Pillet (1 June 1842–1 August 1847); Duponchel, Nestor Roqueplan, Pillet (1 August 1847–Nov. 1847); Duponchel and Roqueplan (Nov. 1847–21 Nov. 1849), Roqueplan (Nov. 1849–Nov. 1854). Wild, *Dictionnaire des Théâtres Parisiens,* 306–7.

CHAPTER FOUR: BALLET-PANTOMIME AND SILENT LANGUAGE

1 Gautier, review of *La Vivandière, La Presse,* 23 Oct. 1848, tr. Guest, *Gautier on Dance,* 205. Mallarmé, qu. by André Levinson in "The Idea of the Dance: From Aristotle to Mallarmé," *What Is Dance? Readings in Theory and Criticism,* 53.

2 Noverre, *Lettres sur la Danse et les Ballets,* 51–53. Two exceptions at the Paris Opéra to the rule of performing ballet-pantomime without intoning words may be found in *La Fille de marbre* (1847), in which a chorus sings in rhymed verse as a group of Salamanders in spangled skirts pose in "attitudes of surprise," and *Griseldis,* in which the title character (created by Carlotta Grisi) sings a *ritornello* from the wings and then, at the end of the ballet, on the stage. See *Gautier on Dance,* 183–84, 197.

3 "[L]'orchestre peint à mesure [l'inscription]." *Psiché* libretto (Paris: P. de Lormel, 1795).

4 When Psiché's mother and her children offer to sacrifice themselves in Psiché's stead, another inscription appears: "Amis, parens s'offrent en vain/ Venus veut qu'au monstre elle donne la main." [Kith and kin offer themselves up in vain/Venus desires Psiché to offer her hand to the monster]. The text of the two inscriptions as given in three surviving published libretti, however (one from Brussels, 1790, and two from Paris, 1795, housed in the Bibliothèque de l'Opéra), are longer than those in the score. The first inscription in these libretti reads: "A Psiché, conduite en coupable, / Avec l'appareil de la mort, / Sur cette roche épouvantable, / Un monstre doit unir son sort." [Pische, the condemned, is led in / Berobed for death/ On this horrible rock / A monster must share her fate]. The second is: "En vain pour expier son crime, / Parens, amis s'offriroient tous, / Vénus, dans son juste courroux, /Veut Psiché seule pour victime." [In vain, to expiate her crime/ Kith and kin would sacrifice themselves/ Venus, in her righteous wrath/ Wants Psiché alone as victim]. The texts given in the score (F-Po A.337a) are: "Psiché pour expier son crime /d'un monstre sur ce roc doit être la victime" and "Amis parens s'offrent en vain/ Venus veut qu'au monstre elle donne la main." It seems unlikely that the words in the libretti matched up precisely with those "played" by the orchestra (though we cannot be certain, because there may be missing versions of the score and libretto).

Bruce Brown discusses a similar use of text in the Viennese ballet *Sémiramis* (1765): "[C]uriously, ... Angiolini is not entirely consistent in substituting gesture for words: at two points he relies on inscriptions—a ghostly hand tracing these words on the wall of [the] queen's chambers: 'mon fils, va me venger: tremble, épouse perfide!' and these which Ninias reads at the bottom of the tomb of Ninus: 'Viens, cours, venge ton pére.'" Gluck sets these verses in speech rhythms, though they do not follow the rules of French prosody. See Bruce Brown, *Gluck and the French Theatre in Vienna,* 163, 337-38.

5 "Le Courage n'a point de sexe," *Achille à Scyros* (Gardel/Cherubini, Méhul, Kreutzer, Rode, Isouard, Boieldieu) libretto (Paris: Roullet, 1817); "A la demande du vaillant Ismaël, le Roi rend la liberté à toutes ses femmes. . . . Zulma seule restera captive," *La Révolte au Sérail* libretto (Paris: J.-N. Barba, 1833); "Veuve Gertrude, aux Noeds galants," "La mère Michaud, meunière," *La Somnambule* libretto (Paris: J.-N. Barba, 1827); "Elle dormira pendant cent ans. . . . Celui qui la reveillera l'épousera, si d'une autre il n'est l'époux," *La Belle au Bois dormant* libretto (Paris: Bezou, 1829).

6 "Haine éternelle aux hommes." *Brézilia ou la Tribu des femmes* libretto (Paris: Librairie Centrale, 1835).

7 The critic writes: "Les Pièces de l'Opéra, on le sait, et surtout les ballets, ont besoin, pour la plupart des spectateurs, d'une explication qui aide à l'intelligence de l'action. Peu de personnes aiment assez la musique pour se passer d'un livret qui les aide à comprendre les situations; c'est ce qui fait que souvent la belle salle de l'Opéra ressemble à un cabinet de lecture où les lecteurs lèvent de temps en temps la tête vers les artistes." [The works performed at the Opéra, as you know, and especially the ballets, need (for most spectators) an explanation that helps in understanding the action. Few people love the music so much that they would pass up a libretto that helps them understand the situations. This often makes the beautiful *salle* of the Opéra house resemble a reading room where the readers look up at the performers from time to time.] *La Revue et Gazette des Théâtres,* 16 March 1845. Gautier remarks, in a similar vein, that "we are not one of those who go to a new ballet and read the scenario during the performance without once raising their eyes because they prefer to understand it rather than to see it." *La Presse,* 21 Feb. 1848, tr. Guest, *Gautier on Dance,* 189. A strange com-

ment is made in *Le Corsaire* of 23 Feb. 1835: "Le poème de *La Juive* est imprimé et se vendra ce soir 1 franc à l'Opéra. Cette innovation utile est de M. Schlesinger acquéreur du poème et de la musique de cet ouvrage." [The libretto of *La Juive* is printed and will be sold tonight for one franc at the Opéra. This useful innovation is that of Schlesinger, who has purchased the libretto and the music of this work.] This latter review was pointed out to me by Cormac Newark, who also notes, together with M. Elizabeth C. Bartlet, that the practice of distributing libretti at the Opéra was in fact common by the 1830s.

8 See Susan Trites Free, "Dance of the Demi-monde," 67.

9 *La Somnambule* libretto (Paris: N. Tresse, 1857), 10.

10 *La Somnambule, Notes de ballet* (pages not numbered), AJ[13] 135. See also the *Fonds Aumer* at the Bibliothèque de l'Opéra.

11 Recitative-like passages also occur in melodramas, as Emilio Sala has pointed out. These consist of spurts of orchestral comment alternating with spoken comments, and in some cases are marked in the scores as recitatives. See Sala, *L'opera senza canto,* 51–54.

12 On the recitative, and the variety of circumstances in which it occurred in eighteenth- and early-nineteenth-century instrumental music—including in ballets—see David Charlton, "Instrumental Recitative: A Study in Morphology and Context, 1700–1808," *Comparative Criticism—A Yearbook,* vol. 4, ed. E. S. Shaffer (Cambridge: Cambridge University Press, 1982), 149–68. He proposes this classification of recitatives in instrumental works: A) Creation of a *persona* for imagined "roles" (including silent characters in ballet); B) Extension of the role of the soloist in a concerto or chamber piece; C) Functions allied to those of the cadenza; and D) Decorative or fanciful reinterpretations of recitative style.

He writes that "the later eighteenth century gave validity to the old shapes and gestures of recitative by setting them in dialectical contexts. Their inherently rhetorical quality was also reinforced . . . by dramatizing their expression: the result coincides closely with Delagrange's formulation of music . . . as an intuitively understood language. Other modes of 'quasi-conceptual' communication can be traced in orchestral music of the time. Since Romantic music's power resided much in the eloquence of instruments, which some saw as a clearer language than words, instrumental recitative could be understood as a neo-classic resource of unusual durability."

See also Charlton, "Orchestra and Image in the Late Eighteenth Century, *Proceedings of the Royal Musical Association* 102 (1976), 1–12.

13 This is described in the libretto, Act One scene v, and is designated as no. 7 in the score.

14 This is described in the libretto, Act Two, Fifth Tableau, scene ix, and is designated in the score as no. 14 of Act Two. An extended trombone solo serves as the voice for a comical street entertainer in *Napoli* in one of this ballet's most memorable scences; choreographed by August Bournonville and first performed in 1842, it is still in the repertory of the Royal Danish Ballet.

15 See Stephanie Jordan, "The Role of the Ballet Composer at the Paris Opéra: 1820–1850," Nicole Wild's discussion of *timbre* in melodrama in "La Musique dans le Mélodrame des Théâtres Parisiens," and Guest's discussion of the *air parlant* or "carillon" in *The Romantic Ballet in Paris,* 10.

16 Annotations in the manuscript conductor's score indicate the entrances of the groups in this fugue. F-Po A.501. On Mark Morris's choreography to a fugue, and correspondence between music and gesture, see the opening remarks in Carolyn Abbate and Roger Parker, "Dismembering Mozart," *Cambridge Opera Journal* 2 no. 2 (July 1990): 187–95.

17 "On peut donc, parfois, recourir aux mélodies tendres et passionnées, aux mouvements larges et solennels, et, sans copier dans toute sa longueur le trio de la *Gazza Ladra* ou la moitié d'un acte de la *Sémiramide,* on peut expliquer le sens de la scène et les gestes des personnages par quelques fragments connus qui réveillent le souvenir d'une situation ou d'un sentiment analogue." *Le Siècle,* 23 Sept. 1836.

18 "Air ou fragment d'air populaire qui rappelle les paroles jointes à la mélodie." Léon et Marie Escudier, *Dictionnaire de Musique Théorique et Historique,* 5th ed., 395.

19 "Le spectateur y retrouve sur les motifs qu'il reconnaît les paroles qu'on ne lui fait pas entendre." *Le Moniteur universel,* 21 Sept. 1827.

20 ". . . les paroles d'un motif connu à l'explication d'une péripétie dramatique." Gustave Chouquet, *Histoire de la Musique Dramatique en France,* 169–71.

21 "La musique unie à la poésie fait une impression si forte sur l'âme, que lors-même qu'ils sont dépouillés du charme des paroles, les airs de chant conservent encore leur signification. Ce ne sont que des souvenirs, mais cette expression mémorative agit d'une manière bien puissante. On a donné par analogie le nom de *proverbes musicaux* aux airs ou fragmens d'airs qui rappellent à l'imagination le trait malin, la pensée ingénieuse, la sentence, le compliment, la déclaration d'amour, le serment, l'invocation, l'expression d'admiration, de désir, de joie, de tristesse, etc., que renfermaient les paroles jointes à leur mélodie. . . . Ces airs que l'on a long-temps répétés . . . sont gravés dans la mémoire de tout le monde. . . ." Castil-Blaze, *Dictionnaire de Musique Moderne* (Paris: Magasin de Musique de la Lyre Moderne, 1821), vol. 2, 178–80.

Ralph P. Locke has shown that the writers of "chansons," or texts, often political, to be sung to well-known tunes, referred to published collections of tunes, which were popular in nineteenth-century Paris. It seems likely that ballet composers referred to them as well. See Locke, "The Music of the French Chanson, 1810–1850," in *Music in Paris in the Eighteen-Thirties,* 431–56. The custom of exploiting known melodies for their referential value dates back at least to the medieval liturgical drama.

22 Other *airs parlants* listed by Castil-Blaze are: "Le Souvenir de notre ardeur," "La Beauté fait toujours voler à la victoire," "Ah! laissez moi la pleurer!" "Venez régner en souveraine," "Du moment qu'on aime, / L'on devient si doux, etc.," "Gardez-vous de la jalousie," "Nous braverons pour lui les plus sanglans hasards," "Je n'ai jamais chéri la vie, / Que pour te prouver mon amour," "Notre général vous appelle," "La victoire est à nous," "Ah! je triomphe de son coeur!" "Ne va pas me tromper," "Ne crois pas m'échapper," "Lorsqu'on est si bien ensemble," "Devrait-on jamais se quitter?" "C'est ici que Rose respire," "Femme jolie et du bon vin: / Voilà les vrais biens de la vie," "Eh mais, oui dà, [sic] / Comment trouver du mal à ça?" "Ils sont passés ces jours de fêtes," "Quoi! c'est vous qu'elle préfère?" "Adieu Marton, adieu Lisette," "Serviteur à monsieur d'Lafleur," "L'Amour est un enfant trompeur," "Ça n'dur'ra pas toujours," "Va-t-en voir s'ils viennent, Jean."

23 Roland John Wiley, *Tchaikovsky's Ballets,* 149–50, 292. As Wiley points out, Yuri Slonimsky claims that it was the idea of the Francophile Ivan Vsevolozhsky to use this tune, though, if so, "it would be reasonable to expect the idea to reach Tchaikovsky through Petipa's instructions, in which, however, there is no mention of it. That it was

Tchaikovsky's own idea cannot be ruled out; he possessed a copy of a French songbook which contained it."

24 My emphasis. " . . . ingénieuses allusions et l'on ne manque jamais d'applaudir le musicien qui les fait exécuter à-propos dans une sérénade, un divertissement, une fête publique. La clarinette fait entendre le motif, et les paroles volent de bouche en bouche. L'emploi de ces airs parlants, de ces *proverbes musicaux,* est d'un grand secours pour l'intelligence de la pantomime des ballets. Ils ajoutent au piquant de certains couplets de vaudeville. Il n'est point d'action dans la vie, point de passion qui n'ait son expression dans la musique, et, qui plus est, son expression consacrée. Il faudrait être tout-à-fait étranger à notre scène lyrique pour ne pas comprendre ce qui signifient la plus grande partie de ces airs."

25 "Il se tourne du côté du Minerve, l'orchestre continue le même air, et dit: *que de Majesté.* Enfin, il fixe Vénus, et toujours en suivant le même air l'orchestre prononce: *que de grâces! que de beauté!" Le Journal de Paris,* 8 March 1793. According to Patrick Barbier, when Marie Antoinette attendait l'Opéra, it was customary for the chorus to sing "Que d'attraits, que de majesté" in her honor. Barbier, *Opera in Paris 1800–1850— A Lively History,* tr. Robert Luoma (Portland: Amadeus Press, 1995), 125.

26 "Elle exprime qu'elle *peut braver les coups du sort, mais non pas les regards d'un père.* . . .Les larmes la suffoquent." *Clari* libretto (Paris: Rue Neuve St.-Marc, 1820). See also *Le Journal des débats,* 22 June 1820.

27 See *La Gazette Musicale de Paris,* 21 Sept. 1834.

28 Castil-Blaze, *La Danse et les Ballets depuis Bacchus jusqu'à Mlle. Taglioni,* 320–21.

29 The source of the Beethoven melody is not identified. *La France Musicale,* 17 August 1845.

30 *Le Corsaire,* 5 May 1830.

31 Composing scores (for instance, those by Hérold and Adam preserved at the Bibliothèque nationale) sometimes include annotations with the words of the actors written into the music. Such words may also be found occasionally in *répetiteurs,* principal violin parts (preserved at the Bibliothèque de l'Opéra), and scores prepared by copyists at the Paris Opéra for export to other houses. See Chapter Two, note 33.

32 David Charlton, "Instrumental recitative: A study in morphology and context, 1700–1808," 149–68. As noted above (see note 12), the subsuming of recitative into instrumental music in the eighteenth century, as Charlton suggests, may well have been "understood as a neoclassical resource of unusual durability" in the Romantic era.

Charlton also points out that some theorists formulated "a modern view of instrumental music, free of necessary imitative associations." He cites the words of P. A. Delagrange, in the *Essai sur la musique considérée dans les rapports avec la Médecine* (Paris, 1804), 14: "La Musique agit comme un beau tableau dont souvent on ne connaît pas le sujet . . . c'est un langage magique qui, par une imitation fidèle, dira tout, en gardant le secret" [Music acts like a beautiful picture of which the subject is often unknowable . . . it is a magic language that, by imitating faithfully, will say everything while keeping it secret], 165–67.

33 "Tout à coup le bruit d'une marche se fait entendre dans le lointain" [All of a sudden the sound of a march is heard in the distance], *Manon Lescaut* libretto, 41; "A ce moment on entend un grand bruit. Tout le monde se lève" [At this moment a big noise is heard. Everyone rises], *Manon Lescaut* libretto, 12; "Un léger bruit se fait entendre à la fenêtre" [A soft sound is heard at the window], *La Somnambule* libretto, 8; "Tableau bruyant et animé de la joie populaire, interrompue par les accords d'une musique religieuse et grave" [Noisy and animated tableau of the people's joy, interrupted by the sounds of solemn religious music], *La Révolte des femmes* (also called *La Révolte au sérail*) (Paris: J.-N. Barba, 1833), 18; "Béatrix . . . s'éloigne de son ancienne amie avec une sort de dédain. Celle-ci se met à rire. . . ." [Béatrix . . . withdraws from her old friend with a sort of disdain. This causes her friend to laugh. . . ." *La Jolie Fille de Gand* (Paris, 1842), 14; "Bruit, tumulte, explosions, querelle générale" [Noise, tumult, outbursts, general quarrel], *La Jolie Fille de Gand,* 14.

I would argue that recitative in both opera and ballet-pantomime (as well as more abstract types of *parlante* music in the latter) was heard by the characters as talking. See Ellen Rosand, "Operatic ambiguities and the power of music," *Cambridge Opera Journal* 4 no. 1 (March 1992): 75–80. On the distinctions between phenomenal and noumenal music, see Carolyn Abbate, *Unsung Voices* (Princeton: Princeton University Press, 1991), especially 119–23 and 131–35.

34 "La musique a été arrangée avec infiniment de grâce," *Le Figaro,* 20 Sept. 1827; "Ce ballet, il est . . . d'une musique choisie et arrangée avec un goût exquis," *Le Constitutionnel,* 21 Sept. 1827; "La musique est de M. Persuis, qui a choisi avec beaucoup de goût parmi les airs déjà connus, ceux qui s'appliquoient le mieux de la situation," *Le Journal de l'Empire,* 25 Nov. 1813; *The Times,* after a performance of 16 April 1825 in London of the Parisian ballet *Les Amours d'Antoine et de Cléopâtre,* qu. by Beaumont, *Complete Book of Ballets,* 59.

35 ". . . melodies faciles qui s'échappaient de sa plume comme l'eau d'une source." *La Revue musicale,* 10 Nov 1832.

36 "*La Fille de Marbre* a été faite en quinze jours, et il y a là bien des motifs que d'autres compositeurs n'auraient pas trouvés en six mois de temps," *La France Musicale,* 24 Oct. 1847.

37 "La musique . . . abonde en motifs élégans et elle fournira une longue carrière de valses, de fantaisies et de contredanses. . . . Dans le second acte surtout, les mélodies sont fraîches et originales. . . ." *La France Musicale,* 2 May 1847.

38 "La musique de la *Péri* . . . se distingue, surtout dans le premier acte, par une succession de motifs, sinon neufs et saillans du moins élégans et distingués." *Le Ménestrel,* 23 July 1843.

39 "L'innovation n'est pas heureuse, vu surtout que trois compositeurs prennent, dans ce cas-là, pour collaborateurs, tous les compositeurs célèbres" [The innovation is unfortunate, mainly because the three composers of the score had all taken famous composers as their collaborators]. *La France Musicale,* 31 Jan. 1839.

40 "La musique de ballet est d'ordinaire d'assez peu d'importance; c'est à peine si dans la quantité innombrable de ballets représentés à l'Opéra, on en peut citer trois où le musicien ait fait quelques frais d'imagination" [Ballet music is ordinarily of rather little importance; one could scarcely cite two or three ballets, out of the innumerable ballets performed at the Opéra, in which the composer had invested any imagination]. *La France Musicale,* 4 July 1841. Escudier goes on to call the *Giselle* score "entirely original," pointing out that it borrowed only eight bars from a romance by one Mlle Puget, and three bars of the huntsmen's chorus from *Euryanthe* of Weber.

41 "J'ai entendu quelques personnes lui reprocher de n'être pas assez fournie d'airs connus. . . . Je crois, pour ma part, que ce qui manque en plagiats à MM. Réber et

Benoist, ils l'ont amplement gagné en expression dramatique" *La Sylphide,* 26 Sept. 1840.

42 "Le ballet est une oeuvre anti-littéraire et anti-musicale. Je ne comprends pas que des gens de bons sens viennent s'asseoir sur les banquettes de l'Opéra et restent là plantés pendant quatre heures devant des entrechats. La musique, pour quoi la comptez-vous? Si les entrechats, les ailes de pigeon, les bouffantes, les grimaces niaises et les petites menottes passées sous le menton vous ennuient, tant pis pour vous. Mais on va au ballet pour entendre de la musique.—J'avais prévu cette formidable objection. Cela serait fort bon s'il y avait de la musique dans les ballets les plus nouveaux. Mais, je vous le demande à mon tour, où est la musique de ballet? qui est-ce qui connaît la musique de ballet? qui a ouï de la musique de ballet? Je supplie tous les honnêtes gens qui auraient quelque connaissance de cette prétendu musique de se présenter immédiatement au bureau de la *France musicale;* il leur sera donné une récompense honnête ou une circulaire de M. Maurice Schlesinger, à leur choix.

Assurément je ne connais pas de meilleure plaisanterie que celle-là: de la musique de ballet! C'est-a-dire que, lorsqu'on veut représenter un ballet nouveau, on s'adresse à un compositeur connu et on l'invite à mettre des accompagnemens là-dessous. Le compositeur connu s'adresse à des compositeurs encore plus connus que lui, à tous les compositeurs connus; il ouvre toutes les partitions connues; il choisit une foule d'air connus; il fait une marqueterie de Mozart, de Haydn, de Beethoven, de M. Doche, de M. Adolphe Adam, de M. Monpou, de Gluck, de Rossini, d'Auber, et ajoute une tête et une queue, plusieurs queues, et, je vous souhaite bien du plaisir, voilà un ballet nouveau." *La France musicale,* 3 Feb. 1839.

43 "Depuis qu'il est convenu que cette musique ne doit être qu'un arrangement, le compositeur trouve qu'il est bien plus commode d'avoir de la mémoire que de l'inspiration. La musique de ballet est une véritable mosaïque dans laquelle on enchâsse pêle-mêle des airs de Rossini, de Boiëldieu, d'Auber, de Meyerbeer, etc., etc. Seulement ces airs sont le plus souvent dénaturés, parce qu'il a fallu en changer le rythme et en altérer les nuances. Ainsi les choses les plus respectables et les plus sacrées sont confondues dans un mélange de morceaux sans cohésion et sans suite; les plus grands maîtres ont payé leur tribut à ce genre bâtard, et il n'est pas jusqu'à Mozart et Beethoven qu'on n'ait dépouillé pour couvrir la nudité . . . " *La France musicale,* 30 June 1839. In this review Escudier does call Gide, the composer of *La Tarentule,* "perhaps the only composer today who knows how to arrange ballet music in a fitting manner." He writes, "M. Casimir Gide est peut-être le seul compositeur, aujourd'hui, qui sache arranger d'une manière convenable la musique de ballet. . . . Nous devons reconnaître qu'il y a une certaine habilité dans les arrangemens de la *Tarentule.* Ils sont faits avec esprit et à propos: puisque c'est tout ce que l'on exige pour former ce que l'on appelle un ballet, n'en demandons pas d'avantage à M. Gide. Il n'a eu qu'un tort, celui de reproduire des motifs trop modernes et trop connus. Nous savons que les compositeurs, loin de s'opposer à cette spoliation, sont les premiers à la solliciter pour la satisfaction de leur amour-propre. C'est donc à eux seuls qu'il faut faire remonter le dégoût que l'on éprouve à entendre des motifs étranglés et qui perdent toute leur beauté en sortant de leur cadre. Ce qui distinguera toujours M. Gide des autres compositeurs de ballet, c'est le bon goût, le choix heureux des idées, et l'élégante simplicité de l'orchestration" [We must recognize that there is a certain skill in the arrangements of *La Tarentule.* They are made with wit, and are appropriate—since that is all that one requires to form that which is called a ballet, and we ask no more than that from Monsieur Gide. He has only done one thing wrong: he has reproduced motifs that are too modern and too well known. We know that the composers, far from opposing this abuse, are the first to solicit it for the satisfaction of their own egos. Thus we must show *them* the disgust we experience on hearing the motifs, which are ruined, losing all their beauty when they leave their context. M. Gide will always be distinguished from other ballet composers for his good taste, fortunate choice of ideas, and the elegant simplicity of the orchestration]. The ambivalence expressed on the matter by Escudier in this review is a good indication that the custom, though still considered praiseworthy in some cases, was held in lower esteem than it once had been.

44 "Mais ces sortes de contributions qu'on peut dire forcées ont été permises de tout temps et sont entièrement autorisées par l'usage. Le public qui n'est pas accoutumé à voir citer les auteurs que des auteurs pillent peut s'y tromper et croire que Beethoven est ressuscité pour régler des pas de danse, il peut s'imaginer que Rossini qui semblait ne plus vouloir écrire d'opéras rentre dans la carrière par un galop ou une marche. Conçoit-on la confusion? Ce même public qui ne s'y connaît pas pourra prendre la musique de M. Carlini pour celle de Rossini, le travail de M. Gide pour celui de Beethoven. Erreur fâcheuse quelquefois pour MM. Gide et Carlini; plus souvent déplorable pour Beethoven et Rossini." *La Revue musicale,* 16 August 1835.

45 It is impossible to know to what extent these critics are exaggerating when they describe mimed performances. In any case it is clear that they are responding to stylized movements that looked ridiculous to them. Ironically, some of the most detailed descriptions of choreography and stage actions of Parisian ballet-pantomime from this period come from derogatory and satirical accounts; Serge Lifar, for example, uses "Grise-Aile" from the satirical journal *La Musée Philipon* in *Giselle—Apothéose d'un ballet Romantique* (Paris: Albin Michel, 1942, repr. Editions d'Aujourd'hui, 1982), 95.

46 "J'ai en aversion les ballets; je pense que ce spectacle, dans lequel les gestes sans paroles sont les seuls interprètes de la pensée (quand pensée il y a), est excessivement absurde, plus absurde cent fois qu'un drame parlé d'où les gestes seraient exclus. On n'a jamais songé pourtant à introduire sur la scène un pareil mode d'exécution pour les poètes.... Nous voyons tous les jours ... des acteurs se disloquer les bras, s'exposer à des luxations de la colonne vertébrale, se défigurer à force de roulements d'yeux et de contorsions ridicules, pour nous faire comprendre quelque lieu commun dramatique. Y parviennent ils, au moins tant de pénibles efforts sont-ils couronnés de succès? Si peu, que toutes les fois qu'il s'agit d'une idée d'où l'intelligence générale de la pièce dépend, on se voit forcée de l'écrire en toutes lettres sur quelques tableau placé bien en évidence, où les spectateurs peuvent lire, comme dans la *Belle au Bois, dormant: Elle dormira cent ans....* Un jeune Arabe, nouvellement arrivé à Paris, me disait un jour: «Je suis allé voir jouer les muets, hier soir.—Les muets! que voulez-vous dire?—Oui, je suis allé à L'Académie Royale de Musique. On y représentait une pièce qui m'a un peu ennuyé, parce que, n'ayant jamais étudié le langage des signes, je n'y comprenais presque rien. J'ai été surpris de la beauté de vos femmes muettes; il est rare que ces êtres incomplets ne joignent pas à ce défaut quelque autre infirmité plus ou moins apparente.—Mais je vous jure qu'il n'y a pas de muets ni surtout de muettes à l'opéra. Placé un peu près de la scène, le babil immodéré de ces dames vous eût rassuré, beaucoup plus peut-être que vous ne l'eussiez désiré.—Alores pourquoi les acteurs de la pièce que j'ai vue ne parlaient-ils donc pas?— Parce que, dans ce genre de spectacle, la parole est prohibée.— Vous vous raillez de moi; comment croirai-je jamais qu'un peuple aussi avancée en civilisation, aussi spirituel que le peuple français, adopte comme genre spécial une aussi énorme bêtise. Autant vaudrait me dire que vous défendez à vos littérateurs d'employer dans leurs écrits plus d'un certain nombre de mots, à l'exclusion du reste de la langue; aque dans certains théâtres de Paris, vous avez des danseurs qui ne doivent danser que sur un pied, des chanteurs qui n'emploient que six notes et un public pour applaudir à cette folle mutilation de leurs facultés.» «On voit que mon interlocuteur, quoique fort instruit dans la langue française, n'avait pas encore eu le temps de se façonner aux habitudes européennes. . . . Quoi qu'il en soit, comme nous partageons sa manière de voir à l'égard des ballets-pantomimes . . ." *La Gazette Musicale de Paris*, 21 Sept. 1834.

47 "Aussitôt arrive une vieille femme qui tarabuste l'amoureux. Au théâtre et dans un ballet, toute vieille femme qui tarabuste un amoureux est la mère de l'amoureuse. Erreur! dans le livret cette femme est une bienfaitrice qui a recueilli Fleur-des-champs sur la rive du Danube, et à laquelle la pauvre fille n'a pas dire qui elle était attendu qu'elle est muette. En vérité, le livret es fort intéressant!

A peine l'amant est-il renvoyé par la mère de Fleur-des-champs, qu'arrive un écuyer avec des trompettes. L'écuyer dit: . . . —Monsieur, qu'est-ce qu'il dit? —Je ne sais pas—Avez-vous un livret? —Non. Je ne comprends pas. —Ni moi non plus. —Voici un livret.—Merci. Ah! c'est un officier du baron qui annonce que son maître appelle toutes les jeunes filles dans son château pour choisir entre elles une épouse qui ne meure pas comme celles de son frère aîné.—Pardieu! j'aime beaucoup ce livret . . . La voilà, c'est elle en personne, avec un voile.—Lisez donc le livret, maladroit! ce n'est pas elle, c'est son ombre.—Puisque le livret me le dit, je n'en doute pas . . ." *La Presse*, 26 Sept. 1836.

48 "Écrire le programme d'un ballet n'est pas chose for difficile en soi; il est bien plus mal aisé d'en faire l'analyse, surtout quand on a le malheur de ne rien comprendre à la pantomime et de ne vouloir as consulter le livret. Je me trouve précisément dans ce cas-là. Des expériences sans nombre m'ont prouvé que l'art mimique était lettre close pour moi, et que je pourrais voir cent et cent fois lever l'index de la main droite vers le front, sans qu'il me fût possible de deviner que cela veut dire: «Vous voyez bien ce bonnet; eh bien! ce bonnet est un bonnet magique; quand on le garde sur la tête, comme je le porte à présent, on n'en a pas plus d'esprit pour cela; mais quand on le retourne, on a tous les esprits à ses ordres, on devient puissant sur eux, ils vous obéissent sans murmure ni retard, et eût-on la fantaisie de changer en femme une bête, une chienne, une chatte, ce souhait serait accompli aussitôt que formé.» Oui, je l'avoue, je ne saurais pas encore, à l'heure qu'il est, que ce simple mouvement du doigt veut dire tout cela, sans l'obligeance de mes confrères . . . qui nous a raconté d'une charmante manière toute l'intrigue. . . . Je n'avais jamais pu me persuader jusqu'ici que mon sens mimique fût assez obtus pour qu'à la première représentation d'une oeuvre de la nature de celle qui absorbe en ce moment toute notre attention, il ne pût me suffire pour en découvrir l'idée fondamentale, l'idée mère, l'IDÉE enfin. Voilà pourquoi je m'obstinais à me passer du livret. Vanité! vanité! tout n'est que vanité!" *Revue et Gazette Musicale*, 22 Oct. 1837.

49 "La pantomime, ce sublime langage polyglotte, qui dit tant de choses en si peu de mots, nous apprend que la scène se passe à Thuringe.—qu'il fait à peine jour, et que le monsieur qui arrive, tout de vert habillé, se nomme monsieur *Hi, hi, là, rions*. . . . Remarquez l'immense avantage de la pantomime sur la langue parlée! Quelques ronds de jambe, quelques ronds de bras et quelques légers tortillements viennent de nous dire le nom de tous ces personnages, leur âge, leur profession, le lieu de leur naissance, et une foule d'autres choses . . ." *La Musée Philipon*, "Grise-Aile", n.d. [1841].

50 "Tandis que tous les acteurs se disloquent de la façon la plus désagréable sur un air que vous connaissez depuis votre plus tendre enfance, on a l'audace de distribuer dans la salle des brochures in-octavo, intitulés, par exemple, *la Gypsy,* ballet-pantomime en trois actes et en je ne sais combien de tableaux; et, dans cette brochure, vous lisez: «Sténio dit aux Bohémiens: J'ai de bons bras; je suis jeune, courageux, voulez-vous que je sois des vôtres? —Mais qui es-tu? mais qui es-tu, toi? lui demande-t-on.—Un malheureux poursuivi, sans argent, sans asile, sans espoir. —Voilà juste ce qu'il faut pour entrer parmi nous»—Vous avez remarqué les expressions du ballet broché: Sténio *DIT,* etc. . . . C'est bientôt dit cela. Sténio, au lieu de *dire,* commence par exécuter un moulinet effrayant avec ses deux bras, et puis il donne un grand coup de poing dans l'oeil au premier bohémien.—Traduction littérale: J'ai de bons bras.—Puis il passe agréablement la main sur ses mollets, comme s'il éprouvait des démangeaisons; il se pince la taille; il se caresse le menton; il se frise légèrement le toupet, se magnétise lui-même—Traduction: Je suis jeune. —Puis il tire son sabre, s'il en a un, et va faire peur à deux ou trois petits enfans situés dans la coulisse.—Traduction: Je suis courageux.—Enfin il se pose fièrement à la manière de don César. . . . Translation: Voulez-vous que je sois des vôtres?

Les trente ou quarante Bohémiens commencent par frapper tous du pied gauche, tenant le pied droit suspendu . . . ; puis ils frappent tous également du pied droit, laissant le pied gauche suspendu . . . ; ils roulent des yeux terribles, ah les gaillards! ils gesticulent avec une véhémence inouïe, et les lancent leurs avant-bras comme s'ls voulaient décrocher les toiles peintes qui leur fournissent un ciel sans nuages.—Traduction: Qui es-tu? qui es-tu? . . .

C'est ainsi qu'on dialogue pendant quatre heures. Et savez-vous que c'est bien long quatre heures, que cela fait deux cent quarante minutes, et que les minutes de ballet sont plus longues que les autres, et que les deux cent quarante minutes forment quatorze mille quatre cents secondes . . . ?" *La France Musicale,* 3 Feb. 1839.

51 "Le ballet de nos jours n'est qu'une parodie de l'ancien ballet, du véritable ballet, du seul ballet qui puisse mériter ce nom. Autrefois un ballet n'était pas autre chose qu'un grand opéra où on chantait beaucoup et où l'on dansait peu. Aujourd'hui, un ballet est quelque chose où l'on danse beaucoup et où l'on ne chante jamais. Toute oeuvre chantée prend un rang considérable dans les beaux-arts. On pouvait se permettre de composer des ballets chantés. Mais depuis que le ballet en est réduit à la pantomime, cette inconcevable mystification, pendant laquelle une foule de gens se courent après comme s'ils voulaient s'attacher de petits morceaux de papier sur le dos avec des épingles, il faut avouer que le ballet n'est plus qu'un songe, une illusion, un rien qui est au-dessous de quoi que ce soit." *La France musicale,* 3 Feb. 1839.

52 Emphasis mine. "J'avouerai toutefois que je n'approuve pas le système adopté par M. Schneitzhoeffer dans la musique de ses ballets. Le langage de la pantomime est bien imparfait; il laisse beaucoup de choses vagues, incertaines, et la musique seule peut suppléer à ce qui lui manque de clarté. Mais la musique est elle-même un art vague qui a besoin du secours de la parole pour rendre des idées positives. Privée de ce secours dans les ballets, elle peut du moins rappeler des situations ou des sentimens analogues à ce qu'elle doit exprimer par des thèmes connus de tout le monde: c'est en effet par ce procédé que plusieurs compositeurs de musique de ballets ont su rendre l'action mimique intelligible; mais ce n'est point ainsi que M. Schneitzhoeffer compose les siens. Considérant la musique comme un art d'expression, il paraît attribuer à ses moyens plus de puissance qu'ils n'en ont, en sorte qu'il dédaigne, en général, les airs connus, et compose consciencieusement toute la musique de ses ouvrages. De là un défaut de clarté qui a peut-être nui plus qu'il ne le pense à ses succès. . . ." *La Revue Musicale,* 17 March 1832.

53 My emphasis. "Un ballet dont les airs sont originaux, c'est-à-dire composés exprès pour la pièce, est ordinairement peu remarquable sous le rapport musical. Des contredanses plus ou moins triviales, des marches bruyantes, sans dessins et sans goût, une sorte de *from from* d'orchestre qui accompagne les gestes du mime.... Tels sont les élémens dont la musique des ballets se compose....

Nos anciens ballets, tels que *le Jugement de Paris, Psyché, Persée et Andromède* étoient composés avec des airs connus. Le musicien, pouvant choisir dans le riche répertoire des symphonistes et des compositeurs dramatiques, ne connoit que l'excellent. Où trouve-t-on des contredanses plus élégantes que les *andantes,* les finales de Haydn, les rondeaux de Steibelt et de Viotti, des morceaux d'action plus dramatiques, plus fortement conçus que l'ouverture de *Démophoon,* le magnifique *agitato* en *fa mineur,* tiré d'un duo de violon de Viotti, l'air d'*Ariodan* placé par Méhul lui-même dans *Persée et Andromède,* et mille autres que je pourrois citer? Les spectateurs étoient-ils fatigués par l'insipide monotonie de la danse, l'orchestre les consoloit; les engageoit à prendre patience en leur faisant entendre de très belle musique admirablement exécutée. Un ballet étoit un concert plein d'intérêt, où tous les genres de musique se réunissoient pour plaire au moyen d'une séduisante variété. Les amateurs du nouveau style y applaudissoient Mozart et Beethoven. Ceux qui ont conservée leur vénération pour nos vieux airs les retrouvoient quelquefois, mais embellis et présentés avec une harmonie plus riche et de meilleur goût.

Je laisse à penser l'effet que produiroient certains morceaux de Rossini, s'ils étoient introduits avec art dans nos ballets. D'ailleurs les airs d'opéra, même, après avoir perdu leurs paroles, conservent une expression mémorative bien précieuse pour expliquer les énigmes du langage mimique, tandis qu'une musique neuve et sans originalité ne frappe point assez l'imagination pour que son expression soit sentie; et son esprit, si toutefois elle en a, échappe à l'auditeur distrait." *Le Journal des Débats,* 28 Sept. 1822. Castil-Blaze expresses similar enthusiasm for the practice of borrowing in his *Dictionnaire,* vol. 1, 44–46: "Je donne la préférence aux [les belles symphonies de Haydn, les ouvertures, la musique dramatique, les concertos, les duos de violons, les sonates, les romances, les barcarolles ...], en ce que les airs de situation ont une expression mémorative très précieuse pour expliquer les énigmes du langage mimique; et tous les autres étant choisis dans le riche répertoire des symphonistes et des compositeurs dramatiques, il y a à parier qu'on ne nous donnera que de l'excellent; tandis que celui qui crée la musique d'un *ballet,* fatigué par l'immensité de son oeuvre, admet beaucoup de choses faibles ou communes, et garde quelquefois en portefeuille de beaux morceaux qu'il craindrait de sacrifier dans un tel ouvrage, les réservant pour un opéra où ils seront placés avec plus d'avantage" [I prefer the beautiful symphonies of Haydn, overtures, dramatic music, concertos, violin duos, sonatas, romances, barcarolles ... music in which the airs of situation have a memorative expression, which is very valuable for explaining the enigmas of the mimic language, and the other airs [are] chosen from the rich repertory of symphonists and dramatic composers; the odds are that they will only give us the excellent, while the creator of ballet music is tired by the immensity of his artistic production and lets many weak and common things in, and sometimes keeps in his portfolio the beautiful passages which he fears to sacrifice to such a work, keeping them for an opera, where they will be placed to greater advantage.]

54 My emphasis. "On ne composait pas autrefois la musique d'un ballet; on l'arrangeait, on la compilait. L'arrangeur prenait des motifs d'opéras ou des mélodies quelconques bien connus qu'il adaptait aux situations du livret et qui expliquaient celles-ci par le sens des paroles que supportaient habituellement ces motifs et ces mélodies. De cette manière la musique donnait l'intelligence de la pantomime, ce qui n'est point du tout inutile. . . . Aujourd'hui, la musique, composée tout entière d'après la fantaisie des auteurs, a tout autant besoin d'explication que le programme, et ce qu'on y a gagné c'est que tous deux sont devenus inintelligibles." *La Revue Musicale,* 16 August 1835.

55 See Chapter One, notes 12 and 14.

56 See Marvin Carlson, "Hernani's Revolt from the Tradition of French Stage Composition," *Theatre Survey* 13 no. 1 (May, 1972): 1–27.

57 Gautier *La Presse,* 11 July 1837, tr. Guest, *Gautier on Dance,* 9–10.

58 Quoted above; see note 50. On the subject of stage acting in the eighteenth century, see Dene Barnett, "The Performance Practice of Acting: The Eighteenth Century," *Theatre Research International* 2, no. 3 (May 1977): 157–85; 3 no. 1 (Oct. 1977): 1–19; 3 no. 2 (Feb. 1978): 79–92; 5 no. 1 (Winter 1979–80): 1–36; and 6 no. 1 (Winter 1980–81): 1–32. See also Dene Barnett (with the assistance of Jeanette Massy Westropp), *The Art of Gesture: The Practices and Principles of 18th-Century Acting* (Heidelberg: Carl Winter Universitätsverlag, 1987), and Giannandrea Poesio and Marian Smith, "Ecoutez-moi," in *Preservation Politics* (forthcoming).

59 The story of this ballet, along with a small handful of others from the nineteenth century, have become familiar enough (in their broadest outlines, at least) that even the summary seems unneccessary. Since only a few Romantic ballets remain in the repertory, in fact, today's audiences are presented with the same handful of old stories over and over and thus have less practical need of libretti than audiences during the July Monarchy at the Opéra, who were constantly presented with new ballet-pantomimes and expected to learn their stories.

Even those audiences familiar with the broad outlines of the plots of the three Tchaikovsky ballets, however, would be astounded to read the long and complicated original libretti. John Wiley has translated them into English; they appear in his *Tchaikovsky's Ballets,* Appendix A, 321–41.

60 Anna Kisselgoff, *The New York Times,* "The Virtues and Pitfalls of Telling No Stories," 7 July 1991. Balanchine's approach to story and music is described well by the dancers Suzanne Farrell and Toni Bentley in *Holding on to the Air—Suzanne Farrell, an Autobiography* (New York and London: Penguin Books, 1990). For example, "*Serenade* was the first ballet Balanchine choreographed on American dancers, on American soil. It is one of his most famous and is considered one of the New York City Ballet's signature works. With its shadowy lighting, girls in long, pale blue tulle skirts, and implications of great emotion and passion, it exemplifies Balanchine's reaction to Tschaikovsky . . . and to plot. There is no story, yet there are many stories, many moods, many emotions, many loves. But they are abstract, the dancers aren't human, their movements represent forces, energies, and these energies are disturbed, whirling like forces of nature and then subsiding before rising again" (59). "In Balanchine's world the dancers were in service to him, but everyone, including him, was in service to the music. Even today this priority more than any other single element separates the New York City Ballet from other companies" (152–53). "Beginning with *Apollo* in 1928, Balanchine had learned the art of elimination. By removing the theatrical distractions of stories, scenery, costumes, and preconceived interpretations, he revealed the essence of the music itself. He never wanted to impose an idea—or himself—on the work of a composer, and it was in this profound respect for the identity of the music that he was so radically different from other choreographers. Above all else, he wanted the audience to hear the music, really hear it, and if his dances enhanced that experience, he considered his job well done" (230).

61 This is not to say that no abstract ballets were created in Europe during the 1830s and 1840s (Perrot's famous *Pas de Quatre,* for example, was produced in London in 1845, and abstract divertissements, such as "The Four Seasons" or the "Four Corners of the World" had long been included as entertainments for onstage characters within larger narrative works). But the self-standing plotless ballet as we know it today had not yet taken hold at the Opéra.

CHAPTER FIVE: HYBRID WORKS AT THE OPÉRA

1 In the famous third-act cloister scene of *Robert le diable,* too, characters portrayed by singers and dancers interact (namely, Robert and the Reverend Mother Hélène, played in the original cast by the tenor Adolphe Nourrit and the dancer Marie Taglioni). I am reserving my comments in this chapter, however, to works in which the mute characters appear in more than one act. On silent characters in the Parisian theater, see Sarah Hibbard, *Magnetism, Muteness, Magic: Spectacle and the Parisian Lyric Stage circa 1830.*

2 R. M. Longyear, "Daniel-François-Esprit Auber," in *The New Grove Dictionary of Music and Musicians.* Bartlet, "Grand opéra," *The New Grove Dictionary of Opera.*

3 Jane Fulcher, *The Nation's Image,* p. 46. See also John W. Klein, "Daniel-François Auber (1782–1871)," *Opera* 22 (1971): 684–90; Karin Pendle, *Eugène Scribe and French Opera of the Nineteenth Century,* 395–426; S. Slatin, "Opera and Revolution: La Muette de Portici and the Belgian Revolution of 1830 Revisited," *The Journal of Musicological Research* 3 (1979): 45–52; Ludwig Finscher, "Aubers La muette de Portici und die Anfänge der Grand-Opéra," *Festschrift Heinz Becker* (Laaber: Laaber-Verlag, 1982), 87–105; Jean Mongrédien, "Variations sur un thème: Masaniello. Du héros de l'histoire à celui de la Muette de Portici," *Jahrbuch für Opernforschung* (Frankfurt and New York: P. Lang, 1985), 90–121; Herbert Schneider and Nicole Wild, *La Muette de Portici—Kritische Ausgabe des Librettos und Dokumentation der ersten Inszenierung* (Tübingen: Stauffenburg Verlag, 1993); and Cormac Newark, "'Mille sentiments confus l'agitent'—understanding *La Muette de Portici,*" conference paper, American Musicological Society national meeting, Phoenix, November 1997. Mr. Newark was kind enough to give me a copy of this paper.

4 *Die Verstäderung der Oper,* 111–31.

5 *Deux Mots ou Une Nuit dans la Forêt,* opera in one act by B. J. Marsollier, music by Nicolas Dalayrac, first performed 9 June 1806 at the Opéra-Comique. See note 19. Among other earlier texted stage works with a mute protagonist are the Pixérécourt melodrama (ca. 1790s) *Coelina ou l'Enfant de mystère* (based on a novel by Curcay-Muminil) and Weber's opera *Silvana* (1810), in which a girl forbidden to speak to strangers expresses herself in gestures. See Pendle, *Scribe and French Opera,* 413.

6 Eugene de Mirecourt, *Scribe* (Paris: G. Havard, 1860), 26, quoted by Guest, *The Romantic Ballet in Paris,* 83. This incident is said to have taken place in 1823. See also Rey Longyear, "La Muette de Portici" *Music Review* 19 (1958); Fulcher, *The Nation's Image,* 25–26; Hanslick, *Die Moderne Oper* (Berlin: A. Hofmann, 1880), 123–37; Chouquet, *Histoire de la Musique Dramatique en France,* 393; and Gerhard, *Die Verstäderung der Oper,* 132.

7 Speagle, "Making Mute Things Speak: Opera and Mélodrame" (conference paper, American Musicological Society national meeting, Phoenix, November 1997). Mr. Speagle kindly allowed me to have a copy of this paper.

8 The story of Tomasso Aniello had been set many times for the stage. Productions include the opera by Reinhard Keiser *Masagniello furioso* (1706), *Masaniello* (Sir Henry Bishop, 1825, based on Samuel Croxall's *Memoirs of a Most Remarkable Révolution in Naples*), and *Masaniello* by Carafa with libretto by Moreau and Lafortelle (1827), based on Raimond de Moirmoiron's *Memoires sur la revolution de Naples de 1647*. Pendle, *Eugène Scribe and French Opera of the Nineteenth Century*, 395.

9 "Dans l'opéra comique [*Masaniello*] la révolution de Naples était présentée dans toute sa crudité, si je puis m'exprimer ainsi. Le peuple souverain et son héros Masaniello y parlaient trop d'insurrection, de liberté, de patrie et de tout le fatras démagogique, et la teinte de l'ouvrage était généralement triste et sombre.

On distingue au contraire dans l'opéra [*La Muette de Portici*] la touche fine et délicate d'un peintre habile, qui connaît bien tous les secrets de son art. Rien de plus ingénieux que l'ordonnance de ses tableaux, rien de plus gracieux que ses constructions. Masaniello n'est plus sur le premier plan. La révolte des lazzaronis ne devient plus qu'épisodique. Le danger de l'autorité légitime, le tumulte populaire, les clameurs de la rébellion, tout se perd et s'oublie, ou plutôt se confond dans l'intérêt qu'inspire un seul personnage. C'est une femme, cette femme est muette, et, fait dit sans épigramme, elle n'en est que plus intéressante. Pour elle tout s'anime, tout se vivifie, sa présence amène toujours une péripétie nouvelle. Enfin c'est sur elle que se portent tous les regards, c'est à elle que s'attachent tous les coeurs. Il me semble difficile d'inventer un ressort qui sauve avec plus d'adresse les inconvénients du sujet. L'invention n'est pas nouvelle. Le sourd et muet de l'Abbé d l'Epée après date, mais ce qui est nouveau, c'est d'avoir détourné l'attention d'un sujet un peu trop grave pour lui même, en s'usant aussi habilement d'un artifice aussi agréable." The *premier plan* was the part of the stage closest to the audience. F-Pa AJ 13 1050. Transcribed in Herbert Schneider and Nicole Wild, *La Muette de Portici—Kritische Ausgabe des Librettos und Dokumentation der ersten Inszenierung* (Tübingen: Stauffenburg Verlag, 1993), 204. Fulcher suggests that the censors' approach was clearly an intellectual one, and they naively believed that "the opera's message would largely inhere in the text." See Fulcher, *The Nation's Image*, 31–32. See also Gerhard, *Die Verstäderung der Oper*, 116–17.

10 Her solo appearances occur in Act Four (No. 14, Choeur et cavatine) and in Act Five (no. 18, Finale).

11 In the libretto Alphonse sings these words (expunged from the Troupenas score) immediately before the mime scene of Fénella described here: "Ah! que par mon trépas/ Ta vengeance soit assouvie!/ Mais le destin d'une autre à mon sort est lié: / Pour une autre que moi j'implore ta pitié! / Prends mes jours, épargne sa vie!" [Ah, may your desire for revenge / Be satisfied by my death! But the fate of another is tied to my own; / For another, I implore your pity! / Take my life, but spare hers!] The plaintive musical phrase immediately preceding Elvire's line "Fénella, sauvez mon époux!" seems to say "je l'épargne, je l'épargne." John Speagle has made a compelling interpretation of this passage based on melodic analysis in "Making Mute Things Speak: Opera and Mélodrame."

12 See also, for example, the review of *Le Dieu et la Bayadère* in *La Revue et Gazette des Théâtres*, 17 April 1845.

13 "Tous les acteurs ont bien joué." *Le Courrier des Théâtres,* 1 March 1828.
14 *Le Moniteur,* 2 March 1828, tr. and qu. by Guest, *The Romantic Ballet in Paris,* 84.
15 "Le mutisme de Fénella est, de plus en plus, un sujet de causerie et de curiosité." *Le Courrier des Théâtres,* 26 April 1828.
16 "Le rôle de la muette se présente d'abord à mon esprit. Quoiqu'il puisse paraître plaisant de citer comme une des bonnes choses le rôle d'un personnage qui ne chante pas, je déclare que je parle sérieusement, et que la musique mélodramatique qui exprime ce que *Fénella* ne peut dire que par ses gestes, fait le plus grand honneur à M. Auber. Il était impossible de mieux rendre les nuances délicates des sentimens qui agitent le coeur de cette jeune fille. Ce genre de mérite n'est pas celui que le public apprécie le mieux, mais il en ressent à son insu toutes les impressions; et, tandis qu'il croit n'accorder son attention qu'aux gestes de l'actrice, la musique l'éclaire ou l'émeut." *La Revue musicale,* 1828, 179-82.
17 *La Presse,* 2 Oct. 1837. Gautier wrote these words on the occasion of *La Muette*'s revival, with Fanny Elssler in the title role, Duprez in the role of Masaniello, and the Noblet sisters (Lise Noblet and Mme Alexis Dupont, née Félicité Noblet) dancing a new Spanish *pas*. In the same review, he wrote that "the great success of the evening was the Spanish dance by the Mmes. Noblet. Their entrance was eagerly awaited. They appeared in white satin basquines, threaded and bespangled with silver. . . ." tr. Guest, *Gautier on Dance,* 19.
18 *La Presse,* 2 October 1837, tr. Guest, *Gautier on Dance,* p. 19.
19 The nineteenth-century publishers of both the *La Muette de Portici* and *Le Dieu et la Bayadère* scores assured potential buyers that the lead roles created (respectively) by Noblet and Taglioni in Paris could be performed by actresses instead of dancers, no doubt in an attempt to allay the reservations of provincial conductors. "Dans les grandes villes ce rôle appartient aux dames de la danse; dans les troupes où il n'y a point de ballets, à celle des actrices qui pourra le mieux le remplir: c'est donc à MM. les directeurs à la distribuer. Mais toutes les actrices qui jouent le rôle de *Muet* de l'*Abbé de d'Epée,* ou *Rose,* dans la pièce des *Deux Mots,* rempliront avec succès ce rôle." [In large cities, this role is given to female dancers; in companies lacking a ballet, it is given to actresses who will best be able to fulfill it. It is therefore up to the directors to cast this role. But all the actresses who play the role of the Mute in l'*Abbé de l'Epée,* or Rose in *Deux Mots,* will do so with success.] *La Muette de Portici,* staging manual, reprinted in *The Original Staging Manuals,* 3 [15]. See also note 33.
20 *La Muette de Portici* libretto (Paris: Imprimerie de Dubuisson et Cie., n.d.), *La Muette de Portici* full score (Paris: Troupenas, 1828[?], repr. New York and London: Garland Publishing Co., 1980), and *La Muette de Portici livret de mise en scène* (repr. in *The Original Staging Manuals for Twelve Parisian Operatic Premières,* 13-72).
21 This work was inspired in part by Goethe's ballad *Der Gott und die Bajadere*. Castil-Blaze, *L'Académie Impériale de Musique,* vol. 2, 220-21. See also Guest, *The Romantic Ballet in Paris,* 103.
22 Charles Maurice, for instance, wrote, "Mlle Taglioni ne mime pas; quand elle veut s'exprimer par ce moyen, on ne sent en elle que la danseuse à qui ce langage n'est point familier. Tout le haut de son corps, si gracieux quand elle cède a sa vocation, est étroit, sec et sans charme lorsqu'elle est privée de mouvement. Sa figure n'est pas comédienne; on y lit par fois une sensation, mais jamais un sentiment. En un mot la pantomime n'est

point du domaine de Mlle Taglioni, dont le rare mérite dans la danse n'en est pas moins, pour elle, le garant d'une haute réputation." [Mlle Taglioni doesn't mime; when she wants to express herself by these means, one senses only a dancer to whom this language is not at all familiar. The whole of her upper body, so graceful when she dances, is tight, dry, and lacking in charm when it is deprived of movement. Her face is not that of a comedienne; one can sometimes detect a sensation there, but never a sentiment. In a word, pantomime is not at all the domain of Mlle Taglioni, whose rare abilities as a dancer guarantee her great reputation.] It must be noted, however, that Maurice was generally disposed against Taglioni and her family. *Le Courrier des Théâtres,* 15 October 1830.

The singing roles, according to some critics at least, were less demanding and featured music more on the order of comic opera (a criticism leveled earlier at *La Muette* and later at *La Tentation* as well). Castil-Blaze calls *La Muette* "un grand opéra dans de petites proportions, un opéra comique avec récitatifs et sans finale, sans *prima donna,* puisqu'elle exécute un *tacet* continu" [a grand opera in small proportions; a comic opera with recitatives and without a finale, without a prima donna, because she executes a continuous tacet]. *L'Académie impériale,* vol. 2, 208.

23 *Dance Index,* July-August, 1944: 118, qu. in Guest, *The Romantic Ballet in Paris,* 103–4.

24 "Il adresse la parole à Zoloé qui ne répond point, alors sa compagne chantante avertit le juge que Zoloé venant d'une contrée lointaine comprend le langage indien, mais ne le parle pas. Alifour [sic] interroge sa belle, et lui demande quel est son état. Zoloé répond par une suite de jetés battus.—Sa consolation dans les chagrins.—Un pas de rigaudon—Sa ressource contre les malheurs qui peuvent lui arriver.—Un pas de basque assaisonné de quelques pirouettes.—Suis-je assez heureux pour vous plaire? — Signe négatif.—Comment faut-il être pour avoir ce bonheur? Zoloé montre alors l'étranger qui a pris sa défense contre la tyrannie capricieuse du juge. Nouvelle colère d'Alifour; Fatmé l'apaise en conseillant à son amie de répondre aux voeux du galant suranné." *Le Journal des Débats,* 15 October 1830.

25 "Les rôles muets, la pantomime qui vient se mêler au chant, au récitatif, sont d'un résultat déplaisant et mesquin. Les musiciens ne voient pas sans dépit et sans impatience une ballérine serpenter à travers un opéra, pour faire boiter les morceaux d'ensemble, pour éborgner les duos, et montrer un rond de jambe à la place de la note qui manque à l'accord vocal." Castil-Blaze, *L'Académie Impériale de Musique,* vol. 2, 220.

26 "L'idée singulière de faire d'une femme qui ne parle pas le personnage principal d'un opéra, avait réussi à M. Scribe dans la *Muette de Portici,* c'était une bonne fortune dont il aurait fallu profiter en ne tentant point une deuxième épreuve du même moyen.... le malheur de la jeune fille inspire de la pitié; mais le silence de la *Bayadère amoureuse* a quelque chose de ridicule, et ce ridicule est d'autant plus sensible qu'elle ne quitte pas le scène et qu'elle y occupe la première place. Qu'importe, dit-on, puisque c'est Mlle Taglioni, et puisque Mlle Taglioni charme le public; mais qui vous empêche de faire pour Mlle Taglioni un ballet où elle serait placée plus convenablement, et dans lequel le musicien n'aurait point à rougir du rôle secondaire qu'on lui fait jouer. Un jour viendra où Mlle Taglioni ne dansera plus; alors la partition du *Dieu et la Bayadère,* livrée à l'histoire de la musique, sera dépouillée de son prestige." Fétis, *La Revue Musicale,* 16 October 1830.

27 Guest, *The Romantic Ballet in Paris,* 233–34.
28 Castil-Blaze, *L'Académie Impériale de Musique,* 229.

29 A score for this work was sent from the Opéra to Brussels. My thanks to David A. Day, who is cataloguing the collection of the Archives de la Ville de Bruxelles, for allowing me to examine it.

30 *Le Dieu et la Bayadère* libretto, "nouvelle edition conforme à la représentation" (Paris: Bezou, 1830), manuscript full score. F-Po A.496a I-IV, and Auber's annotated copy of a printed score (Paris: Troupenas, n. d.), F-Po A.496c.

Some of the text in the libretto varies slightly from that in the scores; for instance, in Act Two scene iii, No. 9, some of the dialogue in the libretto does not appear in the score.

31 *La Tentation* was even referred to in the official memo authorizing its performance as "un mélange de l'opéra et de ballet, des deux genres exploités jusqu'à ce jour sur notre premier théâtre" [a mixture of opera and ballet, the two genres performed up to the present day on our first stage]. F-Pa AJ13 183. This echoes the official language of the directors' contracts, which say that "il ne pourra être exploité sur la scène de l'Opéra que les genres attribués jusqu'à ce jour à ce théâtre" [On the stage of the Opéra, only the genres allocated up to the present day to this theater will be performed], i.e., opera and ballet-pantomime. Quoted in Véron, *Mémoires d'un bourgeois de Paris,* vol. 3, 174. See Chapter Two, note 2.

32 Véron, *Mémoires d'un bourgeois de Paris,* tr. Huckenpahler as "Confessions of an Opera Director," 83.

33 In order to make *Le Dieu et la Bayadère* workable without dancers, the editor of the score even listed necessary cuts and suggested that the role of Fatmé could be eliminated. "Cet ouvrage pouvant être monté dans tous les théâtres où il n'y point de ballet, nous indiquons les changemens qui sont nécessaires pour la mise en scène. . . . Au moyen de ces changemens le rôle de Fatmé n'existe plus et celui de Zoloé quoique crée à Paris par Mlle Taglioni, peut facilement, comme celui de Fénella dans *La Muette de Portici,* être monté par toute autre que par une danseuse." [This work can be mounted in all theaters lacking a ballet; we indicate the changes that are neccesary to stage it . . . With the help of these changes, the role of Fatmé no longer exists, and that of Zoloé, though created in Paris by Mlle Taglioni, can like that of Fénella in *La Muette de Portici* be played as well by anyone else as by a ballerina.] *Le Dieu et la Bayadère* (Paris: Brandus, n.d.).

34 The character known as the hermit in this piece was referred to in the press and in the score as that sufferer of temptation, Saint Anthony.

35 ". . . luxe . . . d'habits, de décors, de musique, de chevaux, d'orchestre, d'anges, de démons, de fumée, de poussière, de bruit et de gloire"; "[a]ucune description . . . ne peut rendre l'éclat et la magnificence de ce spectacle qui se termine par un combat miltonien dans les nuages, entre les légions du ciel et celles de l'enfer." *Le Courrier des Théâtres,* 26 June 1832, and 21 June 1832. See also Guest, *The Romantic Ballet in Paris,* 120.

36 "tout le luxe de chant, d'orchestre, de costumes et de décorations de notre temps." *La Revue musicale,* 23 June 1832.

37 "Ce mélange de bruit et de silence, de gestes et de mélodies vocales, est d'un mauvais effet. Les voix du choeur augmentent l'explosion de la musique, et voilà tout; des choeurs, des airs même n'expliquent rien au public, qui ne peut comprendre des paroles qu'on n'entend pas. Le récitatif seul porterait la clarté dans les scènes d'une action mimique; mais la psalmodie des récitatif serait-elle préférable aux écriteaux dont les chorégraphes se servaient quelquefois? Ces écriteaux étaient au moins en rapport avec le langage adopté; ils étaient muets comme les acteurs. Le ballet-opéra aussi absurde, aussi

ridicule que l'opéra-comique français, dans lequel on chante, on parle tour à tour. Il faut qu'une statue soit entièrement de marbre, de pierre ou de bois: elle ne saurait être mi partie de marbre et de carton." [This mixture of sound and of silence, of gestures and vocal melodies, creates a poor effect. The voices of the choir serve only to augment the explosion of the music; choirs and even arias explain nothing to the public, who cannot understand the words that they can't hear. Recitative alone would impart clarity to scenes with mimic action, but the psalmody of the recitative—would it be preferable to the *écriteaux* that choreographers sometimes used? These *écriteaux* at least were in accord with the adopted language; they were silent like the actors. Ballet-opera is as absurd and ridiculous as French comic opera, in which they alternate singing and speaking. A statue must be entirely of marble, stone, or wood; it cannot be part marble and part cardboard.] Castil-Blaze, *La Danse et les Ballets depuis Bacchus jusqu'à Mlle Taglioni*, 359.

38 "Ce mélange de bruit et de silence, ces personnages muets suivis d'un truchement qui parle pour eux, ne me paraît pas heureux, quoique je sois forcé d'avouer que dans deux ou trois endroits les voix arrivent très habilement pour donner une nouvelle vie, une action irrésistible à l'effet scénique." *Le Journal des Débats*, 23 June 1832.

39 "L'ouvrage le plus originale qui ait été joué sur le Théâtre de l'Opéra et celui dont M. Véron a su tirer le meilleur parti, est sans contredit le Ballet-opéra de la Tentation. Faire un spectacle attrayant sans le secours d'aucun premier sujet du chant et de la Danse, réussir pendant cinquante représentations, à remplir la salle avec une seule pièce longue et dépourvue d'un intérêt puissant, en utiliser ensuite avec bonheur les actes et presque les morceaux pour soutenir la représentation des ouvrages les plus usés du repertoire; telle a été la mission de cette oeuvre ... appelée Bâtarde par la critique et qui a contribué [?] autant qu'un chef d'oeuvre à la fortune du premier entrepreneur de l'Opéra." *Chronique de l'Académie Royale de Musique*, vol. 2, 293. Shortly thereafter in the *Chronique,* there appears a satire on *La Tentation,* complete with eunuchs, gladiators, Roman citizens, senators, slaves, and the Apostle Paul. It is called "Néron" [Nero], in a spoof of Véron's name.

40 See Evlyn Gould, "Why Go to the Theater?" *Journal of Dramatic Theory and Criticism* 2 (1987): 69–86.

41 These works do not constitute the only examples of postbaroque hybrid "operaballets"; *Mlada* (1892; Rimsky-Korsakov and Gedeonov), for example, features both singers and dancers in major roles. However, the ballet characters in the Parisian works of the July Monarchy were far more closely bound to language than the ballet characters in later nineteenth-century works, as the libretti make clear; Mlada is given actual lines of dialogue to mime only in the climactic second scene of Act Three.

42 Fétis, *La Revue Musicale,* 16 October 1830. See note 26.

CHAPTER SIX: *GISELLE*

1 These films include *The Turning Point* (1977) and *Dancers* (1987).

2 Giannandrea Poesio writes, "Links with the operatic tradition ... can be found almost everywhere in Adam's score—considering that he was mainly an opera composer." "Giselle—Part III," *Dancing Times* 84 no. 1003 (April 1994): 698. See also Poesio, "Giselle, Part I," and "Giselle, Part II," in *Dancing Times* 84 nos. 1001 and 1002 (February and March 1994): 454–61, 563–72.

3 Like *Faust,* too, this ballet features a daisy-plucking scene.
Faust: What do you murmur?

Margaret: . . . Loves me—not—loves me—not (*tearing out the last leaf in utter joy:*)
He loves me!
Faust: Yes, my child. Let this sweet flower's word
Be as God's word to you. He loves you.
Goethe, *Faust*, trans. and ed. Walter Kaufmann (New York: Doubleday, 1963), 304–7.

4 Many Parisians had the opportunity to see *Lucia di Lammermoor*, which was produced at the Théâtre Italien in December 1837, at the Théâtre de la Renaissance in August of 1839 and at the Opéra (in a production based on that of the Théâtre de la Renaissance) in February 1846.

5 See Table 6.2, note. Prayer scenes may be found in several popular opera finales of the day. Raoul, Saint-Bris, and Nevers pray for peace in the finale of *Les Huguenots* Act Two; Fénella prays for protection in the finale of *La Muette de Portici* Act Five; Elvire, in a cavatine, prays for Robert in the Act Four finale of *Robert le diable*.

6 Adam, letter to Saint-Georges, in Lifar, *Giselle—Apothéose du Ballet Romantique,* 281–84.

7 I use the original libretto, the annotated *répétiteur* RU-SPtob 7114/8 and Adam's autograph manuscript, F-Pn MS 2639.

8 This account relies on Gautier, *Histoire de l'art dramatique* (Paris: Magnin, Blanchard et Cie., 1858–59), vol. 2, 133–42; Lifar, *Giselle—Apothéose du Ballet Romantique,* passim, Beaumont, *The Ballet Called Giselle* (London: Cyril W. Beaumont, rev. ed.; repr., Princeton: Dance Horizons, 1988), 18–27; Guest, *The Romantic Ballet in Paris,* 206–16.

9 Victor Hugo, "Fantômes," from *Les Orientales* (Paris: Charles Gosselin, 1829). These excerpts are from the critical edition, edited by Élisabeth Barineau (Paris: Librairier Marcel Didier, 1968), vol. 2, 134–37. Translation by Henry Carrington, in Carrington, *Translations from the Poems of Victor Hugo* (London: Walter Scott, 1887), 63–64.

10 *De l'allemagne* (published in France in 1835) had been serialized in the Parisian journal *Europe Littéraire* in 1833 and published in Germany the same year as *Zur Geschichte der neuen schönen Literatur.* The passage quoted here was also printed in the libretto for *Giselle.* See Appendix Two for the original French, and Beaumont, *The Ballet Called Giselle,* 19.

The legend of the Wilis, the phantoms who kill innocent victims by dancing them to death, exists in many versions, according to Lifar. Lifar disagrees with Heine's contention that the wilis of Serbian legend are vengeful; he maintains that wilis are not evil and not inclined to attack innocent people. In fact, he says, they tend to right wrongs and act as a sort of manifestation of immanent justice. Not until the legend became a part of German folklore, says Lifar, did Wilis become such vicious characters. See Lifar, *Giselle—Apothéose du Ballet Romantique,* 117–18.

Beaumont, on the other hand, suggests that the Serbian Wili was a sort of vampire, pointing out that the Slav word "vila" means "vampire"; the plural is "vile" and the word "wilis," he says, is probably the German version of "vile". He points out that Meyer's *Konversationslexikon* makes no distinction between Serbian and Teutonic wilis, defining "Wiles" or Wilis as "a species of vampire consisting of the spirits of betrothed girls who have died as a reult of their being jilted by faithless lovers." Beaumont, *The Ballet Called Giselle,* 18–20.

11 Gautier, *Histoire de l'art dramatique,* vol. 2, 133–34, tr. Guest, *Gautier on Dance,* 94–95.

12 Guest, *The Romantic Ballet in Paris,* 203.

13 Adam, unpublished memoirs, quoted by Pougin, *Adolphe Adam,* 162. The title of *La Rosière de Gand* was later changed to *La Jolie Fille de Gand.*

14 Apparently, the authors took the finished libretto to the famed dancer and choreographer Jules Perrot, who in turn showed it to Adam, who brought it to the attention of Pillet and persuaded him to begin working on *Giselle* right away. This was a departure from the usual practice, which was for the director to choose from among several libretti submitted for his consideration and then to assign a choreographer and a composer to the task of creating the ballet and a score.

According to Adam (Pougin, *Adolphe Adam,* 162) Jules Perrot actually choreographed much of the ballet. This is generally believed nowadays, but exactly which segments he choreographed we cannot be entirely sure. See Lifar, *Giselle—Apothéose du Ballet Romantique,* 131–48.

15 In his unpublished memoirs, in response to those who had criticized him for working too fast, Adam wrote, "J'ai composé *le Chalet* en quinze jours, *le Toreador* en huit, *Giselle* en trois semaines et *Si j'étais Roi* en deux mois; sont-ce mes plus faibles ouvrages?" [I composed *Le Chalet* in fifteen days, *Le Toreador* in eight, *Giselle* in three weeks, and *Si j'étais roi* in two months; are these my weakest works?] Quoted by Arthur Pougin in *Adolphe Adam,* 95–96. See also 161–62.

This exaggeration about *Giselle* is pointed out as such by Richard Bonynge in the liner notes of his recording of *Giselle* (Decca SET433–34, 1970, reissued on compact disk as London 433 007-2, 1987), though it later found its way into the *New Grove* article on Adolphe Adam. Stanley Sadie, ed., *The New Grove Dictionary of Music and Musicians,* 20 vols. (London: Macmillan Publishers Limited, 1980), vol. 1, 90.

16 Adam, unpublished memoirs, quoted by Pougin, *Adolphe Adam,* 162.

17 Gautier, *Histoire de l'art dramatique,* vol. 2, 137–38.

Several hints about Giselle's weak heart are given in the final version of the libretto. In Act One scene iv, immediately after the daisy-petal scene, Giselle tells Loys of a dream she had, in which he loved a beautiful lady more than Giselle. "*C'est que si tu me trompais,* lui dit la jeune fille, *je le sens, j'en mourrais. Elle porte la main à son coeur comme pour lui dire qu'elle en souffre souvent. Loys la rassure par de vives caresses.*" ["If you deceived me," the young girl tells him, "I should die; I feel it." She presses her hand to her heart as if to show him how often it aches. Loys calms her with loving caresses.] (Adam composed music for this passage, though it appears to have been cut before the première.) In Act One scene vi, Berthe first tells Giselle that dancing is not good for her, and then tells Albrecht that the doctor has warned Giselle that dancing may do her harm. (This scene remains in place today although the detail about the doctor is usually left out.) Finally, in Act One scene viii, immediately after Giselle tells Bathilde that she loves to dance, Berthe interjects that it is foolish; for this passage (over which the annotation "oui, dit Berthe, c'est la folie" [yes, says Berthe, it is foolish] may be found in the autograph score), Adam repeats the ominous music that had expressed Berthe's anxieties about this subject two scenes earlier. In most modern productions, a less subtle contrivance is usually introduced: during the waltz scene, Giselle experiences a moment of dizziness, puts her hand on her heart, and temporarily quits dancing—an action unmentioned in the original libretto or the *répétiteur.*

On the subject of Giselle's heart condition and the cause of her death, see my "What Killed Giselle?" *Dance Chronicle* 13 no. 1 (1990): 68–81.

18 Gautier, *Histoire de l'art dramatique,* vol. 2, 137–38. A group of Indian dancers, including Amani-Ammalle, made a great impression on Gautier when they performed with a group in Paris in 1838. See his descriptions in *La Presse,* 20 August 1838 and 27 August 1838, tr. by Guest, *Gautier on Dance,* 39–50.

19 Though Gautier included *Giselle* in the complete edition of his dramatic works, he did acknowledge his debt to Saint-Georges, and even credited him, according to Lifar, with being the sole author of Act One. According to Jules Janin, "C'est M. de Saint-Georges, qui a attaché le fil grâce auquel M. Théophile Gauthier [*sic*] ne s'est pas égaré dans ce labyrinthe enchanté de verdure, de gaze, de sourires, de gambades, de fleurs, d'épaules nues, d'aurore naissant, de crépuscule flamboyant, de poésie, de rêverie, de passions, de musique et d'amour" [It is M. Saint-Georges who provided the thread that prevented Théophile Gautier from losing himself in this labyrinth enchanted by verdure, gauze, smiles, gamboling, flowers, bare shoulders, nascent dawns, flaming twilights, poetry, reverie, passions, music, and love]. *Journal des Débats,* 30 June 1841.

The *oeuvre* of Jules Henri Vernoi, Marquis de Saint-Georges (1801–1875) includes twelve ballets and about eighty operas, including some written in collaboration with Eugene Scribe. Before *Giselle,* he had written a novel and eleven libretti (two for ballets and nine for operas).

20 The portentous significance of Giselle's love for dancing may be much more readily understood when considered in the light of Gautier's initial story idea, wherein Giselle's love for dancing—if enhanced by an evil spell—kills her (like the girl in Hugo's poem: "Elle aimait trop le bal, c'est ce qui l'a tuée . . . " [She loved dancing too much; that's what killed her]). But in the final version, despite Berthe's certainty that dancing will kill her daughter, it is Giselle's love for Albrecht that proves fatal. (As one critic flippantly wrote, "Giselle dies for a reason other than dancing too much: what kills her is her chagrin upon learning suddenly that Loys is a disguised prince; that someone she believed to be her equal is actually Duke Albrecht of Silesia! Didn't she know that kings can marry shepherdesses? . . . One should not raise a child with such an incomplete education!" *La Revue et Gazette Musicale,* 4 July 1841.)

21 I arrived at these figures first by determining what was danced and what was mimed (by reading annotations in the autograph score and in the *répétiteur*) and then by adding up the timings as heard in the Bonynge recording (see note 15), which is the most faithful to the autograph and early Parisian sources, both in its inclusion of passages usually deleted in todays' performances of this ballet, and in its tempi. I subtracted Giselle's Act Two variation (added in Russia later in the nineteenth century), and included the Act One peasant *pas de deux* by Bergmüller, which was interpolated before the première. Note that the total length of Bonynge's recording is over two hours and five minutes; my total is about one hour and fifty-six minutes because I also excluded from consideration the two overtures as well as the one-minute dream-description sequence which was intended to take place in Act One scene iv, but which I believe was cut before the première. Note further that miming and dancing were often mixed within single scenes of *Giselle;* I have taken this into consideration. See also Poesio, "Giselle, Part II," 565.

22 Another incidental consequence is the elimination of the early warnings about the Wilis, whose murderous power is made obvious now only when they begin menacing Hilarion and Albrecht.

23 Levinson wrote these words in 1927, in "The Idea of the Dance: From Aristotle to Mallarmé," in *What Is Dance? Readings in Theory and Criticism,* 47–48. See also "The Idea of the Dance: From Aristotle to Mallarmé," in *André Levinson on Dance: Writings from Paris in the Twenties,* ed. Joan Acocella and Lynn Garafola (Middletown, Conn: Wesleyan University Press, 1991), 80.

24 According to the libretto, the two men emerge from Albrecht's cottage as this scene opens. This surely helped explain their identity, for Hilarion had pointed out this cottage angrily only seconds before, declaring that his rival lived there. Nowadays, by contrast, Albrecht and Wilfride usually make their entrance by dashing in from the wings, an entrance that does not help to demonstrate that Albrecht has established a domicile in Giselle's village.

25 In some productions, too, Berthe's miming suggests the crosses of a cemetery. This was in the Ballet Russe version of the scene as taught by Tamara Karsavina to the Royal Ballet.

26 In one filmed version of *Giselle* Berthe stands stock-still during this erstwhile dialogue as the camera alternates close-ups of her face with images of the Wilis. Thereby the filmmaker takes advantage of his medium's capacity to show internal visions, ridding this particular passage of all semblance of miming or dialogue. See *Giselle,* directed by Hugo Niebeling and David Blair, 1969, released on videodisc by Philips Classic Productions, 1987.

27 In the Royal Ballet production, based on Tamara Karsavina's teachings of this scene as it was performed by the Ballet Russe, this perky dance music is used to express the motions of a jaunty man (imitated by Berthe as she explains the Wilis' habits to the village girls) who is walking innocently in the woods and is set upon by the Wilis.

28 Note that Giselle in today's productions does usually dance a bit of the waltz as the waltz music is played toward the beginning of this scene, though the sixteen measures of waltz music are usually reduced to eight.

29 As the libretto puts it, Berthe describes "une apparition des morts revenant au monde, et dansant ensemble" [an apparition of the dead returning to the world, and dancing together]. *Giselle* libretto, 10.

30 Note, for example, that Berthe's mime scene is longer on the Bonynge recording than on a videotaped American Ballet Theatre production (based on David Blair's production, taped in 1977 and distributed by Bel Canto Paramount Home Video), and longer than on a videotaped Kirov Ballet production (distributed by Thorn EMI Video). Bear in mind, too, that the original version was even longer than that in Bonynge's recording, since the eight measures of waltz music are repeated in the original scores of *Giselle* but not in the recording.

31 *Répétiteur,* 25.

32 According to the *répétiteur,* the *feux follets* (will o' the wisps) appear as this music is played in Act Two.

33 In some cases the music is cut out of Act Two as well, for instance the American Ballet Theatre (hereafter referred to as ABT) production taped in 1977 (distributed by Bel Canto Paramount Home Video).

34 This practice may be found in the Blair production, which has been performed by ABT and the Atlanta Civic Ballet, among other companies. In this production Hilarion makes his first appearance during a newly created scene that transpires during the overture, thus losing his connection with his "signature" motif. Inserting a new scene during the overture is now a widespread practice (followed, for example, by the Eugene Ballet in Eugene, Oregon).

35 This music is quite similar to the giggling music in Act Two scene i of *le Diable boiteux* (see Chapter Four, Example 4.6).

36 It is difficult to tell whether the laughter is in the strings or the low brass; it is probably in the strings, in keeping with the customs for writing instrumental female laughter (e.g., the laughing of the witches in the Symphonie fantastique of Berlioz).

37 It is true that, when the line for "va-t-en, va-t-en" recurs in mm. 50–52, the annotator writes the words "Loys vient sors" [Loys comes—go away]. But I would argue that the emphatic utterance expressed the first time through supplied the idea for the second set of accented quarter notes as well. This is in keeping with composers' practice of allowing a single line of text to inspire the rhythm for an entire dialogue's worth of music—see Chapter Four, Example 10.

38 *Giselle* libretto, 10.

39 This is the version recorded, for example, by Herbert von Karajan, Vienna Philharmonic Orchestra, London CS 6251.

Of this scene, Poesio writes, "The brief jealousy scene that follows the *scène d'amour* with Albrecht challenged by Hilarion, is musically structured on the typical motifs of tempestuous clashes between the principal character and the villain of many operas." "Giselle—Part III," 698.

40 In the course of this conversation, according to the *répétiteur*, Bathilde provided a bit of irony by inviting Giselle to her wedding, a detail now missing from most productions.

41 In a La Scala production (starring Alessandra Ferri, distributed by Bel Air Media and broadcast on the Arts and Entertainment network), Hilarion is given more than the usual amount of dancing to perform. For example, he dances in the opening scenes of Act Two when the *feux follets* appear.

42 See Chapter Two, note 62.

43 This newly contrived scene is usually enacted during the music composed for the overture.

44 See Lifar, *Giselle,* 78. Note that Lifar refers to this scene as "Pantomime d'Hilarion," and calls the second scene of the second act "Récit d'Hilarion." Ibid., 128.

45 I refer to the Blair production as recorded by ABT in 1977. Also, the 146 measures originally written for the action from the end of scene vi until Wilfride knocks on Berthe's door in scene viii are shrunk to eighty-three in this production, eliminating (among other things) a rendition of Hilarion's musical motif.

46 According to the *répétiteur*, the two objects are a sword and a gold chain. In the libretto Hilarion emerges from the cottage with Albrecht's sword and mantle.

47 These are usually members of the noble hunting party, and they are sometimes accompanied by reveling peasants.

48 Lichtenthal, *Dictionnaire*, vol. I, pp. 115–16.

49 Gautier, *Histoire de l'Art Dramatique*, vol. 2, 133, tr. and qu. by Beaumont, *The Ballet Called Giselle,* 18.

50 *La Péri* libretto (Paris: Mme Vve Jonas, 1843).

51 Adam, letter to Saint-Georges, in Lifar, *Giselle—Apothéose du Ballet Romantique,* 281–84.

52 *La France Musicale,* 4 July 1841.

53 *La France Musicale,* 17 August 1845.

54 The librettists referred to the Wilis' opening danced scene (Act Two scene iv) as a "fantastic ball," and of the villagers' scene (Act Two scene vi) wrote that the Wilis

resorted to voluptuous poses and "les figures de leur danse native" in their attempts to ensnare these innocent passersby.

55 *Giselle* libretto (Paris, 1841).

56 In the "Second Night" of Heine's *Les Nuits florentines (Florentine nights)*, the storyteller recalls his obsession with a beautiful woman he had seen dancing on Waterloo Bridge: "Was it some national dance from the South of France or Spain? These were recalled by the violence with which the dancer threw her body to and fro, and the abandon with which she tossed back her head like a bold bacchante. . . . Her dancing had a spontaneous and intoxicating quality, something darkly inevitable or fatalistic, for she danced like Fate itself." Tr. and qu. Guest, *Jules Perrot: Master of the Romantic Ballet* (2nd ed. rev. New York: Dance Horizons, 1984), 66.

57 The Spanish segment is sixteen bars long if the repeats are taken.

58 For a picture of at least one "national" Wili, see Arkin and Smith, "National Dance in the Romantic Ballet," 50.

59 Jone Bergquist Hallmark, personal communication, 28 August 1996. Ms. Hallmark performed this part in the Basel Ballet under the tutelege of Peter Appel, who "instructed me to sweep the floor with my hand, and also told me that my right arm should almost be touching the right toe behind me as I turned."

60 Gautier, qu. Guest, *Fanny Elssler* (Middletown, Conn.: Wesleyan University Press, 1970), 76; Hallmark, personal communication, 28 August 1996; Gautier, *Voyage en Espagne,* ed. and trans. Guest, "Théophile Gautier on Spanish Dancing," *Dance Chronicle* 10, no. 1 (1987): 6–7. Gautier goes on to say: "They dance with their whole body, they arch their backs, bend sideways and twist their torsos with the suppleness of an almeh or a grass snake."

61 This passages calls for 22 measures in the La Scala and ABT productions, and 26 in the Kirov production.

The productions by the Kirov Ballet, La Scala, and ABT to which I refer are those noted above and distributed on video (respectively) by Thorn EMI, Bel Air Media, and Bel Canto Paramount Home Video.

62 This segment is 56 measures long in the La Scala and ABT productions and 50 measures long in the Kirov production.

63 See note 73.

64 This passage calls for 19 measures in the ABT production, 19 in the La Scala production and 22 in the Kirov production.

65 This scene has appeared in a few productions in the past few decades, including those staged by Heinz Spoerli for the Basel Stadttheater Ballet, Pierre Lacotte for the Ballet de l'Opéra du Rhin, and Kirk Peterson for the Hartford Ballet.

When he produced it for the Ballet de l'Opéra du Rhin, Lacotte referred to an annotated nineteenth-century score for *Giselle* which he believed to have been annotated by Marius Petipa in 1842 but did not attempt to reconstruct the ballet as it had been in 1842. As Jean-Pierre Pastori has written of this production, "The *pretense* of producing the "original version" [of *Giselle*] is not viable. It is more a question of tending towards it." Original emphasis. Pastori, *Pierre Lacotte—Tradition* (Paris: Favre, 1987, bilingual text with translation by Jacqueline Gartmann), 80. See also Lacotte, "Giselle: Le style romantique," in *L'Avant-scène Ballet/Danse* 1 no. 1 (January/March 1980): 25, in which Lacotte discusses the annotated *Giselle* score that he consulted. It appears, however, that this score is the *répétiteur* discussed in this volume (RU-SPtob 7114/8), a score Denis Dabbadie says was annotated by Antoine Titus. (See Dabbadie's introduction to Yuri

Slonimski, "L'ère Petipa" in the same issue of *L'Avant-scène Ballet/Danse*, 95.) Lacotte provides a photograph of this score in this same issue of *L'Avant-scène Ballet/Danse*, 96–97, mistakenly attributing the annotations to Petipa.

See also in the same issue of *L'Avant-scène Ballet/Danse* Gérard Mannoni, "Commentaire musical de la partition," 58–80, but note that he misidentifies the theme of Hilarion and mistakenly attributes Friedrich Burgmüller's first-act divertissement to Ludwig Minkus.

66 *La Presse*, 5 July 1841, tr. Ivor Guest, *Gautier on Dance*, 101.

67 It is true that Myrtha's magic branch still spontaneously breaks in most productions today, thus giving her a reason to be angry. But it is not always clear why her branch has broken, and its breaking even occasionally causes a few nervous laughs in the audience. Confusion may be attributed, perhaps, to the fact that the role of the cross is now minimized; the cross of early productions—large enough for Albrecht to cling to—has given way in some cases to a very small cross, which is not effectively presented as an object capable of repelling Wilis or breaking branches.

68 I have used the traditional terms of the *pas de deux* subsections here; these terms, however, do not appear in the *répétiteur*, full score, or autograph of *Giselle* (though the words "variation" and "coda" do appear sometimes in other scores of the period, which indicates that composers and performers did use such terms for such conventional forms even if they did not always feel compelled to write the words down). Please note that the "adagio" section of a *pas de deux* could be in any slow tempo (e.g., larghetto). On the *grand pas d'action*, see Roland John Wiley, *Tchaikovsky's Ballets*, 18.

69 Text in the *répétiteur* (Entrance): "Myrtha ordonne à Giselle de danser Giselle la supplie Myrtha il faut que tu danse" [Myrtha orders Giselle to dance; Giselle begs her; Myrtha: you must dance.]

70 Text in the *répétiteur* (Adagio): "Albert quitte la croix Giselle prie Myrtha Myrtha refuse Myrthe touche Giselle de la main pour la faire danser" [Albrecht leaves the cross; Giselle begs Myrtha; Myrtha refuses; Myrtha touches Giselle's hand to make her dance].

71 Text in the *répétiteur* (Andante): "Myrtha touche Albert de la main ce qui le force a danser" [Myrtha touches Albrecht's hand, forcing him to dance]. The last 8 measures of this 18-measure andante are meant to be repeated once or twice, extending the overall length of Albrecht's variation to 26 or 34 measures.

72 Text in the *répétiteur* (Coda): "Giselle prie Myrtha d'épargner Albert Myrtha non il faut qu'il meure Giselle se jette dans les bras d'Albert Myrtha l'en arrache et ordonne à Giselle de danser Giselle danse" [Giselle begs Myrtha to spare Albrecht; Myrtha: no, he must die; Giselle throws herself into Albrecht's arms; Myrtha pulls them apart and orders Giselle to dance; Giselle dances.] N.B. The first two pages of the coda have been wrongly labeled as pages 135–36 in the *répétiteur*.

Though Albrecht is not mentioned in the annotations in the coda in the *répétiteur*, it is certain that he dances in it, for upon its completion the *répétiteur* says "Albert tombe epuisé" [Albrecht falls, exhausted].

73 According to Giannandrea Poesio, this variation was added in a 1864 Russian production danced by Adèle Grantzow, with music by (according to Lifar) Ludwig Minkus. Poesio, "Giselle—Part III," 691. See also Ries, "Travels with a Chameleon Romantic," 73.

74 This added variation, as noted above, is based on the "harvest dance" motif from Act One.

75 Gautier, *La Presse* 23 Oct. 1848. See Chapter One, note 1.

INDEX

Abbé de l'Épée, L', 128–29, 290n.19
Académie royale de musique. *See* Paris Opéra
Achille à Scyros, 98, 105
Adam, Adolphe, 20, 245n.4, 276n.104
Africaine, L', 27, 60
air parlant, 101–3, 108–10
Albert (François Decombe), 275n.97
Albrecht. See *Giselle*
Alexandre chez Apelles, 105
Ali-Baba, 24, 27, 61, 203
Aline, Reine de Golconde, 75, 77
Alma, 23
Amazones, Les, 24
Ame en peine, L', 24, 50, 209
Angiolini, Gasparo, 241n.2, 277n.4
Annette et Lubin, 73, 104
Antoinette, Marie, 280n.25
Apollo, 287n.60
Apparition, L', 23, 210
Ashton, Frederick, 122
Astolphe et Joconde, 75, 77, 106, 201
Auber, Daniel-François-Esprit, 115, 125, 135, 138, 140, 142
Aumer, Jean, 84, 86–90

Bach, J.S., 103
Balanchine, George, 122, 287n.60
ballet blanc, xi, 177–78, 242, n.5
ballet d'action, xi, 57, 77, 97, 123, 244n.2
ballet en action. See *ballet d'action*
ballet music. *See* ballet-pantomime music
ballet parodies. *See* parodies of comic opera and *Giselle*, lampoon of
Ballet-pantomime, xxi, 21; 244n.2
ballet-pantomime libretto, 3, 99–101, 154–55, 277n.7
ballet-pantomime music, composition of, 4; listeners' expectations of, 6, 18; types of, 6; jettisoning of vocal music, 21, 119; complaints about absence of borrowed music in, 119–21; in *La Tentation*, 155
ballroom dance. *See* social dance
bamboula, 83, 272n.81
Barbier de Seville, Le, 73
Baron, Alfred, 65–66
Bayadère, La, 24

Beaumarchais, Pierre-Augustin Caron de, 78, 84, 86–90, 94, 273n.89
Beethoven, Ludwig van, Fifth symphony in *Le Page Inconstant*, 85, 90–91; piano sonata, op. 13. in *La Tentation*, 161 Fifth Symphony in *La Tentation*, 161; listed as contributor to *L'Ile des Pirates*, 115; unnamed sonata in *L'Ile des Pirates*, 121; unnamed melody used at the Gymnase theater, 109
Belle au bois dormant, La, 35, 40, 75, 98, 106, 201, 202, 116, 253n.24,
Bellini, Vincenzo, 168
Benvenuto Cellini, 23, 49, 61, 206
Berlioz, Hector, 117–18, 250–51n.7
Berthe. See *Giselle*
Betty, 26, 27, 50, 52, 60, 209
Bigottini, Emilie, 125, 136
black people, 47–49, 83, 271n.75, 271–72n.77
Blasis, Carlo, 5, 246, n. 8
Boïeldieu, François-Adrien, 115
bolero, 131, 191
Bonynge, Richard, 295n.15, 296n.21, 297n.30
borrowed music, use of 104–107; decline of, 112–114; complaints about, 114–16; complaints about absence of, 119–21
boulevard theaters, 124
Bouquetière, La, 22, 50, 210
Bournonville, August, 278n.14
bravura dancing, 15–16
Brézilia, 24, 49, 62, 204

cachucha, 68, 71, 249n.29. *See also* Spanish dance
Camargo, Marie, 261n.6
carillon, 103
Carnaval de Venise, Le, 23
Castil-Blaze (Francois-Henri-Joseph-Blaze), 36, 37, 66, 93–94, 108, 120, 142, 144, 164–65, 290–91n.22
Cendrillon, 74
censors, 128–29, 273n.88
chansons (texts), 279n.21
character dance, 18, 191–95. *See also* Spanish dance
Charles VI, 22, 23, 49, 50, 65, 207

INDEX

chartron, 45
Chatte metamorphosée en femme, La, 17, 24, 26, 49, 75, 107, 117, 205
Chercheuse d'Esprit, La, 73, 78–80, 104. *See also* parodies of comic opera
Chouquet, Gustave, 66
Cinq Sens, Les, 24
claque, 260n.68
Clari, 74, 106
class differences, 260–61n.4
Coelina ou l'Enfant de mystère, 288n.5
Comédie-française, 121
comédies mêlée d'ariettes, 78
comic opera, 78, 276n.104
Comte de Carmagnola, Le, 23, 26, 27, 50, 207
Comte Ory, Le, 22, 27, 202
Coq au Village, Le. See Coq du Village, Le
Coq du Village, Le, 73, 77, 104, 269n.43
coquettishness, 15–16, 263n.22
Corsaire, Le, 248n.24
costumes, 211n.1, 212 nn.12, 14, 23, 32, 33, 254 nn. 31, 32, 35
Cracovienne, 18
Crosten, William, 53

dance music, 15. *See also* ballet-pantomime music
Daphnis et Pendrose, 105
DaPonte, Lorenzo, 86–90, 274n.92
Dauberval, Jean, 273n.89
David, 50, 209
De Mille, Agnes, 122
de Boigne, Charles, 68
Decombe, François. *See* Albert
Delaforest, A., 77, 93, 94
Déserteur, Le, 73, 77, 270n.54
Deux mots, Les, 125, 288n.5, 290n.19
Diable à Quatre, Le, 11–12, 24, 27, 35, 50, 54, 61, 75, 107, 109, 209
Diable amoureux, Le, 23, 24, 27, 50, 55, 107, 206
Diable boiteux, Le, 11–13, 17, 23, 49, 54–55, 56, 61, 66–67, 107, 111, 205
Dieu et la Bayadère, Le, 26, 27, 52, 124, 138–49, 165, 202, 292n.33
director, 19, 276n.106. *See also* Louis Véron and *metteur en scène*
divertissement, 16–18, 34–35, 54, 287n.61
Dom Sébastien, 23, 24, 27, 50, 54, 55, 56, 61, 208
Don Giovanni. See Don Juan

Don Juan [Don Giovanni], 17, 23, 35, 47, 204
Don Quixote, 248n.24
Don Sanche, 201
Donizetti, Gaetano, *Donizetti Variations,* 248n.24. *See also La Favorite* and *Les Martyrs*
dramatic music. *See* pantomime music
Drapier, Le, 22, 26, 27, 49, 206
Dumilâtre, Adèle, 173
Duponchel, Edmond, 276n.106
Duvernoy, Alphonse, 5

éclat, 53–4, 55
Ecole de Mouvement, 52,
écriteaux, 165, 292n.37
Enfant prodigue, L', 24, 25, 105, 211
Enlèvement des Sabines, L', 105
Épreuve villageois, L', 74
Erinnerungsmotiv. See reminiscence theme.
Escudier brothers, 36
Esmeralda, 22, 49, 205
Etoile du Séville, 23, 50, 209
Eucharis, 24, 50, 208
Euryanthe, 202

Fanal, Le, 22, 211
Faust, 293n.3
Favart, Charles-Simon, 79
Favorite, La, 23, 26, 50, 56, 61, 64, 172, 206
Fernand Cortez, 23
Fête de Mirza, La, 104
Fétis, François-Joseph, 144, 164, 165,
Feuillet notation, xvii
feux follets. See will o' the wisp,
Figaro ou la Précaution inutile, 73
Filets de vulcain. See Mars et Vénus
Fille de Marbre, La, 23, 50, 210
Fille du Danube, La, 17, 23, 26, 27, 48, 49, 55, 61, 62, 111, 117, 205
Fille Mal gardée, La, 22, 26, 106, 202
Filleule des fées, La, 24, 211
Flore et Zéphire, 106, 109
Fokine, Michel, 5
foyer de la danse, 68, 71
François I à Chambord, 202
Freyschutz, Le, 23, 24, 50, 207
Fronde, La, 22
Fuoco, Sofia, 52

Gardel, Maximilien, 72
Gardel, Pierre, 82, 248n.25, 270n.56

Gautier, Théophile, 4, 19, 37, 67, 68, 94, 97, 121, 138, 172, 174, 296n.18
Gentil, Louis, 165, 245n.3; 251n.9
Gide, Casimir, 161
Gipsy, La, 17, 23, 26, 27, 35, 49, 55, 102, 107, 114, 118, 206
Giselle répétiteur, Act One, scene ii excerpt, 187–88; Act One, scene vii excerpt, 189; Act One, scene ix excerpt, 190; descriptions of closing scenes of Act Two, 195–96; naming of objects taken from Loys' cottage in, 298n.46; annotations in, 299n.65
Giselle, squeamish defense of score, xv–xvi; recurring melodies in, 13; Act One, 29–32; Albrecht as landowner, 60; plot as exoneration for Opéra's male patrons, 71; lampoon of, 118, 283n.45; shared motifs, 168; finale of Act One, 168; Markova and Dolin in, 169; genesis of, 170–75; completion of score, 173; final plot, 174–75; scenes often cut in, 176; sacrifice of character development in, 177; missing mime scenes in Act Two, 177–78; Wilfride vs. Albrecht, 178–80; Berthe vs. Giselle, 180–83; Hilarion, 66, 187–91; ethnic music in, 191–95; character dancing in, 191–95, 299n.58; closing scenes of Act Two, 195–98; Act Two *pas de deux* as Myrthe's last resort, 196–99; Act Two Finale, 198–99; bringing back the old *Giselle*? 199–200; libretto, 213–38; reviewed by Wagner, 248 n.22; Giselle's weak heart, 295n.17; in various tables, 17, 23, 26, 27, 50, 61, 63, 207. See also *Giselle répétiteur*
Gluck, Christoph Willibald, 109
Grantzow, Adèle, 300n.73
Grétry, André-Ernest-Modeste, 72, 109
Griseldis, 24, 50, 201
Grisi, Carlotta, 149, 173
group as choreographic category, 247–48n.47
guarache, 131
Guérillero, Le, 24, 50, 207
Guido et Ginevra, 23, 26, 49, 205
Guillaume Tell, 17, 23, 35, 43, 44, 47, 202
Gustave III, 23, 47, 56, 61, 63, 203
Gyrowetz, Adalbert, 85

Halévy, Jacques-Fromental, 161
Haydn, Joseph, 270
Heine, Heinrich, 172, 294n.10, 299n.56
Henry, Louis (Luigi), 212, nn. 17, 21, 251n.10;

Héro et Léandre, 105
Hérold, Ferdinand, 276,104
Heureux Retour, L', 105
Hilarion. See *Giselle*
Hilverding, Franz, 241,n.2
Hugo, Victor, "Fantômes," 171–72; *Hernani*, 121
Huguenots, Les, 17, 22, 26, 29–34, 48, 49, 51, 54, 55, 60, 64, 168, 205

Ile des Pirates, L', 23, 26, 38, 48, 49, 61, 62, 107, 121, 204
instrumental recitative, 101–3, 110, 278n.11, 280n.32
Iphigénie en Aulide, 24
Iphigénie en Tauride, 24

Jaleo de Xeres, 18
Jeanne la Folle, 23, 26, 27, 210
Jérusalem, 22, 24, 50
jig, 191
Jockey Club, 68
Joconde, 75
Jolie Fille de Gand, La, 23, 27, 48, 50, 54, 55, 56, 63, 66–67, 75, 99, 207
Jugement de Paris, Le, 104, 108–9
Juif errant, Le, 23, 24, 26, 27
Juive, La, 17, 23, 26, 27, 35, 41, 47, 49, 56, 61, 64, 204

Karsavina, Tamara, 297nn.25, 27
Kreutzer, Rodolphe, 272n.83

Lac des Fées, Le, 23, 27, 206
Lady Henriette, 7, 23, 27, 50, 56, 75, 208
Lazzarone, Le, 23, 50, 208
Léocadie, 75
Levinson, André, 178
Lifar, Serge, 283n.44
lithographs, 250n.3
livret de mise en scène, 255–56n.39
Loys. See *Giselle*, Wilfride vs. Albrecht,
Lucie de Lammermoor, 23, 50, 209, 293–94n.3
Luisa Miller, 23
Lydie, 106, 202

MacBeth, 201
magic branch, 168, 300n.67
Malbrouck s'en va-t'en-guerre, 163
Manon Lescaut, 22, 38, 39, 47, 56, 60, 61, 106, 109, 202

Mariage de Figaro, Le, 75
Marie Stuart, 23, 50, 61, 65, 208
Mars et Vénus, 24, 106, 201
Martyrs, Les, 17, 24, 50, 61, 64, 206, 258n.48
Masaniello, 128-29, 288n.8
Maurice, Charles, 136, 138
Medée et Jason, 104
melodrama, 242n.4, 278n.11
metteur en scène, 53, 258n.52
Meyerbeer, Giacomo, 115
Milon, Louis, 72
mime. *See* pantomime,
minuet, 191-92
Mirsa, 104
Mohicans, Les, 17, 37, 49, 61, 63, 205
Moïse, 24, 201
Montez, Lola, 20, 71
Morris, Mark, 278-9n.16
Mozart, Wolfgang Amadeus, *Requiem,* 103; *Don Giovanni,* 71; 247n.18; in *La Tarentule,* 115. *See also Le Nozze di Figaro* and *Don Juan*
Muette de Portici, La, 23, 26, 27, 60, 124, 125-38, 202
Musée Philipon, La, 118
musicology, xv

Napoli, 278n.14
Nathalie, 17, 23, 26, 47, 62, 203
national dance. *See* character dance
Native Americans, 47, 263-4n.25
Nayades, Les, 24
Nerval, Gérard de, 59
Nijinska, Bronislava, 52
Nina ou la Folle par Amour, 74, 77
Ninette à la Cour, 73, 104
Nisida, 210
Noblet, Lise, 136, 138
Nonne sanglante, La, 27
notes de ballet, 100
Nourrit, Adolphe, 20
Noverre, Jean-Georges, xi, 21, 66, 97, 241n.2; *Nozze di Figaro, Le,* 85, 86-90, 92-93, 162. *See also* parodies of comic opera, *Le Page Inconstant,* and *Le Mariage de Figaro*
Nutcracker, 122, 198

Oedipe, 24
onstage sign, 98, 110
opera and ballet-pantomime, plots 22, 26-27; settings, 22-25; form, 28; music, 35-37; staging, 37, 43, 45-57; sensational scenes in opera, 60; urban vs. pastoral settings, 61-65, 125
opera-ballet, 164, 244n.3
opéra bouffon, 78
Opéra Comique, pipeline to Opéra, 72; bitterness of shareholders, 267-8n.40; dispute with the Nouveautés, 267-8n.40; at the Théâtre Feydeau, 269n.34; wrangling over genres, 275n.103
Orgie, L', 23, 26, 27, 47, 75, 111, 203
Orphée, 24
Othello (Otello), 23, 50, 208
Ozaï, 22, 27, 50, 210

Paganini, Niccolò, 251n.8
Page Inconstant, Le, 75, 84-93, 106
Pages du Duc de Vendôme, 74
Palianti, Louis, xv, 244n.15
Pantomime, 45, 51, 255 nn. 34, 38, 39; 267n.39, 269n.47, 287n.58
pantomime music, 8-12, 154, 155
pantomime, complaints about, 116-19, 122
pantomimic intelligibility, 53
Paquerette, 22
Paquita, 23, 27, 50, 63, 209
Paris Opéra, illustrations, xii-xii, 69-70; locations, 244n.1; shared purpose, 19-20
parlante music, use in ballet, 5; 36; shift to the more subtle, 111-14; in *La Muette de Portici,* 135, 137; for Hilarion, 168; for Wilfride and Albrecht,179; for Berthe, 180; unacknowledged in choreography, 183-86
parodies of comic opera, overview, 72-79; *La Chercheuse d'Esprit,* 72, 79-81; *Paul et Virginie,* 81-84; *Le Page Inconstant,* 84-93; decline of the parody ballet, 93-96; ballet-to-opera parodies, 167n.38; *pas de deux,* 13, 16, 28, 45, 85, 129, 156, 248n.24. *See also* Act Two, *pas de deux*
Paul et Virginie, 73, 82-84, 105. *See also* parodies of comic opera
Péri, La, 24, 50, 68, 114, 208
Perrot, Jules, 287n.61, 295n.14
Persée et Andromède, 105
Pharamond, 201
Philtre, Le, 22, 26, 27, 203
Pillet, Léon, 172, 276n.106
plot synopsis vs. visual description, 258n.48
pointing at houses, 187, 188, 259n.62, 297n.24

polka, 249n.29
pose as choreographic category, 52–53, 257n.46
Premier Navigateur, Le, 104
Prévost [Prévôt], Françoise, 248n.25
production costs at the Opéra, 249–50n.2
Promesses du Mariage, Les, 74
proper comportment of women, 71, 266n. 33, 34
Prophète, Le, 17, 23, 24, 35, 51, 55, 60, 211
proverbe musicale, 103
Psiché, 98, 104

rationales for dancing, 17, 66
rehearsal score. See *répétiteur*
Reine de Chypre, La, 23, 48, 50, 207
reminiscence theme, 13–14, 247, n. 20
répétiteur (rehearsal score), 7, 239–40, 254n.33
Révolte au sérail, La, 15–16, 17, 24, 27, 35, 36, 39, 40, 47, 52, 62, 66, 98, 204
Richard en Palestine, 23, 50, 208
Robert Bruce, 23, 50, 209
Robert le diable, 22, 27, 35, 42, 47, 51, 55, 56–57, 168, 169, 203, 288
Rodolphe, Johann Joseph, 248n.25
Roi David, 24
Roqueplan, Nestor, 276n.106
Rossini, Gioacchino, 109, 115, 121

Salieri, Antonio, 109
Sallé, Marie, 261n.6
Sapho, 24
Sauvages, Les, 106
Schneitzhoeffer, Jean-Madeleine, 4, 120
Scribe, Eugène, 125, 129, 134, 138, 140, 142
Serment, Le, 22, 26, 27, 203
Servante Justifiée, La, 22, 74
Sicilien, Le, 201
Siège de Corinthe, Le, 24, 201
Simfonizm, 243 n. 11; 247 n. 17;
Sleeping Beauty (Tchaikovsky), 108, 111, 198. See also *La belle au bois dormant*
social dance, 18, 249n.29
solo melodies for dancing, 248n.25
Somnambule, La, 9–11, 22, 98, 100–101, 106, 109, 202
Spanish dance, 193–4, 251n.14, 263n.24, 290n.17
staging manuals, xvii. See also *livrets de mise en scène*

Stella, 23, 211
Sténochorégraphie, xvii
Stoltz, Rosine, 57
"story ballet," 2, 122
Stradella, 23, 48, 49, 205
stupefaction, 259nn. 54, 55
Swan Lake, 36, 122
Sylphide, La, xi, 8, 17, 21, 23, 26, 42, 43, 55, 56, 61, 97, 103, 107, 110, 203

tableau, 54, 258–59n.53. See also stupefaction
tableau vivant, 256n.40,
Taglioni, Marie, xi, 138, 140, 148–49, 290n.22
Tannhäuser, xv
tarantella, 132
Tarentule, La, 23, 26, 27, 49, 63, 206
Tchaikovsky, Pyotr Illyich, xv, 108, 197–98, 287n.59
Tempête, La, 23, 35, 49, 61, 107, 204
Tentation, La 24, 101–2, 124, 149–61, 203
Théâtre de la Porte Saint-Martin, 242, n.4
Théâtre Italien, 242, n. 4
timbres, 78, 269n.51
tragédie-lyrique, 123

urban and pastoral settings. See opera and ballet-pantomime

Vaisseau-fantôme, La, 23, 50, 207
Vendetta, La, 23, 49, 206
Vénus et Adonis, 105
Vêpres siciliennes, Les, 26, 27
Verdi, Giuseppe, *Four Seasons,* 248n.24. See also *Jérusalem, Luisa Miller,* and *Les Vêpres siciliennes*
verisimilitude, 65
Véron, Louis, 59, 68, 71, 95,165, 293n.39
Vert-Vert, 22
Vertumne et Pomone, 105
Vestale, La, 24
Victorine, 75
Violin du diable, Le, 22, 211
Vivandière, La, 24, 210
Vive Henri Quatre, 105, 108
Volière, La, 15–16, 24, 26, 49, 63, 206
voyeurism, 69–70, 259n.58, 265n.27

Wagner, Richard, 13, xv, 243n.7
waltz, 191–92

well-made libretto, 25
well-made play, 252n.16
white ballet. *See* ballet blanc,
Wild Boy of Aveyron, 128
Wilfride. See *Giselle*
will o' the wisp, 161, 174, 221, 234 297n.32, 298n.41

Willis, Nathaniel, 140

Xacarilla, La, 27, 49, 206

Zémire et Azore, 75
Zerline, 26

GPSR Authorized Representative: Easy Access System Europe - Mustamäe tee 50, 10621 Tallinn, Estonia, gpsr.requests@easproject.com

www.ingramcontent.com/pod-product-compliance
Lightning Source LLC
Chambersburg PA
CBHW061427300426
44114CB00014B/1577